THE OFFICIAL PRICE GUIDE

Royal Doulton

BY
RUTH M. POLLARD

We have compiled the information contained herein through a *patented computerized process* which relies primarily on a nationwide sampling of information provided by noteworthy collectible experts, auction houses and specialized dealers. This unique retrieval system enables us to provide the reader with the most current and accurate information available.

EDITOR
THOMAS E. HUDGEONS III

THIRD EDITION
THE HOUSE OF COLLECTIBLES, INC., ORLANDO, FLORIDA 32809

TABLE OF CONTENTS

Dedicated to
AUNT KATHRYN
for her encouragement and inspiration departed this world January 3, 1983 and sadly missed.

ACKNOWLEDGEMENTS

For his valuable assistance in pricing and identification the author thanks Fred Dearden, Trenton, NJ, for allowing us to photograph his extensive collection. Mr. Dearden loves to share his vast knowledge of Royal Doulton and has helped many novice and advanced collectors in their acquisitions over the years. He will help dispose of a piece or a collection. If you would like to avail yourself of his expertise in the area of identification, appraisal and in-depth information concerning Royal Doulton, just write: Mr. Fred S. Dearden, P. O. Box 3622, Trenton, NJ 03679.

For their contributions in pricing and identification, we also acknowledge: Mrs. Helen Fortune, Ashtabula Antiques Importing Co. Ltd., Ashtabula, OH; Mr. Ed Pascoe, Pascoe and Company Inc., New York, NY; Mrs. Ann Cook, private collector.

PHOTOGRAPHIC RECOGNITION

Cover Photograph: Photographer — Marc Hudgeons, Orlando, FL 32809
Courtesy of: Mr. Fred Dearden, Trenton, NJ 03679
Color Separations: Shanebrook Graphics, Pontiac, IL 61764

IMPORTANT NOTICE

INTRODUCTION

Like a royal bloodline, Royal Doulton creations of the 1970s and 1980s are as collectible as those originating prior to World War I.

Although Doultons are distributed internationally, they are still uncommon compared to the works of other potteries. Doultons will never be plentiful because they are not manufactured in large quantities. Thus the owner of even a single prized work has something which carries an authentic exclusiveness.

Royal Doultons have always possessed a magical quality which intensifies with time. A good portion of Britain's history is incorporated in Doulton figures of kings, queens, sea captains and adventurers. Not only did the company produce figures of high society but common British citizens as well. For example, the Gardener Character Jug is a faithful creation of a laboring gardener who kept the grounds of noble estates. He was a solid part of Britain's history perhaps ignored in the history books, but not in Royal Doulton porcelain. Doultons have a timelessness because their subjects are vignettes out of history captured dramatically in the porcelain art.

The backbone behind this highly collectible ware is made up of the creative and highly skilled artists. A high standard is always required for each piece that leaves the factory. Therefore since the 1800s, this ware has been collectible. Today in English country estates owned by dukes and earls of the 1800s and 1900s is found Doulton ware. With this high level of perfection found in each piece, saying Doulton will continue to be very collectible is an understatement. No other ceramic ware of the twentieth century, with the possible exception of Goebel Hummel figurines, is as universally sought and esteemed as Doulton ware.

MARKET REVIEW

The last two decades saw remarkable growth in the Doulton collector market. If this rate continues, the price could double in the next few years. Royal Doulton has unimpeachable investment credentials among collector's items. It has the established reputation of being a favorite collectible item for more than 150 years. Releases have been in limited quantities further enticing the market.

When investing in Royal Doultons concentrate on the discontinued models, but be selective about the costly pieces. Sometimes they are not among the most attractive buys for investing. Finding an interested buyer may be difficult because many collectors cannot afford the expensive wares therefore concentrating on lower priced pieces.

Two important events taking place in 1984 will definitely play a major role in the Doulton collectibles market. The golden anniversary of the Bunnykins and the character jug series takes place this year. The Bunnykins, a line of ware started in 1934 featuring rabbits is gaining a mass following by collectors of all ages. Three of the most recent figures include Astro Bunnykins Rocket Man, a rabbit dressed in a space suit with a rocket on his back; Jogging Bunnykins, a bunny dressed in typical jogging attire; and Happy Birthday Bunnykins featuring a rabbit dressed in party clothes sitting behind a table eyeing his birthday cake.

To commemorate the golden anniversary of the character jug series, the Collector Club Gallery of London commissioned a new jug titled "Sir Henry Doulton," which is currently available.

Two recent additions to the celebrity collection should be especially popular with American collectors. A "W. C. Fields" character jug and a "Mae West" character jug were introduced recently. Of particular note is that less than 1,500 W. C. Fields jugs and less than 500 Mae West jugs have a special backstamp which reads, "Premier Edition for American Express." This pair of character jugs with the special backstamp will definitely be in demand.

Flambe ware has proved to be popular among collectors. Animal pieces are especially popular. A wire haired terrier sold for around $320 while a small 3½" duck went for $160. Although animals are doing well other flambe ware is also holding its own. At an auction in London, a large 20" landscape vase sold for $500 while a Sung 6¾" vase featuring a leopard and sunset took $450. Perhaps assisting in the Flambe ware's popularity surge was a major exhibition of over 200 pieces of this ware in London in 1983.

The works of major Doulton artists are also doing well on the collector market. Recently, a George Tinworth clock case modeled in the form of a small theater sold for $1,800. Hannah Barlow's work also seems to draw attention. An 1876 jug with a cat scene recently sold for $650. Frederick Moore, one of the chief artists responsible for the flambe and sung glaze effects, is another artist whose work should be watched. He was responsible for some of the most beautiful pieces of flambe. Peggy Davies is another favorite Doulton artist. She has designed over two hundred figures for the HN series and an exhibition of her work was recently held in London. This could spur additional collector interest.

An informed collector will always make better buys. Therefore, with the many information avenues available, Doulton collectors should be one of the most informed groups in the market.

Two new Royal Doulton galleries were recently established. The Sir Henry Doulton Gallery in Stoke-on-Trent and the refurbished Club Gallery in London have attracted thousands of visitors worldwide. To keep abreast of the Doulton market, collecting groups have sprung up in all parts of the world including the U.S.

All collectors should take advantage of Doulton's own club established to inform collectors. The Royal Doulton International Collector's Club has members worldwide and is constantly growing. Michael Doulton is the honorary president of the club and travels worldwide as ambassador for the company. The club publishes an invaluable Doulton collector's magazine filled with information about new issues, artists, company history and other useful information.

HISTORY

At 12, John Doulton began his distinguished career in pottery. Little did he know that his name would survive almost two centuries and be associated with the most sought after ware in pottery history.

Though the Doulton firm has roots extended into history, admiration for fine pottery had already been established before it came upon the scene. In addition to manufacturing terra-cotta or earthenware for household use, ancient civilizations also worked pottery into artistic forms. The earliest specimens were not cast from molds, but made freehand by the modeler and thus could not be precisely duplicated. They also did not possess a lustrous finish or bright enameling. They were usually left in the basic earth color (reddish) and sometimes painted with decorations. This was firmly believed to be the highest state earthenware could reach. Therefore, the western world was very surprised to find that the Chinese manufactured a far superior type of ceramic: hard, smooth, glossy, and beautifully enameled. It soon acquired the name Chinaware, and became the rage of Europe. By the 1400's it was being imported in very large quantities. The difference in quality between Chinaware and European pottery was so great that demand for the latter dwindled.

For many years, European potters tried to duplicate the imported product but the technique of making true porcelain remained a secret until the early 18th century when porcelain began to be produced at Meissen in Prussia.

The "secret" was the use of a special clay. Though strenuous efforts were made to keep the formula in Prussian hands, porcelain was soon manufactured in far-flung parts of the continent.

The history of Doulton pottery began in the 17th century. The successful commercial sale of Oriental wares had prompted potters to strive for reasonably faithful imitations. One of these was John Dwight of Fulham, a small country village just outside London. Dwight wanted to manufacture porcelain. And, if he could not do that, at least manufacture something more dazzling than earthenware. After much struggle and experimentation, Dwight produced a white stoneware with a lustrous finish. It was not really porcelain, but a better imitation of it than any other Englishman had made up to that time. Bubbling with excitement and a dream of vast riches, Dwight applied to Charles II for a patent in 1671 and received it.

Dwight did prosper. He eventually was running a string of factories in Fulham and was, unquestionably, the town's leading citizen. As far as his works are concerned, their modeling was better than their finishing. Dwight restrained himself from putting out cascades of small inexpensive figures. Instead he stayed mainly with grand concepts, producing large stoneware busts and classical statuary similar in design to bronzes and marbles. Made in limited numbers, they have become quite rare and are often found in museums.

During the following century, numerous major developments occurred in pottery making. Of the British potteries, Staffordshire became the unrivaled leader in figureware. Its figures were not usually as delicate or colorful as those of continental European makers, but had charm and originality. By the late 1700's every British pottery works was getting its inspiration from Staffordshire.

Porcelain popularity was still riding very high in England when John Doulton was born in 1793. The native manufacturers had received a boost from the French Revolution, which had reduced exports from France and aided sales of British ware. Doulton's place of birth was Fulham, not far from Dwight's pottery, which was still in operation. Many youths from the region were automatically apprenticed to the pottery trade. John Doulton was one of them. Doulton went for apprenticeship to Dwight's in 1805 and remained there until reaching age 19 in 1812.

Doulton, like other apprentices, braved the intense heat, the filth-riddled air and the 12-hour working days for seven or eight years to become a master. But even those who successfully completed their apprenticeship had an uncertain future. They were not automatically guaranteed a position at the factory where they served, and it was always questionable whether employment could be found elsewhere.

Doulton did not work for Dwight's after filling out his apprenticeship. He went to Lambeth, another small English village known for pottery, and was employed by the Vauxhall works. This had been a successful organization some years earlier but had struck on lean times because of the owner's death. It was then being run by his widow, Martha Jones. In 1815 Doulton, then 22, and with three years under his belt at Vauxhall, bought a partnership in the factory for 100 pounds of sterling. The partnership gave him one-third ownership, the other two-thirds belonged to Mrs. Jones and another partner named John Watt.

Although this arrangement lasted five years because of a poor economy, Mrs. Jones withdrew from Vauxhall. Doulton and Watt decided to keep the company open.

Things improved considerably thereafter. The early 1820's was a period of significant growth for the company. Watt and Doulton proved amicable partners. Watt handled the business end while Doulton ran factory operations.

The firm's line in this era differed considerably from what we now familiarly recognize as "Doulton." A large part of the trade for potters was garden ornaments. These large creations brought a good profit.

Doulton and Watt also made Toby Jugs, commercial packing jars, and decorative flasks.

In 1826 the firm acquired a new headquarters on High Street in Lambeth — not far from historic Lambeth Palace, built in the middle ages. Growing tourism brought many art-minded visitors to Lambeth Palace, and many stopped to see Doulton's and Watt's company called Lambeth Pottery. A drawing by Thomas Wakeman, made around the time of Queen Victoria's ascent, shows the factory's exterior and a general view of the street. It was not a typical-looking factory but had the appearance of a gentlemen's country estate. The building was made entirely of stone. At the front was a tall stately iron gate, leading into a sculpture garden. The gateposts were surmounted with huge likenesses of eagles, and there were various embellishments on the building itself: classical urns along the roof fronting and a sculptured coat of arms rising high over the door.

Henry Doulton, John's son, joined the staff in 1835 at age 15. He had been primed for a university education but saw no reason why he should not start as early as possible to learn the business he would eventually inherit. Henry was well-schooled in art and not only knew artistic porcelain but was attuned to the artistic tastes of the public. He was a go-getter who thought unceasingly of expansion. In 1877 he bought out a factory in Burslem, England, previously used by the firm of Pinder, Bourne and Co. Five years later the name was changed to Doulton and Co. It was here that most of the firm's figureware was made in the late 19th century.

Doulton's had become one of Britain's major industrial enterprises. Its works had enormous influence, not only on other potteries of the time, but in setting styles and shaping public tastes. Doulton pottery was featured in exhibitions and placed in museums. Both wealthy American and English citizens stocked their homes with Doultons.

Because of his artistic and commercial contributions to Britain, Henry Doulton was knighted by Queen Victoria in 1887. This was the first time a potter had received such distinction.

A change in Doulton pottery occurred in the early 1900s. Instead of the emphasis on vases and ornaments, small decorative figures were introduced. Because of the strong collecting interest for 18th century Staffordshire figures, Doulton Art Director Charles Noke felt the public would be willing to buy fine modern figures for a lower price. Therefore, in 1913 Doulton introduced a series of small models called the HN series named after the firm's head colorist, Harry Nixon. Also in 1913, the firm's name changed to Royal Doulton inspired partially by a visit from King George V and Queen Mary to the Burslem factory.

By the end of 1913, Royal Doulton had placed forty character figurines on the market. The figures were well received by the public. Because of World War I, less than a dozen new numbers were added to the HN line in 1914, and even fewer in 1915. But the output rose in 1916 and continued to rise at the war's conclusion. Although most of the early designs were retained until 1938, they were rare due to limited distribution, lost or damaged specimens, and often low production figures.

Because of the depression, the company knew it had to diversify. Therefore in 1932, a line of miniature figures was introduced. At first, the series carried HN numbers, but later was given M numbers. Later, the number scheme was dropped all together.

The company also introduced limited editions and gave greater attention to its miscellaneous wares.

After World War II, Royal Doulton sped full pace surpassing anything in the company's history. Collecting enthusiasm boomed spurred by the discontinuation of the early HN line and by the scarcity of those figures because of the tremendous destruction suffered by Britain during World War II.

In recent years, Royal Doulton has introduced several new series including Dancers of the World and Soldiers of the Revolution.

DESIGNERS

The success of any manufacturer of artistic porcelain depends in large measure on its designers and artists who create each design and the working models for them.

The serious collector realizes that no degree of manufacturing talent can turn a mediocre model into a public favorite, when the finished work goes on sale. In a company such as Royal Doulton, a high standard is always required; and so is, at the same time, imaginative designing that does not merely repeat what has been done in the past. Thus, experimentation is always a necessity, and designers and artists must constantly bring a high level of quality to their experimental efforts.

The following paragraphs give some brief information on noteworthy Doulton artists and designers.

GEORGE TINWORTH. George Tinworth's influence on the factory and on porcelain making in general is well recognized. Tinworth had a very successful career as an independent sculptor in Britain in addition to his work with Doulton. Born in 1843, he grew up in the dawning years of one of the more memorable classical revivals. Heroic sculptures after the Greek manner were strongly in demand when Tinworth began his career, and he received many commissions for such works. Some of his productions showing warriors, gladiators, etc., were of immense size. At the same time he also sculpted small figures of children and animals. Some of Tinworth's models were cast at Doulton's. They enjoyed great popularity, and Tinworth gained a reputation in Britain on a par with that of John Rogers in America — though the "Tinworths" were much smaller physically. A number of Tinworth's models provided inspiration for Doulton's artists. His most significant connection with the firm came through his set of *Merry Musicians,* a group of children playing various instruments.

LESLIE HARRADINE. Leslie Harradine was born in 1887 and came to Doulton as an apprentice modeler at age 15. His great creativity proved a driving force in the organization and resulted in many imaginative creations. Harradine was responsible for a number of the character jugs issued in the early 1900s including Sam Weller, Pickwick, Sairey Gamp and Micawber. His personal tastes in modeling ran strongly in the direction of figureware, but the firm's trade then consisted heavily of vases and garden ornaments, so his talents were directed toward them as well. In 1912, when still very young and on the threshold of an apparently bright career, Harradine decided that factory life did not appeal to him. He bought a farm in Canada and refused all offers to return to Doulton's. However, an arrangement was worked out. For nearly forty years, Harradine modeled figures in clay and shipped them across the Atlantic for use in the Doulton line. In this fashion Doulton gained some of its most popular models including Polly Peachum, The Goose Girl, Contentment, and others.

RICHARD GARBE. Richard Garbe worked at Royal Doulton during the 1930's and created many of its Limited Editions of that era, such as Spirit of the Wind, Beethoven, Salome, and Lady of the Snows. He also modeled wall-masks. Garbe had the important distinction of being instructor in sculpture at London's Royal College of Art. The letters "RA," often shown after his name, signify Royal Artist.

CHARLES NOKE. Charles Noke was Art Director of Doulton's for many years during in the late 19th and early 20th centuries. He had previously been with Worcester, a rival factory, and joined Doulton in 1889. Noke receives credit for shaping Doulton into its present form. He conceived the idea of Fancy Character Figures and instituted the HN series. Noke was extremely partial to figureware and even before the HN series he was adding figures to the Doulton line. He was originally a modeler.

MARGARET M. DAVIES. Peggy Davies, as she is known, has been responsible for designing and modeling many of Royal Doulton's postwar creations. She joined the firm in 1939 just as the war was beginning. Trade was naturally curtailed by the war, and Peggy's home was damaged by German air raids. But she continued her interest in art, and after the war became a very successful independent sculptress. Though not employed by Doulton thereafter, she executed many works for the firm on a contract arrangement. Her Royal Doultons have included Lady Musicians, Figures of Williamsburg, and the much-heralded Dancers of the World, in which each piece has a low limited number of just 750 specimens.

ERIC GRIFFITHS. A sculptor of considerable skill and reputation, Eric Griffiths is noted for his masterful Soldiers of the Revolution series. His early background was in industrial sculpturing. Griffiths now serves as Head of Sculpture for Royal Doulton.

MARY NICOLL. Mary Nicoll contributed many works to the HN series during the 1960's and 1970's, until her death in 1974. Her figures were mainly "general types" rather than historical or fictional characters. They included a number of nautical types, in which she had a special interest.

PRODUCING FIGURINES

Any Royal Doulton article is a work of art. From its inception to finished product, the pieces are carefully produced by exceptionally skilled and dedicated workers. This high level of perfection is the exception rather than the rule in twentieth century pottery making. The following step by step process shows the manufacture of figurines.

Each item entering the Royal Doulton figurine line begins with an idea usually formed by one of the factory's artists. When working up a design, an artist must consider if a work is compatible with the products already in the line, if it can be rendered with genuine visual appeal, and if it is decorative enough to stand on its own merits. Royal Doultons need not be pretty, but must be captivating.

After deciding on a design, sketches are made showing several poses or attitudes. The sketched idea is then formed into a clay working model. The working model must be the exact size and design of the future porcelain model. To make the working model, soft non-hardening clay is used. The clay of the finished model is quite different. Its ingredients are selected to provide maximum hardness. Each ingredient is inspected to assure proper texture and quality and blended together at the factory according to rigid procedures.

When the working model is approved, a cast made from plaster of paris is taken of it. The cast is used as the figurine's mold. After it hardens, the cast is sawed into several pieces making several small molds. Clay slip is then poured into each mold. When hardened, the molds are assembled into figures and then dried. The model is then fired in an oven heated to as high as 1,240 degrees centigrade.

Since most Royal Doulton figurines are highly translucent, the piece is dipped into a vat of liquid glaze which has an appearance of buttermilk. However, when the piece is again fired in the kiln, it emerges with a crystal-like coating. After the second firing, it is hand painted. This step in porcelain factories is called enameling. After the figures are painted, several pieces are inspected. Any defects will deem the piece unsatisfactory.

CARE AND REPAIR

A broken Royal Doulton is worth just a fraction of the normal value of a mint condition specimen because mint condition pieces are easily attainable.

Do not buy a broken Royal Doulton believing if it is repaired it will be worth the same as a mint condition specimen. Unfortunately, it will not. If a specimen breaks, repair it to serve as a filler until another piece can be purchased. If the break is particularly bad, for example if it shatters, discarding it may be wiser than having it repaired, since the expense of the repair may cost more than the broken Doulton is worth.

To fix a clean break between two pieces, apply rubber cement with a brush to the areas that will be fitted together. Let it dry for a minute, then press together gently until fully dry. With a fast drying cement, also hold the pieces together until fully dry.

A professional restorer will usually apply enamel to the joined areas to conceal the break. Again, consider the cost of professional restoration before having the piece repaired. Although the break may not be noticeable, the piece is still damaged and will not retain the value of a mint condition piece.

CLEANING: Royal Doultons may require a periodical cleaning. If the surface is simply dusty, brush with a dry soft cloth. If the surface needs a thorough cleaning, immerse the piece in lukewarm water. Never use hot water which could damage the enamel. Next, soak the piece for several minutes in lukewarm soapy water. Do not use bleach or other harsh detergents, instead use a mild hand soap. After this step, rinse with lukewarm water. If the piece is extremely dirty, the same procedure is used but repeated several times.

TRADEMARKS

Generally, porcelain markings have a reputation for being confusing. Although there are questions about old Doulton marks from the 1800s, fortunately after 1913 Doulton ware is distinctly marked.

In the 1850's the familiar marking was a terse "DOULTON, LAMBETH." It gave the manufacturer's name and location as shown in illustrations 1-6.

1

2

3

4

5

6

After expansion in 1877, the backstamps referred to either the Lambeth or Burslem factories. The coronet was added at the Burslem factory in 1886. After 1891, the word "England" was added. In 1902, Royal was added to the company's name. The marking system became more detailed through the years arriving at its present form of a lion and crown. See illustration 12.

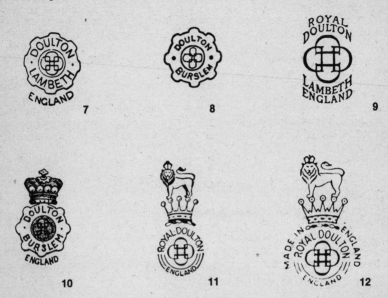

7   8   9

10   11   12

In 1913, the HN numbering system was instituted. The letters HN stood for Doulton's chief colorist Harry Nixon. The plan was to have the HN prefix on every model followed by a serial number and the official name of the model. At first the model names were applied by hand, then later they were stamped. Occasionally specimens turn up which bear the model name without the series number.

In addition, many pieces are hand marked "Potted by Doulton & Co." Usually pieces after 1913 carry a stamped lion and crown symbol.

Bone china products after 1928 are marked "BONE CHINA" with the artist's signature and often a number enclosed by a rectangle. Sometimes an Rd. No. is shown, which is the figure's registration number at the British Patent Office.

In the 1950s and 1960s, script stamped lettering was used to give the appearance of hand lettering. This practice was discontinued.

Revisions of lettering styles naturally created a situation in which identical figures do not always bear identical markings. This is a useful aid in dating. Illustration 17 shows the current marking of "THE BALLOON MAN," the same figure pictured in Illustration 18. In this case the numbering is alike but the style of lettering different.

13

14

15

16

17

18

Examples of the same figures with the same names bearing different numbers are also found. Royal Doulton changes the series number whenever it makes revisions in a figure's color scheme. Therefore, the same figure could have several different numbers. *Kate Hardcastle* exists with numbers HN1718, HN1719, HN1734, HN1919 and HN2028. If a date appears impressed into the mold, this could signify the date of that model's introduction to the line. These dates are occasionally found on older figures only. Molds for HN564, *Parson's Daughter,* carried a dating of 3-1-31. This work remained in the line from then until 1949. When reading these dates, it is important to remember that the British give the DAY before the MONTH. Thus, 3-1-31 is January 3, 1931.

Generally, the HN series runs in sequence and the numerical order roughly indicates the chronological order in which figures were issued. Do not assume the HN numbers follow a precise chronological order. Although recent HN models are numbered in the 2,800s, there are not 2,800 different

ROYAL
DOULTON
FLAMBÉ

pieces produced. Gaps have occurred in the numbering system for several reasons. Groups of numbers are reserved for pieces which will be made in the future or are never made.

The M series comprises miniature figures 4½ " tall introduced in 1932. Some of the works in this series are reduced versions of HN figures, while others were created expressly for the M series and have no HN counterpart. When Royal Doulton began this series, the M prefix was not used. The early miniatures carried HN numbers and were serialized as part of the regular HN series. The last miniatures to carry HN numbers appeared in 1949. Today, *numbering has been abandoned* for the miniature figures; they now bear only the model name. They are readily identified by the standard Royal Doulton markings. Some of the earliest miniatures are marked "DOULTON" or "DOULTON C.," but those in current production have the same stamping as the HN figures.

Royal Doulton marks its special series and editions with unique backstamp information which identifies a particular item or series. Dickensware, which was first introduced in 1908, was marked with a brown backstamp until 1930 when it became a black backstamp until 1960. The Rouge Flambe trademarks vary. Sometimes several marks are found on one piece while others have only one marking along with the traditional Royal Doulton emblem.

Recommended Reading . . .

The Official Price Guide to Royal Doulton is designed for the novice as well as the seasoned collector. Information on price trends, industry development, investing, and collecting techniques such as care and repair, storage, or building a collection is written in a way a beginning hobbyist will understand yet gives specific details and helpful hints the hard-core collector will find useful.

This guide also offers up-to-date prices for both rare and common collectibles that are available in the current secondary market. This guide will give any collector confidence when determining what articles to purchase at what price. With the knowledge gained from this guide, a collector will move from flea market to auction house with ease knowing which items are "hot" and which articles are definitely overpriced.

As your interest in collecting grows, you may want to start a reference library of your favorite areas. For the collector who needs more extensive coverage of the collectibles market, The House of Collectibles publishes a complete line of comprehensive companion guides which are itemized at the back of this book. They contain full coverage on buying, selling, and caring of valuable articles, plus listings with thousands of prices for rare, unusual, and common antiques and collectibles.

$9.95-2nd Edition, 672 pgs., Order #393-7

The House of Collectibles recommends *The Official Price Guide to Collector Plates,* second edition, as the companion to this guide.

- *Over 18,000 current collector values* — The most complete listing of all U.S. and Foreign plate manufacturers and distributors in print!
- **COMPARE CURRENT MARKET VALUES WITH THE ORIGINAL ISSUE PRICE** — Our special price column will enable you to spot the best investment potential in one glance!
- **INVESTMENT REVIEW** — Certain types of plates, artists and manufacturers are more valuable . . . learn which ones are and why!
- **EVERY KNOWN COLLECTOR PLATE, FROM 1895 TO DATE** — Each plate listing includes title and series, the original release date, designing artist, production methods used, quantities issued, issue price and the current value price range.
- **EXPANDED GALLERY OF ARTISTS** — Read about the legendary artists who create collector plates including tributes to the late Ted De Grazia and Frances Hook.
- **FULLY ILLUSTRATED.**

Available from your local dealer or order direct from:
THE HOUSE OF COLLECTIBLES, see order blank

RECOMMENDED READING

Doulton Pottery, Parts I and II by Richard Dennis
The Doulton Lambeth Wares by Desmond Eyles
Royal Doulton 1815-1965 by Desmond Eyles
Royal Doulton Figures by Desmond Eyles and Richard Dennis
Royal Doulton Character & Toby Jugs by Desmond Eyles
The Doulton Story by Paul Atterbury and Louise Irvine
Limited Edition Loving-Cups and Jugs by Richard Dennis
Doulton Flambe Animals by Jocelyn Lukins
Royal Doulton Figurines and Character Jugs by Katherine Morrison McClinton
Royal Doulton Series Ware by Louise Irvine
Doulton Stoneware Pottery by Richard Dennis
Royal Doulton Figurines by Chilton Press

HOW TO USE THIS BOOK

The HN series which comprises the majority of the Royal Doulton line is listed both numerically and alphabetically. The numerical list records the HN figures with their dates of introduction and discontinuance. In the alphabetical list, a brief description of the pieces is given. Subjects in the HN series are highly diversified representing the works of many different artists at different time periods. This series is good for topical collecting. Basically, there are three categories: historical characters, fictional characters, and general characters. Historical characters include kings, queens and other individuals taken from history. Fictional characters are best exemplified by the Dickens characters. General characters, which is the largest of the groups, include trades people and ladies in flowing gowns.

Following the numerical listing of the HN series is the numerical listing of the M series which contains miniature fancy and character figures. The numerical listings of both groups include all objects bearing those prefix letters including those which belong to sub series of their own. The numerical listings are designed for quick easy reference. More detailed information on these works is contained in the alphabetical listings.

Through the years, Royal Doulton has issued many wildlife figurines. The majority, while carrying HN prefix numbers, were grouped into a sub series of their own. In addition to these HN figures of animals and birds, a K series or miniature animal and bird figures was also produced. The HN animal and bird figures are listed numerically followed by a numerical listing of the K animal and bird figures. These numerical listings are then followed by a priced alphabetical listing of both groups.

Following is a combined alphabetical listing of the HN and M series. The book also includes different series of limited editions, toby jugs, plates, rouge flambe and miscellaneous items.

PRICES. Prices shown in this book represent average retail selling prices compiled from dealers' catalogues, auction results, magazine ads, and other sources. Price ranges are given for out-of-production items while those in current production are listed at the retail price. Although extreme care has been made to be accurate, the prices listed should be used as guidelines. Prices vary throughout the country, therefore discovering prices higher or lower than those listed is possible, although unusual.

"HN" NUMERICAL LISTINGS OF FANCY AND CHARACTER FIGURES

	Date	Price Range	
HN 1			
□ Darling (1st version)	1913-1928	1000.00	1150.00
HN 2			
□ Elizabeth Fry	1913-1938	4000.00	4500.00
HN 3			
□ Milking Time	1913-1938	3000.00	3500.00
HN 4			
□ Picardy Peasant (female)	1913-1938	1500.00	2000.00
HN 5			
□ Picardy Peasant (female)	1913-1938	1500.00	2000.00
HN 6			
□ Dunce	1913-1938	2750.00	3000.00
HN 7			
□ Pedlar Wolf	1913-1938	2000.00	2500.00
HN 8			
□ The Crinoline	1913-1938	1300.00	1450.00
HN 9			
□ The Crinoline	1913-1938	1300.00	1450.00
HN 9A			
□ The Crinoline	1913-1938	1300.00	1450.00
HN 10			
□ Madonna of the Square	1913-1938	1450.00	1600.00
HN 10A			
□ Madonna of the Square	1913-1938	1350.00	1500.00
HN 11			
□ Madonna of the Square	1913-1938	1450.00	1700.00
HN 12			
□ Baby	1913-1938	2050.00	2200.00
HN 13			
□ Picardy Peasant (male)	1913-1938	1950.00	2000.00
HN 14			
□ Madonna of the Square	1913-1938	1450.00	1700.00
HN 15			
□ The Sleepy Scholar	1913-1938	1650.00	1800.00
HN 16			
□ The Sleepy Scholar	1913-1938	1550.00	1700.00
HN 17			
□ Picardy Peasant (male)	1913-1938	1850.00	2000.00
HN 17A			
□ Picardy Peasant (female)	1913-1938	1850.00	2000.00
HN 18			
□ Pussy	1913-1938	2400.00	2600.00
HN 19			
□ Picardy Peasant (male)	1913-1938	1600.00	1850.00
HN 20			
□ The Coquette	1913-1938	2500.00	3000.00

	Date	Price Range	
HN 21 ☐ The Crinoline	1913-1938	1300.00	1450.00
HN 21A ☐ The Crinoline	1913-1938	1250.00	1400.00
HN 22 ☐ The Lavender Woman	1913-1938	1750.00	2000.00
HN 23 ☐ The Lavender Woman	1913-1938	1750.00	2000.00
HN 23A ☐ The Lavender Woman	1913-1938	1750.00	2000.00
HN 24 ☐ Sleep	1913-1938	2000.00	2250.00
HN 24A ☐ Sleep	1913-1938	2200.00	2400.00
HN 25 ☐ Sleep	1913-1938	2500.00	2800.00
HN 25A ☐ Sleep	1913-1938	2500.00	2800.00
HN 26 ☐ The Diligent Scholar	1913-1938	1750.00	2000.00
HN 27 ☐ Madonna of the Square	1913-1938	1650.00	1800.00
HN 28 ☐ Motherhood	1913-1938	1750.00	2000.00
HN 29 ☐ The Sleepy Scholar	1913-1938	1450.00	1600.00
HN 30 ☐ Motherhood	1913-1938	2250.00	2500.00
HN 31 ☐ The Return of Persephone..........	1913-1938	4000.00	5000.00
HN 32 ☐ Child and Crab	1913-1938	1750.00	2000.00
HN 33 ☐ An Arab	1913-1938	1600.00	1800.00
HN 34 ☐ Moorish Minstrel	1913-1938	2000.00	2200.00
HN 35 ☐ Charley's Aunt (1st version)	1914-1938	700.00	800.00
HN 36 ☐ The Sentimental Pierrot............	1914-1938	1750.00	1900.00
HN 37 ☐ The Coquette	1914-1938	2500.00	3000.00
HN 38 ☐ The Carpet Vendor (1st version)	1914-1938	2750.00	3000.00
HN 38A ☐ The Carpet Vendor (1st version)	1914A-1938	2750.00	3000.00
HN 39 ☐ The Welsh Girl	1914-1938	2500.00	2750.00

	Date	Price Range	
HN 40			
☐ A Lady of the Elizabethan Period (1st version)	1914-1938	1750.00	2000.00
HN 40A			
☐ A Lady of the Elizabethan Period (1st version)	1914-1938	1750.00	2000.00
HN 41			
☐ A Lady of the Georgian Period	1914-1938	2000.00	2300.00
HN 42			
☐ Robert Burns	1914-1938	3000.00	3500.00
HN 43			
☐ A Lady of the Time of Henry VI	1914-1938	2750.00	3250.00
HN 44			
☐ A Lilac Shawl	1915-1938	1250.00	1500.00
HN 44A			
☐ A Lilac Shawl	1915-1938	1250.00	1500.00
HN 45			
☐ A Jester (1st version)	1915-1938	1250.00	1500.00
HN 45A			
☐ A Jester (2nd version)	1915-1938	1250.00	1500.00
HN 45B			
☐ A Jester (2nd version)	1915-1938	1250.00	1500.00
HN 46			
☐ The Gainsborough Hat	1915-1938	1200.00	1350.00
HN 46A			
☐ The Gainsborough Hat	1915-1938	1200.00	1350.00
HN 47			
☐ The Gainsborough Hat	1915-1938	1200.00	1350.00
HN 48			
☐ Lady of the Fan	1916-1938	1650.00	1800.00
HN 48A			
☐ Lady with Rose	1916-1938	1650.00	1800.00
HN 49			
☐ Under the Gooseberry Bush	1916-1938	1250.00	1500.00
HN 50			
☐ A Spook	1916-1938	1100.00	1200.00
HN 51			
☐ A Spook	1916-1938	1250.00	1400.00
HN 51A			
☐ A Spook	1916-1938	1250.00	1400.00
HN 51B			
☐ A Spook	1916-1938	1250.00	1400.00
HN 52			
☐ Lady of the Fan	1916-1938	1650.00	1800.00
HN 52A			
☐ Lady with Rose	1916-1938	1650.00	1800.00
HN 53			
☐ Lady of the Fan	1916-1938	1650.00	1800.00

	Date	Price Range	
HN 53A			
☐ Lady of the Fan	1916-1938	1650.00	1800.00
HN 54			
☐ Lady Ermine	1916-1938	1250.00	1500.00
HN 55			
☐ A Jester (2nd version)	1916-1938	1300.00	1500.00
HN 56			
☐ The Land of Nod	1916-1938	1750.00	2000.00
HN 56A			
☐ The Land of Nod	1916-1938	2000.00	2300.00
HN 56B			
☐ The Land of Nod	1916-1938	1750.00	2000.00
HN 57			
☐ The Curtsey	1916-1938	1500.00	1750.00
HN 57A			
☐ The Flounced Skirt	1916-1938	1650.00	1800.00
HN 57B			
☐ The Curtsey	1916-1938	1500.00	1750.00
HN 58			
☐ A Spook	1916-1938	1250.00	1400.00
HN 59			
☐ Upon her Cheeks she Wept	1916-1938	1500.00	1600.00
HN 60			
☐ Shy Anne	1916-1938	1500.00	1700.00
HN 61			
☐ Katharine	1916-1938	1500.00	1700.00
HN 62			
☐ A Child's Grace	1916-1938	1400.00	1600.00
HN 62A			
☐ A Child's Grace	1916-1938	1500.00	1700.00
HN 63			
☐ The Little Land	1916-1938	2000.00	2500.00
HN 64			
☐ Shy Anne	1916-1938	1500.00	1600.00
HN 65			
☐ Shy Anne	1916-1938	1550.00	1700.00
HN 66			
☐ The Flounced Skirt	1916-1938	1650.00	1800.00
HN 66A			
☐ The Curtsey	1916-1938	1550.00	1700.00
HN 67			
☐ The Little Land	1916-1938	1750.00	2000.00
HN 68			
☐ Lady with a Rose	1916-1938	1650.00	1800.00
HN 69			
☐ Pretty Lady	1916-1938	1250.00	1500.00
HN 70			
☐ Pretty Lady	1916-1938	1250.00	1500.00

	Date	Price Range	
HN 71			
☐ A Jester (1st version)	1917-1938	1250.00	1500.00
HN 71A			
☐ A Jester (1st version)	1917-1938	1250.00	1500.00
HN 72			
☐ An Orange Vendor	1917-1938	950.00	1100.00
HN 73			
☐ A Lady of the Elizabethan Period (1st version).....................	1917-1938	1800.00	2000.00
HN 74			
☐ Katharine	1917-1938	1650.00	1800.00
HN 75			
☐ Blue Beard (1st version)	1917-1938	2550.00	3000.00
HN 76			
☐ Carpet Vendor (2nd version)	1917-1938	3000.00	3500.00
HN 77			
☐ The Flounced Skirt	1917-1938	1650.00	1800.00
HN 78			
☐ The Flounced Skirt	1917-1938	1650.00	1800.00
HN 79			
☐ Shylock	1917-1938	2500.00	2750.00
HN 80			
☐ Fisherwomen	1917-1938	3000.00	3500.00
HN 81			
☐ A Shepherd (1st version)	1918-1938	2250.00	2500.00
HN 82			
☐ The Afternoon Call	1918-1938	2250.00	2500.00
HN 83			
☐ The Lady Anne	1918-1938	2750.00	3000.00
HN 84			
☐ A Mandarin (1st version)	1918-1938	2250.00	2500.00
HN 85			
☐ Jack Point	1918-1938	2000.00	2200.00
HN 86			
☐ Out for a Walk...................	1918-1936	2250.00	2500.00
HN 87			
☐ The Lady Anne	1918-1938	2750.00	3000.00
HN 88			
☐ Spooks	1918-1936	1400.00	1650.00
HN 89			
☐ Spooks	1918-1936	1400.00	1650.00
HN 90			
☐ Doris Keene as Cavallini (1st version)	1918-1936	2000.00	2500.00
HN 91			
☐ Jack Point	1918-1938	2000.00	2250.00
HN 92			
☐ The Welsh Girl	1918-1938	2500.00	2750.00
HN 93			
☐ The Lady Anne	1918-1938	2750.00	3000.00

	Date	Price Range	
HN 94			
☐ The Young Knight	1918-1936	2750.00	3250.00
HN 95			
☐ Europa and the Bull	1918-1938	3000.00	3500.00
HN 96			
☐ Doris Keene as Cavallini (2nd version)	1918-1938	2250.00	2500.00
HN 97			
☐ The Mermaid	1918-1936	650.00	750.00
HN 98			
☐ Guy Gawkes	1918-1949	1300.00	1500.00
HN 99			
☐ Jack Point	1918-1938	2000.00	2250.00
HN 100 — HN 299 ANIMAL AND BIRD MODELS			
HN 300			
☐ The Mermaid	1918-1936	850.00	1000.00
HN 301			
☐ Moorish Piper Minstrel	1918-1938	2750.00	3000.00
HN 302			
☐ Pretty Lady	1918-1938	1350.00	1600.00
HN 303			
☐ Motherhood	1918-1938	2250.00	2500.00
HN 304			
☐ Lady with Rose	1918-1938	1650.00	1800.00
HN 305			
☐ A Scribe	1918-1936	1100.00	1200.00
HN 306			
☐ Milking Time	1913-1938	2750.00	3000.00
HN 307			
☐ The Sentimental Pierrot	1918-1938	1750.00	1900.00
HN 308			
☐ A Jester (2nd version)	1918-1938	1250.00	1500.00
HN 309			
☐ A Lady of the Elizabethan Period (2nd version)	1918-1938	1750.00	2000.00
HN 310			
☐ Dunce	1918-1938	2750.00	3000.00
HN 311			
☐ Dancing Figure	1918-1938	3500.00	4000.00
HN 312			
☐ Spring (1st version) The Seasons	1918-1938	1500.00	1800.00
HN 313			
☐ Summer (1st version) The Seasons . .	1918-1938	1650.00	1800.00
HN 314			
☐ Autumn (1st version) The Seasons . . .	1918-1938	1200.00	1400.00
HN 315			
☐ Winter (1st version) The Seasons	1918-1938	1500.00	1800.00
HN 316			
☐ A Mandarin (1st version)	1918-1938	2250.00	2500.00

	Date	Price Range	
HN 317			
☐ Shylock	1918-1938	2500.00	2750.00
HN 318			
☐ A Mandarin (1st version)	1918-1938	2250.00	2500.00
HN 319			
☐ A Gnome	1918-1938	1000.00	1200.00
HN 320			
☐ A Jester (1st version)	1918-1938	1250.00	1500.00
HN 321			
☐ Digger (New Zealand)	1918-1938	1250.00	1500.00
HN 322			
☐ Digger (Australian)	1918-1938	1250.00	1500.00
HN 323			
☐ Blighty	1918-1938	1250.00	1500.00
HN 324			
☐ A Scribe	1918-1938	1100.00	1200.00
HN 325			
☐ Pussy	1918-1938	2450.00	2650.00
HN 326			
☐ Madonna of the Square	1918-1938	1650.00	1800.00
HN 327			
☐ The Curtsey	1918-1938	1550.00	1700.00
HN 328			
☐ Moorish Piper Minstrel	1918-1938	2750.00	3000.00
HN 329			
☐ The Gainsborough Hat	1918-1938	1200.00	1350.00
HN 330			
☐ Pretty Lady	1918-1938	1450.00	1600.00
HN 331			
☐ A Lady of the Georgian Period	1918-1938	2000.00	2300.00
HN 332			
☐ Lady Ermine	1918-1938	1450.00	1750.00
HN 333			
☐ The Flounced Skirt	1918-1938	1550.00	1700.00
HN 334			
☐ The Curtsey	1918-1938	1450.00	1600.00
HN 335			
☐ Lady of the Fan	1919-1938	1650.00	1800.00
HN 336			
☐ Lady with Rose	1919-1938	1700.00	1800.00
HN 337			
☐ The Parson's Daughter	1919-1938	800.00	900.00
HN 338			
☐ The Parson's Daughter	1919-1938	800.00	900.00
HN 339			
☐ In Grandma's Days (A Lilac Shawl) ...	1919-1938	1250.00	1500.00
HN 340			
☐ In Grandma's Days (A Lilac Shawl) ...	1919-1938	1250.00	1500.00

	Date	Price Range	
HN 341			
☐ Katherine	1919-1938	1250.00	1500.00
HN 342			
☐ The Lavender Woman	1919-1938	1650.00	1800.00
HN 343			
☐ An Arab	1919-1938	1750.00	2000.00
HN 344			
☐ Henry Irving as Cardinal Wolsey.....	1919-1949	2000.00	2500.00
HN 345			
☐ Doris Keene as Cavallini (2nd version)	1919-1949	2750.00	3000.00
HN 346			
☐ Tony Weller (1st version)	1919-1938	1800.00	2000.00
HN 347			
☐ Guy Fawkes	1919-1938	1250.00	1400.00
HN 348			
☐ The Carpet Vendor (1st version)	1919-1938	1750.00	2000.00
HN 349			
☐ Fisherwomen	1919-1968	2750.00	3000.00
HN 350			
☐ The Carpet Vendor (1st version)	1919-1938	3000.00	3500.00
HN 351			
☐ Picardy Peasant (female)...........	1919-1938	3000.00	3250.00
HN 352			
☐ The Gainsborough Hat	1919-1938	1750.00	2000.00
HN 353			
☐ Digger (Australian)	1919-1938	1350.00	1600.00
HN 354			
☐ A Geisha (1st version)	1919-1938	2250.00	2500.00
HN 355			
☐ Dolly	1919-1938	1250.00	1500.00
HN 356			
☐ Sir Thomas Lovell.................	1919-1938	1500.00	1700.00
HN 357			
☐ Dunce	1919-1938	2750.00	3000.00
HN 358			
☐ An Old King.....................	1919-1938	1150.00	1300.00
HN 359			
☐ Fisherwomen	1919-1938	3000.00	3500.00
HN 360 NO DETAILS AVAILABLE			
HN 361			
☐ Pretty Lady	1919-1938	1450.00	1600.00
HN 362			
☐ In Grandma's Days................	1919-1938	1550.00	1700.00
HN 363			
☐ The Curtsey.....................	1919-1938	1600.00	1700.00
HN 364			
☐ Moorish Minstrel	1920-1938	2750.00	3000.00

	Date	Price Range	
HN 365			
☐ Double Jester	1920-1938	2750.00	3250.00
HN 366			
☐ A Mandarin (2nd version)	1920-1938	1400.00	1550.00
HN 367			
☐ A Jester (1st version)	1920-1938	1400.00	1500.00
HN 368			
☐ Tony Weller (1st version)	1920-1938	1800.00	2000.00
HN 369			
☐ Cavalier (1st version)	1920-1938	2100.00	2400.00
HN 370			
☐ Henry VIII (1st version)	1920-1938	2350.00	2600.00
HN 371			
☐ The Curtsey	1920-1938	1650.00	1800.00
HN 372			
☐ Spooks	1920-1936	1400.00	1650.00
HN 373			
☐ Boy on a Crocodile	1920-1938	4000.00	4500.00
HN 374			
☐ Lady and Blackamoor (1st version) . .	1920-1936	2500.00	2700.00
HN 375			
☐ Lady and Blackamoor (2nd version) . .	1920-1938	2500.00	2700.00
HN 376			
☐ A Geisha (1st version)	1920-1938	2300.00	2500.00
HN 377			
☐ Lady and Blackamoor (2nd version) . .	1920-1938	2500.00	2700.00
HN 378			
☐ An Arab	1920-1938	1500.00	1750.00
HN 379			
☐ Ellen Terry as Queen Catherine	1920-1949	2750.00	3000.00
HN 380			
☐ A Gnome	1920-1938	1000.00	1200.00
HN 381			
☐ A Gnome	1920-1938	1000.00	1200.00
HN 382			
☐ A Mandarin (1st version)	1920-1938	2250.00	2500.00
HN 383			
☐ The Gainsborough Hat	1920-1938	1150.00	1300.00
HN 384			
☐ Pretty Lady	1920-1938	1450.00	1600.00
HN 385			
☐ St. George (1st version)	1920-1938	4500.00	5000.00
HN 386			
☐ St. George (1st version)	1920-1938	4500.00	5000.00
HN 387			
☐ A Geisha (1st version)	1920-1938	2250.00	2500.00
HN 388			
☐ In Grandma's Days	1920-1938	1650.00	1800.00

	Date	Price Range	
HN 389			
☐ The Little Mother (1st version)	1920-1938	2500.00	2700.00
HN 390			
☐ The Little Mother (1st version)	1920-1938	2500.00	2700.00
HN 391			
☐ A Princess	1920-1938	2750.00	3000.00
HN 392			
☐ A Princess	1920-1938	2750.00	3000.00
HN 393			
☐ Lady Without Bouquet	1920-1938	2000.00	2500.00
HN 394			
☐ Lady Without Bouquet	1920-1938	2000.00	2500.00
HN 395			
☐ Contenment	1920-1938	1850.00	2000.00
HN 396			
☐ Contenment	1920-1938	1850.00	2000.00
HN 397			
☐ Puff and Powder	1920-1938	2000.00	2200.00
HN 398			
☐ Puff and Powder	1920-1938	2000.00	2200.00
HN 399			
☐ Japanese Fan	1920-1938	1450.00	1600.00
HN 400			
☐ Puff and Powder	1920-1938	2000.00	2200.00
HN 401			
☐ Marie (1st version)	1920-1938	2250.00	2500.00
HN 402			
☐ Betty (1st version)	1920-1938	2000.00	2250.00
HN 403			
☐ Betty (1st version	1920-1938	2000.00	2250.00
HN 404			
☐ King Charles	1920-1951	1750.00	2000.00
HN 405			
☐ Japanese Fan	1920-1938	1250.00	1500.00
HN 406			
☐ The Bouquet	1920-1938	1500.00	1700.00
HN 407			
☐ Omar Khayyam and the Beloved	1920-1938	3500.00	4000.00
HN 408			
☐ Omar Khayyam (1st version)	1920-1938	2250.00	3000.00
HN 409			
☐ Omar Khayyam (1st version)	1938-1938	2250.00	3000.00
HN 410			
☐ Blue Beard (1st version)	1920-1938	3000.00	3500.00
HN 411			
☐ A Lady of the Elizabethan Period (1st version)	1920-1938	2000.00	2500.00
HN 412			
☐ A Jester (1st version)	1920-1938	1350.00	1300.00

	Date	Price Range	
HN 413			
☐ The Crinoline	1920-1938	1700.00	1950.00
HN 414			
☐ The Bouquet	1920-1938	1550.00	1700.00
HN 415			
☐ Moorish Minstrel	1920-1938	2750.00	3000.00
HN 416			
☐ Moorish Piper Minstrel	1920-1938	2750.00	3000.00
HN 417			
☐ One of the Forty (1st version)	1920-1938	1100.00	1200.00
HN 418			
☐ One of the Forty (2nd version)	1920-1938	1100.00	1200.00
HN 419			
☐ Omar Khayyam and the Beloved.....	1920-1938	3500.00	4000.00
HN 420			
☐ A Princess......................	1920-1938	2750.00	3000.00
HN 421			
☐ Contentment....................	1920-1938	1500.00	1700.00
HN 422			
☐ The Bouquet	1920-1938	1550.00	1700.00
HN 423			
☐ One of the Forty (3rd and 8th version)	1921-1938	450.00	500.00
HN 424			
☐ Sleep	1921-1938	2000.00	2200.00
HN 425			
☐ The Goosegirl	1921-1938	2750.00	3000.00
HN 426			
☐ A Jester (1st version)	1921-1938	1250.00	1500.00
HN 427			
☐ One of the Forty (9th version)	1921-1938	1100.00	1200.00
HN 428			
☐ The Bouquet	1921-1938	1550.00	1700.00
HN 429			
☐ The Bouquet	1921-1938	1550.00	1700.00
HN 430			
☐ A Princess......................	1921-1938	2750.00	3000.00
HN 431			
☐ A Princess......................	1921-1938	2750.00	3000.00
HN 432			
☐ Puff and Powder..................	1921-1938	2000.00	2200.00
HN 433			
☐ Puff and Powder..................	1921-1938	2000.00	2200.00
HN 434			
☐ Marie (1st version)	1921-1938	2250.00	2500.00
HN 435			
☐ Betty (1st version)................	1921-1938	2000.00	2250.00
HN 436			
☐ The Goosegirl	1921-1938	2500.00	3000.00

	Date	Price Range	
HN 437			
☐ The Goosegirl	1921-1938	2500.00	3000.00
HN 438			
☐ Betty (1st version).................	1921-1938	2000.00	2250.00
HN 439			
☐ Japanese Fan	1921-1938	1500.00	1600.00
HN 440			
☐ Japanese Fan	1921-1938	1500.00	1600.00
HN 441			
☐ The Parson's Daughter	1921-1938	850.00	950.00
HN 442			
☐ In Grandma's Days................	1921-1938	1650.00	1800.00
HN 443			
☐ Out for a Walk....................	1921-1938	2250.00	2500.00
HN 444			
☐ A Lady of the Georgian Period	1921-1938	2100.00	2300.00
HN 445			
☐ Guy Fawkes	1921-1938	1250.00	1400.00
HN 446			
☐ A Jester (1st version)	1921-1936	1350.00	1500.00
HN 447			
☐ Lady with Shawl	1921-1936	3250.00	3500.00
HN 448			
☐ The Goosegirl	1921-1936	2750.00	3000.00
HN 449			
☐ Fruit Gathering	1921-1938	2750.00	3000.00
HN 450			
☐ A Mandarin (3rd version)	1921-1938	1500.00	1750.00
HN 451			
☐ An Old Man	1921-1938	2250.00	2500.00
HN 452 NO DETAILS AVAILABLE			
HN 453			
☐ The Gainsborough Hat	1921-1938	1250.00	1400.00
HN 454			
☐ The Smiling Buddha...............	1921-1938	1250.00	1400.00
HN 455			
☐ A Mandarin (2nd version)	1921-1938	1750.00	2000.00
HN 456			
☐ The Welsh Girl	1921-1938	2500.00	2700.00
HN 457			
☐ Crouching Nude	1921-1938	1100.00	1300.00
HN 458			
☐ Lady with Shawl	1921-1938	3000.00	3500.00
HN 459			
☐ Omar Khayyam and the Beloved.....	1921-1938	3500.00	4000.00
HN 460			
☐ A Mandarin (3rd version)	1921-1938	2250.00	2500.00
HN 461			
☐ A Mandarin (3rd version)	1921-1938	2250.00	2500.00

	Date	Price Range	
HN 462			
☐ Woman Holding Child	1921-1938	2000.00	2200.00
HN 463			
☐ Polly Peachum (1st version)	1921-1949	600.00	700.00
HN 464			
☐ Captain MacHeath	1921-1949	750.00	850.00
HN 465			
☐ Polly Peachum	1921-1949	500.00	600.00
HN 466			
☐ Tulips..........................	1921-1938	1600.00	1700.00
HN 467			
☐ Doris Keane as Cavallini (1st version)......................	1921-1936	2000.00	2200.00
HN 468			
☐ Contentment.....................	1921-1938	1750.00	2000.00
HN 469			
☐ The Little Mother (1st version).......	1921-1938	1750.00	2000.00
HN 470			
☐ Lady and Blackamoor (2nd version) ..	1921-1938	2500.00	2700.00
HN 471			
☐ Katharine	1921-1938	2000.00	2500.00
HN 472			
☐ Spring (1st version) The Seasons	1921-1938	1500.00	1800.00
HN 473			
☐ Summer (1st version) The Seasons ..	1921-1938	1650.00	1800.00
HN 474			
☐ Autumn (1st version) The Seasons ...	1921-1938	1300.00	1400.00
HN 475			
☐ Winter (1st version) The Seasons	1921-1938	1500.00	1800.00
HN 476			
☐ Fruit Gathering	1921-1938	2650.00	2800.00
HN 477			
☐ Betty (1st version)................	1921-1938	2500.00	3000.00
HN 478			
☐ Betty (1st version)................	1921-1938	2500.00	3000.00
HN 479			
☐ The Balloon Seller	1921-1938	2250.00	2500.00
HN 480			
☐ One of the Forty (10th version)	1921-1938	800.00	900.00
HN 481			
☐ One of the Forty (11th version)	1921-1938	1100.00	1200.00
HN 482			
☐ One of the Forty (12th version)	1921-1938	1100.00	1200.00
HN 483			
☐ One of the Forty (11th version)	1921-1938	1100.00	1200.00
HN 484			
☐ One of the Forty (12th version)	1921-1938	1100.00	1200.00
HN 485			
☐ Lucy Lockett (1st version)	1921-1949	800.00	900.00

	Date	Price Range	
HN 486			
☐ The Balloon Seller	1921-1938	1500.00	1700.00
HN 487			
☐ Pavlova	1921-1938	1500.00	1700.00
HN 488			
☐ Tulips..........................	1921-1938	1500.00	1700.00
HN 489			
☐ Polly Peachum (2nd version)	1921-1938	400.00	500.00
HN 490			
☐ One of the Forty (1st version)	1921-1938	1100.00	1200.00
HN 491			
☐ One of the Forty (11th version)	1921-1938	1100.00	1200.00
HN 492			
☐ One of the Forty (12th version)	1921-1938	1100.00	1200.00
HN 493			
☐ One of the Forty (10th version)	1921-1938	1100.00	1200.00
HN 494			
☐ One of the Forty (2nd version)	1921-1938	1100.00	1200.00
HN 495			
☐ One of the Forty (1st version)	1921-1938	1100.00	1200.00
HN 496			
☐ One of the Forty (13th version)	1921-1938	1100.00	1200.00
HN 497			
☐ One of the Forty (10th version)	1921-1938	1100.00	1200.00
HN 498			
☐ One of the Forty (2nd version)	1921-1938	1100.00	1200.00
HN 499			
☐ One of the Forty (10th version)	1921-1938	1100.00	1200.00
HN 500			
☐ One of the Forty (13th version)	1921-1938	1100.00	1200.00
HN 501			
☐ One of the Forty (1st version)	1921-1938	1100.00	1200.00
HN 502			
☐ Marie (1st version)	1921-1938	2250.00	2500.00
HN 503			
☐ Fruit Gathering...................	1921-1938	2500.00	3000.00
HN 504			
☐ Marie (1st version)	1921-1938	2250.00	2500.00
HN 505			
☐ Marie (1st version)	1921-1938	2250.00	2500.00
HN 506			
☐ Marie (1st version)	1921-1938	2250.00	2500.00
HN 507			
☐ Pussy..........................	1921-1938	2400.00	2600.00
HN 508			
☐ An Orange Vendor	1921-1938	1000.00	1100.00
HN 509			
☐ Lady of the Fan..................	1921-1938	1650.00	1800.00

	Date	Price Range	
HN 510			
☐ A Child's Grace....................	1921-1938	1650.00	1800.00
HN 511			
☐ Upon her Cheeks she Wept	1921-1938	1500.00	1600.00
HN 512			
☐ A Spook........................	1921-1938	1250.00	1400.00
HN 513			
☐ Picardy Peasant (female)...........	1921-1938	1750.00	2000.00
HN 514			
☐ The Welsh Girl	1921-1938	2500.00	2700.00
HN 515			
☐ Lady with Rose...................	1921-1938	1650.00	1800.00
HN 516			
☐ The Welsh Girl	1921-1938	2500.00	2700.00
HN 517			
☐ Lady with Rose...................	1921-1938	1650.00	1800.00
HN 518			
☐ The Curtsey.....................	1921-1938	1650.00	1800.00
HN 519			
☐ The Welsh Girl	1921-1938	2500.00	2700.00
HN 520			
☐ The Welsh Girl	1921-1938	2500.00	2700.00
HN 521			
☐ An Orange Vendor	1921-1938	1000.00	1100.00
HN 522			
☐ Upon her Cheeks she Wept	1921-1938	1500.00	1600.00
HN 523			
☐ Sentinel........................	1921-1938	4500.00	5000.00
HN 524			
☐ Lucy Lockett....................	1921-1938	850.00	950.00
HN 525			
☐ The Flower Seller's Children........	1921-1949	650.00	750.00
HN 526			
☐ The Beggar (1st version)	1921-1949	600.00	700.00
HN 527			
☐ The Highwayman	1921-1949	700.00	800.00
HN 528			
☐ One of the Forty (1st version)	1921-1938	1100.00	1200.00
HN 529			
☐ Mr. Pickwick (1st version)	1922-	45.00	60.00
renumbered as miniature	1932-		
HN 530			
☐ The Fat Boy (1st version)	1922-	45.00	60.00
renumbered as miniature	1932-		
HN 531			
☐ Sam Weller	1922-	45.00	60.00
renumbered as miniature	1932-		

	Date	Price Range	
HN 532			
☐ Mr. Micawber (1st version)	1922-	45.00	60.00
renumbered as miniature	1932-		
HN 533			
☐ Sairey Gamp (1st version)	1922-	45.00	60.00
renumbered as miniature	1932-		
HN 534			
☐ Fagin	1922-	45.00	60.00
renumbered as miniature	1932-		
HN 535			
☐ Pecksniff (1st version)	1922-	45.00	60.00
renumbered as miniature	1932-		
HN 536			
☐ Stiggins	1922-	45.00	60.00
renumbered as miniature	1932-		
HN 537			
☐ Bill Sykes	1922-	45.00	60.00
renumbered as miniature	1932-		
HN 538			
☐ Buz Fuz	1922-	45.00	60.00
renumbered as miniature	1932-		
HN 539			
☐ Tiny Tim	1922-	45.00	60.00
renumbered as miniature	1932-		
HN 540			
☐ Little Nell	1922-	45.00	60.00
renumbered as miniature	1932-		
HN 541			
☐ Alfred Jingle	1922-	45.00	60.00
renumbered as miniature	1932-		
HN 542			
☐ The Cobbler (1st version)	1922-1939	1100.00	1200.00
HN 543			
☐ The Cobbler (1st version)	1922-1938	1200.00	1300.00
HN 544			
☐ Tony Weller (2nd version)	1922-	45.00	60.00
renumbered as miniature	1932-		
HN 545			
☐ Uriah Heep (1st version)	1922-	45.00	60.00
renumbered as miniature	1932-		
HN 546			
☐ The Artful Dodger	1922-	45.00	60.00
renumbered as miniature	1932-		
HN 547			
☐ The Curtsey	1922-1938	1450.00	1600.00
HN 548			
☐ The Balloon Seller	1922-1938	800.00	900.00
HN 549			
☐ Polly Peachum (2nd version)	1922-1949	450.00	500.00

	Date	Price Range	
HN 550			
☐ Polly Peachum (1st version)	1922-1949	500.00	600.00
HN 551			
☐ The Flower Seller's Children	1922-1949	500.00	600.00
HN 552			
☐ A Jester (1st version)	1922-1938	1350.00	1500.00
HN 553			
☐ Pecksniff (2nd version)	1923-1939	400.00	500.00
HN 554			
☐ Uriah Heep (2nd version)	1923-1939	400.00	500.00
HN 555			
☐ The Fat Boy (2nd version)	1923-1939	400.00	500.00
HN 556			
☐ Mr. Pickwick (2nd version)	1923-1939	400.00	500.00
HN 557			
☐ Mr. Micawber (2nd version)	1923-1939	400.00	500.00
HN 558			
☐ Sairey Gamp (2nd version)	1923-1939	400.00	500.00
HN 559			
☐ The Goosegirl	1923-1938	2750.00	3000.00
HN 560			
☐ The Goosegirl	1923-1938	2750.00	3000.00
HN 561			
☐ Fruit Gathering	1923-1938	2500.00	3000.00
HN 562			
☐ Fruit Gathering	1923-1938	2500.00	3000.00
HN 563			
☐ Man in Tudor Costume	1923-1938	1400.00	1750.00
HN 564			
☐ The Parson's Daughter	1923-1949	350.00	400.00
HN 565			
☐ Pretty Lady	1923-1938	1450.00	1600.00
HN 566			
☐ The Crinoline	1923-1938	1250.00	1400.00
HN 567			
☐ The Bouquet	1923-1938	1550.00	1700.00
HN 568			
☐ Shy Anne	1923-1949	1450.00	1600.00
HN 569			
☐ The Lavender Woman	1924-1928	1150.00	1300.00
HN 570			
☐ Woman Holding Child	1923-1938	2000.00	2200.00
HN 571			
☐ Falstaff (1st version)	1923-1938	700.00	800.00
HN 572			
☐ Contentment	1923-1938	1750.00	2000.00
HN 573			
☐ Madonna of the Square	1913-1938	1650.00	1800.00
HN 574 NO DETAILS AVAILABLE			

	Date	Price Range	
HN 575			
☐ Falstaff (1st version)	1923-1938	700.00	800.00
HN 576			
☐ Madonna of the Square	1923-1938	1650.00	1800.00
HN 577			
☐ The Chelsea Pair (female)	1923-1938	700.00	800.00
HN 578			
☐ The Chelsea Pair (female)	1923-1938	700.00	800.00
HN 579			
☐ The Chelsea Pair (male)	1923-1938	725.00	800.00
HN 580			
☐ The Chelsea Pair (male)	1923-1938	725.00	800.00
HN 581			
☐ The Perfect Pair	1923-1938	1000.00	1100.00
HN 582			
☐ Grossmith's "Tsang Ihang" Perfume . of Tibet (also called "Tibetian Lady")	1923-Unknown	650.00	700.00
HN 583			
☐ The Balloon Seller	1923-1949	500.00	600.00
HN 584			
☐ Lady with Rose	1923-1938	1650.00	1800.00
HN 585			
☐ Harlequinade	1923-1938	850.00	950.00
HN 586			
☐ Boy with Turban	1923-1938	550.00	650.00
HN 587			
☐ Boy with Turban	1923-1938	550.00	650.00
HN 588			
☐ Girl with Yellow Frock	1923-1938	1350.00	1500.00
HN 589			
☐ Polly Peachum (1st version)	1924-1949	500.00	600.00
HN 590			
☐ Captain MacHeath	1924-1949	750.00	850.00
HN 591			
☐ The Beggar (1st version)	1924-1949	650.00	750.00
HN 592			
☐ The Highwayman	1924-1949	700.00	800.00
HN 593			
☐ Nude on Rock	1924-1938	950.00	1000.00
HN 594			
☐ Madonna of the Square	1924-1938	1650.00	1800.00
HN 595			
☐ Grief	1924-1938	900.00	1000.00
HN 596			
☐ Despair	1924-1938	1400.00	1650.00
HN 597			
☐ The Bather (1st version)	1924-1938	900.00	1000.00
HN 598			
☐ Omar Khayyam and the Beloved	1924-1938	3500.00	4000.00

	Date	Price Range	
HN 599			
☐ Masquerade (male, 1st version)	1924-1949	750.00	800.00
HN 600			
☐ Masquerade (female, 1st version)	1924-1949	750.00	800.00
HN 601			
☐ A Mandarin (3rd version)	1924-1938	2250.00	2500.00
HN 602 NO DETAILS AVAILABLE			
HN 603a			
☐ Child Study	1924-1938	275.00	325.00
HN 603b			
☐ Child Study	1924-1938	300.00	350.00
HN 604a			
☐ Child Study	1924-1938	300.00	350.00
HN 604b			
☐ Child Study	1924-1938	300.00	350.00
HN 605a			
☐ Child Study	1924-1938	300.00	350.00
HN 605b			
☐ Child Study	1924-1938	300.00	350.00
HN 606a			
☐ Child Study	1924-1949	300.00	350.00
HN 606b			
☐ Child Study	1924-1949	300.00	350.00
HN 607 NO DETAILS AVAILABLE			
HN 608			
☐ Falstaff (1st version)	1924-1938	700.00	800.00
HN 609			
☐ Falstaff (1st version)	1924-1938	700.00	800.00
HN 610			
☐ Henry Lytton as Jack Point	1924-1949	800.00	900.00
HN 611			
☐ A Mandarin (3rd version)	1924-1938	2000.00	2500.00
HN 612			
☐ Poke Bonnett	1924-1938	1350.00	1500.00
HN 613			
☐ Madonna of the Square	1924-1938	1650.00	1800.00
HN 614			
☐ Polly Peachum (1st version)	1924-1938	600.00	700.00
HN 615			
☐ Katharine	1924-1938	1650.00	1800.00
HN 616			
☐ A Jester (1st version)	1924-1938	1350.00	1500.00
HN 617			
☐ A Shepherd (1st version)	1924-1938	1750.00	2000.00
HN 618			
☐ Falstaff (2nd version)	1924-1938	700.00	800.00
HN 619			
☐ Falstaff (1st version)	1924-1938	700.00	800.00

	Date	Price Range	
HN 620			
☐ Polly Peachum (2nd version)	1924-1938	450.00	500.00
HN 621			
☐ Pan on Rock	1924-1938	1100.00	1200.00
HN 622			
☐ Pan on Rock	1924-1938	1100.00	1200.00
HN 623			
☐ An Old King.	1924-1938	1300.00	1500.00
HN 624			
☐ Lady with Rose	1924-1938	1650.00	1800.00
HN 625			
☐ A Spook	1924-1938	1250.00	1400.00
HN 626			
☐ Lady with Shawl	1924-1938	3000.00	3500.00
HN 627			
☐ A Jester (1st version)	1924-1938	1350.00	1500.00
HN 628			
☐ The Crinoline	1924-1938	1350.00	1500.00
HN 629			
☐ The Curtsey.	1924-1938	1650.00	1800.00
HN 630			
☐ A Jester (2nd version).	1924-1938	1350.00	1500.00
HN 631			
☐ Fisherwomen	1924-1938	3000.00	3500.00
HN 632			
☐ A Shepherd (1st version)	1924-1938	1750.00	2000.00
HN 633			
☐ A Princess.	1924-1938	2750.00	3000.00
HN 634			
☐ A Geisha (1st version)	1924-1938	2250.00	2500.00
HN 635			
☐ Harlequinade	1924-1938	1150.00	1300.00
HN 636			
☐ Masquerade (male, 1st version)	1924-1938	1000.00	1250.00
HN 637			
☐ Masquerade (female, 1st version)	1924-1938	1000.00	1250.00
HN 638			
☐ Falstaff (1st version)	1924-1938	700.00	800.00
HN 639			
☐ Elsie Maynard.	1924-1949	800.00	900.00
HN 640			
☐ Charley's Aunt (1st version)	1924-1938	900.00	1000.00
HN 641			
☐ A Mandarin	1924-1938	1100.00	1200.00
HN 642			
☐ Pierrette (1st version)	1924-1938	900.00	1000.00
HN 643			
☐ Pierrette (1st version)	1924-1938	900.00	1000.00

	Date	Price Range	
HN 644			
☐ Pierrette (1st version)	1924-1938	800.00	900.00
HN 645			
☐ One of the Forty (12th version)	1924-1938	1100.00	1200.00
HN 646			
☐ One of the Forty (11th version)	1924-1938	1100.00	1200.00
HN 647			
☐ One of the Forty (2nd version)	1924-1938	1100.00	1200.00
HN 648			
☐ One of the Forty (1st version)	1924-1938	1100.00	1200.00
HN 649			
☐ One of the Forty (13th version)	1924-1938	1100.00	1200.00
HN 650			
☐ Crinoline Lady (miniature)	1924-1938	550.00	650.00
HN 651			
☐ Crinoline Lady (miniature)	1924-1938	550.00	650.00
HN 652			
☐ Crinoline Lady (miniature)	1924-1938	550.00	650.00
HN 653			
☐ Crinoline Lady (miniature)	1924-1938	550.00	650.00
HN 654			
☐ Crinoline Lady (miniature)	1924-1938	550.00	650.00
HN 655			
☐ Crinoline Lady (miniature)	1924-1938	550.00	650.00
HN 656			
☐ The Mask	1924-1938	850.00	950.00
HN 657			
☐ The Mask	1924-1938	850.00	950.00
HN 658			
☐ Mam'selle	1924-1938	850.00	950.00
HN 659			
☐ Mam'selle	1924-1938	900.00	1000.00
HN 660			
☐ The Welsh Girl	1924-1938	2500.00	2750.00
HN 661			
☐ Boy with Turban	1924-1938	500.00	600.00
HN 662			
☐ Boy with Turban	1924-1938	500.00	600.00
HN 663			
☐ One of the Forty (12th version)	1924-1938	1100.00	1200.00
HN 664			
☐ One of the Forty (10th version)	1924-1938	1100.00	1200.00
HN 665			
☐ One of the Forty (13th version)	1924-1938	1100.00	1200.00
HN 666			
☐ One of the Forty (2nd version)	1924-1938	1100.00	1200.00
HN 667			
☐ One of the Forty (11th version)	1924-1938	1100.00	1200.00

	Date	Price Range	
HN 668			
☐ The Welsh Girl	1924-1938	2500.00	2700.00
HN 669			
☐ The Welsh Girl	1924-1938	2500.00	2700.00
HN 670			
☐ The Curtsey	1924-1938	1450.00	1600.00
HN 671			
☐ Lady Ermine	1924-1938	1650.00	1800.00
HN 672			
☐ Tulips	1924-1938	1550.00	1700.00
HN 673			
☐ Henry VIII (1st version)	1924-1938	2350.00	2600.00
HN 674			
☐ Masquerade (female, 1st version)	1924-1938	700.00	800.00
HN 675			
☐ The Gainsborough Hat	1924-1938	1350.00	1500.00
HN 676			
☐ Pavlova	1924-1938	1500.00	1700.00
HN 677			
☐ One of the Forty (1st version)	1924-1938	1100.00	1200.00
HN 678			
☐ Lady with Shawl	1924-1938	3250.00	3500.00
HN 679			
☐ Lady with Shawl	1924-1938	3250.00	3500.00
HN 680			
☐ Polly Peachum (1st version)	1924-1949	600.00	700.00
HN 681			
☐ The Cobbler (2nd version)	1924-1938	600.00	700.00
HN 682			
☐ The Cobbler (1st version)	1924-1938	700.00	800.00
HN 683			
☐ Masquerade (male, 1st version)	1924-1938	700.00	800.00
HN 684			
☐ Tony Weller (1st version)	1924-1938	1650.00	1800.00
HN 685			
☐ Contentment	1923-1938	1900.00	2000.00
HN 686			
☐ Contentment	1924-1938	1900.00	2000.00
HN 687			
☐ The Bather (1st version)	1924-1949	675.00	775.00
HN 688			
☐ A Yeoman of the Guard	1924-1938	950.00	1050.00
HN 689			
☐ A Chelsea Pensioner	1924-1938	1250.00	1400.00
HN 690			
☐ A Lady of the Georgian Perod	1925-1938	2150.00	2300.00
HN 691			
☐ Pierrette (1st version)	1925-1938	1250.00	1500.00

	Date	Price Range	
HN 692			
☐ Sleep	1925-1938	2050.00	2200.00
HN 693			
☐ Polly Peachum (1st version)	1925-1949	600.00	700.00
HN 694			
☐ Polly Peachum (2nd version)	1925-1949	400.00	500.00
HN 695			
☐ Lucy Lockett (2nd version).	1925-1949	650.00	750.00
HN 696			
☐ Lucy Lockett (2nd version	1925-1949	650.00	750.00
HN 697			
☐ The Balloon Seller	1925-1938	800.00	900.00
HN 698			
☐ Polly Peachum (3rd version, miniature)	1925-1949	400.00	500.00
HN 699			
☐ Polly Peachum (3rd version, miniature)	1925-1949	400.00	500.00
HN 700			
☐ Pretty Lady	1925-1938	1500.00	1750.00
HN 701			
☐ The Welsh Girl	1925-1938	2500.00	2700.00
HN 702			
☐ A Lady of the Georgian Period	1925-1938	2150.00	2300.00
HN 703			
☐ Woman Holding Child	1925-1938	2000.00	2200.00
HN 704			
☐ One of the Forty (2nd version)	1925-1938	1100.00	1200.00
HN 705			
☐ The Gainsborough Hat	1925-1938	1200.00	1350.00
HN 706			
☐ Fruit Gathering	1925-1938	2500.00	3000.00
HN 707			
☐ Fruit Gathering	1925-1938	3000.00	3500.00
HN 708			
☐ Shepherdess (1st version, miniature) .	1925-1948	650.00	750.00
HN 709			
☐ Shepherd (1st version, miniature)	1925-1938	550.00	650.00
HN 710			
☐ Sleep	1925-1938	2050.00	2200.00
HN 711			
☐ Harlequinade	1925-1938	850.00	950.00
HN 712			
☐ One of the Forty (11th version)	1925-1938	1100.00	1200.00
HN 713			
☐ One of the Forty (12th version)	1925-1938	1100.00	1200.00
HN 714			
☐ One of the Forty (10th version)	1925-1938	1100.00	1200.00

	Date	Price Range	
HN 715			
☐ Proposal (lady)	1925-1938	950.00	1000.00
HN 716			
☐ Proposal (lady)	1925-1938	950.00	1000.00
HN 717			
☐ Lady Clown	1925-1938	1300.00	1450.00
HN 718			
☐ Lady Clown	1925-1938	1300.00	1450.00
HN 719			
☐ Butterfly	1925-1938	900.00	1050.00
HN 720			
☐ Butterfly	1925-1938	900.00	1050.00
HN 721			
☐ Pierrette (1st version)	1925-1938	900.00	1000.00
HN 722			
☐ Mephisto	1925-1938	1350.00	1500.00
HN 723			
☐ Mephisto	1925-1938	1500.00	1600.00
HN 724			
☐ Mam'selle	1925-1938	900.00	1000.00
HN 725			
☐ The Proposal (male)	1925-1938	950.00	1000.00
HN 726			
☐ A Victorian Lady	1925-1938	350.00	400.00
HN 727			
☐ A Victorian Lady	1925-1938	350.00	400.00
HN 728			
☐ A Victorian Lady	1925-1952	300.00	350.00
HN 729			
☐ The Mask........................	1925-1938	850.00	950.00
HN 730			
☐ Butterfly	1925-1938	1000.00	1100.00
HN 731			
☐ Pierrette (1st version)	1925-1938	900.00	1000.00
HN 732			
☐ Pierrette (1st version)..............	1925-1938	900.00	1000.00
HN 733			
☐ The Mask........................	1925-1938	850.00	950.00
HN 734			
☐ Polly Peachum (2nd version)	1925-1949	450.00	500.00
HN 735			
☐ Shepherdess (2nd version)	1925-1938	1500.00	1750.00
HN 736			
☐ A Victorian Lady	1925-1938	450.00	500.00
HN 737 NO DETAILS AVAILABLE			
HN 738			
☐ Lady Clown	1925-1938	1300.00	1450.00
HN 739			
☐ A Victorian Lady	1925-1938	650.00	750.00

	Date	Price Range	
HN 740			
☐ A Victorian Lady	1925-1938	450.00	500.00
HN 741			
☐ A Geisha (1st version)	1925-1938	2250.00	2500.00
HN 742			
☐ A Victorian Lady	1925-1938	450.00	500.00
HN 743			
☐ Woman Holding Child	1925-1938	2050.00	2200.00
HN 744			
☐ The Lavender Woman	1925-1938	1750.00	2000.00
HN 745			
☐ A Victorian Lady	1925-1938	450.00	500.00
HN 746			
☐ A Mandarin (1st version)	1926-1938	2250.00	2500.00
HN 747			
☐ Tulips	1925-1938	1550.00	1700.00
HN 748			
☐ Out for a Walk	1925-1936	2350.00	2500.00
HN 749			
☐ London Cry, Strawberries	1925-1938	900.00	1000.00
HN 750			
☐ Shepherdess (2nd version)	1925-1938	1500.00	1750.00
HN 751			
☐ Shepherd (3rd version)	1925-1938	1500.00	1750.00
HN 752			
☐ London Cry, Turnips and Carrots	1925-1938	900.00	1000.00
HN 753			
☐ The Dandy	1925-1938	1100.00	1250.00
HN 754			
☐ The Belle	1925-1938	1150.00	1250.00
HN 755			
☐ Mephistopheles and Marguerite	1925-1949	1350.00	1500.00
HN 756			
☐ The Modern Piper	1925-1938	1650.00	1800.00
HN 757			
☐ Polly Peachum (3rd version)	1925-1949	350.00	400.00
HN 758			
☐ Polly Peachum (3rd version)	1925-1949	350.00	400.00
HN 759			
☐ Polly Peachum (3rd version)	1925-1949	350.00	400.00
HN 760			
☐ Polly Peachum (3rd version miniature)	1925-1949	350.00	400.00
HN 761			
☐ Polly Peachum (3rd version miniature)	1925-1949	350.00	400.00
HN 762			
☐ Polly Peachum (3rd version miniature)	1925-1949	350.00	400.00

	Date	Price Range	
HN 763			
☐ Pretty Lady	1925-1938	1450.00	1600.00
HN 764			
☐ Madonna of the Square	1925-1938	1650.00	1800.00
HN 765			
☐ The Poke Bonnet	1925-1938	1500.00	1600.00
HN 766			
☐ Irish Colleen	1925-1938	1650.00	1800.00
HN 767			
☐ Irish Colleen	1925-1938	1650.00	1800.00
HN 768			
☐ Harlequinade Masked	1925-1938	1350.00	1450.00
HN 769			
☐ Harlequinade Masked	1925-1938	1350.00	1450.00
HN 770			
☐ Lady Clown	1925-1938	1300.00	1450.00
HN 771			
☐ London Cry, Turnips and Carrots	1925-1938	900.00	1000.00
HN 772			
☐ London Cry, Strawberries	1925-1938	900.00	1000.00
HN 773			
☐ The Bather (2nd version)	1925-1938	900.00	1100.00
HN 774			
☐ The Bather (2nd version)	1925-1938	900.00	1100.00
HN 775			
☐ Mephistopheles and Marguerite	1925-1949	1350.00	1500.00
HN 776			
☐ The Belle	1925-1938	1250.00	1350.00
HN 777			
☐ Bo-Peep (1st version)	1926-1938	1250.00	1350.00
HN 778			
☐ Captain (1st version)	1926-1938	1250.00	1400.00
HN 779			
☐ A Geisha (1st version)	1926-1938	2250.00	2500.00
HN 780			
☐ Harlequinade	1926-1938	850.00	950.00
HN 781			
☐ The Bather (1st version)	1926-1938	800.00	900.00
HN 782			
☐ The Bather (1st version)	1926-1938	800.00	900.00
HN 783			
☐ Pretty Lady	1926-1938	1450.00	1600.00
HN 784			
☐ Pierette (1st version)	1926-1938	900.00	1000.00
HN 785			
☐ The Mask	1926-1938	850.00	950.00
HN 786			
☐ Mam'selle	1926-1938	900.00	1000.00

	Date	Price Range	
HN 787			
☐ A Mandarin (1st version)	1926-1938	2250.00	2500.00
HN 788			
☐ Proposal (lady)	1926-1938	900.00	1000.00
HN 789			
☐ The Flower Seller	1926-1938	600.00	700.00
HN 790			
☐ The Parson's Daughter	1926-1938	550.00	600.00
HN 791			
☐ A Mandarin (1st version)	1926-1938	2250.00	2500.00
HN 792			
☐ The Welsh Girl	1926-1938	2550.00	2700.00
HN 793			
☐ Katharine	1926-1938	1650.00	1800.00
HN 794			
☐ The Bouquet	1926-1938	1550.00	1700.00
HN 795			
☐ Pierrette (2nd version, miniature)	1926-1938	650.00	750.00
HN 796			
☐ Pierrette (2nd version, miniature)	1926-1938	650.00	750.00
HN 797			
☐ Moorish Minstrel	1926-1949	2150.00	2300.00
HN 798			
☐ Tete-a-Tete (1st version)..........	1926-1938	1150.00	1300.00
HN 799			
☐ Tete-a-Tete (1st version)..........	1926-1938	1150.00	1300.00
HN 800 — HN 1200 ANIMAL AND BIRD MODELS			
HN 1201			
☐ Hunts Lady	1926-1938	1100.00	1200.00
HN 1202			
☐ Bo-Peep (1st version)	1926-1938	1050.00	1200.00
HN 1203			
☐ Butterfly	1926-1938	1100.00	1250.00
HN 1204			
☐ Angela	1926-1938	675.00	850.00
HN 1205			
☐ Miss 1926	1926-1938	2050.00	2200.00
HN 1206			
☐ The Flower Seller's Children	1926-1949	450.00	500.00
HN 1207			
☐ Miss 1926	1926-1938	2050.00	2200.00
HN 1208			
☐ A Victorian Lady	1926-1938	450.00	500.00
HN 1209			
☐ The Proposal (male)	1926-1938	900.00	1000.00
HN 1210			
☐ Boy with Turban	1926-1938	500.00	600.00
HN 1211			
☐ Quality Street	1926-1938	1100.00	1200.00

	Date	Price Range	
HN 1212			
☐ Boy with Turban	1926-1938	550.00	650.00
HN 1213			
☐ Boy with Turban	1926-1938	500.00	600.00
HN 1214			
☐ Boy with Turban	1926-1938	500.00	600.00
HN 1215			
☐ The Pied Piper...................	1926-1938	800.00	900.00
HN 1216			
☐ Falstaff (1st version)	1926-1949	700.00	800.00
HN 1217			
☐ The Prince of Wales	1926-1938	1450.00	1600.00
HN 1218			
☐ A Spook........................	1926-1938	1250.00	1400.00
HN 1219			
☐ Negligee	1927-1938	1100.00	1200.00
HN 1220			
☐ Lido Lady.......................	1927-1938	1000.00	1100.00
HN 1221			
☐ Lady Jester (1st version)	1927-1938	1350.00	1500.00
HN 1222			
☐ Lady Jester (1st version)	1927-1938	1350.00	1500.00
HN 1223			
☐ A Geisha (2nd version)	1927-1938	900.00	1000.00
HN 1224			
☐ The Wandering Minstrel	1927-1938	1250.00	1400.00
HN 1225			
☐ Boy with Turban	1927-1938	500.00	600.00
HN 1226			
☐ The Huntsman (1st version)........	1927-1938	1350.00	1500.00
HN 1227			
☐ The Bather (2nd version)	1927-1938	900.00	1000.00
HN 1228			
☐ Negligee	1927-1938	1100.00	1200.00
HN 1229			
☐ Lido Lady.......................	1927-1938	1100.00	1200.00
HN 1230			
☐ Baba	1927-1938	600.00	650.00
HN 1231			
☐ Cassim (1st version)..............	1927-1938	550.00	600.00
HN 1232			
☐ Cassim (1st version)..............	1927-1938	550.00	600.00
HN 1233			
☐ Susanna	1927-1938	1100.00	1200.00
HN 1234			
☐ A Geisha (2nd version)	1927-1938	900.00	1000.00
HN 1235			
☐ A Scribe........................	1927-1938	1100.00	1200.00

	Date	Price Range	
HN 1236			
☐ Tete-a-Tete (2nd version)	1927-1938	650.00	750.00
HN 1237			
☐ Tete-a-Tete (2nd version)	1927-1938	650.00	750.00
HN 1238			
☐ The Bather (1st version)	1927-1938	900.00	1000.00
HN 1239 · HN 1241 ANIMAL and BIRD MODELS			
HN 1242			
☐ The Parson's Daughter	1927-1938	550.00	600.00
HN 1243			
☐ Baba	1927-1927	600.00	650.00
HN 1244			
☐ Baba	1927-1938	600.00	650.00
HN 1245			
☐ Baba	1927-1938	600.00	650.00
HN 1246			
☐ Baba	1927-1938	600.00	650.00
HN 1247			
☐ Baba	1928-1938	600.00	650.00
HN 1248			
☐ Baba	1927-1938	600.00	650.00
HN 1249			
☐ Circe	1927-1938	1200.00	1400.00
HN 1250			
☐ Circe	1927-1938	1200.00	1400.00
HN 1251			
☐ The Cobbler	1927-1938	600.00	700.00
HN 1252			
☐ Kathleen	1927-1938	800.00	850.00
HN 1253			
☐ Kathleen	1927-1938	800.00	850.00
HN 1254			
☐ Circe	1927-1938	1200.00	1400.00
HN 1255			
☐ Circe	1927-1938	1200.00	1400.00
HN 1256			
☐ Captain MacHeath	1927-1949	700.00	800.00
HN 1257			
☐ The Highwayman	1927-1949	600.00	700.00
HN 1258			
☐ A Victorian Lady	1927-1938	450.00	500.00
HN 1259			
☐ The Alchemist	1927-1938	1450.00	1650.00
HN 1260			
☐ Carnival	1927-1938	1500.00	1650.00
HN 1261			
☐ Sea Sprite (1st version)	1927-1938	600.00	650.00
HN 1262			
☐ Spanish Lady	1927-1938	900.00	1000.00

	Date	Price Range	
HN 1263			
☐ Lady Clown	1927-1938	1300.00	1450.00
HN 1264			
☐ Judge and Jury	1927-1938	3000.00	3500.00
HN 1265			
☐ Lady Fayre	1928-1938	550.00	650.00
HN 1266			
☐ Ko-Ko.	1928-1949	650.00	750.00
HN 1267			
☐ Carmen (1st version)	1928-1938	600.00	725.00
HN 1268			
☐ Yum-Yum.	1928-1938	650.00	750.00
HN 1269			
☐ Scotch Girl	1928-1938	1350.00	1500.00
HN 1270			
☐ The Swimmer	1928-1938	1100.00	1200.00
HN 1271			
☐ The Mask.	1928-1938	950.00	1050.00
HN 1272			
☐ Negligee	1928-1938	1100.00	1200.00
HN 1273			
☐ Negligee	1928-1938	1100.00	1200.00
HN 1274			
☐ Harlequinade Masked	1928-1938	1350.00	1450.00
HN 1275			
☐ Kathleen	1928-1938	800.00	850.00
HN 1276			
☐ A Victorian Lady	1928-1938	350.00	400.00
HN 1277			
☐ A Victorian Lady	1928-1938	350.00	400.00
HN 1278			
☐ Carnival.	1928-1938	1400.00	1550.00
HN 1279			
☐ Kathleen	1928-1938	800.00	850.00
HN 1280			
☐ Blue Bird	1928-1938	650.00	750.00
HN 1281			
☐ Scotties.	1928-1938	1100.00	1200.00
HN 1282			
☐ The Alchemist.	1928-1938	1450.00	1650.00
HN 1283			
☐ The Cobbler (2nd version)	1928-1949	600.00	700.00
HN 1284			
☐ Lady Jester (2nd version)	1928-1938	750.00	850.00
HN 1285			
☐ Lady Jester (2nd version)	1928-1938	750.00	850.00
HN 1286			
☐ Ko-Ko.	1938-1949	600.00	750.00

	Date	Price Range	
HN 1287			
☐ Yum-Yum........................	1928-1939	650.00	750.00
HN 1288			
☐ Susanna	1928-1938	1100.00	1200.00
HN 1289			
☐ Midinette (1st version)	1928-1938	1500.00	1600.00
HN 1290			
☐ Spanish Lady	1928-1938	900.00	1000.00
HN 1291			
☐ Kathleen	1928-1938	850.00	950.00
HN 1292			
☐ A Geisha (2nd version)	1928-1938	900.00	1000.00
HN 1293			
☐ Spanish Lady	1928-1938	900.00	1000.00
HN 1294			
☐ Spanish Lady	1928-1938	900.00	1000.00
HN 1295			
☐ A Jester (1st version)	1928-1949	900.00	1000.00
HN 1296			
☐ Columbine (1st version)	1928-1938	700.00	800.00
HN 1297			
☐ Columbine (1st version)	1928-1938	700.00	800.00
HN 1298			
☐ Sweet and Twenty (1st version)......	1928-1969	200.00	275.00
HN 1299			
☐ Susanna	1928-1938	1100.00	1200.00
HN 1300			
☐ Carmen (1st version)	1928-1938	750.00	850.00
HN 1301			
☐ Gypsy Woman with Child	1928-1938	2250.00	2400.00
HN 1302			
☐ Gypsy Girl with Flowers	1928-1938	2250.00	2400.00
HN 1303			
☐ Angela	1928-1938	950.00	1100.00
HN 1304			
☐ Harlequinade Masked	1928-1938	1350.00	1450.00
HN 1305			
☐ Siesta	1928-1938	1350.00	1500.00
HN 1306			
☐ Midinette (1st version)	1928-1938	1500.00	1600.00
HN 1307			
☐ An Irishman.....................	1928-1938	1150.00	1250.00
HN 1308			
☐ The Moor	1928-1938	1500.00	1750.00
HN 1309			
☐ Spanish Lady	1928-1938	900.00	1000.00
HN 1310			
☐ A Geisha (2nd version)	1929-1938	800.00	900.00

	Date	Price Range	
HN 1311			
☐ Cassim (2nd version)	1929-1938	700.00	800.00
HN 1312			
☐ Cassim (2nd version)	1929-1938	700.00	800.00
HN 1313			
☐ Sonny	1929-1938	600.00	700.00
HN 1314			
☐ Sonny	1929-1938	600.00	700.00
HN 1315			
☐ Old Balloon Seller	1929-	185.00	
HN 1316			
☐ Toys...........................	1929-1938	1200.00	1500.00
HN 1317			
☐ The Snake Charmer	1929-1938	900.00	1000.00
HN 1318			
☐ Sweet Anne.....................	1929-1949	200.00	250.00
HN 1319			
☐ Darling (1st version)	1929-1959	150.00	200.00
HN 1320			
☐ Rosamund (1st version)	1929-1938	1500.00	2000.00
HN 1321			
☐ A Geisha (1st verson)	1929-1938	2250.00	2500.00
HN 1322			
☐ A Geisha (1st version)	1929-1938	2250.00	2500.00
HN 1323			
☐ Contentment....................	1929-1938	1550.00	1700.00
HN 1324			
☐ Fairy	1929-1938	850.00	950.00
HN 1325			
☐ The Orange Seller................	1929-1949	900.00	1000.00
HN 1326			
☐ The Swimmer	1929-1938	1300.00	1400.00
HN 1327			
☐ Bo-Peep (1st version)	1929-1938	1050.00	1200.00
HN 1328			
☐ Bo-Peep (1st version)	1929-1938	1050.00	1200.00
HN 1329			
☐ The Swimmer	1929-1938	1300.00	1400.00
HN 1330			
☐ Sweet Anne.....................	1929-1949	325.00	375.00
HN 1331			
☐ Sweet Anne.....................	1929-1949	300.00	350.00
HN 1332			
☐ Lady Jester (1st version)	1929-1938	1250.00	1350.00
HN 1333			
☐ A Jester (2nd version)..............	1929-1949	1350.00	1500.00
HN 1334			
☐ Tulips..........................	1929-1938	1550.00	1700.00

	Date	Price Range	
HN 1335			
☐ Folly...........................	1929-1938	1600.00	1750.00
HN 1336			
☐ One of the Forty (11th version)	1929-1938	1100.00	1200.00
HN 1337			
☐ Priscilla........................	1929-1938	500.00	600.00
HN 1338			
☐ The Courtier	1929-1938	1200.00	1350.00
HN 1339			
☐ Covent Garden	1929-1938	1000.00	1200.00
HN 1340			
☐ Priscilla........................	1929-1949	325.00	375.00
HN 1341			
☐ Marietta........................	1929-1949	700.00	800.00
HN 1342			
☐ The Flower Seller's Children	1929-	395.00	
HN 1343			
☐ Dulcinea	1929-1938	900.00	1050.00
HN 1344			
☐ Sunshine Girl	1929-1938	1400.00	1500.00
HN 1345			
☐ A Victorian Lady	1929-1949	250.00	300.00
HN 1346			
☐ Iona	1929-1938	2500.00	3000.00
HN 1347			
☐ Moira	1929-1938	2750.00	3000.00
HN 1348			
☐ Sunshine Girl	1929-1938	1400.00	1500.00
HN 1349			
☐ Scotties........................	1929-1949	1500.00	1600.00
HN 1350			
☐ One of the Forty (11th version)	1929-1949	1100.00	1200.00
HN 1351			
☐ One of the Forty (1st version)	1920-1949	1100.00	1200.00
HN 1352			
☐ One of the Forty (1st version)	1929-1949	1100.00	1200.00
HN 1353			
☐ One of the Forty (2nd version)	1929-1949	1100.00	1200.00
HN 1354			
☐ One of the Forty (13th version)	1929-1949	1100.00	1200.00
HN 1355			
☐ The Mendicant	1929-1938	350.00	400.00
HN 1356			
☐ The Parson's Daughter	1929-1938	475.00	550.00
HN 1357			
☐ Kathleen	1929-1938	800.00	850.00
HN 1358			
☐ Rosina	1929-1938	750.00	850.00

	Date	Price Range	
HN 1359			
☐ Two-A-Penny.....................	1929-1938	1200.00	1300.00
HN 1360			
☐ Sweet and Twenty (1st version)......	1929-1938	450.00	500.00
HN 1361			
☐ Mask Seller......................	1929-1938	650.00	700.00
HN 1362			
☐ Pantalettes......................	1929-1938	350.00	400.00
HN 1363			
☐ Doreen..........................	1929-1938	900.00	1000.00
HN 1364			
☐ Rosina..........................	1929-1938	750.00	850.00
HN 1365			
☐ The Mendicant	1929-1969	300.00	350.00
HN 1366			
☐ The Moor........................	1930-1949	1500.00	1750.00
HN 1367			
☐ Kitty............................	1930-1938	1000.00	1100.00
HN 1368			
☐ Rose............................	1930-	65.00	
HN 1369			
☐ Boy on Pig	1930-1938	900.00	1000.00
HN 1370			
☐ Marie (2nd version)	1930-	65.00	
HN 1371			
☐ Darling (1st version)	1930-1938	275.00	325.00
HN 1372			
☐ Darling (1st verson)	1930-1938	275.00	325.00
HN 1373			
☐ Sweet Lavender	1930-1949	225.00	275.00
HN 1374			
☐ Fairy	1930-1938	850.00	950.00
HN 1375			
☐ Fairy	1930-1938	750.00	850.00
HN 1376			
☐ Fairy	1930-1938	650.00	750.00
HN 1377			
☐ Fairy	NOT ISSUED		
HN 1378			
☐ Fairy	1930-1938	550.00	650.00
HN 1379			
☐ Fairy	1930-1938	550.00	650.00
HN 1380			
☐ Fairy	1930-1938	850.00	950.00
HN 1381 · HN 1386 FAIRIES — NOT ISSUED			
HN 1387			
☐ Rose............................	1930-1938	250.00	300.00
HN 1388			
☐ Marie (2nd version)	1930-1938	250.00	300.00

	Date	Price Range	
HN 1389			
☐ Doreen..........................	1930-1938	600.00	700.00
HN 1390			
☐ Doreen..........................	1929-1938	600.00	700.00
HN 1391			
☐ Pierrette (3rd version)..............	1930-1938	1000.00	1100.00
HN 1392			
☐ Paisley Shawl (1st version)	1930-1949	570.00	670.00
HN 1393			
☐ Fairy	1930-1938	650.00	750.00
HN 1394			
☐ Fairy	1930-1938	550.00	650.00
HN 1395			
☐ Fairy	1930-1938	750.00	850.00
HN 1396			
☐ Fairy	1930-1938	550.00	650.00
HN 1397			
☐ Gretchen	1930-1938	650.00	700.00
HN 1398			
☐ Derrick.........................	1930-1938	650.00	750.00
HN 1399			
☐ The Young Widow	1930-1930	1250.00	1500.00
HN 1400			
☐ The Windmill Lady	1930-1938	1550.00	1700.00
HN 1401			
☐ Chorus Girl	1930-1938	1650.00	1800.00
HN 1402			
☐ Miss Demure.....................	1930-1975	250.00	300.00
HN 1403			
☐ The Old Huntsman	NOT ISSUED		
HN 1404			
☐ Betty (2nd version)	1930-1938	500.00	600.00
HN 1405			
☐ Betty (2nd version)	1930-1938	500.00	600.00
HN 1406			
☐ The Flower Seller's Children	1930-1938	550.00	650.00
HN 1407			
☐ The Winner	1930-1938	3000.00	3500.00
HN 1408			
☐ John Peel	1930-1937	2750.00	3000.00
HN 1409			
☐ Hunting Squire	1930-1938	2000.00	2500.00
HN 1410			
☐ Abdullah	1930-1938	800.00	950.00
HN 1411			
☐ Charley's Aunt (2nd version)	1930-1938	1375.00	1425.00
HN 1412			
☐ Pantalettes	1930-1949	350.00	400.00

	Date	Price Range	
HN 1413			
☐ Margery	1930-1949	350.00	400.00
HN 1414			
☐ Patricia	1930-1949	550.00	650.00
HN 1415 NO DETAILS AVAILABLE			
HN 1416			
☐ Rose.	1930-1949	150.00	200.00
HN 1417			
☐ Marie (2nd version)	1930-1949	250.00	300.00
HN 1418			
☐ The Little Mother (2nd version)	1930-1938	1100.00	1200.00
HN 1419			
☐ Dulcinea	1930-1938	1000.00	1150.00
HN 1420			
☐ Phyllis	1930-1949	575.00	675.00
HN 1421			
☐ Barbara	1930-1938	600.00	750.00
HN 1422			
☐ Joan.	1930-1949	450.00	550.00
HN 1423			
☐ Babette	1930-1938	500.00	600.00
HN 1424			
☐ Babette	1930-1938	550.00	650.00
HN 1425			
☐ The Moor	1930-1949	1500.00	1750.00
HN 1426			
☐ The Gossips	1930-1949	500.00	750.00
HN 1427			
☐ Darby	1930-1949	325.00	400.00
HN 1428			
☐ Calumet.	1930-1949	1000.00	1100.00
HN 1429			
☐ The Gossips	1930-1949	525.00	575.00
HN 1430			
☐ Phyllis	1930-1938	700.00	800.00
HN 1431			
☐ Patricia	1930-1949	550.00	650.00
HN 1432			
☐ Barbara	1930-1938	700.00	825.00
HN 1433			
☐ The Little Bridesmaid (1st version) . . .	1930-1951	175.00	225.00
HN 1434			
☐ The Little Bridesmaid (1st version) . . .	1930-1949	225.00	275.00
HN 1435			
☐ Betty (2nd version)	1930-1938	500.00	600.00
HN 1436			
☐ Betty (2nd version)	1930-1938	500.00	600.00
HN 1437			
☐ Sweet and Twenty (1st version).	1930-1938	400.00	450.00

	Date	Price Range	
HN 1438			
☐ Sweet and Twenty (1st version)......	1930-1938	450.00	500.00
HN 1439			
☐ Columbine (1st version)............	1930-1938	700.00	800.00
HN 1440			
☐ Miss Demure.....................	1930-1949	350.00	400.00
HN 1441			
☐ Child Study	1931-1938	350.00	400.00
HN 1442			
☐ Child Study	1931-1938	350.00	400.00
HN 1443			
☐ Child Study	1931-1938	350.00	400.00
HN 1444			
☐ Pauline	1931-1938	400.00	450.00
HN 1445			
☐ Biddy	1931-1938	300.00	350.00
HN 1446			
☐ Marietta.........................	1931-1949	700.00	800.00
HN 1447			
☐ Marigold	1931-1949	450.00	500.00
HN 1448			
☐ Rita	1931-1938	600.00	700.00
HN 1449			
☐ The Little Mistress	1931-1949	500.00	550.00
HN 1450			
☐ Rita	1931-1938	600.00	700.00
HN 1451			
☐ Marigold	1931-1938	450.00	500.00
HN 1452			
☐ A Victorian Lady..................	1931-1949	250.00	300.00
HN 1453			
☐ Sweet Anne......................	1931-1949	325.00	375.00
HN 1454			
☐ Negligee	1931-1938	1100.00	1200.00
HN 1455			
☐ Molly Malone	1931-1938	1350.00	1500.00
HN 1456			
☐ Butterfly	1931-1938	1000.00	1100.00
HN 1457			
☐ All-A-Blooming	1931-Unknown	900.00	1000.00
HN 1458			
☐ Monica	1931-1949	200.00	250.00
HN 1459			
☐ Monica	1931-Unknown	200.00	250.00
HN 1460			
☐ Paisley Shawl (1st version)	1931-1949	400.00	450.00
HN 1461			
☐ Barbara	1931-1938	650.00	725.00

	Date	Price Range	
HN 1462			
☐ Patricia	1931-1938	550.00	650.00
HN 1463			
☐ Miss Demure	1931-1949	350.00	400.00
HN 1464			
☐ The Carpet Seller	1931-1969	300.00	375.00
HN 1464A			
☐ The Carpet Seller	1969-Unknown	275.00	350.00
HN 1465			
☐ Lady Clare	1931-1938	700.00	800.00
HN 1466			
☐ All-A-Blooming	1931-1938	1000.00	1100.00
HN 1467			
☐ Monica	1931-	100.00	
HN 1468			
☐ Pamela	1931-1938	750.00	850.00
HN 1469			
☐ Pamela	1931-1938	650.00	750.00
HN 1470			
☐ Chloe	1931-1949	300.00	350.00
HN 1471			
☐ Annette	1931-1938	275.00	325.00
HN 1472			
☐ Annette	1931-1949	400.00	450.00
HN 1473			
☐ Dreamland	1931-1938	1850.00	2000.00
HN 1474			
☐ In the Stocks (1st version)	1931-1938	1300.00	1500.00
HN 1475			
☐ In the Stocks (1st version)	1931-1938	1000.00	1250.00
HN 1476			
☐ Chloe	1931-1938	275.00	325.00
HN 1477 NO DETAILS AVAILABLE			
HN 1478			
☐ Sylvia	1931-1938	700.00	800.00
HN 1479			
☐ Chloe	1931-1949	250.00	300.00
HN 1480			
☐ Newhaven Fishwife	1931-1938	1350.00	1500.00
HN 1481			
☐ Dreamland	1931-1938	1850.00	2000.00
HN 1482			
☐ Pearly Boy (1st version)	1931-1949	350.00	400.00
HN 1483			
☐ Pearly Girl (1st version)	1931-1949	350.00	400.00
HN 1484			
☐ Jennifer	1931-1949	400.00	500.00
HN 1485			
☐ Greta	1931-1953	300.00	350.00

	Date	Price Range	
HN 1486			
☐ Phyllis	1931-1949	650.00	750.00
HN 1487			
☐ Suzette	1931-1950	300.00	350.00
HN 1488			
☐ Gloria	1932-1938	900.00	1000.00
HN 1489			
☐ Marie (2nd version)	1932-1949	250.00	300.00
HN 1490			
☐ Dorcas	1932-1938	450.00	500.00
HN 1491			
☐ Dorcas	1932-1938	450.00	500.00
HN 1492			
☐ Old Lavender Seller	1932-1949	600.00	700.00
HN 1493			
☐ The Potter	1932-	325.00	
HN 1494			
☐ Gwendolen	1932-1938	775.00	850.00
HN 1495			
☐ Priscilla	1932-1949	500.00	600.00
HN 1496			
☐ Sweet Anne	1932-1967	225.00	275.00
HN 1497			
☐ Rosamund (2nd version)	1932-1938	800.00	1000.00
HN 1498			
☐ Chloe	1932-1938	300.00	350.00
HN 1499			
☐ Miss Demure	1932-1938	400.00	450.00
HN 1500			
☐ Biddy	1932-1938	300.00	350.00
HN 1501			
☐ Priscilla	1932-1938	500.00	600.00
HN 1502			
☐ Lucy Ann	1932-1951	300.00	350.00
HN 1503			
☐ Gwendolen	1932-1949	700.00	800.00
HN 1504			
☐ Sweet Maid (1st version)	1932-1938	900.00	1000.00
HN 1505			
☐ Sweet Maid (1st version)	1932-1938	900.00	1000.00
HN 1506			
☐ Rose	1932-1938	250.00	300.00
HN 1507			
☐ Pantalettes	1932-1949	450.00	500.00
HN 1508			
☐ Helen	1932-1938	650.00	800.00
HN 1509			
☐ Helen	1932-1938	650.00	800.00

	Date	Price Range	
HN 1510			
☐ Constance......................	1932-1938	1500.00	1700.00
HN 1511			
☐ Constance......................	1932-1938	1500.00	1700.00
HN 1512			
☐ Kathleen	1932-1938	700.00	800.00
HN 1513			
☐ Biddy	1932-1951	160.00	225.00
HN 1514			
☐ Dolly Vardon	1932-1938	700.00	800.00
HN 1515			
☐ Dolly Vardon	1932-1949	800.00	900.00
HN 1516			
☐ Cicely..........................	1932-1949	1100.00	1200.00
HN 1517			
☐ Veronica (1st version)	1932-1951	350.00	400.00
HN 1518			
☐ The Potter	1932-1949	425.00	475.00
HN 1519			
☐ Veronica (1st version)	1932-1938	400.00	450.00
HN 1520			
☐ Eugene	1932-1938	575.00	675.00
HN 1521			
☐ Eugene	1932-1938	575.00	675.00
HN 1522			
☐ The Potter	1932-1949	425.00	475.00
HN 1523			
☐ Lisette..........................	1932-1938	900.00	1000.00
HN 1524			
☐ Lisette..........................	1932-1938	900.00	1000.00
HN 1525			
☐ Clarissa (1st version)	1932-1938	625.00	700.00
HN 1526			
☐ Anthea..........................	1932-1938	500.00	600.00
HN 1527			
☐ Anthea..........................	1932-1949	575.00	675.00
HN 1528			
☐ Bluebeard (2nd version)	1932-1949	1000.00	1100.00
HN 1529			
☐ A Victorian Lady..................	1932-1938	400.00	450.00
HN 1530			
☐ The Little Bridesmaid	1932-1938	200.00	250.00
HN 1531			
☐ Marie (2nd version)...............	1932-1938	250.00	350.00
HN 1532			
☐ Fairy	1932-1938	550.00	650.00
HN 1533			
☐ Fairy	1932-1938	550.00	650.00

	Date	Price Range	
HN 1534			
☐ Fairy	1932-1938	550.00	650.00
HN 1535			
☐ Fairy	1932-1938	550.00	650.00
HN 1536			
☐ Fairy	1932-1938	550.00	650.00
HN 1537			
☐ Janet (1st version)	1932-	125.00	
HN 1538			
☐ Janet (1st version)	1932-1949	275.00	325.00
HN 1539			
☐ A Saucy Nymph	1933-1949	275.00	325.00
HN 1540			
☐ 'Little Child so Rare and Sweet'	1933-1949	425.00	475.00
HN 1541			
☐ 'Happy Joy, Baby Boy'	1933-1949	300.00	350.00
HN 1542			
☐ 'Little Child so Rare and Sweet'	1933-1949	375.00	425.00
HN 1543			
☐ 'Dancing Eyes and Sunny Hair'	1933-1949	225.00	300.00
HN 1544			
☐ 'Do you Wonder where Fairies are that Folk Declare Have Vanished' ...	1933-1949	300.00	350.00
HN 1545			
☐ 'Called Love, a Little Boy, almost Naked, Wanton, Blind, Cruel now, and then as Kind'	1933-1949	325.00	375.00
HN 1546			
☐ 'Here a Little Child I Stand'	1933-1949	300.00	350.00
HN 1547			
☐ Pearly Boy (1st version)	1933-1949	400.00	450.00
HN 1548			
☐ Pearly Girl (1st version)	1933-1949	375.00	425.00
HN 1549			
☐ Sweet and Twenty (1st version)	1933-1949	350.00	400.00
HN 1550			
☐ Annette	1933-1949	425.00	475.00
HN 1551			
☐ Rosamund (2nd version)	1933-1938	450.00	500.00
HN 1552			
☐ Pinkie..........................	1933-1938	450.00	500.00
HN 1553			
☐ Pinkie..........................	1933-1938	450.00	500.00
HN 1554			
☐ Charley's Aunt (2nd version)	1933-1938	1200.00	1350.00
HN 1555			
☐ Marigold	1933-1949	450.00	500.00
HN 1556			
☐ Rosina	1933-1938	500.00	600.00

	Date	Price Range	
HN 1557			
☐ Lady Fayre	1933-1938	750.00	850.00
HN 1558			
☐ Dorcas..........................	1933-1952	350.00	400.00
HN 1559			
☐ Priscilla	1933-1949	400.00	500.00
HN 1560			
☐ Miss Demure....................	1933-1949	350.00	400.00
HN 1561			
☐ Willy-Won't He	1933-1949	500.00	550.00
HN 1562			
☐ Gretchen	1933-1938	700.00	800.00
HN 1563			
☐ Sweet and Twenty (1st version)......	1933-1938	450.00	500.00
HN 1564			
☐ Pamela	1933-1938	650.00	750.00
HN 1565			
☐ Lucy Ann	1933-1938	325.00	375.00
HN 1566			
☐ Estelle	1933-1938	800.00	900.00
HN 1567			
☐ Patricia	1933-1949	650.00	750.00
HN 1568			
☐ Charmain	1933-1938	650.00	750.00
HN 1569			
☐ Charmain	1933-1938	650.00	750.00
HN 1570			
☐ Gwendolen	1933-1949	675.00	750.00
HN 1571			
☐ Old Lavender Seller	1933-1949	600.00	700.00
HN 1572			
☐ Helen	1933-1938	550.00	700.00
HN 1573			
☐ Rhoda	1933-1949	575.00	650.00
HN 1574			
☐ Rhoda	1933-1938	500.00	550.00
HN 1575			
☐ Daisy	1933-1949	250.00	300.00
HN 1576			
☐ Tildy...........................	1933-1938	700.00	800.00
HN 1577			
☐ Suzette	1933-1949	500.00	550.00
HN 1578			
☐ The Hinged Parasol	1933-1949	350.00	450.00
HN 1579			
☐ The Hinged Parasol	1933-1949	350.00	450.00
HN 1580			
☐ Rosebud (1st version)..............	1933-1938	600.00	700.00

	Date	Price Range	
HN 1581			
☐ Rosebud (1st version)..............	1933-1938	600.00	700.00
HN 1582			
☐ Marion	1933-1938	700.00	800.00
HN 1583			
☐ Marion	1933-1938	700.00	800.00
HN 1584			
☐ Willy-Won't He	1933-1949	350.00	400.00
HN 1585			
☐ Suzette	1933-1938	500.00	600.00
HN 1586			
☐ Camille	1933-1949	650.00	700.00
HN 1587			
☐ Fleurette	1933-1949	625.00	700.00
HN 1588			
☐ The Bride (1st version)	1933-1938	750.00	850.00
HN 1589			
☐ Sweet and Twenty (2nd version)	1933-1949	225.00	275.00
HN 1590 - HN 1597 WALL MASKS			
HN 1598			
☐ Clothilde	1933-1949	550.00	650.00
HN 1599			
☐ Clothilde	1933-1949	550.00	650.00
HN 1600			
☐ The Bride (1st version)	1933-1949	650.00	750.00
HN 1601 - HN 1603 WALL MASKS			
HN 1604			
☐ The Emir	1933-1949	900.00	1000.00
HN 1605			
☐ The Emir	1933-1949	900.00	1000.00
HN 1606			
☐ Falstaff (1st version)	1933-1949	700.00	800.00
HN 1607			
☐ Cerise	1933-1949	300.00	375.00
HN 1608 - HN 1609 WALL MASKS			
HN 1610			
☐ Sweet and Twenty (2nd version)	1933-1938	275.00	325.00
HN 1611 - HN 1614 WALL MASKS			
HN 1615			
☐ BOOKEND, MICAWBER		350.00	400.00
HN 1616			
☐ BOOKEND, TONY WELLER		350.00	400.00
HN 1617			
☐ Primroses	1934-1949	525.00	575.00
HN 1618			
☐ Maisie	1934-1949	475.00	525.00
HN 1619			
☐ Maisie	1934-1949	475.00	525.00

	Date	Price Range	
HN 1620			
☐ Rosabell	1934-1938	900.00	1000.00
HN 1621			
☐ Irene.	1934-1951	350.00	400.00
HN 1622			
☐ Evelyn	1934-1949	700.00	850.00
HN 1623			
☐ BOOKEND, PICKWICK		350.00	400.00
HN 1624			
☐ NO DETAILS AVAILABLE			
HN 1625			
☐ BOOKEND, SAIREY GAMP		350.00	400.00
HN 1626			
☐ Bonnie Lassie	1934-1953	250.00	300.00
HN 1627			
☐ Curly Knob	1934-1949	525.00	575.00
HN 1628			
☐ Margot.	1934-1938	700.00	800.00
HN 1629			
☐ Grizel	1934-1938	550.00	650.00
HN 1630 WALL MASK			
HN 1631			
☐ Sweet Anne.	1934-1938	300.00	400.00
HN 1632			
☐ A Gentlewoman	1934-1949	675.00	775.00
HN 1633			
☐ Clemency	1934-1938	650.00	750.00
HN 1634			
☐ Clemency	1934-1949	650.00	750.00
HN 1635			
☐ Marie (2nd version)	1934-1949	250.00	300.00
HN 1636			
☐ Margot.	1934-1938	700.00	800.00
HN 1637			
☐ Evelyn	1934-1938	850.00	950.00
HN 1638			
☐ Ladybird	1934-1949	900.00	1000.00
HN 1639			
☐ Dainty May	1934-1949	400.00	450.00
HN 1640			
☐ Ladybird	1934-1938	900.00	1000.00
HN 1641			
☐ The Little Mother (2nd version)	1934-1949	900.00	1000.00
HN 1642			
☐ Granny's Shawl	1934-1949	400.00	500.00
HN 1643			
☐ Clemency	1934-1938	650.00	750.00
HN 1644			
☐ Herminia	1934-1938	850.00	950.00

	Date	Price Range	
HN 1645			
☐ Aileen	1934-1938	750.00	850.00
HN 1646			
☐ Herminia	1934-1938	900.00	1000.00
HN 1647			
☐ Granny's Shawl	1934-1949	350.00	400.00
HN 1648			
☐ Camille	1934-1949	600.00	675.00
HN 1649			
☐ Sweet and Twenty (1st version)......	1934-1949	450.00	500.00
HN 1650			
☐ Veronica (1st version)	1934-1949	500.00	550.00
HN 1651			
☐ Charmain	1934-1938	800.00	900.00
HN 1652			
☐ Janet (1st version)	1934-1949	300.00	350.00
HN 1653			
☐ Margot.........................	1934-1938	700.00	800.00
HN 1654			
☐ Rose...........................	1934-1938	250.00	300.00
HN 1655			
☐ Marie (2nd version)...............	1934-1938	250.00	300.00
HN 1656			
☐ Dainty May	1934-1949	300.00	350.00
HN 1657			
☐ The Moor.......................	1934-1949	1500.00	1750.00
HN 1658 - HN 1661 WALL MASKS			
HN 1662			
☐ Delicia.........................	1934-1938	550.00	650.00
HN 1663			
☐ Delicia.........................	1934-1938	550.00	650.00
HN 1664			
☐ Aileen	1934-1938	850.00	950.00
HN 1665			
☐ Miss Winsome	1934-1949	600.00	700.00
HN 1666			
☐ Miss Winsome	1934-1938	650.00	750.00
HN 1667			
☐ Blossom	1934-1949	700.00	800.00
HN 1668			
☐ Sibell	1934-1949	600.00	700.00
HN 1669			
☐ Anthea.........................	1934-1938	575.00	675.00
HN 1670			
☐ Gillian	1934-1949	700.00	800.00
HN 1671 - HN 1676 WALL MASKS			
HN 1677			
☐ Tinkle Bell	1935-	75.00	

	Date	Price Range	
HN 1678			
☐ Dinky Doo	1934-	65.00	
HN 1679			
☐ Babie	1935-	75.00	
HN 1680			
☐ Tottles	1935-1975	60.00	125.00
HN 1681			
☐ Delicia	1935-1938	600.00	700.00
HN 1682			
☐ Teresa	1935-1949	800.00	900.00
HN 1683			
☐ Teresa	1935-1938	900.00	1000.00
HN 1684			
☐ Lisette	1935-1938	900.00	1000.00
HN 1685			
☐ Cynthia	1935-1949	500.00	600.00
HN 1686			
☐ Cynthia	1935-1949	500.00	600.00
HN 1687			
☐ Clarissa (1st version)	1935-1949	675.00	750.00
HN 1688			
☐ Rhoda	1935-1949	550.00	650.00
HN 1689			
☐ Calumet	1935-1949	800.00	900.00
HN 1690			
☐ June	1935-1949	450.00	500.00
HN 1691			
☐ June	1935-1949	350.00	400.00
HN 1692			
☐ Sonia	1935-1949	650.00	750.00
HN 1693			
☐ Virginia	1935-1949	650.00	750.00
HN 1694			
☐ Virginia	1935-1949	650.00	750.00
HN 1695			
☐ Sibell	1935-1949	600.00	700.00
HN 1696			
☐ Suzette	1935-1949	400.00	450.00
HN 1697			
☐ Irene	1935-1949	400.00	475.00
HN 1698			
☐ Phyllis	1935-1949	750.00	850.00
HN 1699			
☐ Marietta	1935-1949	900.00	1000.00
HN 1700			
☐ Gloria	1935-1938	1000.00	1100.00
HN 1701			
☐ Sweet Anne	1935-1938	300.00	400.00

	Date	Price Range	
HN 1702			
☐ A Jester (1st version)	1935-1949	900.00	1000.00
HN 1703			
☐ Charley's Aunt (3rd version)	1935-1938	800.00	900.00
HN 1704			
☐ Herminia	1935-1938	850.00	950.00
HN 1705			
☐ The Cobbler (3rd version)	1935-1949	550.00	600.00
HN 1706			
☐ The Cobbler (3rd version)	1935-1949	275.00	325.00
HN 1707			
☐ Paisley Shawl (1st version)	1935-1949	525.00	575.00
HN 1708			
☐ The Bather (1st version)	1935-1938	1250.00	1450.00
HN 1709			
☐ Pantalettes	1935-1938	500.00	600.00
HN 1710			
☐ Camilla	1935-1949	700.00	800.00
HN 1711			
☐ Camilla	1935-1949	700.00	800.00
HN 1712			
☐ Daffy Down Dilly..................	1935-1975	225.00	300.00
HN 1713			
☐ Daffy Down Dilly..................	1935-1949	425.00	500.00
HN 1714			
☐ Millicent	1935-1949	1050.00	1150.00
HN 1715			
☐ Millicent	1935-1949	1050.00	1150.00
HN 1716			
☐ Diana...........................	1935-1949	300.00	375.00
HN 1717			
☐ Diana...........................	1935-1949	300.00	375.00
HN 1718			
☐ Kate Hardcastle	1935-1949	475.00	575.00
HN 1719			
☐ Kate Hardcastle	1935-1949	475.00	575.00
HN 1720			
☐ Frangcon.......................	1935-1949	650.00	750.00
HN 1721			
☐ Frangcon.......................	1935-1949	650.00	750.00
HN 1722			
☐ The Coming of Spring	1935-1949	1250.00	1400.00
HN 1723			
☐ The Coming of Spring	1935-1949	1250.00	1400.00
HN 1724			
☐ Ruby	1935-1949	300.00	350.00
HN 1725			
☐ Ruby	1935-1949	300.00	350.00

	Date	Price Range	
HN 1726			
☐ Celia	1935-1949	750.00	850.00
HN 1727			
☐ Celia	1935-1949	750.00	850.00
HN 1728			
☐ The New Bonnet	1935-1949	525.00	575.00
HN 1729			
☐ Vera	1935-1938	500.00	600.00
HN 1730			
☐ Vera	1935-1938	500.00	600.00
HN 1731			
☐ Daydreams	1935-	155.00	
HN 1732			
☐ Daydreams	1935-1949	275.00	325.00
HN 1733 WALL MASK			
HN 1734			
☐ Kate Hardcastle	1935-1949	500.00	600.00
HN 1735			
☐ Sibell	1935-1949	800.00	850.00
HN 1736			
☐ Camille	1935-1949	700.00	800.00
HN 1737			
☐ Janet (1st version)	1935-1949	300.00	350.00
HN 1738			
☐ Sonia	1938-1949	750.00	850.00
HN 1739			
☐ Paisley Shawl (1st version)	1935-1949	400.00	450.00
HN 1740			
☐ Gladys	1935-1949	550.00	600.00
HN 1741			
☐ Gladys	1935-1938	575.00	625.00
HN 1742			
☐ Sir Walter Raleigh	1935-1949	550.00	700.00
HN 1743			
☐ Mirabel	1935-1949	750.00	850.00
HN 1744			
☐ Mirabel	1935-1949	750.00	850.00
HN 1745			
☐ The Rustic Swain	1935-1949	1750.00	2250.00
HN 1746			
☐ The Rustic Swain	1935-1949	1850.00	2350.00
HN 1747			
☐ Afternoon Tea....................	1935-1982	300.00	400.00
HN 1748			
☐ Afternoon Tea....................	1935-1949	450.00	550.00
HN 1749			
☐ Pierrette (3rd version).............	1936-1949	1000.00	1100.00
HN 1750			
☐ Folly..........................	1936-1949	1100.00	1250.00

	Date	Price Range	
HN 1751			
☐ Sir Walter Raleigh	1936-1949	1000.00	1100.00
HN 1752			
☐ Regency	1936-1949	600.00	700.00
HN 1753			
☐ Eleanore	1936-1949	700.00	850.00
HN 1754			
☐ Eleanore	1936-1949	700.00	850.00
HN 1755			
☐ The Court Shoemaker	1936-1949	1500.00	1700.00
HN 1756			
☐ Lizana	1936-1949	650.00	750.00
HN 1757			
☐ Romany Sue	1936-1949	700.00	800.00
HN 1758			
☐ Romany Sue	1936-1949	700.00	800.00
HN 1759			
☐ The Orange Lady	1936-1975	250.00	300.00
HN 1760			
☐ 4 o'Clock	1936-1949	475.00	575.00
HN 1761			
☐ Lizana	1936-1938	650.00	750.00
HN 1762			
☐ The Bride (1st version)	1936-1949	700.00	800.00
HN 1763			
☐ Windflower (1st version)	1936-1949	350.00	400.00
HN 1764			
☐ Windflower (1st version)	1936-1949	425.00	475.00
HN 1765			
☐ Chloe	1936-1950	250.00	300.00
HN 1766			
☐ Nana	1936-1949	275.00	325.00
HN 1767			
☐ Nana	1936-1949	275.00	325.00
HN 1768			
☐ Ivy............................	1936-1949	50.00	75.00
HN 1769			
☐ Ivy............................	1936-1938	350.00	400.00
HN 1770			
☐ Maureen	1936-1959	250.00	325.00
HN 1771			
☐ Maureen	1936-1949	600.00	700.00
HN 1772			
☐ Delight.........................	1936-1967	150.00	200.00
HN 1773			
☐ Delight.........................	1936-1949	375.00	425.00
HN 1774			
☐ Spring (2nd version) (Limited Edition, Figurines)........................	1933-	2500.00	3000.00

	Date	Price Range	
HN 1775			
☐ Salome (Limited Editon, Figurines)...	1933-	4500.00	5000.00
HN 1776			
☐ West Wind (Limited Edition, Figurines)........................	1933-	4500.00	5000.00
HN 1777			
☐ Spirit of the Wind (Limited Edition, Miscellaneous)...................	1933-	3500.00	4000.00
HN 1778			
☐ Beethoven (Limited Edition, Figurines).......................	1933-	6000.00	6500.00
HN 1779			
☐ BIRD MODEL (Macaw by R. Garbe)			
HN 1780			
☐ Lady of the Snows (withdrawn date not available)	1933-	3500.00	4000.00
HN 1781 - HN 1786 WALL MASKS			
HN 1787 - HN 1790 NO DETAILS AVAILABLE			
HN 1791			
☐ Old Balloon Seller and Bulldog......	1932-1938	1250.00	1500.00
HN 1792			
☐ Henry VIII (2nd version) (Limited Edition, Figurines).........	1933-	1750.00	2000.00
HN 1793			
☐ This Little Pig	1936-	75.00	
HN 1794			
☐ This Little Pig	1936-1949	300.00	350.00
HN 1795			
☐ M'Lady's Maid	1936-1949	1150.00	1300.00
HN 1796			
☐ Hazel	1936-1949	350.00	400.00
HN 1797			
☐ Hazel	1936-1949	300.00	350.00
HN 1798			
☐ Lily.............................	1936-1949	100.00	150.00
HN 1799			
☐ Lily.............................	1936-1949	100.00	150.00
HN 1800			
☐ St. George (1st version)	1934-1950	3000.00	3500.00
HN 1801			
☐ An Old King.....................	1937-1954	950.00	1150.00
HN 1802			
☐ Esteile	1937-1949	700.00	800.00
HN 1803			
☐ Aileen	1937-1949	700.00	800.00
HN 1804			
☐ Granny..........................	1937-1949	850.00	950.00
HN 1805			
☐ To Bed	1937-1959	110.00	175.00

	Date	Price Range	
HN 1806			
☐ To Bed	1937-1949	150.00	200.00
HN 1807			
☐ Spring Flowers	1937-1959	275.00	350.00
HN 1808			
☐ Cissie	1937-1951	225.00	275.00
HN 1809			
☐ Cissie	1937-	100.00	
HN 1810			
☐ Bo-Peep (2nd version)	1937-1949	250.00	300.00
HN 1811			
☐ Bo-Peep (2nd version)	1937-	100.00	
HN 1812			
☐ Forget-me-not	1937-1949	550.00	650.00
HN 1813			
☐ Forget-me-not	1937-1949	550.00	650.00
HN 1814			
☐ The Squire	1937-1949	2100.00	2600.00
HN 1815			
☐ The Huntsman (2nd version)	1937-1949	2300.00	2500.00
HN 1816 - HN 1817 WALL MASKS			
HN 1818			
☐ Miranda	1937-1949	750.00	850.00
HN 1819			
☐ Miranda	1937-1949	750.00	850.00
HN 1820			
☐ Reflections	1937-1938	1000.00	1100.00
HN 1821			
☐ Reflections	1937-1938	1000.00	1100.00
HN 1822			
☐ M'Lady's Maid	1937-1949	1150.00	1300.00
HN 1823 - HN 1824 WALL MASKS			
HN 1825			
☐ Spirit of the Wind	1937-1949	3500.00	4000.00
HN 1826			
☐ West Wind	1937-1949	4500.00	5000.00
HN 1827			
☐ Spring (2nd version)	1937-1949	2500.00	3000.00
HN 1828			
☐ Salome	1937-1949	4500.00	5000.00
HN 1829			
☐ BIRD MODEL (Macaw)			
HN 1830			
☐ Lady of the Snows	1937-1949	3500.00	4000.00
HN 1831			
☐ The Cloud	1937-1949	4000.00	4500.00
HN 1832			
☐ Granny	1937-1949	850.00	950.00

	Date	Price Range	
HN 1833			
☐ Top o' the Hill	1937-1971	225.00	275.00
HN 1834			
☐ Top o' the Hill	1937-	170.00	
HN 1835			
☐ Verena	1938-1949	750.00	850.00
HN 1836			
☐ Vanessa	1938-1949	600.00	700.00
HN 1837			
☐ Mariquita.......................	1938-1949	1400.00	1750.00
HN 1838			
☐ Vanessa	1938-1949	600.00	700.00
HN 1839			
☐ Christine (1st version)	1938-1949	650.00	750.00
HN 1840			
☐ Christine (1st version)	1938-1949	650.00	750.00
HN 1841			
☐ The Bride (1st version)	1938-1949	800.00	900.00
HN 1842			
☐ Babie	1938-1949	150.00	200.00
HN 1843			
☐ Biddy Penny Farthing	1938-	175.00	
HN 1844			
☐ Odds and Ends	1938-1949	800.00	900.00
HN 1845			
☐ Modena	1938-1949	750.00	850.00
HN 1846			
☐ Modena	1938-1949	750.00	850.00
HN 1847			
☐ Reflections	1938-1949	1000.00	1100.00
HN 1848			
☐ Reflections	1938-1949	1000.00	1100.00
HN 1849			
☐ Top o' the Hill	1938-1975	175.00	225.00
HN 1850			
☐ Antoinette (1st version)	1938-1949	800.00	900.00
HN 1851			
☐ Antoinette (1st version)	1938-1949	800.00	900.00
HN 1852			
☐ The Mirror	1938-1949	800.00	1000.00
HN 1853			
☐ The Mirror	1938-1949	800.00	1000.00
HN 1854			
☐ Verena	1938-1949	750.00	850.00
HN 1855			
☐ Memories	1938-1949	450.00	500.00
HN 1856			
☐ Memories	1938-1949	450.00	500.00

	Date	Price Range	
HN 1857			
☐ Memories	1938-1949	450.00	500.00
HN 1858			
☐ Dawn	1938-1949	1350.00	1500.00
HN 1859			
☐ Tildy	1938-1949	800.00	900.00
HN 1860			
☐ Millicent	1938-1949	1050.00	1150.00
HN 1861			
☐ Kate Hardcastle	1938-1949	500.00	600.00
HN 1862			
☐ Jasmine..........................	1938-1949	625.00	675.00
HN 1863			
☐ Jasmine..........................	1938-1949	625.00	675.00
HN 1864			
☐ Sweet and Fair	1938-1949	650.00	700.00
HN 1865			
☐ Sweet and Fair	1938-1949	650.00	700.00
HN 1866			
☐ Wedding Morn	1938-1949	1200.00	1300.00
HN 1867			
☐ Wedding Morn	1938-1949	1200.00	1300.00
HN 1868			
☐ Serena	1938-1949	1100.00	1200.00
HN 1869			
☐ Dryad of the Pines	1938-1949	2750.00	3000.00
HN 1870			
☐ Little Lady Make Believe	1938-1949	500.00	550.00
HN 1871			
☐ Annabella	1938-1949	450.00	525.00
HN 1872			
☐ Annabella	1938-1949	450.00	525.00
HN 1873			
☐ Granny's Heritage	1938-1949	450.00	500.00
HN 1874			
☐ Granny's Heritage	1938-1949	450.00	500.00
HN 1875			
☐ Annabella	1938-1949	450.00	525.00
HN 1876			
☐ Jasmine..........................	1938-1949	650.00	700.00
HN 1877			
☐ Jean	1938-1949	475.00	525.00
HN 1878			
☐ Jean	1938-1949	375.00	450.00
HN 1879			
☐ Bon Jour	1938-1949	650.00	750.00
HN 1880			
☐ The Lambeth Walk	1938-1949	1300.00	1400.00

	Date	Price Range	
HN 1881			
☐ The Lambeth Walk	1938-1949	1300.00	1400.00
HN 1882			
☐ Nell Gwynn	1938-1949	600.00	700.00
HN 1883			
☐ Prudence.......................	1938-1949	750.00	800.00
HN 1884			
☐ Prudence.......................	1938-1949	750.00	800.00
HN 1885			
☐ Nadine........................	1938-1949	650.00	750.00
HN 1886			
☐ Nadine........................	1938-1949	650.00	750.00
HN 1887			
☐ Nell Gwynn	1938-1949	600.00	700.00
HN 1888			
☐ Bon Jour	1938-1949	600.00	700.00
HN 1889			
☐ Goody Two Shoes	1938-1949	250.00	300.00
HN 1890			
☐ Lambing Time...................	1938-1980	100.00	150.00
HN 1891			
☐ Pecksniff (2nd version)	1938-1952	400.00	450.00
HN 1892			
☐ Uriah Heep (2nd version)	1938-1952	275.00	325.00
HN 1893			
☐ Fat Boy (2nd version)	1938-1952	325.00	375.00
HN 1894			
☐ Mr. Pickwick (2nd version)	1938-1952	400.00	450.00
HN 1895			
☐ Mr. Micawber (2nd version)	1938-1952	400.00	450.00
HN 1896			
☐ Sairey Gamp (2nd version).........	1938-1952	325.00	375.00
HN 1897			
☐ Miss Fortune....................	1938-1949	400.00	450.00
HN 1898			
☐ Miss Fortune....................	1938-1949	400.00	450.00
HN 1899			
☐ Midsummer Noon.................	1939-1949	550.00	600.00
HN 1900			
☐ Midsummer Noon.................	1939-1949	550.00	600.00
HN 1901			
☐ Penelope	1939-1975	300.00	350.00
HN 1902			
☐ Penelope	1939-1949	550.00	600.00
HN 1903			
☐ Rhythm	1939-1949	1000.00	1100.00
HN 1904			
☐ Rhythm	1939-1949	1000.00	1100.00

	Date	Price Range	
HN 1905			
□ Goody Two Shoes	1939-1949	225.00	275.00
HN 1906			
□ Lydia	1939-1949	300.00	350.00
HN 1907			
□ Lydia	1939-1949	300.00	350.00
HN 1908			
□ Lydia	1939-	125.00	
HN 1909			
□ Honey	1939-1949	350.00	400.00
HN 1910			
□ Honey	1939-1949	375.00	450.00
HN 1911			
□ Autumn Breezes	1939-1976	150.00	200.00
HN 1912			
□ Old Balloon Seller and Bulldog	1939-1949	1350.00	1500.00
HN 1913			
□ Autumn Breezes	1939-1971	195.00	245.00
HN 1914			
□ Paisley Shawl (2nd version)	1939-1949	300.00	350.00
HN 1915			
□ Veronica (2nd version)	1939-1949	400.00	450.00
HN 1916			
□ Janet (2nd version)	1939-1949	350.00	400.00
HN 1917			
□ Meryll	1939-1949	1200.00	1350.00
HN 1918			
□ Sweet Suzy	1939-1949	650.00	750.00
HN 1919			
□ Kate Hardcastle	1939-1949	800.00	900.00
HN 1920			
□ Windflower (2nd version)	1939-1949	500.00	550.00
HN 1921			
□ Roseanna	1940-1949	400.00	450.00
HN 1922			
□ Spring Morning	1940-1973	175.00	225.00
HN 1923			
□ Spring Morning	1940-1949	275.00	325.00
HN 1924			
□ Fiona (1st version)	1940-1949	550.00	650.00
HN 1925			
□ Fiona (1st version)	1940-1949	550.00	650.00
HN 1926			
□ Roseanna	1940-1959	275.00	325.00
HN 1927			
□ The Awakening	1940-1949	2050.00	2200.00
HN 1928			
□ Marguerite	1940-1959	300.00	350.00

	Date	Price Range	
HN 1929			
☐ Marguerite	1940-1949	500.00	600.00
HN 1930			
☐ Marguerite	1940-1949	550.00	650.00
HN 1931			
☐ Meriel.........................	1940-1949	850.00	950.00
HN 1932			
☐ Meriel.........................	1940-1949	850.00	950.00
HN 1933			
☐ Fiona (1st version)	1940-1949	650.00	750.00
HN 1934			
☐ Autumn Breeezes	1940-	170.00	
HN 1935			
☐ Sweeting	1940-1973	100.00	150.00
HN 1936			
☐ Miss Muffet.....................	1940-1967	150.00	200.00
HN 1937			
☐ Miss Muffet.....................	1940-1952	300.00	350.00
HN 1938			
☐ Sweeting	1940-1949	275.00	350.00
HN 1939			
☐ Windflower (2nd version)	1940-1949	500.00	550.00
HN 1940			
☐ Toinette	1940-1949	1450.00	1750.00
HN 1941			
☐ Peggy.........................	1940-1949	150.00	200.00
HN 1942			
☐ Pyjams........................	1940-1949	325.00	375.00
HN 1943			
☐ Veronica	1940-1949	400.00	450.00
HN 1944			
☐ Daydreams	1940-1949	350.00	400.00
HN 1945			
☐ Spring Flowers	1940-1949	500.00	550.00
HN 1946			
☐ Marguerite	1940-1949	400.00	500.00
HN 1947			
☐ June..........................	1940-1949	450.00	500.00
HN 1948			
☐ Lady Charmain	1940-1973	275.00	325.00
HN 1949			
☐ Lady Charmain	1940-1975	275.00	325.00
HN 1950			
☐ Claribel	1940-1949	350.00	400.00
HN 1951			
☐ Claribel	1940-1949	325.00	375.00
HN 1952			
☐ Irene..........................	1940-1950	500.00	600.00

	Date	Price Range	
HN 1953			
☐ Orange Lady	1940-1975	200.00	250.00
HN 1954			
☐ The Balloon Man	1940-	185.00	
HN 1955			
☐ Lavinia.........................	1940-1979	85.00	125.00
HN 1956			
☐ Chloe...........................	1940-1949	400.00	450.00
HN 1957			
☐ The New Bonnet..................	1940-1949	500.00	550.00
HN 1958			
☐ Lady April	1940-1959	250.00	300.00
HN 1959			
☐ The Choice	1941-1949	850.00	950.00
HN 1960			
☐ The Choice	1941-1949	850.00	950.00
HN 1961			
☐ Daisy	1941-1949	275.00	325.00
HN 1962			
☐ Genevieve	1941-1975	160.00	225.00
HN 1963			
☐ Honey	1941-1949	400.00	450.00
HN 1964			
☐ Janet (2nd version)	1941-1949	350.00	400.00
HN 1965			
☐ Lady April	1941-1949	300.00	350.00
HN 1966			
☐ Orange Vendor	1941-1949	700.00	800.00
HN 1967			
☐ Lady Betty......................	1941-1951	250.00	325.00
HN 1968			
☐ Madonna of the Square	1941-1949	850.00	950.00
HN 1969			
☐ Madonna of the Square	1941-1949	850.00	950.00
HN 1970			
☐ Milady	1941-1949	900.00	950.00
HN 1971			
☐ Springtime	1941-1949	900.00	950.00
HN 1972			
☐ Regency Beau...................	1941-1949	850.00	950.00
HN 1973			
☐ The Corinthian	1941-1949	950.00	1050.00
HN 1974			
☐ Forty Winks.....................	1945-1973	165.00	250.00
HN 1975			
☐ The Shepherd (4th version)	1945-1975	150.00	200.00
HN 1976			
☐ Easter Day......................	1945-1951	425.00	475.00

	Date	Price Range	
HN 1977			
☐ Her Ladyship	1945-1959	250.00	325.00
HN 1978			
☐ Bedtime........................	1945-	55.00	
HN 1979			
☐ Gollywog.....................	1945-1959	300.00	350.00
HN 1980			
☐ Gwynneth	1945-1952	250.00	325.00
HN 1981			
☐ The Ermine Coat................	1945-1967	200.00	275.00
HN 1982			
☐ Sabbath Morn..................	1945-1959	265.00	325.00
HN 1983			
☐ Rosebud (2nd version)	1945-1952	450.00	500.00
HN 1984			
☐ The Patchwork Quilt	1945-1959	450.00	500.00
HN 1985			
☐ Darling (2nd version)	1946-	55.00	
HN 1986			
☐ Diana.......................	1946-1975	125.00	175.00
HN 1987			
☐ Paisley Shawl (1st version)	1946-1959	250.00	300.00
HN 1988			
☐ Paisley Shawl (2nd version)........	1946-1975	150.00	225.00
HN 1989			
☐ Margaret	1947-1959	350.00	400.00
HN 1990			
☐ Mary Jane	1947-1959	375.00	425.00
HN 1991			
☐ Market Day (Country Lass)	1947-1955	275.00	325.00
HN 1991			
☐ Country Lass	1975-1981	125.00	175.00
HN 1992			
☐ Christmas Morn	1947-	155.00	
HN 1993			
☐ Griselda.....................	1947-1953	500.00	600.00
HN 1994			
☐ Karen.......................	1947-1955	350.00	400.00
HN 1995			
☐ Olivia.......................	1947-1951	300.00	400.00
HN 1996			
☐ Prue........................	1947-1955	275.00	325.00
HN 1997			
☐ Belle o' the Ball................	1947-1979	225.00	275.00
HN 1998			
☐ Collinette	1947-1949	450.00	500.00
HN 1999			
☐ Collinette	1947-1949	425.00	475.00

	Date	Price Range	
HN 2000			
☐ Jacqueline	1947-1951	400.00	450.00
HN 2001			
☐ Jacqueline	1947-1951	425.00	475.00
HN 2002			
☐ Bess...........................	1947-1969	225.00	275.00
HN 2003			
☐ Bess...........................	1947-1950	350.00	400.00
HN 2004			
☐ A'Courting......................	1947-1953	650.00	750.00
HN 2005			
☐ Henrietta Maria	1948-1953	550.00	650.00
HN 2006			
☐ The Lady Anne Nevill	1948-1953	800.00	900.00
HN 2007			
☐ Mrs. Fitzherbert	1948-1953	600.00	700.00
HN 2008			
☐ Philippa of Hainault..............	1948-1953	650.00	725.00
HN 2009			
☐ Eleanor of Provence..............	1948-1953	600.00	700.00
HN 2010			
☐ The Young Miss Nightingale........	1948-1953	700.00	800.00
HN 2011			
☐ Matilda	1948-1953	600.00	700.00
HN 2012			
☐ Margaret of Anjou	1948-1953	500.00	600.00
HN 2013			
☐ Angelina	1948-1951	700.00	800.00
HN 2014			
☐ Jane............................	1948-1951	600.00	700.00
HN 2015			
☐ Sir Walter Raleigh	1948-1955	750.00	800.00
HN 2016			
☐ A Jester (1st version)	1949-	200.00	
HN 2017			
☐ Silks and Ribbons	1949-	150.00	
HN 2018			
☐ Parson's Daughter	1949-1953	350.00	400.00
HN 2019			
☐ Minuet	1949-1971	225.00	275.00
HN 2020			
☐ Deidre	1949-1955	350.00	400.00
HN 2021			
☐ Blithe Morning	1949-1971	150.00	225.00
HN 2022			
☐ Janice	1949-1955	450.00	500.00
HN 2023			
☐ Joan...........................	1949-1959	350.00	400.00

	Date	Price Range	
HN 2024			
☐ Darby	1949-1959	300.00	375.00
HN 2025			
☐ Gossips	1949-1967	350.00	400.00
HN 2026			
☐ Suzette	1949-1959	300.00	350.00
HN 2027			
☐ June.	1949-1952	325.00	375.00
HN 2028			
☐ Kate Hardcastle	1949-1952	500.00	600.00
HN 2029			
☐ Windflower (1st version)	1949-1952	400.00	450.00
HN 2030			
☐ Memories	1949-1959	400.00	450.00
HN 2031			
☐ Granny's Heritage	1949-1969	400.00	450.00
HN 2032			
☐ Jean.	1949-1959	225.00	300.00
HN 2033			
☐ Midsummer Noon.	1949-1955	475.00	525.00
HN 2034			
☐ Madonna of the Square	1949-1951	800.00	900.00
HN 2035			
☐ Pearly Boy (2nd version)	1949-1959	150.00	225.00
HN 2036			
☐ Pearly Girl (2nd version)	1949-1959	150.00	225.00
HN 2037			
☐ Goody Two Shoes	1949-	100.00	
HN 2038			
☐ Peggy.	1949-1979	75.00	125.00
HN 2039			
☐ Easter Day.	1949-1969	275.00	325.00
HN 2040			
☐ Gollywog	1949-1959	225.00	275.00
HN 2041			
☐ The Broken Lance	1949-1975	500.00	600.00
HN 2042			
☐ Owd Willum.	1949-1973	175.00	250.00
HN 2043			
☐ The Poacher	1949-1959	250.00	325.00
HN 2044			
☐ Mary Mary	1949-1973	125.00	175.00
HN 2045			
☐ She Loves Me Not	1949-1962	150.00	200.00
HN 2046			
☐ He Loves Me	1949-1962	175.00	225.00
HN 2047			
☐ Once Upon a Time	1949-1955	200.00	250.00

	Date	Price Range	
HN 2048			
☐ Mary Had a Little Lamb	1949-	100.00	
HN 2049			
☐ Curly Locks	1949-1953	250.00	300.00
HN 2050			
☐ Wee Willie Winkie	1949-1953	225.00	250.00
HN 2051			
☐ St. George (2nd version)	1950-	475.00	
HN 2052			
☐ Grandma	1950-1959	325.00	400.00
HN 2053			
☐ The Gaffer	1950-1959	350.00	400.00
HN 2054			
☐ Falstaff (2nd version)	1950-	150.00	
HN 2055			
☐ The Leisure Hour	1950-1965	400.00	500.00
HN 2056			
☐ Susan	1950-1959	300.00	350.00
HN 2057			
☐ The Jersey Milkmaid	1950-1959	275.00	325.00
HN 2057			
☐ The Milkmaid	1975-1981	135.00	185.00
HN 2058			
☐ Hermione	1950-1952	600.00	700.00
HN 2059			
☐ The Bedtime Story	1950-	215.00	
HN 2060			
☐ Jack	1950-1971	125.00	175.00
HN 2061			
☐ Jill	1950-1971	150.00	200.00
HN 2062			
☐ Little Boy Blue	1950-1973	115.00	175.00
HN 2063			
☐ Little Jack Horner	1950-1953	225.00	275.00
HN 2064			
☐ My Pretty Maid	1950-1954	250.00	300.00
HN 2065			
☐ Blithe Morning	1950-1973	200.00	225.00
HN 2066			
☐ Minuet	1950-1955	225.00	275.00
HN 2067			
☐ St. George (1st version)	1950-1976	3750.00	4500.00
HN 2068			
☐ Calumet	1950-1953	625.00	725.00
HN 2069			
☐ Farmer's Wife	1951-1955	400.00	500.00
HN 2070			
☐ Bridget	1951-1973	250.00	325.00

	Date	Price Range	
HN 2071			
☐ Bernice	1951-1953	600.00	700.00
HN 2072			
☐ The Rocking Horse.	1951-1953	1450.00	1750.00
HN 2073			
☐ Vivienne.	1951-1967	200.00	300.00
HN 2074			
☐ Marianne	1951-1953	475.00	550.00
HN 2075			
☐ French Peasant	1951-1955	600.00	700.00
HN 2076			
☐ Promenade	1951-1953	1150.00	1350.00
HN 2077			
☐ Rowena	1951-1955	550.00	650.00
HN 2078			
☐ Elfreda.	1951-1955	600.00	700.00
HN 2079			
☐ Damaris.	1951-1952	800.00	950.00
HN 2080			
☐ Jack Point (Prestige Series)	1952-	1500.00	
HN 2081			
☐ Princess Badoura (Prestige Series) . .	1952-	14000.00	15000.00
HN 2082			
☐ The Moor (Prestige Series)	1952-	1450.00	
HN 2083 NO DETAILS AVAILABLE			
HN 2084			
☐ King Charles I (Prestige Series)	1952-	1500.00	
HN 2085			
☐ Spring (3rd version)	1952-1959	400.00	450.00
HN 2086			
☐ Summer (2nd version)	1952-1959	500.00	550.00
HN 2087			
☐ Autumn (2nd version)	1952-1959	500.00	550.00
HN 2088			
☐ Winter (2nd version)	1952-1959	350.00	425.00
HN 2089			
☐ Judith . . . . .'.	1952-1959	225.00	300.00
HN 2090			
☐ Midinette (2nd version)	1952-1965	225.00	300.00
HN 2091			
☐ Rosemary	1952-1959	350.00	450.00
HN 2092			
☐ Sweet Maid (2nd version).	1952-1955	350.00	400.00
HN 2093			
☐ Georgiana	1952-1955	600.00	700.00
HN 2094			
☐ Uncle Ned	1952-1965	400.00	450.00
HN 2095			
☐ Ibrahim	1952-1955	700.00	800.00

	Date	Price Range	
HN 2096			
☐ The Fat Boy (3rd version)	1952-1967	300.00	350.00
HN 2097			
☐ Mr. Micawber (3rd version)	1952-1967	325.00	375.00
HN 2098			
☐ Pecksniff (3rd version)	1952-1967	300.00	350.00
HN 2099			
☐ Mr. Pickwick (3rd version)	1952-1967	325.00	375.00
HN 2100			
☐ Saiey Gamp (3rd version)	1952-1967	275.00	325.00
HN 2101			
☐ Uriah Heep (3rd version)	1952-1967	300.00	350.00
HN 2102			
☐ Pied Piper	1953-1976	250.00	300.00
HN 2103			
☐ Mask Seller	1953-	175.00	
HN 2104			
☐ Abdullah	1953-1962	550.00	700.00
HN 2105			
☐ Bluebeard (2nd version)	1953-	375.00	
HN 2106			
☐ Linda	1953-1976	120.00	150.00
HN 2107			
☐ Valerie	1953-	100.00	
HN 2108			
☐ Baby Bunting	1953-1959	225.00	275.00
HN 2109			
☐ Wendy	1953-	75.00	
HN 2110			
☐ Christmas Time	1953-1967	350.00	400.00
HN 2111			
☐ Betsy	1953-1959	325.00	375.00
HN 2112			
☐ Carolyn	1953-1965	350.00	400.00
HN 2113			
☐ Maytime	1953-1967	225.00	300.00
HN 2114			
☐ Sleepyhead	1953-1955	850.00	1000.00
HN 2115			
☐ Coppelia	1953-1959	600.00	700.00
HN 2116			
☐ Ballerina	1953-1973	250.00	325.00
HN 2117			
☐ The Skater	1953-1971	275.00	350.00
HN 2118			
☐ Good King Wenceslas	1953-1976	250.00	300.00
HN 2119			
☐ Town Crier	1953-1976	250.00	300.00

	Date	Price Range	
HN 2120			
☐ Dinky Do	1983-	65.00	
HN 2121			
☐ Babie	1983-	75.00	
HN 2122			
☐ Yoeman of the Guard	1954-1959	650.00	750.00
HN 2123			
☐ Rose.	1983-	65.00	
HN 2124 - HN 2127 NOT ISSUED			
HN 2128			
☐ River Boy	1962-1975	150.00	200.00
HN 2129 - HN 2131 NOT ISSUED			
HN 2132			
☐ The Suitor	1962-1971	400.00	475.00
HN 2133			
☐ Faraway	1958-1962	300.00	350.00
HN 2134			
☐ An Old King.	1954-	475.00	
HN 2135			
☐ Gay Morning	1954-1967	225.00	300.00
HN 2136			
☐ Delphine	1954-1967	275.00	325.00
HN 2137			
☐ Lilac Time	1954-1969	250.00	300.00
HN 2138			
☐ La Sylphide	1956-1965	325.00	400.00
HN 2139			
☐ Giselle	1954-1969	300.00	350.00
HN 2140			
☐ Giselle, Forest Glade	1954-1965	300.00	375.00
HN 2141			
☐ Choir Boy	1954-1975	75.00	125.00
HN 2142			
☐ Rag Doll.	1954-	75.00	
HN 2143			
☐ Friar Tuck	1954-1965	500.00	600.00
HN 2144			
☐ The Jovial Monk	1954-1967	175.00	225.00
HN 2145			
☐ Wardrobe Mistress.	1954-1967	475.00	525.00
HN 2146			
☐ The Tinsmith	1962-1967	450.00	500.00
HN 2147			
☐ Autumn Breezes	1955-1971	325.00	375.00
HN 2148			
☐ The Bridesmaid (2nd version)	1955-1959	175.00	225.00
HN 2149			
☐ Love Letter	1958-1976	250.00	300.00

	Date	Price Range	
HN 2150			
☐ Willy Won't He	1955-1959	250.00	300.00
HN 2151			
☐ Mother's Help	1962-1969	175.00	225.00
HN 2152			
☐ Adrienne	1964-1976	175.00	225.00
HN 2153			
☐ The One That Got Away	1955-1959	225.00	275.00
HN 2154			
☐ A Child from Williamsburg	1964-1983	75.00	115.00
HN 2155 NOT ISSUED			
HN 2156			
☐ The Polka	1955-1969	250.00	300.00
HN 2157			
☐ A Gypsy Dance (1st version)	1955-1957	350.00	400.00
HN 2158			
☐ Alice...........................	1960-1980	95.00	125.00
HN 2159			
☐ Fortune Teller	1955-1967	425.00	475.00
HN 2160			
☐ The Apple Maid..................	1957-1962	350.00	425.00
HN 2161			
☐ The Hornpipe	1955-1962	750.00	850.00
HN 2162			
☐ The Foaming Quart	1955-	165.00	
HN 2163			
☐ In the Stocks (2nd version)	1955-1959	600.00	700.00
HN 2164 NOT ISSUED			
HN 2165			
☐ Janice	1955-1965	450.00	500.00
HN 2166			
☐ The Bride (2nd version)	1956-1976	175.00	225.00
HN 2167			
☐ Home Again	1956-	125.00	
HN 2168			
☐ Esmeralda......................	1956-1959	350.00	400.00
HN 2169			
☐ Dimity	1956-1959	300.00	350.00
HN 2170			
☐ Invitation.......................	1956-1975	110.00	150.00
HN 2171			
☐ The Fiddler	1956-1962	650.00	800.00
HN 2172			
☐ Jolly Sailor	1956-1965	600.00	700.00
HN 2173			
☐ The Organ Grinder	1956-1965	650.00	700.00
HN 2174			
☐ The Tailor	1956-1959	600.00	700.00

	Date	Price Range	
HN 2175			
☐ The Beggar (2nd version)	1956-1962	550.00	625.00
HN 2176 NOT ISSUED			
HN 2177			
☐ My Teddy	1962-1967	250.00	300.00
HN 2178			
☐ Enchantment	1957-1982	155.00	
HN 2179			
☐ Noelle	1957-1967	350.00	400.00
HN 2180 NOT ISSUED			
HN 2181			
☐ Summer's Day	1957-1962	375.00	450.00
HN 2182 NOT ISSUED			
HN 2183			
☐ Boy from Williamsburg	1969-1983	75.00	115.00
HN 2184			
☐ Sunday Morning	1963-1969	265.00	325.00
HN 2185			
☐ Columbine (2nd version)	1957-1969	225.00	275.00
HN 2186			
☐ Harlequin	1957-1969	225.00	275.00
HN 2187 - HN 2190 NOT ISSUED			
HN 2191			
☐ Sea Sprite (2nd version)	1958-1962	475.00	525.00
HN 2192			
☐ Wood Nymph	1958-1962	300.00	350.00
HN 2193			
☐ Fair Lady	1963-	155.00	
HN 2194 - HN 2195 NOT ISSUED			
HN 2196			
☐ The Bridesmaid (3rd version)	1960-1976	100.00	125.00
HN 2197 - HN 2201 NOT ISSUED			
HN 2202			
☐ Melody	1957-1962	200.00	275.00
HN 2203			
☐ Teenager	1957-1962	225.00	275.00
HN 2204			
☐ Long John Silver	1957-1965	425.00	500.00
HN 2205			
☐ Master Sweep	1957-1962	600.00	700.00
HN 2206			
☐ Sunday Best	1979-	295.00	
HN 2207			
☐ Stayed at Home	1958-1969	150.00	200.00
HN 2208			
☐ Silversmith of Williamsburg	1960-1983	125.00	200.00
HN 2209			
☐ Hostess of Williamsburg	1960-1983	135.00	200.00

	Date	Price Range	
HN 2210			
☐ Debutante	1963-1967	375.00	425.00
HN 2211			
☐ Fair Maiden	1967-	195.00	
HN 2212			
☐ Rendezvous	1962-1971	350.00	400.00
HN 2213			
☐ Contemplation, white	1983-	75.00	
HN 2214			
☐ Bunny	1960-1975	125.00	175.00
HN 2215			
☐ Sweet April	1965-1967	325.00	400.00
HN 2216			
☐ Pirouette	1959-1967	200.00	250.00
HN 2217			
☐ Old King Cole	1963-1967	750.00	850.00
HN 2218			
☐ Cookie	1958-1975	125.00	175.00
HN 2219 NOT ISSUED			
HN 2220			
☐ Winsome	1960-	155.00	
HN 2221			
☐ Nanny	1958-	175.00	
HN 2222			
☐ Camellia	1960-1971	200.00	275.00
HN 2223			
☐ Schoolmarm	1958-1980	110.00	175.00
HN 2224 NOT ISSUED			
HN 2225			
☐ Make Believe	1962-	100.00	
HN 2226			
☐ The Cellist	1960-1967	450.00	500.00
HN 2227			
☐ Gentleman from Williamsburg	1960-1983	100.00	175.00
HN 2228			
☐ Lady from Williamsburg	1960-1983	110.00	200.00
HN 2229			
☐ Southern Belle	1958-	185.00	
HN 2230			
☐ A Gypsy Dance (2nd version)	1959-1971	200.00	275.00
HN 2231			
☐ Sweet Sixteen	1958-1965	275.00	325.00
HN 2232 NOT ISSUED			
HN 2233			
☐ Royal Governor's Cook . . . . :	1960-1983	115.00	200.00
HN 2234			
☐ Michelle	1967-	155.00	
HN 2235			
☐ Dancing Years	1965-1971	375.00	425.00

	Date	Price Range	
HN 2236			
☐ Affection	1962-	**100.00**	
HN 2237			
☐ Celeste	1959-1971	**200.00**	**250.00**
HN 2238			
☐ My Pet	1962-1975	**100.00**	**150.00**
HN 2239			
☐ Wigmaker of Williamsburg	1960-1983	**115.00**	**200.00**
HN 2240			
☐ Blacksmith of Williamsburg	1960-1983	**125.00**	**200.00**
HN 2241			
☐ Contemplation, black . . . . , . . .	1983-	**75.00**	
HN 2242			
☐ First Steps	1959-1965	**500.00**	**550.00**
HN 2243			
☐ Treasure Island.	1962-1975	**150.00**	**200.00**
HN 2244			
☐ Newsboy	1959-1965	**525.00**	**625.00**
HN 2245			
☐ The Basket Weaver	1959-1962	**500.00**	**600.00**
HN 2246			
☐ Cradle Song	1959-1962	**400.00**	**450.00**
HN 2247			
☐ Omar Khayyam (2nd version)	1965-1983	**115.00**	**165.00**
HN 2248			
☐ Tall Story.	1968-1975	**150.00**	**200.00**
HN 2249			
☐ The Favourite	1960-	**165.00**	
HN 2250			
☐ The Toymaker	1959-1973	**425.00**	**475.00**
HN 2251			
☐ Masquerade (2nd version)	1960-1965	**350.00**	**400.00**
HN 2252 NOT ISSUED			
HN 2253			
☐ The Puppetmaker	1962-1973	**400.00**	**475.00**
HN 2254			
☐ Shore Leave	1965-1979	**200.00**	**250.00**
HN 2255			
☐ Teatime	1972-1983	**165.00**	
HN 2256			
☐ Twilight	1971-1976	**125.00**	**200.00**
HN 2257			
☐ Sea Harvest	1969-1976	**150.00**	**200.00**
HN 2258			
☐ A Good Catch	1966-	**165.00**	
HN 2259			
☐ Masquerade (2nd version)	1960-1965	**300.00**	**350.00**
HN 2260			
☐ The Captain (2nd version)	1965-1982	**175.00**	**225.00**

	Date	Price Range	
HN 2261			
☐ Marriage of Art and Industry (Limited Edition, Figurines)	1958-	7000.00	8000.00
HN 2262			
☐ Lights Out	1965-1969	225.00	275.00
HN 2263			
☐ Seashore	1961-1965	250.00	300.00
HN 2264			
☐ Elegance	1961-	155.00	
HN 2265			
☐ Sara	1980-	215.00	
HN 2266			
☐ Ballad Seller	1968-1973	325.00	375.00
HN 2267			
☐ Rhapsody	1961-1973	135.00	200.00
HN 2268			
☐ Daphne	1963-1975	210.00	260.00
HN 2269			
☐ Leading Lady	1965-1976	150.00	225.00
HN 2270			
☐ Pillow Fight.....................	1965-1969	200.00	250.00
HN 2271			
☐ Melanie	1965-1980	125.00	175.00
HN 2272			
☐ Repose	1972-1979	150.00	200.00
HN 2273			
☐ Denise.........................	1964-1971	275.00	325.00
HN 2274			
☐ Golden Days	1964-1973	125.00	175.00
HN 2275			
☐ Sandra.........................	1969-	155.00	
HN 2276			
☐ Heart to Heart..................	1961-1971	400.00	500.00
HN 2277 · HN 2278 NOT ISSUED			
HN 2279			
☐ The Clockmaker	1961-1975	300.00	350.00
HN 2280			
☐ The Mayor	1963-1971	400.00	500.00
HN 2281			
☐ The Professor	1965-1980	150.00	200.00
HN 2282			
☐ The Coachman	1963-1971	475.00	550.00
HN 2283			
☐ Dreamweaver	1972-1976	250.00	300.00
HN 2284			
☐ The Craftsman	1961-1965	475.00	525.00
HN 2285 · HN 2286 NOT ISSUED			
HN 2287			
☐ Symphony	1961-1965	250.00	325.00

	Date	Price Range	
HN 2288 - HN 2303 NOT ISSUED			
HN 2304			
☐ Adrienne	1964-	155.00	
HN 2305			
☐ Dulcie	1981-	185.00	
HN 2306			
☐ Reverie	1964-1981	225.00	275.00
HN 2307			
☐ Coralie.........................	1964-	155.00	
HN 2308			
☐ Picnic..........................	1965-	100.00	
HN 2309			
☐ Buttercup	1964-	145.00	
HN 2310			
☐ Lisa	1969-1982	200.00	225.00
HN 2311			
☐ Lorna	1965-	125.00	
HN 2312			
☐ Soiree	1967-	170.00	
HN 2313 NOT ISSUED			
HN 2314			
☐ Old Mother Hubbard	1964-1975	300.00	350.00
HN 2315			
☐ Last Waltz......................	1967-	185.00	
HN 2316 NOT ISSUED			
HN 2317			
☐ The Lobster Man.................	1964-	165.00	
HN 2318			
☐ Grace...........................	1966-1980	110.00	155.00
HN 2319			
☐ The Bachelor....................	1964-1975	225.00	275.00
HN 2320			
☐ Tuppence a Bag	1968-	165.00	
HN 2321			
☐ Family Album	1966-1973	350.00	400.00
HN 2322			
☐ The Cup of Tea	1964-1983	115.00	150.00
HN 2323 NOT ISSUED			
HN 2324			
☐ Matador and Bull (Prestige Series) ...	1964-	10500.00	
HN 2325			
☐ The Master	1967-	165.00	
HN 2326			
☐ Antoinette (2nd version).............	1967-1979	150.00	175.00
HN 2327			
☐ Katrina.........................	1965-1969	250.00	300.00
HN 2328			
☐ Queen of Sheba	1982-	1250.00	

	Date	Price Range	
HN 2329			
☐ Lynne............................	1971-	**170.00**	
HN 2330			
☐ Meditation......................	1971-1983	**225.00**	**300.00**
HN 2331			
☐ Cello (Limited Edition, Lady Musicians)	1970-	**750.00**	**800.00**
HN 2332 NOT ISSUED			
HN 2333			
☐ Jacqueline	1983-	**145.00**	
HN 2334			
☐ Fragrance	1966-	**170.00**	
HN 2335			
☐ Hilary...........................	1967-1980	**95.00**	**150.00**
HN 2336			
☐ Alison	1966-	**155.00**	
HN 2337			
☐ Loretta.........................	1966-1980	**100.00**	**150.00**
HN 2338			
☐ Penny...........................	1968-	**65.00**	
HN 2339			
☐ My Love	1969-	**185.00**	
HN 2340			
☐ Belle (2nd version)	1968-	**65.00**	
HN 2341			
☐ Cherie	1966-	**100.00**	
HN 2342 NOT ISSUED			
HN 2343			
☐ Premiere	1969-1979	**175.00**	**225.00**
HN 2344 NOT ISSUED			
HN 2345			
☐ Clarissa (2nd version)	1968-1981	**125.00**	**175.00**
HN 2346			
☐ Kathy (Kate Greenaway)	1981-	**75.00**	
HN 2347			
☐ Nina............................	1969-1976	**125.00**	**175.00**
HN 2348			
☐ Geraldine	1972-1976	**125.00**	**175.00**
HN 2349			
☐ Flora	1966-1973	**175.00**	**225.00**
HN 2350 · HN 2351 NOT ISSUED			
HN 2352			
☐ A Stitch In Time	1966-1980	**95.00**	**150.00**
HN 2353 · HN 2355 NOT ISSUED			
HN 2356			
☐ Ascot...........................	1968-	**185.00**	
HN 2357 · HN 2358 NOT ISSUED			
HN 2359			
☐ The Detective	1977-1983	**125.00**	**165.00**

	Date	Price Range	
HN 2360 NOT ISSUED			
HN 2361			
☐ The Laird	1969-	175.00	
HN 2362			
☐ The Wayfarer	1970-1976	200.00	250.00
HN 2363 - HN 2367 NOT ISSUED			
HN 2368			
☐ Fleur	1968-	185.00	
HN 2369			
☐ Fleur	1984-	185.00	
HN 2370			
☐ Sir Edward.	1979-	750.00	
HN 2371			
☐ Sir Ralph	1979-	750.00	
HN 2372			
☐ Sir Thomas	1979-	750.00	
HN 2373			
☐ Joan.	1982-	95.00	
HN 2374			
☐ Mary.	1984-	95.00	
HN 2375			
☐ The Viking	1973-1976	250.00	300.00
HN 2376			
☐ Indian Brave (Limited Edition, Figurines.	1967-	4000.00	5000.00
HN 2377			
☐ Georgina (Kate Greenaway)	1981-	75.00	
HN 2378			
☐ Simone	1971-1981	125.00	185.00
HN 2379			
☐ Ninette	1971-	185.00	
HN 2380			
☐ Sweet Dreams	1971-	150.00	
HN 2381			
☐ Kirsty.	1971-	185.00	
HN 2382			
☐ Secret Thoughts	1971-	215.00	
HN 2383			
☐ Breton Dancer (Limited Edition, Dancers of the World)	1981-	850.00	
HN 2384			
☐ West Indian Dancer (Limited Edition, Dancers of the World)	1981-	850.00	
HN 2385			
☐ Debbie	1969-1982	115.00	135.00
HN 2386			
☐ Prince Phillip (Limited Edition, Figurines.	1981-	750.00	

	Date	Price Range	
HN 2387			
☐ Helen of Troy (Limited Edition, Femme Fatale Series)	1981-	1250.00	
HN 2388			
☐ Karen..........................	1982-	185.00	
HN 2389			
☐ Angela	1982-	95.00	
HN 2390 - NOT ISSUED			
HN 2391			
☐ TZ 'U-HSI Empress Dowager	1983-	1250.00	
HN 2392			
☐ Jennifer	1982-	155.00	
HN 2393			
☐ Rosalind	1970-1975	150.00	200.00
HN 2394			
☐ Lisa	1983-	125.00	
HN 2395 - NOT ISSUED			
HN 2396			
☐ Wistful.........................	1979-	325.00	
HN 2397			
☐ Margaret	1982-	95.00	
HN 2398			
☐ Alexandra	1970-1976	175.00	225.00
HN 2399			
☐ Buttercup	1983-	145.00	
HN 2400			
☐ Debbie.........................	1983-	75.00	
HN 2401			
☐ Sandra.........................	1984-	155.00	
HN 2402 - 2409 NOT ISSUED			
HN 2410			
☐ Breton Dancer	1981-	850.00	
HN 2411 - 2416 NOT ISSUED			
HN 2417			
☐ The Boatman	1971-	165.00	
HN 2418 - HN 2420 NOT ISSUED			
HN 2421			
☐ Charlotte.......................	1972-	185.00	
HN 2422			
☐ Francine	1972-1980	50.00	100.00
HN 2423 - NOT ISSUED			
HN 2424			
☐ Penny..........................	1983-	65.00	
HN 2425			
☐ Southern Belle	1984-	185.00	
HN 2426			
☐ Tranquility, (Image Series) (black) ...	1980-	75.00	

	Date	Price Range	
HN 2427			
☐ Virginals (Limited Edition, Lady Musicians)	1971-	750.00	800.00
HN 2428			
☐ The Palio (Limited Edition, Miscellaneous)	1971-	N/A	
HN 2429			
☐ Elyse	1972-	185.00	
HN 2430			
☐ Romance	1972-1980	90.00	150.00
HN 2431			
☐ Lute (Limited Edition, Lady Musicians)	1972-	750.00	800.00
HN 2432			
☐ Violin (Limited Edition, Lady Musicians)	1972-	750.00	800.00
HN 2433			
☐ Peace (Image Series)	1980-	50.00	
HN 2434			
☐ Fair Maiden	1983-	95.00	
HN 2435			
☐ Queen of the Ice	1984-	125.00	
HN 2436			
☐ Scottish Highland Dancer (Limited Edition, Dancers of the World)	1978-	600.00	650.00
HN 2437			
☐ Queen of the Dawn................	1984-	125.00	
HN 2438			
☐ Sonata..........................	1984-	125.00	
HN 2439			
☐ Phillippine Dancer (Limited Edition, Dancers of the World)	1978-	550.00	650.00
HN 2440			
☐ Cynthia	1984-	125.00	
HN 2441			
☐ Pauline	1984-	155.00	
HN 2442			
☐ Sailor's Holiday	1972-1979	200.00	250.00
HN 2443			
☐ The Judge	1972-	175.00	
☐ The Judge, Matte Finish	1972-1976	175.00	225.00
HN 2444			
☐ Bon Appetit......................	1972-1976	150.00	225.00
HN 2445			
☐ Parisian.........................	1972-1975	130.00	200.00
HN 2446			
☐ Thanksgiving	1972-1976	200.00	250.00
HN 2447 — HN 2454 NOT ISSUED			

	Date	Price Range	
HN 2455			
☐ The Seafarer	1972-1976	225.00	275.00
HN 2456 — HN 2460 NOT ISSUED			
HN 2461			
☐ Janine	1971-	170.00	
HN 2462 NOT ISSUED			
HN 2463			
☐ Olga............................	1972-1975	175.00	225.00
HN 2464 — HN 2465 NOT ISSUED			
HN 2466			
☐ Eve.............................	1984-	1250.00	
HN 2467			
☐ Melissa	1981-	170.00	
HN 2468 NOT ISSUED			
HN 2469			
☐ Tranquility (Image Series)	1980-	75.00	
HN 2470			
☐ Peace (Image Series)	1980-	50.00	
HN 2471			
☐ Victoria	1973-	170.00	
HN 2472 NOT ISSUED			
HN 2473			
☐ At Ease	1973-1979	175.00	225.00
HN 2474 NOT ISSUED			
HN 2475			
☐ Vanity	1973-	100.00	
HN 2476			
☐ Mandy..........................	1982-	65.00	
HN 2477 — HN 2481 NOT ISSUED			
HN 2482			
☐ Harp (Limited Edition, Lady Musicians)	1973-	1100.00	1200.00
HN 2483			
☐ Flute (Limited Edition, Lady Musicians)	1973-	750.00	800.00
HN 2484			
☐ Past Glory	1973-1979	200.00	250.00
HN 2485			
☐ Lunchtime.......................	1973-1980	150.00	200.00
HN 2486 NOT ISSUED			
HN 2487			
☐ Beachcomber	1973-1976	160.00	225.00
HN 2488 — HN 2491 NOT ISSUED			
HN 2492			
☐ The Huntsman (3rd version)	1974-1979	135.00	200.00
HN 2493 NOT ISSUED			
HN 2494			
☐ Old Meg........................	1974-1976	325.00	375.00
HN 2495 — HN 2498 NOT ISSUED			

	Date	Price Range	
HN 2499			
☐ Helmsman......................	1974-	200.00	
HN 2500 — HN 2670 ANIMAL MODELS			
HN 2502			
☐ Queen Elizabeth II (Limited Edition, now sold out)	1973-	2000.00	2500.00
HN 2503 — HN 2519 ANIMAL MODELS			
HN 2520			
☐ The Farmers Boy	1938-1960	1000.00	1250.00
HN 2521 — HN 2541 ANIMAL MODELS			
HN 2542			
☐ Boudoir (Haute Ensemble)	1974-1979	325.00	375.00
HN 2543			
☐ Eliza (Haute Ensemble)	1974-1979	175.00	225.00
HN 2544			
☐ A la Mode (Haute Ensemble)	1974-1979	175.00	250.00
HN 2545			
☐ Carmen (Haute Ensemble) (2nd version)	1974-1979	200.00	250.00
HN 2546			
☐ Buddies	1973-1976	200.00	250.00
HN 2547 — HN 2553 BIRD MODELS			
HN 2554			
☐ Masque	1973-1982	170.00	
HN 2555 — HN 2670 ANIMAL and BIRD MODELS			
HN 2671			
☐ Good Morning...................	1974-1976	325.00	375.00
HN 2672 — HN 2676 NOT ISSUED			
HN 2677			
☐ Taking Things Easy	1975-	200.00	
HN 2678 NOT ISSUED			
HN 2679			
☐ Drummer Boy	1976-1981	325.00	375.00
HN 2680 — HN 2682 NOT ISSUED			
HN 2683			
☐ Stop Press......................	1977-1980	150.00	200.00
HN 2684 — HN 2693 NOT ISSUED			
HN 2694			
☐ Fiona (2nd version)...............	1974-1980	95.00	150.00
HN 2695 — HN 2698 NOT ISSUED			
HN 2699			
☐ Cymbals (Limited Editions, Lady Musicians)	1974-	650.00	700.00
HN 2700			
☐ Chitarrone (Limited Editions, Lady Musicians)	1974-	650.00	700.00
HN 2701 — HN 2703 NOT ISSUED			
HN 2704			
☐ Pensive Moments................	1974-1981	150.00	200.00

	Date	Price Range	
HN 2705			
☐ Julia...........................	1975-	155.00	
HN 2706 — HN 2708 NOT ISSUED			
HN 2709			
☐ Regal Lady	1975-1983	115.00	170.00
HN 2710			
☐ Jean...........................	1984-	95.00	
HN 2711 NOT ISSUED			
HN 2712			
☐ Mantilla........................	1974-1979	300.00	350.00
HN 2713			
☐ Tenderness (White)	1983-	75.00	
HN 2714			
☐ Tenderness (Black)...............	1983-	75.00	
HN 2715			
☐ Patricia	1982-	95.00	
HN 2716			
☐ Cavalier (2nd version).............	1976-1982	200.00	
HN 2717			
☐ Private, 2nd South Carolina Regiment 1781, (Limited Edition, Soldiers)	1975-	750.00	
HN 2718			
☐ Lady Pamela	1974-1980	150.00	200.00
HN 2719			
☐ Laurianne	1974-1979	150.00	200.00
HN 2720			
☐ Family (Image Series) (White)	1980-	95.00	
HN 2721			
☐ Family (Image Series) (Black)	1980-	95.00	
HN 2722			
☐ Veneta.........................	1974-1980	100.00	150.00
HN 2723			
☐ Grand Manner...................	1975-1981	250.00	300.00
HN 2724			
☐ Clarinda........................	1975-1980	175.00	225.00
HN 2725			
☐ Santa Claus	1982-	195.00	
HN 2726			
☐ The Centurion...................	1982-	150.00	
HN 2727			
☐ Little Miss Muffet	1984-		
HN 2728			
☐ Rest Awhile.....................	1981-	200.00	
HN 2729			
☐ Song of the Sea	1983-	150.00	
HN 2730 NOT ISSUED			
HN 2731			
☐ Thanks Doc	1975-	200.00	

	Date	Price Range
HN 2732		
❏ Thank You	1983-	**145.00**
HN 2733		
❏ Officer of the Line	1983-	**195.00**
HN 2734		
❏ Sweet Seventeen	1975-	**185.00**
HN 2735		
❏ Young Love	1975-	**695.00**
HN 2736		
❏ Tracy	1983-	**95.00**
HN 2737		
❏ Harlequin	1982-	**750.00**
HN 2738		
❏ Columbine.	1982-	**750.00**
HN 2739		
❏ Ann	1984-	**95.00**
HN 2740 — HN 2741 NOT ISSUED		
HN 2742		
❏ Sheila	1984-	**125.00**
HN 2743 — HN 2751 NOT ISSUED		
HN 2752		
❏ Major, 3rd New Jersey Regiment, 1776 (Limited Edition, Soldiers)	1975-	**750.00**
HN 2753		
❏ Serenade	1984-	**95.00**
HN 2754		
❏ Private, 3rd North Carolina Regiment, 1778 (Limited Edition, Soldiers)	1976-	**750.00**
HN 2755		
❏ Captain, 2nd New York Regiment, 1775 (Limited Edition, Soldiers)	1976-	**750.00**
HN 2756		
❏ Musicale	1984-	**125.00**
HN 2757		
❏ Lyric.	1984-	**95.00**
HN 2758		
❏ Linda	1984-	**95.00**
HN 2759		
❏ Private, Rhode Island Regiment, 1781 (Limited Edition, Soldiers)	1977-	**750.00**
HN 2760		
❏ Private, Massachusetts Regiment, 1778 (Limited Edition, Soldiers)	1977-	**750.00**
HN 2761		
❏ Private, Delaware Regiment, 1776 (Limited Edition, Soldiers)	1977-	**750.00**
HN 2762		
❏ Lovers (Image Series) (White)	1979-	**95.00**

	Date	Price Range	
HN 2763			
☐ Lovers (Image Series) (Black)	1979-	95.00	
HN 2764 NOT ISSUED			
HN 2765			
☐ Punch & Judy Man	1981-	250.00	
HN 2766 — HN 2767 NOT ISSUED			
HN 2768			
☐ Pretty Polly	1984-	100.00	
HN 2769 NOT ISSUED			
HN 2770			
☐ New Companions.................	1982-	185.00	
HN 2771 — HN 2778 NOT ISSUED			
HN 2779			
☐ Private, 1st Georgia Regiment, 1777 (Limited Edition, Soldiers)	1975-	750.00	
HN 2780			
☐ Corporal, 1st New Hampshire Regiment 1778 (Limited Edition, Soldiers).	1975-	750.00	
HN 2781 — HN 2787 NOT ISSUED			
HN 2788			
☐ Marjorie........................	1980-	185.00	
HN 2789			
☐ Kate	1978-	155.00	
HN 2790 NOT ISSUED			
HN 2791			
☐ Elaine	1980-	185.00	
HN 2792			
☐ Christine (2nd version).............	1978-	250.00	
HN 2793			
☐ Clare	1980-	250.00	
HN 2794 NOT ISSUED			
HN 2795			
☐ French Horn (Limited Editions, Lady Musicians)	1976-	650.00	700.00
HN 2796			
☐ Hurdy Gurdy (Limited Editions, Lady Musicians)	1975-	650.00	750.00
HN 2797			
☐ Viola d'Amore (Limited Editions, Lady Musicians)	1976-	650.00	700.00
HN 2798			
☐ Dulcimer (Limited Edition, Lady Musicians).........................	1975-	650.00	700.00
HN 2799			
☐ Ruth (Kate Greenaway)	1976-1982	65.00	100.00
HN 2800			
☐ Carrie (Kate Greenaway)	1976-1981	65.00	100.00
HN 2801			
☐ Lori (Kate Greenaway)	1976-	75.00	

	Date	Price Range	
HN 2802			
☐ Anna (Kate Greenaway)	1976-	65.00	100.00
HN 2803			
☐ First Dance	1977-	170.00	
HN 2804 NOT ISSUED			
HN 2805			
☐ Rebecca	1980-	325.00	
HN 2806			
☐ Jane	1983-	135.00	
HN 2807			
☐ Stephanie	1977-1982	175.00	225.00
HN 2808			
☐ Balinese Dancer	1982-	950.00	
HN 2809			
☐ North American Indian Dancer	1982-	950.00	
HN 2810			
☐ Solitude	1977-1983	165.00	215.00
HN 2811			
☐ Stephanie	1983-	170.00	
HN 2812 — HN 2813 NOT ISSUED			
HN 2814			
☐ Eventide	1977-	165.00	
HN 2815			
☐ Sergeant, 6th Maryland Regiment 1777 (Limited Edition, Soldiers)	1976-	750.00	
HN 2816			
☐ Votes for Women	1978-1981	200.00	250.00
HN 2817 NOT ISSUED			
HN 2818			
☐ Balloon Girl	1982-	125.00	
HN 2819 — HN 2823 NOT ISSUED			
HN 2824			
☐ Harmony	1978-	170.00	
HN 2825			
☐ Lady and the Unicorn	1982-	2500.00	
HN 2826			
☐ Leda and the Swan	1983-	2500.00	
HN 2827			
☐ Juno and the Peacock	1984-	1250.00	
HN 2828 — HN 2829 NOT ISSUED			
HN 2830			
☐ Indian Temple Dancer (Limited Edition, Dancers of the World)	1977-	800.00	850.00
HN 2831			
☐ Spanish Flamenco Dancer (Limited Edition, Dancers of the World)	1977-	800.00	850.00
HN 2832			
☐ Fair Lady	1977-	155.00	

	Date	Price Range	
HN 2833			
☐ Sophie (Kate Greenaway)	1977-	**75.00**	
HN 2834			
☐ Emma (Kate Greenaway)	1977-1982	**65.00**	**100.00**
HN 2835			
☐ Fair Lady	1977-	**155.00**	
HN 2836			
☐ Polish Dancer (Limited Edition, Dancers of the World)	1980-	**750.00**	
HN 2837			
☐ Awakening (Image Series) (Black) ...	1980-	**50.00**	
HN 2838			
☐ Sympathy (Image Series) (Black)	1980-	**75.00**	
HN 2839			
☐ Nicola	1978-	**250.00**	
HN 2840			
☐ Chinese Dancer (Limited Edition, Dancers of the World)	1980-	**750.00**	
HN 2841			
☐ Mother & Daughter (Image Series) ...	1980-	**95.00**	
HN 2842			
☐ Innocence	1979-1983	**110.00**	**150.00**
HN 2843			
☐ Mother & Daughter (Image Series) ...	1980-	**95.00**	
HN 2844			
☐ Sergeant, Virginia 1st Regiment Continental Light Dragoons, 1777 (Limited Edition, Soldiers)	1978-	**1750.00**	
HN 2845			
☐ Private, Connecticut Regiment, 1777 (Limited Edition, Soldiers)	1978-	**750.00**	
HN 2846			
☐ Private, Pennsylvania Rifle Battalion 1776, (Limited Edition, Soldiers)	1978-	**750.00**	
HN 2847 — HN 2850 NOT ISSUED			
HN 2851			
☐ Christmas Parcels	1978-1982	**165.00**	**200.00**
HN 2852 — HN 2854 NOT ISSUED			
HN 2855			
☐ Embroidering	1980-	**225.00**	
HN 2856			
☐ St. George (3rd version) (Prestige Series)	1978-	**6500.00**	
HN 2857 NOT ISSUED			
HN 2858			
☐ The Doctor	1979-	**225.00**	
HN 2859 — HN 2860 NOT ISSUED			

	Date	Price Range	
HN 2861			
☐ George Washington at Prayer (Limited Edition, Soldiers)	1977-	1800.00	2000.00
HN 2862			
☐ First Waltz.......................	1979-1983	165.00	225.00
HN 2863			
☐ Lucy (Kate Greenaway)	1980-	75.00	
HN 2864			
☐ Tom (Kate Greenaway).............	1978-1981	85.00	110.00
HN 2865			
☐ Tess (Kate Greenaway)	1978-1983	65.00	100.00
HN 2866			
☐ Mexican Dancer (Limited Edition, Dancers of the World)	1979-	550.00	
HN 2868			
☐ Kurdish Dancer (Limited Edition, Dancers of the World)	1979-	550.00	
HN 2868			
☐ Cleopatra and Slave (Limited Edition, Femmes Fatales Series)	1979-	1100.00	1300.00
HN 2869			
☐ Louise (Kate Greenaway)...........	1980-	75.00	
HN 2870			
☐ Beth (Kate Greenaway)	1980-1983	75.00	100.00
HN 2871			
☐ Beat You To It	1980-	350.00	
HN 2872			
☐ The Young Master	1980-	325.00	
HN 2873			
☐ Bride (4th version)	1980-	170.00	
HN 2874			
☐ Bridesmaid (4th version)	1980-	100.00	
HN 2875			
☐ Awakening (Image Series)	1980-	50.00	
HN 2876			
☐ Sympathy (Image Series)	1980-	75.00	
HN 2877			
☐ The Wizard	1979-	215.00	
HN 2878			
☐ Her Majesty Queen Elizabeth II......	1983-		
HN 2879			
☐ Gamekeeper	1984-	125.00	
HN 2880 — HN 2881 NOT ISSUED			
HN 2882			
☐ Queen Mother (Limited Edition, Figurines)	1980-	1250.00	1500.00
HN 2883			
☐ H.R.H. The Prince of Wales.	1982-	750.00	

	Date	Price Range
HN 2884 NOT ISSUED		
HN 2885		
☐ Lady Diana Spencer	1982-	**750.00**
HN 2886 — HN 2887 NOT ISSUED		
HN 2888		
☐ His Holiness Pope John Paul II.	1982-	**150.00**
HN 2889		
☐ Captain Cook	1980-	**365.00**
HN 2890		
☐ The Clown	1979-	**295.00**
HN 2891 NOT ISSUED		
HN 2892		
☐ The Chief	1979-	**200.00**
HN 2893 — HN 2897 NOT ISSUED		
HN 2898		
☐ Ko-Ko (2nd version)	1980-	**750.00**
HN 2899		
☐ Yum-Yum (2nd version)	1980-	**750.00**
HN 2900		
☐ Ruth the Pirate Maid	1981-	**750.00**
HN 2901		
☐ The Pirate King	1981-	**750.00**
HN 2902		
☐ Elsie Maynard	1982-	**750.00**
HN 2903		
☐ Colonel Fairfax	1982-	**750.00**
HN 2904 — HN 2905 NOT ISSUED		
HN 2906		
☐ Paula	1980-	**185.00**
HN 2907		
☐ The Piper	1980-	**250.00**
HN 2908		
☐ Ajax (Limited Edition, Ships Figurehead)	1980-1983	**750.00**
HN 2909		
☐ Benmore (Limited Edition, Ships Figurehead)	1980-1983	**750.00**
HN 2910		
☐ Lalla Rookh (Limited Edition, Ships Figurehead)	1981-1983	**750.00**
HN 2911		
☐ Gandolf (J.R.R. Tolkien Series)	1980-1983	**50.00**
HN 2912		
☐ Frado (J.R.R. Tolkien Series)	1980-1983	**35.00**
HN 2913		
☐ Gollum (J.R.R. Tolkien Series)	1980-1983	**35.00**
HN 2914		
☐ Bilbo (J.R.R. Tolkien Series)	1980-1983	**35.00**

	Date	Price Range	
HN 2915			
☐ Galadrial (J.R.R. Tolkien Series)	1981-1983	45.00	
HN 2916			
☐ Aragorn (J.R.R. Tolkien Series)	1980-1983	45.00	
HN 2917			
☐ Legolas (J.R.R. Tolkien Series)	1981-1983	45.00	
HN 2918			
☐ Boromir (J.R.R. Tolkien Series)	1981-1983	50.00	
HN 2919			
☐ Rachel	1981-	185.00	
HN 2920			
☐ Yearning (White)	1983-	75.00	
HN 2921			
☐ Yearning (Black)	1983-	75.00	
HN 2922			
☐ Gimli (J.R.R. Tolkien Series)	1981-1983	45.00	
HN 2923			
☐ Barliman Butterbur	1982-1983	45.00	
HN 2924			
☐ Tom Bombadil	1982-1983	50.00	
HN 2925			
☐ Samwise	1982-1983	35.00	
HN 2926			
☐ Tom Sawyer	1982-	50.00	
HN 2927			
☐ Huckleberry Finn	1982-	50.00	
HN 2928			
☐ Nelson (Limited Edition, Ships Figureheads)	1981-1983	750.00	
HN 2929 — HN 2932 NOT ISSUED			
HN 2933			
☐ Kathleen	1984-	195.00	
HN 2934			
☐ Balloon Boy	1984-	95.00	
HN 2935			
☐ Balloon Lady	1984-	125.00	
HN 2936 — HN 2939 NOT ISSUED			
HN 2940			
☐ All Aboard	1982-	175.00	
HN 2941			
☐ Tom Brown	1983-	50.00	
HN 2942			
☐ Prized Possessions (Collectors Club figurine)	1982-	125.00	200.00
HN 2943			
☐ The China Repairer	1983-	185.00	
HN 2944			
☐ Rag Doll Seller	1983-	150.00	
HN 2945 NOT ISSUED			

	Date	Price Range	
HN 2946			
☐ Elizabeth	1982-	225.00	
HN 2947 — HN 2951 NOT ISSUED			
HN 2952			
☐ Susan	1982-	175.00	
HN 2953			
☐ Sleepy Darling			
(Collectors Club figurine)	1981-	100.00	150.00
HN 2954			
☐ Samantha	1982-	95.00	
HN 2955			
☐ Nancy	1982-	95.00	
HN 2956			
☐ Heather	1982-	95.00	
HN 2957			
☐ Edith	1982-	75.00	
HN 2958			
☐ Amy	1982-	75.00	
HN 2959			
☐ Save Some For Me	1983-	75.00	
HN 2960			
☐ Laura	1983-	145.00	
HN 2961			
☐ Carol	1982-	95.00	
HN 2962			
☐ Barbara	1982-	95.00	
HN 2963			
☐ It Won't Hurt	1982-	75.00	
HN 2964			
☐ Dressing Up	1982-	75.00	
HN 2965			
☐ Pollyanna	1982-	50.00	
HN 2966			
☐ And So To Bed	1983-	75.00	
HN 2967			
☐ Please Keep Still	1983-	75.00	
HN 2968 — HN 2969 NOT ISSUED			
HN 2970			
☐ And One For You	1982-	75.00	
HN 2971			
☐ As Good As New.................	1982-	75.00	
HN 2972			
☐ Little Lord Fauntleroy	1982-	50.00	
HN 2973 NOT ISSUED			
HN 2974			
☐ Carolyn	1983-	155.00	
HN 2975			
☐ Heidi	1983-	50.00	

	Date	Price Range
HN 2976		
☐ I'm Nearly Ready	1984-	75.00
HN 2977		
☐ Magic Dragon	1984-	75.00
HN 2978 NOT ISSUED		
HN 2979		
☐ Fairyspell	1984-	65.00
HN 2980		
☐ Just One More	1984-	75.00
HN 2981		
☐ Stick 'Em Up	1984-	75.00
HN 2982 — HN 2988 NOT ISSUED		
HN 2989		
☐ The Genie	1983-	95.00
HN 2990 — HN 3012 NOT ISSUED		
HN 3013		
☐ James	1983-	75.00
HN 3014		
☐ Nell	1983-	75.00
HN 3015 NOT ISSUED		
HN 3016		
☐ Graduate, girl	1984-	100.00
HN 3017		
☐ Graduate, boy	1984-	100.00
HN 3018		
☐ Sisters, white	1984-	95.00
HN 3019		
☐ Sisters, black	1984-	95.00
HN 3020		
☐ Ellen...........................	1984-	75.00
HN 3021		
☐ Polly Put the Kettle On............	1984-	95.00
HN 3022 — HN 3023 NOT ISSUED		
HN 3024		
☐ April Showers	1984-	75.00
HN 3025		
☐ Rumplestiltskin	1984-	125.00
HN 3026 — HN 3029 NOT ISSUED		
HN 3030		
☐ Little Bo Peep	1984-	95.00
HN 3031		
☐ Wee Willie Winkie	1984-	95.00
HN 3032		
☐ Tom, Tom the Piper's Son	1984-	95.00
HN 3033		
☐ Springtime (Collectors Club figurine)	1983-	125.00
HN 3034		
☐ Little Jack Horner................	1984-	95.00

	Date	Price Range	
HN 3035			
☐ Little Boy Blue	1984-	95.00	
HN 3036 — HN 3046 NOT ISSUED			
HN 3047			
☐ Sharon	1984-	85.00	

"M" NUMERICAL LISTINGS OF MINIATURE FANCY & CHARACTER FIGURINES

	Date	Price Range	
M 1			
☐ Victorian Lady	1932-1945	300.00	325.00
M 2			
☐ Victorian Lady	1932-1945	300.00	325.00
M 3			
☐ Paisley Shawl	1932-1938	275.00	325.00
M 4			
☐ Paisley Shawl	1932-1945	300.00	350.00
M 5			
☐ Sweet Anne	1932-1945	200.00	275.00
M 6			
☐ Sweet Anne	1932-1945	250.00	325.00
M 7			
☐ Patricia	1932-1945	300.00	350.00
M 8			
☐ Patricia	1932-1938	300.00	350.00
M 9			
☐ Chloe	1932-1945	250.00	300.00
M 10			
☐ Chloe	1932-1945	250.00	300.00
M 11			
☐ Bridesmaid	1932-1938	325.00	375.00
M 12			
☐ Bridesmaid	1932-1945	200.00	275.00
M 13			
☐ Priscilla	1932-1938	400.00	450.00
M 14			
☐ Priscilla	1932-1945	275.00	325.00
M 15			
☐ Pantalettes	1932-1945	250.00	300.00
M 16			
☐ Panalettes	1932-1945	250.00	300.00
M 17			
☐ Shepherd	1932-1938	550.00	700.00
M 18			
☐ Shepherdess	1932-1938	600.00	700.00
M 19			
☐ Shepherd	1932-1938	550.00	700.00

		Date	Price Range	
M 20				
☐ Shepherdess		1932-1938	600.00	700.00
M 21				
☐ Polly Peachum		1932-1945	325.00	375.00
M 22				
☐ Polly Peachum		1932-1938	325.00	375.00
M 23				
☐ Polly Peachum		1932-1938	325.00	375.00
M 24				
☐ Priscilla		1932-1945	300.00	350.00
M 25				
☐ Victorian Lady		1932-1945	300.00	325.00
M 26				
☐ Paisley Shawl		1932-1945	275.00	325.00
M 27				
☐ Sweet Anne		1932-1945	200.00	275.00
M 28				
☐ Patricia		1932-1945	325.00	375.00
M 29				
☐ Chloe		1932-1945	250.00	300.00
M 30				
☐ Bridesmaid		1932-1945	200.00	275.00
M 31				
☐ Pantalettes		1932-1945	250.00	300.00
M 32				
☐ Rosamund		1932-1945	250.00	300.00
M 33				
☐ Rosamund		1932-1945	325.00	375.00
M 34				
☐ Denise		1933-1945	350.00	400.00
M 35				
☐ Denise		1933-1945	350.00	400.00
M 36				
☐ Norma		1933-1945	375.00	425.00
M 37				
☐ Norma		1933-1945	375.00	425.00
M 38				
☐ Robin		1933-1945	300.00	350.00
M 39				
☐ Robin		1933-1945	300.00	350.00
M 40				
☐ Erminie		1933-1945	400.00	500.00
M 41				
☐ Mr. Pickwick		1932-1983	20.00	30.00
M 42				
☐ Mr. Micawber		1932-1983	20.00	30.00
M 43				
☐ Mr. Pecksniff		1932-1983	20.00	30.00

	Date	Price Range	
M 44			
☐ Fat Boy	1932-1983	20.00	30.00
M 45			
☐ Uriah Heep	1932-1983	20.00	30.00
M 46			
☐ Sairey Gamp	1932-1983	20.00	30.00
M 47			
☐ Tony Weller.....................	1932-1983	20.00	30.00
M 48			
☐ Sam Weller	1932-1983	20.00	30.00
M 49			
☐ Fagin	1932-1983	20.00	30.00
M 50			
☐ Stiggins........................	1932-1983	20.00	30.00
M 51			
☐ Little Nell	1932-1983	20.00	30.00
M 52			
☐ Alfred Jingle	1932-1983	20.00	30.00
M 53			
☐ Buz Fuz	1932-1983	20.00	30.00
M 54			
☐ Bill Sykes	1932-1983	20.00	30.00
M 55			
☐ Artful Dodger	1932-1983	20.00	30.00
M 56			
☐ Tiny Tim.........................	1932-1983	20.00	30.00
M 57 — M 62 DICKENS NAPKIN RINGS			
M 63 NOT ISSUED			
M 64			
☐ Veronica	1934-1949	325.00	375.00
M 65			
☐ June...........................	1935-1949	325.00	375.00
M 66			
☐ Monica	1935-1949	275.00	325.00
M 67			
☐ Dainty May	1935-1949	325.00	375.00
M 68			
☐ Mirabel	1936-1949	300.00	350.00
M 69			
☐ Janet	1936-1949	300.00	350.00
M 70			
☐ Veronica	1936-1949	325.00	375.00
M 71			
☐ June...........................	1936-1949	325.00	375.00
M 72			
☐ Monica	1936-1949	300.00	350.00
M 73			
☐ Dainty May	1936-1949	325.00	375.00

	Date	Price Range	
M 74			
☐ Mirabel	1936-1949	**300.00**	**350.00**
M 75			
☐ Janet	1936-1949	**300.00**	**350.00**
M 76			
☐ Bumble	1939-1982	**20.00**	**30.00**
M 77			
☐ Captain Cuttle	1939-1983	**20.00**	**30.00**
M 78			
☐ Windflower	1939-1949	**400.00**	**450.00**
M 79			
☐ Windflower	1939-1949	**500.00**	**550.00**
M 80			
☐ Goody Two Shoes	1939-1949	**400.00**	**450.00**
M 81			
☐ Goody Two Shoes	1939-1949	**350.00**	**400.00**
M 82			
☐ Bo-Peep	1939-1949	**425.00**	**475.00**
M 83			
☐ Bo-Peep	1939-1949	**400.00**	**450.00**
M 84			
☐ Maureen	1939-1949	**350.00**	**400.00**
M 85			
☐ Maureen	1939-1949	**350.00**	**400.00**
M 86			
☐ Mrs. Bardell	1949-1983	**20.00**	**30.00**
M 87			
☐ Scrooge	1949-1983	**20.00**	**30.00**
M 88			
☐ David Copperfield	1949-1983	**20.00**	**30.00**
M 89			
☐ Oliver Twist	1949-1983	**20.00**	**30.00**
M 90			
☐ Dick Swiveller	1949-1983	**20.00**	**30.00**
M 91			
☐ Trotty Veck	1949-1983	**20.00**	**30.00**

"HN" NUMERICAL LISTINGS OF ANIMALS & BIRD MODELS

HN 100
☐ Fox in red frock coat

HN 101
☐ Hare in red coat

HN 102
☐ Hare in white coat

HN 103
☐ Double Penguins

HN 104
☐ Single Penguin

HN 105
☐ Collie (sable)

HN 106
☐ Collie (white and sable)

HN 107
☐ Hare, crouching

HN 108
□ Rabbit
HN 109
□ Cat (white)
HN 110
□ Titanian bowl, jade
HN 111
□ Cockerel on stand
HN 112
□ Alsatian (pale gray)
HN 113
□ Penguin
HN 114
□ Drake (malachite head)
HN 115
□ Drake (blue head)
HN 116
□ Drake (bright colours overall)
HN 117
□ Two Foxes
HN 118
□ Monkey
HN 119
□ Polar Bear, sitting on green cube
HN 120
□ Cat (white)
HN 121
□ Polar Bear, sitting
HN 122
□ Two Turtle Doves
HN 123
□ Pelican
HN 124
□ Cockerel, sitting
HN 125
□ Guinea Fowl
HN 126
□ Hare, crouching
HN 127
□ Pekinese
HN 128
□ Puppy
HN 129
□ Bulldog, sitting
HN 130
□ Fox
HN 131
□ Kingfisher on rock
HN 132
□ Drake on rock

HN 133
□ Double Penguins
HN 134
□ Single Penguin
HN 135
□ Raven on rock
HN 136
□ Robin on rock
HN 137
□ Blue Tit on rock
HN 138
□ Squirrel
HN 139
□ Falcon on rock
HN 140
□ Ape
HN 141
□ Rhinoceros
HN 142
□ Hare, crouching
HN 143
□ Chaffinch on its back
HN 144
□ Wren
HN 145
□ Small yellow bird on rock,
beak open
HN 145A
□ Small yellow bird on rock,
beak closed
HN 146
□ 'Old Bill' Bulldog with helmet
and haversack
HN 147
□ Fox on rock
HN 148
□ Two Drakes
HN 149
□ Swallow on rock
HN 150
□ Duck
HN 151
□ Rabbit
HN 152
□ Kingfisher on rock
HN 153
□ 'Old Bill' Bulldog with tammy
and haversack
HN 154
□ Character Cat

HN 155
☐ Owl

HN 156
☐ Monkey, listening

HN 157
☐ Cockerel

HN 158
☐ Toucan

HN 159
☐ Toucan

HN 160
☐ Owl and Young

HN 161
☐ Four Thrush Chicks

HN 162
☐ Butterfly (blue and gold)

HN 163
☐ Budgerigar

HN 164
☐ Cockerel, crowing

HN 165
☐ Kingfisher

HN 166
☐ Foxhound, seated

HN 167
☐ Tern Duck

HN 168
☐ Tern Drake

HN 169
☐ Owl

HN 170
☐ Brown Bear, Titanian ware

HN 171
☐ Four Baby Birds

HN 172
☐ Buffalo

HN 173
☐ 'Wise Old Owl' in red cloak and Ermine collar

HN 175
☐ Great Crested Grebe

HN 176
☐ Bloodhound

HN 177
☐ Powder Bowl with small ape figure seated on lid

HN 178
☐ Cockerel, crouching

HN 179
☐ Two Foxes

HN 180
☐ Cockerel, crouching

HN 181
☐ Elephant

HN 182
☐ Character Monkey, green jacket

HN 183
☐ Character Monkey, blue jacket

HN 184
☐ Cockerel, crowing

HN 185
☐ Parrot on rock

HN 186
☐ Elephant

HN 187
☐ Character Owl (check shawl, ermine collar)

HN 188
☐ Duckling (yellow and brown)

HN 189
☐ Duckling (black and yellow)

HN 190
☐ Duckling (green and blue)

HN 191
☐ Parrot, baby (blue and purple)

HN 192
☐ Parrot, baby (red and orange)

HN 193
☐ Tortoise

HN 194
☐ Terrier Puppy

HN 195
☐ Tern Duck

HN 196
☐ Toucan

HN 197
☐ Bird on rock

HN 198
☐ Penguin and Young

HN 199
☐ Budgerigar on stand (green and yellow)

HN 200
☐ Parrot, baby (decorated in enamel flowers)

HN 201
☐ Tabby cat and mouse

HN 202
☐ Black cat and mouse

HN 203
☐ Tortoiseshell cat on pillar
HN 204
☐ Tortoiseshell Cat
HN 205
☐ Two Ducklings (black and white)
HN 206
☐ Two Ducklings (brown and white)
HN 207
☐ Character Mouse
HN 208
☐ Character Toucan
HN 209
☐ Two Rabbits
HN 210
☐ Black and White Cat
HN 211
☐ Black-headed Gull
HN 212
☐ Black-headed Gull
HN 213
☐ Two Pigs
HN 214
☐ Bird and four Chicks (black, pink and brown)
HN 215
☐ Bird and four Chicks (gray, blue and lemon)
HN 216
☐ Bird and four Chicks (green, blue and lemon)
HN 217
☐ Two Rabbits (brown patches on faces)
HN 218
☐ Two Rabbits (brown and black patches on faces
HN 219
☐ Two Rabbits (brown, black, and yellow patches on faces)
HN 220
☐ Bird on rock
HN 221
☐ Cat (black and white)
HN 222
☐ Owl in boat
HN 223
☐ Lion, sitting
HN 224
☐ Kingfisher on rock

HN 225
☐ Tiger, lying
HN 226
☐ Character Mouse (blue coat)
HN 227
☐ Tabby Cat, asleep
HN 228
☐ Character Mouse (yellow coat)
HN 229
☐ Teal Duck
HN 231
☐ Foxhound
HN 232
☐ Puppy with bone
HN 233
☐ Kitten
HN 234
☐ Two Cats
HN 235
☐ Duckling
HN 236
☐ Two Baby Birds
HN 237
☐ Character Mouse with basket of babies
HN 238
☐ Two Pigs
HN 239
☐ Two Ducks
HN 240
☐ Bird on Rock
HN 241
☐ Eagle (brown and gold)
HN 242
☐ Eagle (lighter color, white head and neck)
HN 243
☐ Piggy Bowl
HN 244
☐ Cat and Mouse (cat black and white)
HN 245
☐ Cat and Mouse (cat all black)
HN 246
☐ Character Pig
HN 247
☐ Guinea Fowl
HN 248
☐ Drake, large size

HN 249
☐ Mallard Drake, large size
HN 250
☐ Heron
HN 251
☐ Heron
HN 252
☐ Drake, large size
HN 253
☐ Small Ape, sitting
HN 254
☐ Two small Apes
HN 256 — HN 266
☐ Miniature Character Penguins
and Puffins
HN 267
☐ Cockerel, sitting
HN 268
☐ Kingfisher
HN 269
☐ Blue Bird on Rock
HN 270
☐ Brown Bear, sitting up
HN 271
☐ Duck
HN 272
☐ Bird with three Chicks
HN 273
☐ Rabbit
HN 274
☐ Green Bird
HN 275
☐ Two Orange Birds
HN 276
☐ Rabbit
HN 277
☐ Wren
HN 278
☐ Two Green Birds
HN 279
☐ Green Bird on Rock
HN 280
☐ Three Chicks
HN 281
☐ Yellow Bird on Rock
HN 282
☐ Blue Bird
HN 283 — HN 293
☐ Miniature Character Penguins
and Puffins

HN 294
☐ Toucan, large size (black and
white, red beak)
HN 295
☐ Toucan, large size (black and
green, brown beak)
HN 295A
☐ Toucan, large size (black and
green, brown beak)
HN 296
☐ Penguin
HN 297
☐ Penguin and Young
HN 298
☐ Duck, sitting
HN 299
☐ Drake, lying
HN 800
☐ Pig, asleep
HN 801
☐ Pig asleep, larger version
HN 802
☐ Two Pigs
HN 803
☐ Rabbit
HN 804
☐ Miniature Pup, playing
(pale orange)
HN 805
☐ Miniature Pup, playing
(malachite and purple)
HN 806
☐ Miniature Drake (white)
HN 807
☐ Miniature Drake (malachite and
purple)
HN 808 — HN 812
☐ Miniature Character Pups
HN 813
☐ Miniature White Bird
HN 814
☐ Miniature Character Pup
HN 815
☐ Miniature Character Pup
HN 818
☐ Character Cat 'Lucky' (black and
white)
HN 819
☐ Miniature Cat 'Lucky' (white)

HN 820 — HN 825
☐ Miniature Kittens
HN 826
☐ Character Pup
HN 827
☐ Character Cat (tortoiseshell)
HN 828
☐ Character Cat (tabby)
HN 829
☐ Character Cat (black and white)
HN 830
☐ NO RECORD
HN 831
☐ Beagle Puppy
HN 832
☐ Pekinese Puppy (sitting)
HN 833
☐ Pekinese Puppy, standing
HN 834
☐ Pekinese Puppy on stand (black and brown)
HN 835
☐ Pekinesed Puppy on stand (lighter brown)
HN 836
☐ Pekinese Puppy on stand (light color)
HN 837
☐ Chow on stand (brown)
HN 838
☐ Chow on stand (lighter brown)
HN 839
☐ Chow on stand (white and gray)
HN 840 — HN 845
☐ Character Ducks
HN 846
☐ Toucan
HN 847
☐ Yellow Bird
HN 849
☐ Duck and Ladybird
HN 850
☐ Duck, standing on rocks
HN 851
☐ Bird on Tree Stump
HN 852
☐ Penguin, standing on rocks
HN 853
☐ Small Mallard Drake on rocks

HN 854
☐ Budgerigar
HN 855
☐ Small Bird on Tree Stump
HN 856
☐ Penguin on rocks
HN 858
☐ Kingfisher on rock
HN 859
☐ Tortoise on rocks
HN 860
☐ Small Bird on Tree Stump
HN 861
☐ Polar Bear
HN 862A
☐ Kingfisher on stand, with Primroses
HN 862B
☐ Kingfisher on stand, with Kingcups
HN 863
☐ Ducks, quacking
HN 864
☐ Ducks, quacking
HN 865
☐ Ducks, quacking
HN 866
☐ Fox, sitting
HN 867 — HN 874
HN 875
☐ Kingfisher on Tree Stump
HN 876
☐ Tiger On Rock
HN 877
☐ Baby Parrot
HN 878
☐ Cockerel (white)
HN 879
☐ Cockerel (blue and green)
HN 880
☐ Cockerel (brown and orange)
HN 881
☐ Bulldog, sitting
HN 882
☐ Penguin, large size
HN 883
☐ Two Monkeys
HN 884
☐ Cockatoo (blue and orange)

HN 885
- ☐ Cockatoo (pink, purple and orange)

HN 886
- ☐ Cockatoo (red, blue and orange)

HN 888
- ☐ Cockatoo (pale blue and yellow)

HN 889
- ☐ Dog, seated Greyhound (black and white)

HN 890
- ☐ Dog, seated Greyhound (brown)

HN 891
- ☐ Elephant, large size (silver gray)

HN 892
- ☐ Character Pigs, in Clown costume

HN 893
- ☐ Character Pigs, in Clown costume

HN 894
- ☐ Character Pigs, in Clown costume

HN 895
- ☐ Character Pigs, in Clown costume

HN 896
- ☐ Character Pigs, in Clown costume

HN 897
- ☐ Character Pigs, in Clown costume

HN 898
- ☐ Alsatian's Head

HN 899
- ☐ Alsatian, sitting

HN 900
- ☐ Fox Terrier (white and brown)

HN 901
- ☐ Fox Terrier (white and black)

HN 902
- ☐ Character Pigs

HN 903
- ☐ Character Pigs

HN 904
- ☐ Terrier Puppy

HN 905
- ☐ Small Frog

HN 906
- ☐ Spaniel Puppy (black and white)

HN 907
- ☐ Spaniel Puppy (brown and white)

HN 908
- ☐ Spaniel Puppy's Head

HN 909
- ☐ Fox Terrier, standing

HN 910
- ☐ Fox Terrier, sitting

HN 911
- ☐ Tiger, lying

HN 912
- ☐ Tiger, sitting

HN 913 — HN 918
- ☐ Toucan Head on round bowl-like Bodies

HN 919
- ☐ Leopard, sitting

HN 920
- ☐ Two Foxes (brown)

HN 921
- ☐ Alsatian, sitting, large size

HN 922
- ☐ Character Hare

HN 923
- ☐ Fox Terrier, standing

HN 924
- ☐ Fox Terrier, sitting, large size

HN 925
- ☐ Two Foxes (gray and brown)

HN 926
- ☐ Two Foxes (miniature model)

HN 927
- ☐ Two Pekinese Dogs

HN 928
- ☐ Large Toucan Bowl

HN 929
- ☐ Miniature Terrier Pup, sitting

HN 930
- ☐ Miniature Alsatian, sitting

HN 931
- ☐ Miniature Terrier Pup

HN 932
- ☐ Miniature Scotch Terrier

HN 933
- ☐ Miniature Scotch Terrier

HN 934
- ☐ Miniature Scotch Terrier

HN 935
- ☐ Pip, Squeak and Wilfred Ash Tray

HN 936
- ☐ Teal, swimming

HN 937
- ☐ Alsatian on stand

HN 938
☐ Alsatian on stand, sitting
HN 939
☐ Large and small Brown Bears
HN 940
☐ Large and small Brown Bears, (light brown)
HN 941
☐ Elephant, large size (black)
HN 942
☐ Terrier
HN 943
☐ Terrier
HN 944
☐ Fox Terrier
HN 945
☐ Fox Terrier
HN 946
☐ Penguin Chick
HN 947
☐ Penguin Chick
HN 948
☐ Bulldog, large size (brown)
HN 949
☐ Baby Elephants
HN 950
☐ Baby Elephant
HN 951
☐ Baby Elephant
HN 952
☐ Baby Elephant
HN 953
☐ Terrier Pup (brown and black)
HN 954
☐ Terrier Pup (darker brown and black)
HN 955
☐ Brown Bear, Standing
HN 956
☐ Mallard Drake, large size
HN 957
☐ Spaniel (liver and white)
HN 958
☐ Spaniel (black and white)
HN 960
☐ Character Ape with book, eyes open
HN 961
☐ Character Ape with book, eyes closed

HN 962
☐ Terrier's Head
HN 963
☐ Fox, sitting
HN 964
☐ Scotch Terrier, large size (black)
HN 965
☐ Scotch Terrier, large size (brown)
HN 966
☐ Elephant, large size (brown and gray)
HN 967
☐ Tabby Cat
HN 968
☐ Pig, black and white
HN 969
☐ Two Rabbits
HN 970
☐ Dachshund
HN 971
☐ 'Lucky' Cat Ash tray
HN 972
☐ Character Ape in Dunce's cap, reading book
HN 973
☐ Character Duck (orange)
HN 974
☐ Character Duck (lemon yellow)
HN 975
☐ Collie (silver gray)
HN 976
☐ Collie (brown)
HN 977
☐ Duck
HN 978
☐ Fox, lying
HN 979
☐ Hare, lying
HN 980
☐ Scotch Terrier (black)
HN 981
☐ Scotch Terrier (light gray and brown)
HN 982
☐ Sealyham Terrier (black patches on face)
HN 983
☐ Sealyham Terrier (brown patches on face)

HN 984
☐ Hare, lying (white)

HN 985
☐ Hare, lying (gray)

HN 986
☐ Alsatian sitting on lid of Lustre Bowl

HN 987
☐ Bulldog sitting on lid of Lustre Bowl

HN 988
☐ Airedale Terrier (brown)

HN 989
☐ Sealyham Terrier (gray)

HN 990
☐ Tiger, crouching

HN 991
☐ Tiger, crouching (smaller model)

HN 992
☐ Sealyham Terrier (black)

HN 993
☐ Cat asleep on cushion

HN 994
☐ Fox on pedestal

HN 995
☐ Pekinese (brown)

HN 996
☐ Airedale Terrier (black, blue and brown)

HN 997
☐ Terrier, seated (black and brown)

HN 998
☐ Penguin and Baby

HN 999
☐ Persian Cat (black and white)

HN 1000
☐ Cocker Spaniel, large size (black)

HN 1001
☐ Cocker Spaniel and Pheasant, large size

HN 1002
☐ Cocker Spaniel (liver and white)

HN 1003
☐ Pekinese (dark colouring)

HN 1004
☐ Blue Tit on Bough with Blossom

HN 1005
☐ Thrush on Bough with Blossom

HN 1007
☐ Ch. 'Charley Startler' Rough haired Terrier, large size

HN 1008
☐ Ch. 'Albourne Arthur' Scottish Terrier, large size

HN 1009
☐ Hare and Two Leverets

HN 1010
☐ Ch. Biddie of Ifield 'Pekinese', large size

HN 1011
☐ Ch. Biddie of Ifield 'Pekinese', medium size

HN 1012
☐ Ch. Biddie of Ifield 'Pekinese', small size

HN 1013
☐ Ch. 'Charley Hunter' Fox Terrier, medium size

HN 1014
☐ Ch. 'Charley Hunter' Fox Terrier, small size

HN 1015
☐ Ch. 'Albourne Arthur' Scottish Terrier, medium size

HN 1016
☐ Ch. 'Albourne Arthur' Scottish Terrier, small size

HN 1017
☐ Scottish Terrier, sitting (black)

HN 1018
☐ Scottish Terrier, sitting (black)

HN 1019
☐ Scottish Terrier, sitting (black)

HN 1020
☐ Ch. 'Lucky Star of Ware' Cocker Spaniel, medium size

HN 1021
☐ Ch. 'Lucky Star of Ware' Cocker Spaniel, small size

HN 1022
☐ Ch. 'Cotsfold Topsail' Airedale Terrier, large size

HN 1023
☐ Ch. 'Cotsfold Topsail' Airedale Terrier, medium size

HN 1024
☐ Ch. 'Cotsfold Topsail' Airedale Terrier, small size

HN 1025
☐ Ch. 'Tring Rattler' Foxhound, large size

HN 1026
☐ Ch. 'Tring Rattler' Foxhound, medium size

HN 1027
☐ Ch. 'Tring Rattler' Foxhound, small size

HN 1028
☐ Cocker Spaniel and Pheasant, medium size

HN 1029
☐ Cocker Spaniel and Pheasant, small size

HN 1030
☐ Ch. 'Scotia Stylist' Sealyham, large size

HN 1031
☐ Ch. 'Scotia Stylist' Sealyham, medium size

HN 1032
☐ Ch. 'Scotia Stylist' Sealyham, small size

HN 1033
☐ Ch. 'Charming Eyes' Cairn, large size

HN 1034
☐ Ch. 'Charming Eyes' Cairn, medium size

HN 1035
☐ Ch. 'Charming Eyes' Cairn, small size

HN 1036
☐ Cocker Spaniel, medium size, (liver and white)

HN 1037
☐ Cocker Spaniel, small size, (liver and white)

HN 1038
☐ Scottish Terrier, begging

HN 1039
☐ Pekinese, sitting, large size

HN 1040
☐ Pekinese, sitting, small size

HN 1041
☐ Sealyham, lying, large size

HN 1042
☐ Bulldog, large size, (brindle)

HN 1043
☐ Bulldog, medium size, (brindle)

HN 1044
☐ Bulldog, small size, (brindle)

HN 1045
☐ Bulldog, large size, (brown and white)

HN 1046
☐ Bulldog, medium size (brown and white)

HN 1047
☐ Bulldog, small size (brown and white)

HN 1048
☐ West Highland White Terrier, large size

HN 1049
☐ Ch. 'Maesydd Mustard' English Setter, large size

HN 1050
☐ Ch. 'Maesydd Mustard' English Setter, medium size

HN 1051
☐ Ch. 'Maesydd Mustard' English Setter, small size

HN 1052
☐ Sealyham, lying, medium size

HN 1053
☐ Sealyham, lying, small size

HN 1054
☐ Irish Setter, large size

HN 1055
☐ Irish Setter, medium size

HN 1056
☐ Irish Setter, small size

HN 1057
☐ Ch. 'Ashstead Applause' Collie, large size

HN 1058
☐ Ch. 'Ashstead Applause' Collie, medium size

HN 1059
☐ Ch. 'Ashstead Applause' Collie, small size

HN 1062
☐ Cocker Spaniel and Pheasant, (black and white) small size

HN 1063
☐ Cocker Spaniel and Hare, medium size (liver and white)

HN 1064
☐ Cocker Spaniel and Hare, small size (liver and white)

HN 1065
☐ Greyhound, large size (brown)

HN 1066
☐ Greyhound, medium size (brown)

HN 1067
☐ Greyhound, small size (brown)

HN 1068
☐ Smooth-haired Fox Terrier, large size

HN 1069
☐ Smooth-haired Fox Terrier, medium size

HN 1070
☐ Smooth-haired Fox Terrier, small size

HN 1071
☐ Hare, lying

HN 1072
☐ Bulldog, large size (white)

HN 1073
☐ Bulldog, medium size (white)

HN 1074
☐ Bulldog, small size (white)

HN 1075
☐ Greyhound, large size (black and white)

HN 1076
☐ Greyhound, medium size (black and white)

HN 1077
☐ Greyhound, small size (black and white)

HN 1078
☐ Cocker Spaniel, small size (black and white)

HN 1079
☐ Gordon Setter, large size

HN 1080
☐ Gordon Setter, medium size

HN 1081
☐ Gordon Setter, small size

HN 1082
☐ Tiger, stalking, large size

HN 1083
☐ Tiger, stalking, medium size

HN 1084
☐ Tiger, stalking, small size

HN 1085
☐ Lion, large size

HN 1086
☐ Lion, medium size

HN 1087 — HN 1093 A
☐ Ash Tray

HN 1094
☐ Leopard

HN 1095 - 1095 A
☐ Ash Tray

HN 1096
☐ Character Fox with stolen Goose (green cloak and hat)

HN 1097
☐ Character Dog, running with ball

HN 1098
☐ Character Dog

HN 1099
☐ Character Dog, yawning

HN 1100
☐ Character Dog

HN 1101
☐ Character Dog, lying

HN 1102
☐ Character Fox with stolen Goose (red cloak and hat)

HN 1103
☐ Character Dog, with ball

HN 1104
☐ Cairn, large size (black)

HN 1105
☐ Cairn, medium size (black)

HN 1106
☐ Cairn, small size (black)

HN 1107
☐ Cairn, large size (black), (earthenware)

HN 1108
☐ Cocker Spaniel, large size (black and white)

HN 1109
☐ Cocker Spaniel, medium size (black and white)

HN 1111
☐ Ch. 'Goworth Victor' Dalmatian, large size

HN 1112
☐ Lion, large size

HN 1113
☐ Ch. 'Goworth Victor' Dalmatian, medium size

HN 1114
☐ Ch. 'Goworth Victor' Dalmatian, small size

HN 1115
☐ Ch. 'Benign of Picardy' Alsatian, large size

HN 1116
☐ Ch. 'Benign of Picardy' Alsatian, medium size

HN 1117
☐ Ch. 'Benign of Picardy' Alsatian, small size

HN 1118
☐ Tiger on Rock, large size (earthenware)

HN 1119
☐ Lion on Rock, large size (earthenware)

HN 1120
☐ Fighting Elephant, large size (earthenware)

HN 1121
☐ Elephant, large size

HN 1122
☐ Elephant, large size

HN 1123
☐ Elephant, medium size

HN 1124
☐ Elephant, large size

HN 1125
☐ Lion on Alabaster Base

HN 1126
☐ Tiger on Alabaster Base

HN 1127
☐ Ch. 'Shrewd Saint' Dachshund, large size

HN 1128
☐ Ch. 'Shrewd Saint' Dachshund, medium size

HN 1129
☐ Ch. 'Shrewd Saint' Dachshund, small size

HN 1130
☐ Fox, large size

HN 1131
☐ Staffordshire Bull Terrier, large size

HN 1132
☐ Staffordshire Bull Terrier, medium size

HN 1133
☐ Staffordshire Bull Terrier, small size

HN 1134
☐ Cocker Spaniel, large size (liver and white)

HN 1135
☐ Cocker Spaniel, medium size (liver and white)

HN 1136
☐ Cocker Spaniel, small size (liver and white)

HN 1137
☐ Cocker Spaniel and Pheasant, large size (black and white)

HN 1138
☐ Cocker Spaniel and Pheasant, medium size (black and white)

HN 1139
☐ Dachshund, large size

HN 1140
☐ Dachshund, medium size

HN 1141
☐ Dachshund, small size

HN 1142
☐ Ch. 'Bokus Brock' Bull Terrier, large size

HN 1143
☐ Ch. 'Bokus Brock' Bull Terrier, medium size

HN 1144
☐ Ch. 'Bokus Brock' Bull Terrier, small size

HN 1145
☐ Moufflon, standing (green matte)

HN 1146
☐ Calf, sleeping (green matte)

HN 1147
☐ Calf, standing (green matte)

HN 1148
☐ Buffalo (green matte)

HN 1149
☐ Donkey, small size (green matte)

HN 1150
☐ Young Doe (green matte)

HN 1151
☐ Swiss Goat (green matte)
HN 1152
☐ Horse (green matte)
HN 1153
☐ Moufflon, lying (green matte)
HN 1154
☐ Jumping Goat (green matte)
HN 1155
☐ Donkey, large size, (green matte)
HN 1156
☐ Suspicious Doe (green matte)
HN 1157
☐ Antelope (green matte)
HN 1158
☐ Character Dog with plate
HN 1159
☐ Character Dog with bone
HN 1160
☐ Moufflon, standing (cream matte)
HN 1161
☐ Calf, sleeping (cream matte)
HN 1162
☐ Calf, standing (cream matte)
HN 1163
☐ Buffalo (cream matte)
HN 1164
☐ Donkey, small size (cream matte)
HN 1165
☐ Young Doe (cream matte)
HN 1166
☐ Swiss Goat (cream matte)
HN 1167
☐ Horse (cream matte)
HN 1168
☐ Moufflon, lying (cream matte)
HN 1169
☐ Jumping Goat (cream matte)
HN 1170
☐ Donkey, large size (cream matte)
HN 1171
☐ Suspicious Dog (cream matte)
HN 1172
☐ Antelope (cream matte)
HN 1173
☐ Calf, sleeping (natural colors)
HN 1174
☐ Calf, standing (natural colors)
HN 1175
☐ Buffalo (natural colors)

HN 1176
☐ Donkey, small size (natural colors)
HN 1177
☐ Young Doe (natural colors)
HN 1178
☐ Swiss Goat (natural colors)
HN 1179
☐ Moufflon, standing (natural colors)
HN 1180
☐ Horse (natural colors)
HN 1181
☐ Moufflon, lying (natural colors)
HN 1182
☐ Jumping Goat (natural colors)
HN 1183
☐ Donkey, large size (natural colors)
HN 1184
☐ Suspicious Doe (natural colors)
HN 1185
☐ Antelope (natural colors)
HN 1186
☐ Cocker Spaniel, large size (golden brown)
HN 1187
☐ Cocker Spaniel, medium size (golden brown)
HN 1188
☐ Cocker Spaniel, small size (golden brown)
HN 1189
☐ King Penguin
HN 1190
☐ Penguin
HN 1191
☐ Mallard
HN 1192
☐ Duck
HN 1193
☐ Tern
HN 1194
☐ Tern
HN 1195
☐ Seagull
HN 1196
☐ Seagull
HN 1197
☐ Gannet

HN 1198
☐ Drake
HN 1199
☐ Penguin
HN 2500
☐ Cerval
HN 2501
☐ Lynx
HN 2502
☐ Deer (green)
HN 2503
☐ Deer (white)
HN 2504
☐ Lamb (green)
HN 2505
☐ Lamb (white)
HN 2506
☐ Asiatic Elephant
HN 2507
☐ Zebra
HN 2508
☐ Character Dog
HN 2509
☐ Sealyham
HN 2510
☐ Character Dog
HN 2511
☐ Character Dog
HN 2512
☐ Ch. 'Chosen Dan of Notts' smooth haired Terrier, large size
HN 2513
☐ Ch. 'Chosen Dan of Notts' smooth haired Terrier medium size
HN 2514
☐ Ch. 'Chosen Dan of Notts' smooth haired Terrier, small size
HN 2515
☐ Ch. 'Dry Toast' Springer Spaniel, large size
HN 2516
☐ Ch. 'Dry Toast' Springer Spaniel, medium size
HN 2517
☐ Ch. 'Dry Toast' Springer Spaniel, small size

HN 2518
☐ 'Pride of the Shires', mare and foal (brown)
HN 2519
☐ 'The Gude Gray Mare', with foal, large size
HN 2520
☐ The Farmer's Boy on dappled Shire
HN 2521
☐ 'The Dapple Grey' (girl on Shire Pony)
HN 2522
☐ 'The Chestnut Mare' with foal, large size
HN 2523
☐ 'Pride of the Shires' mare and foal (dapple gray)
HN 2524
☐ American Foxhound, large size
HN 2525
☐ American Foxhound, medium size
HN 2526
☐ American Foxhound, small size
HN 2527
☐ Fox (sitting)
HN 2528
☐ 'Pride of the Shires' replacing 2518
HN 2529
☐ English Setter and Pheasant
HN 2530
☐ 'Merely a Minor' large size (brown)
HN 2531
☐ 'Merely a Minor' large size (gray)
HN 2532
☐ 'The Gude Gray Mare' with foal, medium size
HN 2533
☐ 'The Chestnut Mare' with foal, small size
HN 2534
☐ 'Pride of the Shires' mare and foal, small size (brown)

HN 2535
☐ Tiger on Rock
HN 2536
☐ 'Pride of the Shires' mare
and foal, small size (gray)
HN 2537
☐ 'Merely a Minor', medium
size (brown)
HN 2538
☐ 'Merely a Minor', medium
size (gray)
HN 2539
☐ Persian Cat (white)
HN 2540
☐ Kingfisher
HN 2541
☐ Kingfisher
HN 2542
☐ Baltimore Oriole
HN 2543
☐ Blue Bird
HN 2544
☐ Mallard
HN 2545
☐ Pheasant
HN 2546
☐ Yellow Throated Warbler
HN 2547
☐ Budgerigars (pair)
HN 2548
☐ Golden Crested Wren
HN 2549
☐ Robin
HN 2550
☐ Chaffinch
HN 2551
☐ Bullfinch
HN 2552
☐ Young Thrushes (pair)
HN 2553
☐ Young Robins (group)
HN 2554
☐ Cardinal Bird
HN 2555
☐ Drake Mallard
HN 2556
☐ Mallard
HN 2557
☐ Welsh Corgi, large size

HN 2558
☐ Welsh Corgi, medium size
HN 2559
☐ Welsh Corgi, small size
HN 2560
☐ Great Dane, large size
HN 2561
☐ Great Dane, medium size
HN 2562
☐ Great Dane, small size
HN 2563
☐ 'Pride of the Shires' (no foal)
large size (brown)
HN 2564
☐ 'Pride of the Shires' (no foal)
medium size (brown)
HN 2564
☐ 'Pride of the Shires' (no foal)
medium size (brown)
HN 2565
☐ 'The Chestnut Mare' (no foal)
large size
HN 2566
☐ 'The Chestnut Mare' (no foal)
small size
HN 2567
☐ 'Merely a Minor' small size (gray)
HN 2568
☐ 'The Gude Gray Mare' (no foal)
large size
HN 2569
☐ 'The Gude Gray Mare' (no foal)
medium size
HN 2570
☐ 'The Gude Grey Mare' (no foal)
small size
HN 2571
☐ 'Merely a Minor' small size,
(brown)
HN 2572
☐ Drake Mallard small size
HN 2573
☐ Kingfisher, small size
HN 2574
☐ Seagull, small size
HN 2575
☐ Swan
HN 2576
☐ Pheasant, small size

HN 2577
☐ Peacock
HN 2578
☐ Horse without Boy (dapple gray)
HN 2579
☐ Kitten lying on Back (brown)
HN 2580
☐ Kitten, sitting licking hind paw (brown)
HN 2581
☐ Kitten, sleeping (brown)
HN 2582
☐ Kitten, sitting on haunches (tan)
HN 2583
☐ Kitten, sitting licking front paw (tan)
HN 2584
☐ Kitten, sitting, surprised (tan)
HN 2585
☐ Puppy in basket, lying (cocker)
HN 2586
☐ Puppy in basket (cocker)
HN 2587
☐ Puppy in basket (terrier)
HN 2588
☐ Puppies in basket, three (terriers)
HN 2589
☐ Puppy, begging (Cairn)
HN 2590
☐ Cocker Spaniels, sleeping (pair)
HN 2591
☐ Drake Mallard
HN 2592
☐ Hare
HN 2593
☐ Hare
HN 2594
☐ Hare, lying, small size
HN 2595
☐ Lambs
HN 2596
☐ Lambs
HN 2597
☐ Lambs
HN 2598
☐ Lambs
HN 2599
☐ English Setter and Pheasant

HN 2600
☐ Cocker Spaniel and Pheasant, small size
HN 2601
☐ American Great Dane, large size
HN 2602
☐ American Great Dane, medium size
HN 2603
☐ American Great Dane, small size
HN 2604
☐ Peacock Butterfly
HN 2605
☐ Camberwell Beauty Butterfly
HN 2606
☐ Swallowtail Butterfly
HN 2607
☐ Red Admiral Butterfly
HN 2608
☐ Copper Butterfly
HN 2609
☐ Tortoiseshell Butterfly
HN 2610
☐ Hen Pheasant
HN 2611
☐ Chaffinch
HN 2612
☐ Baltimore Oriole
HN 2613
☐ Golden Crested Wren
HN 2614
☐ Blue Bird
HN 2615
☐ Cardinal Bird
HN 2616
☐ Bullfinch
HN 2617
☐ Robin
HN 2618
☐ Yellow Throated Warbler
HN 2619
☐ Grouse
HN 2620
☐ English Setter, large size (liver and white)
HN 2621
☐ English Setter, medium size (liver and white)

HN 2622
☐ English Setter, small size (liver and white)

HN 2623
☐ Horse without boy (brown)

HN 2624
☐ Pointer

HN 2625
☐ Poodle, large size

HN 2626
☐ Poodle, medium size

HN 2627
☐ Poodle, small size

HN 2628
☐ Chow, large size

HN 2629
☐ Chow, medium size

HN 2630
☐ Chow, small size

HN 2631
☐ French Poodle

HN 2632
☐ Cock Pheasant

HN 2633
☐ Penguin, large size

HN 2634
☐ Pheasant, large size

HN 2635
☐ Mallard, large size

HN 2636
☐ Indian Rummer Drake

HN 2637
☐ Polar Bear

HN 2638
☐ Leopard on Rock

HN 2639
☐ Tiger on Rock

HN 2640
☐ Fighter Elephant

HN 2641
☐ Lion on Rock

HN 2642
☐ Squirrel

HN 2643
☐ Ch. 'Warlord of Mazelaine', Boxer

HN 2644
☐ Elephant

HN 2645
☐ Doberman Pinscher

HN 2646
☐ Tiger

HN 2647
☐ Drake

HN 2648
☐ Character Piglets

HN 2649
☐ Character Piglets

HN 2650
☐ Character Piglets

HN 2651
☐ Character Piglets

HN 2652
☐ Character Piglets

HN 2653
☐ Character Piglets

HN 2654
☐ Character Dog with slipper

HN 2655
☐ Siamese Cat, sitting (Chatcull Range)

HN 2656
☐ Pine Martin (Chatcull Range)

HN 2657
☐ Langur Monkey (Chatcull Range)

HN 2658
☐ White-tailed Deer (Chatcull Range)

HN 2659
☐ Brown Bear (Chatcull Range)

HN 2660
☐ Siamese Cat, standing (Chatcull Range)

HN 2661
☐ Mountain Sheep (Chatcull Range)

HN 2662
☐ Siamese Cat, lying (Chatcull Range)

HN 2663
☐ River Hog (Chatcull Range)

HN 2664
☐ Nyala Antelope (Chatcull Range)

HN 2665
☐ Llama (Chatcull Range)

HN 2666
☐ Badger (Chatcull Range)

HN 2667
☐ Ch. 'Bumblikite of Mansergh' Black Labrador (Chatcull Range)

HN 2668
☐ Puffins (Jefferson Sculptures)
HN 2669
☐ Snowy Owl (Jefferson Sculptures)
HN 2670
☐ Snowy Owl (Jefferson Sculptures)
HN 3500
☐ Black Throat Loon (Jefferson Sculptures)
HN 3501
☐ White Winged Crossbills (Jefferson Sculptures)
HN 3502
☐ King Eider (Jefferson Sculptures)
HN 3503
☐ Roseate Terns (Jefferson Sculptures)
HN 3404
☐ Golden-Crowned Kinglet (Jefferson Sculptures)
HN 3505
☐ Winter Wren (Jefferson Sculptures)
HN 3506
☐ Colorado Chipmunks (Jefferson Sculptures)
HN 3507
☐ Harbor Seals (Jefferson Sculptures)
HN 3508
☐ Snowshoe Hares (Jefferson Sculptures)
HN 3509
☐ Downy Woodpecker (Jefferson Sculptures)

HN 3510
☐ Fledgling Bluebird (Jefferson Sculptures)
HN 3511
☐ Chipping Sparrow (Jefferson Sculptures)
HN 3522
☐ The Leap
HN 3523
☐ Capricorn
HN 3524
☐ The Gift of Life
HN 3525
☐ Courtship
HN 3526
☐ Shadowplay
HN 3527
☐ Going Home
HN 3528
☐ Freedom
HN 3529
☐ Bright Water
HN 3530
☐ Clearwater
HN 6406
☐ Bulldog, Union Jack, large
HN 6407
☐ Bulldog, Union Jack, small
HN 6448
☐ Huntsman Fox (Jefferson Sculptures)

"K" NUMERICAL LISTINGS OF MINIATURE ANIMALS & BIRD MODELS

K 1
☐ Bulldog
K 2
☐ Bull Pup
K 3
☐ Sealyham
K 4
☐ Sealyham
K 5
☐ Airedale

K 6
☐ Pekinese
K 7
☐ Foxhound
K 8
☐ Terrier
K 9
☐ Cocker Spaniel
K 10
☐ Scottish Terrier

K 11
☐ Cairn
K 12
☐ Cat
K 13
☐ Alsatian
K 14
☐ Bull Terrier
K 15
☐ Chow Chow
K 16
☐ Welsh Corgi
K 17
☐ Dachshund
K 18
☐ Scottish Terrier
K 19
☐ St. Bernard
K 20
☐ Penguins
K 21
☐ Penguin
K 22
☐ Penguins
K 23
☐ Penguin
K 24
☐ Penguin
K 25
☐ Penguins

K 26
☐ Mallard
K 27
☐ Yellow-Throated Warbler
K 28
☐ Cardinal Bird
K 29
☐ Baltimore Oriole
K 30
☐ Blue Bird
K 31
☐ Bull Finch
K 32
☐ Budgerigar
K 33
☐ Golden Crested Wren
K 34
☐ Magpie
K 35
☐ Jay
K 36
☐ Goldfinch
K 37
☐ Hare, lying
K 38
☐ Hare, sitting, ears down
K 39
☐ Hare, sitting, ears up

ANIMAL AND BIRD MODELS

The following alphabetical listings include all the Royal Doulton Animal and Bird figures in the HN and K series (the HN being full-sized figures and the K miniatures). Keep in mind when using these listings that titles were often similar or identical on a number of different figures, which can be distinguished by further description (as given) or by the difference in serial numbers. Similarity in figures is not necessarily an indication of similarity in value.

Several animal figures, particularly dogs, are known to be in collections although they were not production models. Royal Doulton also issued several items incorporating the K-series dogs, such as calendars, pen holders, and ashtrays. While few head plaques are listed in Royal Doulton references, it is felt that a full dozen were produced. All animal studies are being discontinued as of January 1, 1984.

The difference in pricing is due to the popularity of the breed with collectors. HN No. 2511 and 1100 are both considered by fanciers to be of the bull terrier persuasion. Most of the other are nondescript terriers, except for the Sealyhams.

		Price Range	
☐ Airedale	K 5	75.00	100.00
☐ Airedale, 'Cotsford Topsail', large	HN 1022	350.00	400.00
☐ Airedale, 'Cotsford Topsail', medium	HN 1023	75.00	95.00
☐ Airedale, 'Cotsford Topsail', small	HN 1024	125.00	150.00
☐ Airedale Terrier	HN 988	175.00	215.00
☐ Alsatian	K 13	35.00	45.00
☐ Alsatian, pale gray	HN 112	200.00	300.00
☐ Alsatian, Head	HN 898	150.00	175.00
☐ Alsatian, sitting, large	HN 921	200.00	300.00
☐ Alsatian, 'Benign of Picardy', large	HN 1115	300.00	350.00
☐ Alsatian, 'Benign of Picardy', medium	HN 1116	75.00	95.00
☐ Alsatian, 'Benign of Picardy', small	HN 1117	75.00	125.00
☐ American Foxhound, large	HN 2524	225.00	350.00
☐ American Foxhound, medium	HN 2525	125.00	175.00
☐ American Foxhound, small	HN 2526	100.00	125.00
☐ American Great Dane, large	HN 2601	275.00	350.00
☐ American Great Dane, medium	HN 2602	140.00	175.00
☐ American Great Dane, small	HN 2603	100.00	175.00
☐ Baltimore Oriole	HN 2542	225.00	275.00
☐ Beagle, puppy	HN 831	150.00	175.00
☐ Black Labrador, 'Bumblikite of Mansergh'	HN 2667	85.00	95.00
☐ Bloodhound	HN 176	250.00	300.00
☐ Boxer, 'Warlord of Mazelaine'	HN 2643	75.00	100.00
☐ Brown Bear, Titanian ware	HN 170	250.00	300.00
☐ Budgerigars, pair	HN 2547	125.00	150.00
☐ Bulldog, pup	K 2	35.00	45.00
☐ Bulldog	K 1	35.00	45.00
☐ Bulldog, brown, large	HN 948	250.00	350.00
☐ Bulldog, sitting on lid of Lustre Bowl	HN 987	200.00	225.00

		Price Range	
❒ **Bulldog,** sitting	HN 129	200.00	225.00
❒ **Bulldog,** sitting	HN 881	150.00	165.00
❒ **Bulldog,** Brindle, large	HN 1042	375.00	475.00
❒ **Bulldog,** Brindle, medium	HN 1043	250.00	300.00
❒ **Bulldog,** Brindle, small	HN 1044	150.00	175.00
❒ **Bulldog,** brown and white, large	HN 1045	300.00	400.00
❒ **Bulldog,** brown and white, medium	HN 1046	150.00	200.00
❒ **Bulldog,** brown and white, small	HN 1047	60.00	65.00
❒ **Bulldog,** 'Old Bill' with helmet and haversack	HN 146	300.00	350.00
❒ **Bulldog,** 'Old Bill' with tammy and haversack	HN 153	300.00	350.00
❒ **Bulldog,** Union Jack, large	HN 6406	375.00	400.00
❒ **Bulldog,** Union Jack, medium	—	175.00	200.00
❒ **Bulldog,** Union Jack, small	HN 6407	135.00	160.00
❒ **Bulldog,** white, large	HN 1072	300.00	400.00
❒ **Bulldog,** white, medium	HN 1073	250.00	300.00
❒ **Bulldog,** white, small	HN 1074	60.00	65.00
❒ **Bull Terrier**	K 14	100.00	150.00
❒ **Bull Terrier,** 'Bokus Brock', large	HN 1142	500.00	600.00
❒ **Bull Terrier,** 'Bokus Brock', medium	HN 1143	350.00	400.00
❒ **Bull Terrier,** 'Bokus Brock', small	HN 1144	150.00	250.00
❒ **Bull Terrier,** Staffordshire, white, large	HN 1131	500.00	600.00
❒ **Bull Terrier,** Staffordshire, white, medium	HN 1132	300.00	400.00
❒ **Bull Terrier,** Staffordshire, white, small	HN 1133	150.00	250.00
❒ **Cairn**	K 11	35.00	45.00
❒ **Cairn,** black, large	HN 1104	275.00	300.00
❒ **Cairn,** black, medium	HN 1105	150.00	200.00
❒ **Cairn,** black, small	HN 1106	75.00	100.00
❒ **Cairn,** black, large, earthenware	HN 1107	200.00	300.00
❒ **Cairn,** 'Charming Eyes', large	HN 1033	300.00	350.00
❒ **Cairn,** 'Charming Eyes', medium	HN 1034	150.00	175.00
❒ **Cairn,** 'Charming Eyes', small	HN 1035	60.00	65.00
❒ **Cat**	K 12	35.00	45.00
❒ **Cat,** Persian, black and white	HN 999	45.00	60.00
❒ **Cat,** Persian, white	HN 2539	125.00	150.00
❒ **Cat,** Siamese, standing	HN 2660	55.00	70.00
❒ **Cat,** Siamese, sitting	HN 2665	55.00	70.00
❒ **Cat,** Siamese, lying	HN 2662	55.00	70.00
❒ **Cat,** Tortoiseshell	HN 204	225.00	250.00
❒ **Cat,** two	HN 234	250.00	300.00
❒ **Character Dog,** running with ball	HN 1097	35.00	
❒ **Character Dog,** on back	HN 1098	110.00	140.00
❒ **Character Dog,** yawning	HN 1099	35.00	
❒ **Character Dog,** walking	HN 1100	130.00	160.00
❒ **Character Dog,** lying	HN 1101	110.00	140.00
❒ **Character Dog,** with ball	HN 1103	35.00	

			Price Range
☐ **Character Dog,** with plate	HN 1158	35.00	
☐ **Character Dog,** with bone	HN 1159	35.00	
☐ **Character Dog,** Sealyham sitting	HN 2408	125.00	150.00
☐ **Character Dog,** Sealyham standing	HN 2409	125.00	150.00
☐ **Character Dog,** running	HN 2510	110.00	140.00
☐ **Character Dog,** standing	HN 2511	130.00	160.00
☐ **Character Dog,** with slipper	HN 2654	35.00	
☐ **Chestnut Mare with Foal,** large	HN 2522	300.00	350.00
☐ **Chow Chow**	K 15	35.00	45.00
☐ **Chow,** large	HN 2628	400.00	500.00
☐ **Chow,** medium......................	HN 2629	200.00	300.00
☐ **Chow,** small........................	HN 2630	100.00	200.00
☐ **Chow,** on stand, lighter brown	HN 838	100.00	200.00
☐ **Chow,** on stand, brown	HN 837	100.00	200.00
☐ **Chow,** on stand, white and gray........	HN 839	100.00	200.00
☐ **Cock Pheasant**	HN 2632	425.00	495.00
☐ **Cocker Spaniel**	K 9	35.00	45.00
☐ **Cocker Spaniel,** black, large	HN 1000	200.00	250.00
☐ **Cocker Spaniel,** black and white, large..	HN 1108	150.00	250.00
☐ **Cocker Spaniel,** black and white, medium	HN 1109	75.00	95.00
☐ **Cocker Spaniel,** black and white, small .	HN 1078	80.00	125.00
☐ **Cocker Spaniel,** Golden brown, large ...	HN 1186	200.00	300.00
☐ **Cocker Spaniel,** Golden brown, medium	HN 1187	85.00	100.00
☐ **Cocker Spaniel,** Golden brown, small ...	HN 1188	75.00	100.00
☐ **Cocker Spaniel,** liver and white, large...	HN 1002	200.00	250.00
☐ **Cocker Spaniel,** liver and white, large...	HN 1134	250.00	275.00
☐ **Cocker Spaniel,** liver and white, medium	HN 1135	95.00	110.00
☐ **Cocker Spaniel,** liver and white, small ..	HN 1136	75.00	100.00
☐ **Cocker Spaniel,** liver and white, small ..	HN 1037	50.00	75.00
☐ **Cocker Spaniel,** 'Lucky Star of Ware', medium	HN 1020	85.00	95.00
☐ **Cocker Spaniel,** 'Lucky Star of Ware', small................................	HN 1021	75.00	100.00
☐ **Cocker Spaniels,** sleeping	HN 2590	50.00	75.00
☐ **Cocker Spaniel and Hare,** liver and white, medium......................	HN 1063	100.00	200.00
☐ **Cocker Spaniel and Hare,** liver and white, small	HN 1064	100.00	150.00
☐ **Cocker Spaniel and Pheasant,** large, liver and white	HN 1001	225.00	275.00
☐ **Cocker Spaniel and Pheasant,** large, black and white	HN 1137	250.00	300.00
☐ **Cocker Spaniel and Pheasant,** medium, red and white	HN 1028	110.00	135.00
☐ **Cocker Spaniel and Pheasant,** medium, black and white	HN 1138	95.00	110.00
☐ **Cocker Spaniel and Pheasant,** small, red and white	HN 1029	125.00	150.00

Cocker And Pheasant,
HN1001, large, discontinued
1969, **225.00 - 275.00**

		Price Range	
☐ **Cocker Spaniel and Pheasant,** small, black and white	HN 1062	100.00	125.00
☐ **Cocker Spaniel and Pheasant,** small	HN 2600	100.00	125.00
☐ **Cockerel,** sitting	HN 124	125.00	150.00
☐ **Collie,** Ashstead Applause, large	HN 1057	250.00	350.00
☐ **Collie,** Ashstead Applause, medium	HN 1058	85.00	95.00
☐ **Collie,** Ashstead Applause, small	HN 1059	100.00	125.00
☐ **Collie,** brown	HN 976	225.00	275.00
☐ **Collie,** silver gray	HN 975	350.00	400.00
☐ **Collie,** sable	HN 105	200.00	300.00
☐ **Collie,** sable and white	HN 106	250.00	300.00
☐ **Dachshund**	K 17	35.00	45.00
☐ **Dachshund,** red, large	HN 1139	250.00	300.00
☐ **Dachshund,** red, medium	HN 1140	150.00	200.00
☐ **Dachshund,** red, small	HN 1141	95.00	125.00
☐ **Dachshund,** 'Shrewd Saint', large	HN 1127	200.00	275.00
☐ **Dachshund,** 'Shrewd Saint', medium	HN 1128	75.00	95.00
☐ **Dachshund,** 'Shrewd Saint', small	HN 1129	110.00	135.00
☐ **Dalmatian,** 'Goworth Victor', large	HN 1111	275.00	350.00
☐ **Dalmatian,** 'Goworth Victor', medium	HN 1113	85.00	95.00
☐ **Dalmatian,** 'Goworth Victor', small	HN 1114	95.00	125.00

		Price Range	
☐ **Doberman Pinscher**	HN 2645	85.00	95.00
☐ **Double Doves**	HN 122	300.00	400.00
☐ **Drake,** Mallard, large	HN 956	175.00	200.00
☐ **Drake,** Mallard	HN 2591	90.00	125.00
☐ **Drake,** Mallard on rocks, small	HN 853	75.00	95.00
☐ **Drake,** Miniature, malachite and purple .	HN 807	45.00	65.00
☐ **Drake,** Miniature, white	HN 806	75.00	95.00
☐ **Elephant**........................	HN 2644	80.00	95.00
☐ **Elephant,** trunk up	HN 891 ◄	375.00	425.00
☐ **Elephant,** fighting	HN 2640	1200.00	1350.00
☐ **English Setter,** liver and white, large....	HN 2620	350.00	450.00
☐ **English Setter,** liver and white, medium .	HN 2621	150.00	250.00
☐ **English Setter,** liver and white, small ...	HN 2622	100.00	175.00
☐ **English Setter,** 'Maesydd Mustard', large .	HN 1049	300.00	350.00
☐ **English Setter,** 'Maesydd Mustard', medium	HN 1050	80.00	95.00
☐ **English Setter,** 'Maesydd Mustard', small................................	HN 1051	90.00	110.00
☐ **English Setter and Pheasant**	HN 2529	375.00	395.00
☐ **Fox,** on rock	HN 147	125.00	150.00
☐ **Fox,** Red Frock Coat	HN 100	350.00	400.00
☐ **Fox,** sitting.........................	HN 2634	550.00	650.00
☐ **Foxhound**..........................	K 7	25.00	35.00

Fox-Hound K7,
discontinued 1977,
25.00 – 27.00

☐ **Foxhound**..........................	HN 231	275.00	325.00
☐ **Foxhound,** seated	HN 166	200.00	225.00
☐ **Foxhound,** 'Tring Rattler', large........	HN 1025	300.00	350.00
☐ **Foxhound,** 'Tring Rattler', medium	HN 1026	200.00	250.00
☐ **Foxhound,** 'Tring Rattler', small	HN 1027	175.00	195.00
☐ **Fox Terrier**	HN 942	100.00	200.00
☐ **Fox Terrier**	HN 943	100.00	200.00
☐ **Fox Terrier**	HN 944	100.00	200.00
☐ **Fox Terrier**	HN 945	185.00	225.00
☐ **Fox Terrier,** 'Crackley Hunter', medium .	HN 1013	150.00	200.00
☐ **Fox Terrier,** 'Crackley Hunter', small ...	HN 1014	60.00	65.00

		Price Range	
☐ **Fox Terrier,** smooth-haired, large	HN 1068	350.00	450.00
☐ **Fox Terrier,** smooth-haired, medium	HN 1069	200.00	250.00
☐ **Fox Terrier,** smooth-haired, small	HN 1070	150.00	200.00
☐ **Fox Terrier,** smooth, large, Ch. Chosen Dan of Notts	HN 2513	300.00	400.00
☐ **Fox Terrier,** smooth, medium, Ch. Chosen Dan of Notts	HN 2514	200.00	250.00
☐ **Fox Terrier,** smooth, small, Ch. Chosen Dan of Notts	HN 2515	150.00	200.00
☐ **Fox Terrier,** standing	HN 909	100.00	200.00
☐ **Fox Terrier,** sitting	HN 910	100.00	200.00
☐ **Fox Terrier,** standing	HN 923	150.00	250.00
☐ **Fox Terrier,** sitting, large	HN 924	200.00	275.00
☐ **French Poodle,** medium	HN 2631	85.00	95.00
☐ **Gordon Setter,** large	HN 1079	400.00	500.00
☐ **Gordon Setter,** medium	HN 1080	175.00	200.00
☐ **Gordon Setter,** small	HN 1081	100.00	150.00
☐ **Great Dane,** large	HN 2560	300.00	400.00
☐ **Great Dane,** medium	HN 2561	175.00	200.00
☐ **Great Dane,** medium	HN 2602	225.00	275.00
☐ **Great Dane,** small	HN 2562	100.00	175.00
☐ **Greyhound,** brown, large	HN 1065	300.00	400.00
☐ **Greyhound,** brown, medium	HN 1066	300.00	400.00
☐ **Greyhound,** brown, small	HN 1067	150.00	200.00
☐ **Greyhound,** black and white, large	HN 1075	300.00	400.00
☐ **Greyhound,** black and white, medium . . .	HN 1076	150.00	275.00
☐ **Greyhound,** black and white, small	HN 1077	150.00	200.00
☐ **Greyhound,** black and white, seated	HN 889	200.00	300.00
☐ **Greyhound,** brown, seated	HN 890	200.00	300.00
☐ **Gude Grey Mare,** no foal, medium	HN 2569	250.00	300.00
☐ **Gude Grey Mare,** with foal, medium	HN 2532	200.00	250.00
☐ **Hare,** lying	K 37	35.00	50.00
☐ **Hare,** lying, small	HN 2594	35.00	45.00
☐ **Hare,** sitting, ears down	K 38	40.00	55.00
☐ **Hare,** sitting, ears up	K 39	35.00	40.00
☐ **Huntsman Fox**	HN 6448	40.00	50.00
☐ **Irish Setter,** large	HN 1054	300.00	400.00
☐ **Irish Setter,** medium	HN 1055	85.00	100.00
☐ **Irish Setter,** small	HN 1056	90.00	125.00
☐ **Kingfisher,** small	HN 2573	75.00	100.00
☐ **Kitten,** lying on back, brown	HN 2579	35.00	45.00
☐ **Kitten,** sitting licking hind paw, brown . .	HN 2580	35.00	45.00
☐ **Kitten,** sleeping, brown	HN 2581	35.00	45.00
☐ **Kitten,** sitting on haunches, tan	HN 2582	35.00	45.00
☐ **Kitten,** sitting, licking front paw	HN 2583	35.00	45.00
☐ **Kitten,** sitting, surprised, tan	HN 2584	35.00	45.00
☐ **Langur Monkey**	HN 2657	150.00	175.00
☐ **Leopard on Rock**	HN 2638	1300.00	1500.00

		Price Range	
☐ Lion on Rock	HN 2641	1300.00	1500.00
☐ Mallard	HN 2556	200.00	225.00
☐ Merely a Minor, brown, small	HN 2571	175.00	225.00
☐ Mountain Sheep	HN 2661	150.00	200.00
☐ Nyala Antelope	HN 2664	250.00	300.00
☐ Owl, character, check shawl, ermine collar	HN 187	750.00	850.00
☐ Owl, 'Wise Old', red cloak, ermine collar	HN 173	400.00	500.00
☐ Parrot, on rock	HN 185	250.00	300.00
☐ Peacock	HN 2577	150.00	175.00
☐ Pekinese	K 6	35.00	45.00
☐ Pekinese, 'Biddee of Ifield', large	HN 1010	325.00	375.00
☐ Pekinese, 'Biddee of Ifield', medium	HN 1011	250.00	300.00
☐ Pekinese, 'Biddee of Ifield', small	HN 1012	60.00	65.00
☐ Pekinese, sitting, large	HN 1039	250.00	300.00
☐ Pekinese, sitting, small	HN 1040	125.00	150.00
☐ Pekinese Puppy, sitting	HN 832	125.00	175.00
☐ Pekinese Puppy, standing	HN 833	125.00	185.00
☐ Pekinese Puppy, on stand, black and brown	HN 834	150.00	195.00
☐ Pekinese Puppy, on stand, lighter brown	HN 835	150.00	195.00
☐ Pekinese Puppy, on stand, light color	HN 836	150.00	195.00
☐ Penquins	K 20	100.00	125.00
☐ Penquins	K 21	75.00	100.00
☐ Penquins	K 22	100.00	125.00
☐ Penquins	K 23	75.00	100.00
☐ Penquins	K 24	75.00	100.00
☐ Penquins	K 25	100.00	125.00
☐ Pheasant	HN 2545	235.00	275.00
☐ Pheasant, small	HN 2576	150.00	175.00
☐ Pig, asleep	HN 800	75.00	95.00
☐ Pig, asleep, large	HN 801	125.00	150.00
☐ Piglets, character	HN 2648	100.00	150.00
☐ Piglets, character	HN 2649	100.00	150.00
☐ Piglets, character	HN 2650	100.00	150.00
☐ Piglets, character	HN 2651	100.00	150.00
☐ Piglets, character	HN 2652	100.00	150.00
☐ Piglets, character	HN 2653	100.00	150.00
☐ Pointer	HN 2624	250.00	300.00
☐ Polar Bear, sitting on green cube	HN 119	175.00	250.00
☐ Poodle, large	HN 2625	400.00	500.00
☐ Poodle, medium	HN 2626	200.00	300.00
☐ Poodle, small	HN 2627	100.00	200.00
☐ 'Pride of Shires', mare and foal, gray, small	HN 2536	200.00	250.00
☐ 'Pride of Shires', mare, no foal, brown, medium	HN 2564	185.00	225.00
☐ Puppies in Basket, three, Terriers	HN 2588	45.00	55.00

		Price Range	
☐ **Puppy**	HN 128	135.00	185.00
☐ **Puppy,** begging, Cairn	HN 2589	45.00	55.00
☐ **Puppy,** in basket, Cocker	HN 2586	45.00	55.00
☐ **Puppy,** in basket, lying, Cocker	HN 2585	45.00	55.00
☐ **Puppy,** in basket, Terrier	HN 2587	45.00	55.00
☐ **Rhinoceros**	HN 141	200.00	300.00
☐ **River Hog**	HN 2663	175.00	225.00
☐ **Scottish Terrier**	K 10	35.00	45.00
☐ **Scottish Terrier**	K 18	35.00	- 45.00
☐ **Scottish Terrier,** large	HN 1008	300.00	400.00
☐ **Scottish Terrier,** 'Albourne Arthur', medium	HN 1015	150.00	200.00
☐ **Scottish Terrier,** 'Albourne Arthur', small	HN 1016	65.00	95.00
☐ **Scottish Terrier,** sitting, black	HN 1017	300.00	400.00
☐ **Scottish Terrier,** sitting, black	HN 1018	200.00	250.00
☐ **Scottish Terrier,** sitting, black	HN 1019	100.00	125.00
☐ **Scottish Terrier,** begging	HN 1038	300.00	350.00
☐ **Scottish Terrier,** light gray and brown	HN 981	225.00	250.00
☐ **Sealyham,** begging	K 3	35.00	45.00
☐ **Sealyham,** sleeping	K 4	75.00	100.00
☐ **Sealyham,** character sitting	HN 2508	125.00	150.00
☐ **Sealyham,** character dog standing	HN 2509	125.00	150.00
☐ **Sealyham,** lying, large	HN 1041	275.00	300.00
☐ **Sealyham,** lying, medium	HN 1052	200.00	250.00

Sealy Ham,
HN1030, large,
discontinued 1957,
500.00 – 600.00

		Price Range	
☐ Sealyham, lying, small	HN 1053	150.00	200.00
☐ Sealyham, 'Scotia Stylist', large	HN 1030	500.00	600.00
☐ Sealyham, 'Scotia Stylist', medium	HN 1031	175.00	225.00
☐ Sealyham, 'Scotia Stylist', small	HN 1032	125.00	150.00
☐ Sealyham, Terrier, black patches on face	HN 982	150.00	175.00
☐ Sealyham, Terrier, brown patches on face	HN 983	150.00	175.00
☐ Springer Spaniel, 'Dry Toast', large	HN 2515	225.00	275.00
☐ Springer Spaniel, 'Dry Toast', medium	HN 2516	150.00	175.00
☐ Springer Spaniel, 'Dry Toast', small	HN 2517	50.00	60.00
☐ St. Bernard	K 19	35.00	45.00
☐ Staffordshire Bull Terrier, medium	HN 1132	175.00	225.00
☐ Teal Duck	HN 229	150.00	185.00
☐ Tern Duck	HN 167	150.00	200.00
☐ Terrier	K 8	35.00	45.00
☐ Terrier, seated, black and brown	HN 997	175.00	225.00
☐ Terrier's Head	HN 962	150.00	175.00
☐ Terrier, 'Crackley Startler', rough-haired, large	HN 1007	300.00	400.00
☐ Tiger	HN 2646	750.00	850.00
☐ Tiger, lying	HN 911	375.00	425.00
☐ Tiger, sitting	HN 912	375.00	425.00
☐ Tiger on Rock	HN 2639	1350.00	1500.00
☐ Toucan	HN 159	150.00	200.00
☐ Welsh Corgi	K 16	35.00	45.00
☐ Welsh Corgi, large	HN 2557	350.00	400.00
☐ Welsh Corgi, medium	HN 2558	200.00	250.00
☐ Welsh Corgi, small	HN 2559	45.00	60.00
☐ West Highland White Terrier, large	HN 1048	500.00	600.00
☐ Yellow Bird on Rock, beak closed	HN 145A	100.00	125.00
☐ Yellow Bird on Rock, beak open	HN 145	100.00	125.00

CHATCULL RANGE OF ANIMALS

This is a series bearing standard HN prefix numbers, which originated in 1940. The designer of these appealing portrayals was Joseph Ledger, whose estate was known as "Chatcull Hall" — thus the title for the series. These were not limited editions but the majority are now out of production and are becoming harder to find. Prices are likely to rise more sharply across-the-board on Chatculls when the entire series is out of production.

☐ Badger	HN 2666	225.00	250.00
☐ Black Labrador 'Bumblikite of Mansergh'	HN 2667	85.00	95.00
☐ Brown Bear	HN 2659	250.00	300.00
☐ Langur Monkey	HN 2657	250.00	300.00
☐ Llama	HN 2665	175.00	225.00
☐ Mountain Sheep	HN 2661	150.00	200.00

		Price Range	
☐ **Nyala Antelope**	HN 2664	250.00	300.00
☐ **Pine Martin**	HN 2656	225.00	250.00
☐ **River Hog**	HN 2663	175.00	225.00
☐ **Siamese Cat,** lying	HN 2662	55.00	70.00
☐ **Siamese Cat,** sitting	HN 2655	55.00	70.00
☐ **Siamese Cat,** standing	HN 2660	55.00	70.00
☐ **White-tailed Deer**	HN 2658	250.00	300.00

IMAGES OF NATURE

An exciting new approach has been introduced in the Animal and Bird Models. These figures present a streamlined and modernistic style, each conveying an animal in action. This new Image Collection was introduced in 1982.

THE LEAP   Price
HN 3522
☐ Dolphin rising from the water, designer A. Hughes.................   75.00

Going Home, HN3527, **50.00**

GOING HOME
Price

HN 3527
☐ A pair of flying geese, designer
A. Hughes........................ **50.00**

CAPRICORN
HN 3523
☐ Mountain goat poised on a precipice,
designer A. Hughes................ **50.00**

THE GIFT OF LIFE
HN 3524
☐ A mare with her new born foal,
designer R. Willis. **175.00**

COURTSHIP
HN 3525
☐ Dramatic mating display of two terns,
designer R. Willis. **250.00**

SHADOWPLAY
HN 3526
☐ A playful cat sitting erect, designer
R. Willis. **75.00**

FREEDOM
HN 3528
☐ A pair of otters at play, designer
Robert Jefferson. **195.00**

BRIGHTWATER
HN 3529
☐ Single otter, designer Robert Jeffer-
son. **100.00**

CLEARWATER
HN 3530
☐ Single otter, designer Robert Jeffer-
son. **100.00**

JEFFERSON SCULPTURES

The following wildlife sculptures were created by Robert Jefferson. Beautiful renditions of nature, most were produced in limited edition, however, a few models were unlimited. First limited edition was released in 1974.

	Date	Price
☐ **Black-Throated Loon** Limited edition of 150 . **HN 3500**	1974	2350.00
☐ **Chipping Sparrow** Limited edition of 200 . . . **HN 3511**	1976	950.00
☐ **Colorado Chipmunks** Limited edition of 75 . . **HN 3506**	1974	7500.00
☐ **Downy Woodpecker** Edition unlimited . . . . . **HN 3509**	1975	525.00
☐ **Fledgling Bluebird** Limited edition of 250 . . . **HN 3510**	1976	600.00
☐ **Golden-Crowned Kinglet** Edition unlimited . . **HN 3504**	1974	525.00
☐ **Harbor Seals** Limited edition of 75 . . . . **HN 3507**	1975	1600.00
☐ **Huntsman Fox** Edition unlimited . . . . **HN 6448**	—	50.00
☐ **King Eider** Limited edition of 150 . . . . **HN 3502**	1974	1800.00
☐ **Puffins** Limited edition of 250 . . . . **HN 2668**	1974	1600.00
☐ **Roseate Terns** Limited edition of 150 . . . . . . **HN 3503**	1974	2500.00
☐ **Snowshoe Hares** Limited edition of 75 . . . . . **HN 3508**	1975	2750.00
☐ **Snowy Owl,** Female, Limited edition of 150 . **HN 2670**	1974	2150.00
☐ **Snowy Owl,** Male, Limited edition of 150 . . . . **HN 2669**	1974	1750.00
☐ **White-Winged Cross Bills** Limited edition of 250 . . . . **HN 3501**	1974	1450.00
☐ **Winter Wren** Edition unlimited . . . . **HN 3505**	1974	375.00

FANCY AND CHARACTER FIGURINES

The following ALPHABETICAL listing gives series numbers, dates, descriptions, and current retail selling prices for figues in the HN series. Descriptions indicate the color schemes found on the majority of specimens on each model. Color variations do exist on many models. While some collectors take a special interest in "off-color" models, the market on them is not widespread enough to establish firm values.

ABDULLAH

	Date	Price Range	
HN 1410			
☐ Dark skinned figure seated on blue cushions, green turban, height 5¾", designer L. Harradine	1930-1938	800.00	950.00
HN 2104			
☐ Dark skinned figure seated on black base which has blue rug with red, green, black squares, large cushion of yellow and green gray trousers, black coat, orange shirt, red waistband, orange and red turban with green feather, height 6", designer L. Harradine.	1953-1962	550.00	700.00

	Date	Price Range

A'COURTING
HN 2004

☐ Boy and girl figure on light green base, boy's costume is shaded blues, jacket dark blue with gold buttons, hat black, girl's costume is red dress with white collar, white apron in hand, white head cap with blue ribbon, height 7¼ ", designer L. Harradine. . .   1947-1953   650.00   750.00

ADRIENNE
HN 2152

☐ Gown of purple with yellow scarf, height 7½ ", designer M. Davies.   1964-1976   175.00   225.00

HN 2304

☐ Gown of blue with very light green scarf, height 7½ ", designer M. Davies   1964-   155.00

AFFECTION
HN 2236

☐ Small girl in gown of purple with white trim, seated on bench of green holding small white kitten, height 4¾ ", designer M. Davies.   1962-   100.00

AFTERNOON CALL, The
(sometimes referred to as Lady With Ermine Muff)

HN   82

☐ Lady seated on beige couch, cream gown with green designs, coat of blue with white fur trim and muff, green hat with blue feather, height 6¾ ", designer E. W. Light.   1918-1938   2250.00   2500.00

AFTERNOON TEA
HN 1747

☐ Two ladies seated on sofa, one gown is pink, bonnet of green with blue ribbons, the other gown is white skirt with blue and yellow flower design, jacket is light blue, bonnet is white with red ribbons, height 5¾ ", designer P. Railston.   1935-1982   300.00   400.00

HN 1748

☐ Green dress, height 5¼ ", designer P. Railston.   1935-1949   450.00   550.00

	Date	Price Range

AILEEN
HN 1645
☐ Seated figure in green dress, shawl is light blue with red and blue flowers, white necklace, red shoes, height 6″, designer L. Harradine. 1934-1938 **750.00 850.00**

HN 1664
☐ Pink skirt, height 6″, designer L. Harradine. 1934-1938 **850.00 950.00**

HN 1803
☐ Cream dress, blue shawl, height 6″, designer L. Harradine 1937-1949 **700.00 800.00**

A LA MODE
HN 2544
☐ Tall figure with red hair, green dress with a darker green design, height 12½ ″, designer E. J. Griffiths 1974-1979 **175.00 250.00**

ALL ABOARD
HN 2940
☐ Depicts an old sea captain, standing on a gray base alongside is a clock and a sign telling departure time of deep sea trips. Mans outfit is a blue turtle neck sweater over beige trousers, black boots, height 9¼″, designer R. Tabbenor 1982- **175.00**

ALCHEMIST, The
HN 1259
☐ Mottled robe, red hat, height 11½ ″, designer L. Harradine. 1927-1938 **1450.00 1650.00**

HN 1282
☐ Dark brown robe with multicolored sleeves and red scarf, dark brown hat, holding small object in one hand, height 11¼ ″, designer L. Harradine. . 1928-1938 **1450.00 1650.00**

ALEXANDRA
HN 2398
☐ Green dress with white flowers and flowing yellow cape, height 7¾″, designer M. Davies. 1970-1976 **175.00 225.00**

	Date	Price Range	
ALFRED JINGLE			

HN 541

This was discontinued in 1932 renumbered in 1932 and still produced.

☐ A character from Dickens "Pickwick Papers," height 3¾", designer L. Harradine.	1922-1932	45.00	60.00
☐ **M-52** Renumbered as a miniature, height 3¾", designer L. Harradine. . .	1932-1983	20.00	30.00

ALICE

HN 2158

☐ Blue dress, white ribbon in blonde hair, open book on lap, height 5", designer M. Davies.	1960-1980	95.00	125.00

ALISON

HN 2336

☐ White skirt with small red and green design, blue overdress, height 7½", designer M. Davies.	1966-	155.00	

ALL-A-BLOOMING

HN 1457

☐ Blue dress, height 6½", designer L. Harradine.	1931-Unknown	900.00	1000.00

HN 1466

☐ Lady seated on brown wicker stand, yellow/green basket of flowers beside her, skirt red, apron white, shawl dark blue with shades of yellow and green, hat is shades of blue with green feathers, height 6½", designer L. Harradine.	1931-1938	1000.00	1100.00

AMY

HN 2958

☐ One of the charming Kate Greenaway figures. Young figure in very pale blue dress with darker blue ruffles on bottom, dark blue ribbon at waist. Dark hair with white cap. Figure is holding a doll in red dress, yellow hair, height 6", designer P. Parsons.	1982-	75.00	

	Date	Price Range	

ANGELA
HN 1204
☐ Figure on light colored pedestal, costume of shaded reds and blue, red shoes, holding large fan behind head of dark blue and red, height 7¼", designer L. Harradine. 1926-1938   675.00   850.00

HN 1303
☐ Blue fan and spotted costume, height 7¼", designer L. Harradine. . . . . , 1928-1938   950.00   1100.00

ANGELINA
HN 2013
☐ Red dress trimmed in white, holding green hat with blue ribbon, height 6¾", designer L. Harradine. 1948-1951   700.00   800.00

ANNA (Kate Greenaway)
HN 2802
☐ Small girl, purple dress, white apron and bonnet, holding flower in one hand, on white base, height 5¾", designer M. Davies. 1976-1982   65.00   100.00

ANNABELLA
HN 1871
☐ Small figure in curtsy position, orange skirt with green bodice, holding basket of flowers on arm, hat matches skirt, height 5¼", designer L. Harradine. 1938-1949   450.00   525.00

HN 1872
☐ Green skirt and blue bodice, height 5¼", designer L. Harradine. 1938-1949   450.00   525.00

HN 1875
☐ Red dress, height 4¾", designer L. Harradine. 1938-1949   450.00   525.00

Annabella, HN1871, 450.00 ~ 525.00

ANNETTE	Date	Price Range	
HN 1471			
☐ Dutch figure in blue gown with white apron, white dutch cap carrying light colored basket with red fruit, light wooden shoes, height 6¼ ″, designer L. Harradine.	1931-1938	375.00	425.00
HN 1472			
☐ Gown of green, apron shaded green, red and cream, red basket, height 6 ″, designer L. Harradine.	1931-1949	400.00	450.00
HN 1550			
☐ Green skirt, apron with light stripes, red blouse, height 6¼ ″, designer L. Harradine.	1933-1949	425.00	475.00

	Date	Price Range	

ANTHEA

HN 1526

☐ Green dress with white designs, blue shawl with red flowers, green hat with red feather, carrying parasol, height 6½ ", designer L. Harradine. . . . . | 1932-1938 | 500.00 | 600.00

HN 1527

☐ Gown of shaded blues and reds with cream, shawl white with red and black designs, blue hat with light feather, height 6½ ", designer L. Harradine. . . . . | 1932-1949 | 575.00 | 675.00

HN 1669

☐ Skirt of cream, jacket red, shawl green, hat green, height 6½ ", designer L. Harradine. . . . . | 1934-1938 | 575.00 | 675.00

ANTOINETTE

HN 1850

☐ Black base and pedestal, gown is red with green trim, hat green with black ribbons (1st version), height 8¼ ", designer L. Harradine. . . . . | 1938-1949 | 800.00 | 900.00

HN 1851

☐ Base black, pedestal blue and cream, gown shaded blue and red with blue overdress, blue hat with green ribbons (1st version), height 8¼ ", designer L. Harradine. . . . . | 1938-1949 | 800.00 | 900.00

HN 2326

☐ White gown with gold design and trim, gold shoe, seated figure (2nd version), height 6¼ ", designer M. Davies. . . . . | 1967-1979 | 150.00 | 175.00

APPLE MAID, The

HN 2160

☐ Figure seated on brown wicker chair, black skirt, green blouse, white apron, white head covering, brown basket with apples, height 6½ ", designer L. Harradine. . . . . | 1957-1962 | 350.00 | 425.00

ARAB/MOOR

HN 33

☐ Green costume, blue cloak, height 15¾ ", designer C. J. Noke. . . . . | 1913-1938 | 1600.00 | 1800.00

	Date	Price Range	

HN 343
☐ Striped yellow and purple costume, height 16½ ", designer C. J. Noke. .... 1919-1938 — 1750.00 2000.00

HN 378
☐ Costume of patchwork colors of green, brown, yellow hooded cloak of dark blue, multicolored base, height 16½ ", designer C. J. Noke. .... 1920-1930 — 1500.00 1750.00

ARTFUL DODGER, The

HN 546
☐ A character from Dickens "Oliver Twist," height 3¾ ", designer L. Harradine. .... 1922- — 45.00 60.00
☐ **M-55** Renumbered as a miniature, height 4¼ ", designer L. Harradine. .. 1932-1983 — 20.00 30.00

ASCOT

HN 2356
☐ Seated lady on brown chair, green dress, green hat with blue trim, yellow boa, light blue parasol, height 5¾ ", designer M. Davies. .... 1968- — 185.00

AT EASE

HN 2473
☐ Lady seated on green and brown chaise lounge, dark hair, pale green gown trimmed in brown, height 6", designer M. Davies. .... 1973-1979 — 175.00 225.00

AUTUMN

HN 314
☐ Blue/gray base, pink gown, autumn colored flowers in arm (1st version), height 7¼ ", designer unknown. ...... 1918-1938 — 1200.00 1400.00

HN 474
☐ Patterned robe (1st version), height 7½ ", designer unknown. .... 1921-1938 — 1300.00 1400.00

HN 2087
☐ Green and yellow base, gown of red, blue and white apron, small white cap with blue ribbons, brown broom (2nd version), height 7¼ ", designer M. Davies .... 1952-1959 — 500.00 550.00

At Ease, HN2473, **175.00 – 225.00**

AUTUMN BREEZES	Date	Price Range	
HN 1911			
☐ Pink and pale blue skirt, green bodice and hat, white muff. Earlier mold has two feet, height 7½″, designer L. Harradine.	1939-1976	150.00	200.00
HN 1913			
☐ Green skirt, dark blue bodice, blue hat with black apron, white muff, height 7½″, designer L. Harradine.	1939-1971	195.00	245.00
HN 1934			
☐ Red skirt and bodice, white hat, height 7½″, designer L. Harradine.	1940-	170.00	
HN 2147			
☐ White skirt, black bodice, white hat and muff, height 7½″, designer L. Harradine.	1955-1971	325.00	375.00

Autumn Breezes,
HN, 1913,
195.00 – 245.00

AWAKENING, The	**Date**	**Price Range**	
HN 1927			
☐ Nude figure on light colored base with a full length of light material draped down front, height unknown, designer L. Harradine.	1940-1949	2050.00	2200.00
BABA			
HN 1230			
☐ Small seated figure with striped yellow and purple trousers and cone shaped hat, height 3¼″, designer L. Harradine.	1927-1938	550.00	650.00
HN 1243			
☐ Orange trousers, height 3¼″, designer L. Harradine.	1927-1927	550.00	650.00
HN 1244			
☐ Yellow trousers with green stripes, height 3¼″, designer L. Harradine. . .	1927-1938	550.00	650.00

	Date	Price Range	

HN 1245
☐ White trousers with blue/black markings, height 3¼″, designer L. Harradine 1927-1938   550.00   650.00

HN 1246
☐ Green trousers, height 3¼″, designer L. Harradine 1927-1938   550.00   650.00

HN 1247
☐ White trousers with black spots, height 3¼″, designer L. Harradine . . . 1928-1938   550.00   650.00

HN 1248
☐ Green striped trousers, white striped sleeves, red waistband, white cone shaped hat, height 3¼″, designer L. Harradine 1927-1938   550.00   650.00

BABETTE

HN 1423
☐ Small figure in bathing costume on base with open parasol, blue and white costume, height 5″, designer L. Harradine 1930-1938   500.00   600.00

HN 1424
☐ Yellow costume with red stripes, height 5″, designer L. Harradine 1930-1938   550.00   650.00

BABIE

HN 1679
☐ Small figure in gown of green and cream, blue bonnet with red feather, carrying red parasol, height 4¾″, designer L. Harradine 1935-   75.00

HN 1842
☐ Pink dress, green hat and umbrella, height 4¾″, designer L. Harradine . . 1938-1949   150.00   200.00

HN 2121
☐ Dress is shades of pinks decorated with white summer flowers. Bonnet is pink with gold ribbon, gold parasol, height 4¾″, designer L. Harradine . . 1983-   75.00

BABY

HN 12
☐ Small child figure on base, wrapped entirely in blue/gray robe, height unknown, designer C. J. Noke 1913-1938   2050.00   2200.00

	Date	Price Range	

BABY BUNTING

HN 2108

☐ White child figure with brown covering arms and head, head cover has ears, height 5 ¼ ", designer M. Davies. — 1953-1959 — 225.00 — 275.00

BACHELOR, The

HN 2319

☐ Character figure seated in dark brown chair with foot stool darning blue sock, wears brown trousers, black vest, white shirt, brown tie, blue socks, brown shoes, height 7", designer M. Nicoll .... — 1964-1975 — 225.00 — 275.00

BALLAD SELLER

HN 2266

☐ Skirt and bonnet of pink, bodice white with gold, holding white sheet with printing in one hand, rolled white sheet in other, height 7 ½ ", designer M. Davies. .... — 1968-1973 — 325.00 — 375.00

BALLERINA

HN 2116

☐ White dress with shades of blue and red, red ribbon at waist, red ballet shoes on dark base, blue ribbon and flower trim on gown, height 7 ¼ ", designer M. Davies. .... — 1953-1973 — 250.00 — 325.00

BALLOON BOY

HN 2934

☐ Base resembles cobble street, boy dressed in dark pants, white skirt, green jacket and beige cap, holding a bunch of gaily colored balloons, height 7 ½ ", designer P. Gee. .... — 1984- — 95.00

BALLOON GIRL

HN 2818

☐ Seated blonde girl dressed in gray skirt, yellow blouse, red scarf tied around neck, green shawl with red fringe, hat is black with beige ribbon, colorful balloons in her hand, height 6 ½ ", designer W. K. Harper. .... — 1982- — 125.00

Balloon Boy,
HN2934,
95.00

Balloon Girl,
HN2818,
125.00

	Date	Price Range

BALLOON LADY

HN 2935

☐ Dressed in a burnt ochre skirt and white buttoned apron, white blouse, purple shawl with heavy fringe, black hat with green feather, holding a colorful bunch of balloons, height 8¼″, designer P. Gee.   1984-   125.00

BALLOON MAN, The

HN 1954

☐ Character figure seated on brown box, green trousers, black shoes, black coat, brown vest, white shirt, brown hat, holding multicolored balloons, with red knapsack, height 7¼″, designer L. Harradine.   1940-   175.00

BALLOON SELLER, The

HN 479

☐ Blue dress, white spots, height 9″, designer L. Harradine.   1921-1938   2250.00 2500.00

HN 486

☐ Blue dress, no hat, height 9″, designer L. Harradine.   1921-1938   1500.00 1700.00

HN 548

☐ Black shawl, blue dress, height 9″, designer L. Harradine.   1922-1938   800.00   900.00

HN 583

☐ White skirt with small green design, green shawl with red fringe, red blouse, black hat with green feather, baby in orange and red, balloons multicolored, height 9″, designer L. Harradine.   1923-1949   500.00   600.00

HN 697

☐ Striped red shawl, blue dress, height 9″, designer L. Harradine.   1925-1938   800.00   900.00

BARBARA

HN 1421

☐ Brown base, gown of cream with red and blue flower design, blue and red shawl with black designs, blue and red bonnet, holding small envelope in one hand and small round red and yellow purse, height 7¾″, designer L. Harradine.   1930-1938   600.00   750.00

	Date	Price Range	

HN 1432
☐ Black base, gown of shaded blue, red, green, multicolored shawl and bonnet, small purse, height 7¾", designer L. Harradine. 1930-1938 700.00 825.00

HN 1461
☐ Green dress, height 7¾", designer L. Harradine. 1931-1938 650.00 725.00

BATHER, The

HN 597
☐ Mottled gray robe, blue base (1st version), height 7¾", designer L. Harradine. 1924-1938 900.00 1000.00

HN 687
☐ Royal blue base, also royal blue lining of purple robe which has blue designs, nude white figure with greenish shoes (1st version), height 7¾", designer L. Harradine. 1924-1949 675.00 775.00

HN 773
☐ Pink robe, blue and black markings (2nd version), height 7½", designer L. Harradine. 1925-1938 900.00 1100.00

HN 774
☐ Nude white figure on black base with purple robe which has red lining, black spots (2nd version), height 7¾", designer L. Harradine. 1925-1938 900.00 1100.00

HN 781
☐ Blue and green robe (1st version), height 7¾", designer L. Harradine. . . 1926-1938 800.00 900.00

HN 782
☐ Mottled purple robe, black lining (1st version), height 7¾", designer L. Harradine. 1926-1938 800.00 900.00

HN 1227
☐ Flowered pink robe (2nd version), height 7½", designer L. Harradine. . . 1927-1938 900.00 1000.00

HN 1238
☐ Brown base, white nude figure, black robe with gold design, lining of robe is red (1st version), height 7¾", designer L. Harradine. 1927-1938 900.00 1000.00

	Date	Price Range

HN 1708

☐ Light green base, figure has black bathing suit, black shoes, robe of red with black and green shadings, blue lining (1st version), height 7¾", designer L. Harradine.   1935-1938   **1250.00   1450.00**

BASKET WEAVER, The
HN 2245

☐ Seated figure in light green gown with white trim, light colored basket on lap and at side, height 5¾", designer M. Nicoll.   1959-1962   **500.00   600.00**

BEACHCOMBER
HN 2487

☐ Light colored base, barefooted character figure, gray pants, lavender shirt, green scarf, grey hat, holding shell, matt finish, height 6¼", designer M. Nicoll.   1973-1976   **160.00   225.00**

BEAT YOU TO IT
HN 2871

☐ Blue base, light tan wicker chair, brown dog in chair with blue cushions, girl's gown is white with shaded red and yellow sleeves, tiny flower design at hem line, height 6½", designer M. Davies.   1980-   **350.00**

BEDTIME
HN 1978

☐ Small girl in white nightgown on black base, height 5¾", designer L. Harradine.   1945-   **55.00**

BEDTIME STORY, The
HN 2059

☐ Three figures, lady's gown is red, girl's gown is white skirt with blue design, blue bodice, boy dressed in tan trousers, blue jacket, height 4¾", designer L. Harradine.   1950-   **215.00**

	Date	Price Range	

BEGGAR, The

HN 526

☐ A character from "The Beggar's Opera," with blue trousers, red sash and dark gray cloak (1st version), height 6½", designer L. Harradine. . .   1921-1949   600.00   700.00

HN 591

☐ Different glaze finish (1st version), height 6¾", designer L. Harradine. . .   1924-1949   650.00   750.00

HN 2175

☐ Taller version but with brown trousers, red sash and darker gray cloak (2nd version), height 6¾", designer L. Harradine.   1956-1962   550.00   625.00

BELLE, The

HN 754

☐ 18th century style gown of multicolors, trimmed in green, blue bonnet with red ribbons, red shoes, on green and black base, height 6½", designer L. Harradine.   1925-1938   1150.00   1250.00

HN 776

☐ No color detail available, height 6½", designer L. Harradine.   1925-1938   1250.00   1350.00

BELLE

HN 2340

☐ Small female figure in green tiered dress, trimmed in white (2nd version), height 4½", designer M. Davies.   1968-   65.00

BELLE O' THE BALL

HN 1997

☐ Shaded yellow, red, blue gown with red overdress, small hat, holding masking in one hand, seated on couch of brown and light yellow with shaded blue and red, pillow multicolored.   1947-1979   225.00   275.00

BERNICE

HN 2071

☐ Dress is shaded colors of red with red cloak, black hat with blue feather, height 7¾", designer M. Davies.   1951-1953   600.00   700.00

	Date	Price Range	

BESS
HN 2002
☐ White dress with colored flowers, red cloak, height 7¼″, designer L. Harradine. 1947-1969   225.00   275.00

HN 2003
☐ Pink dress with blue cloak with red lining, height 7¼″, designer L. Harradine. 1947-1950   350.00   400.00

BETH (Kate Greenaway)
HN 2870
☐ Small figure on white base, light lavender dress and white apron with green trim, holding single flower, white bonnet with green ribbon, height 5¾″, designer M. Davies. 1980-1983   75.00   100.00

BETSY
HN 2111
☐ Gown of shaded blues and reds, white apron with blue flower design trimmed in green, white cap, height 7″, designer L. Harradine. 1953-1959   325.00   375.00

BETTY
HN 402
☐ Full pink gown with black collar, tall hat of black with gold feather and trim (1st version), height unknown, designer L. Harradine. 1920-1938   2000.00   2250.00

HN 403
☐ Green skirt, blue, yellow and white border (1st version), height unknown, designer L. Harradine. 1920-1938   2000.00   2250.00

HN 435
☐ Blue skirt with yellow spots (1st version), height unknown, designer L. Harradine. 1921-1938   2000.00   2250.00

HN 438
☐ Green skirt (1st version), height unknown, designer L. Harradine. 1921-1938   2000.00   2250.00

HN 477
☐ Spotted green skirt (1st version), height unknown, designer L. Harradine. 1921-1938   2500.00   3000.00

	Date	Price Range	

HN 478
- [ ] White spotted skirt (1st version), height unknown, designer L. Harradine............................ 1921-1938   2500.00   3000.00

HN 1404
- [ ] Small girl with white dog at feet, gown of white with shaded reds trimmed in blue, with tiny blue figure on dress (2nd version), height 4½ ″, designer L. Harradine..................... 1930-1938   500.00   600.00

HN 1405
- [ ] Green dress (2nd version), height 4½ ″, designer L. Harradine......... 1930-1938   500.00   600.00

HN 1435
- [ ] Mottled multicolored dress (2nd version), height 4½ ″, designer L. Harradine............................. 1930-1938   500.00   600.00

HN 1436
- [ ] Patterned green dress (2nd version), height 4½ ″, designer L. Harradine... 1930-1938   500.00   600.00

BIDDY

HN 1445
- [ ] Green tiered gown with blue shawl, blue bonnet, holding a green parasol, height 5½ ″, designer L. Harradine... 1931-1938   300.00   350.00

HN 1500
- [ ] Yellow dress, height 5½ ″, designer L. Harradine..................... 1932-1938   300.00   350.00

HN 1513
- [ ] Shaded gown of red with blue shawl, blue bonnet, holding shaded blue and yellow parasol, height 5½ ″, designer L. Harradine..................... 1932-1951   160.00   225.00

BIDDY PENNY FARTHING

HN 1843
- [ ] Older lady figure in very light blue skirt, lavender bodice with gold design, dark gray shawl with lavender fringe, holding balloon and basket of flowers, height 9″, designer L. Harradine............................ 1938-   175.00

	Date	Price Range	

BILL SYKES
HN 537
☐ A character from Dicken's "Oliver Twist," height 3¾", designer L. Harradine. 1922- 45.00 60.00
☐ **M-54** Made as a miniature, height 4¼", designer L. Harradine. 1932- 20.00 30.00

BLACKSMITH OF WILLIAMSBURG
HN 2240
☐ Blue trousers, black boots with light top, brown apron and cap, white shirt, gray anvil also on white base, height 6¾", designer M. Davies. 1960- 125.00 200.00

BLITHE MORNING
HN 2021
☐ Pink skirt with blue bodice, red shawl, green hat, height 7¼", designer L. Harradine. 1949-1971 150.00 225.00
HN 2065
☐ Red dress, green and yellow shawl, pale colored hat, height 7¼", designer L. Harradine. 1950-1973 200.00 225.00

BLIGHTY
HN 323
☐ Mottled green and brown costume of British soldier, on same colored base, height 11¼", designer E. W. Light. . . . 1918-1938 1250.00 1500.00

BLOSSOM
HN 1667
☐ Seated lady in light green gown with multicolored shawl, small girl standing in between knees of lady, in gown of shaded blue, white collar, basket of multicolored flowers at lady's side. height 6¾", designer L. Harradine. . . 1934-1949 700.00 800.00

BLUE BEARD
HN 75
☐ Costume of white with blue trim, cloak blue with yellow lining (1st version), height unknown, designer E. W. Light. 1917-1938 2550.00 3000.00

Bluebeard,
HN2105,
375.00

HN 410	Date	Price Range	
☐ Blue costume (1st version), height unknown, designer E. W. Light.	1920-1938	3000.00	3500.00
HN 1528			
☐ Red costume with multicolored robe and turban (2nd version), height 11½ ″, designer L. Harradine.	1932-1949	1000.00	1100.00
HN 2105			
☐ Yellow, green and orange costume with dark blue robe (2nd version), height 11 ″, designer L. Harradine. . . .	1953-	375.00	

BLUE BIRD

HN 1280

	Date	Price Range	
☐ Small kneeling white figure on red and cream colored base, holding dark colored bird on one hand, height 4¾ ″, designer L. Harradine.	1928-1938	650.00	750.00

	Date	Price Range

BOATMAN, The

HN 2417

☐ Character figure seated on gray chest, white life preserver at side, black boots, green trousers, yellow slicker, yellow hat, painting on white preserver, height 6½ ", designer M. Nicoll.   1971-   165.00

BON APPETIT

HN 2444

☐ Character figure on green and yellow base which has small bonfire and tan wicker basket on it, brown costume with long blue coat, blue hat, yellow shirt, brown tie, frying fish in black skillet, matt finish, height 6", designer M. Nicoll.   1972-1976   150.00   225.00

BON JOUR

HN 1879

☐ Green tiered gown with white trim, red shawl with black designs, red bonnet with dark ribbons, height 6¾ ", designer L. Harradine.   1938-1949   650.00   750.00

HN 1888

☐ Red gown trimmed in white, shawl red with darker design, black bonnet with green ribbons, height 6¾ ", designer L. Harradine.   1938-1949   600.00   700.00

BONNIE LASSIE

HN 1626

☐ Seated figure in cream colored gown, red shawl with black stripes, hat to match, black shoes, light colored basket of flowers at feet, pail with flowers, height 5¼ ", designer L. Harradine.   1934-1953   250.00   300.00

BO-PEEP

HN 777

☐ Gown of purple with green design, black hat with red ribbon, black staff, black base with small lamb (1st version), height 6¾ ", designer L. Harradine.   1926-1938   1250.00   1350.00

	Date	Price Range	

HN 1202
☐ Skirt is purple with green, pink and black trim (1st version), height 6¾", designer L. Harradine.   1926-1938   **1050.00**   **1200.00**

HN 1327
☐ Flowered multicolored costume (1st version), height 6¾", designer L. Harradine.   1929-1938   **1050.00**   **1200.00**

HN 1328
☐ Cream skirt with black and blue small squares, overlay is red with black designs, bodice is dark with green squares, bonnet light with dark ribbon, staff is brown, base black with small lamb (1st version), height 6¾", designer L. Harradine.   1929-1938   **1050.00**   **1200.00**

HN 1810
☐ White, blue and red shirt, blue overlay, blue bonnet with red ribbon, holding staff in both hands (2nd version), height 5", designer L. Harradine.   1937-1949   **250.00**   **300.00**

HN 1811
☐ Red skirt with dark red overlay, green bonnet with green ribbons, staff light green (2nd version), height 5", designer L. Harradine.   1937-   **100.00**

☐ **M-82** Made as a miniature, red gown, height 4", designer L. Harradine.   1939-1949   **425.00**   **475.00**

☐ **M-83** Gown of blue, height 4", designer L. Harradine.   1939-1949   **400.00**   **450.00**

BOUDOIR

HN 2542
☐ Tall figure in greyest blue with white design gown, height 12¼", designer E. J. Griffiths.   1974-1979   **325.00**   **375.00**

BOUQUET, The

HN 406
☐ No record of coloring, height 9", designer G. Lambert.   1920-1938   **1500.00**   **1700.00**

HN 414
☐ Pink and yellow shawl, height 9", designer G. Lambert.   1920-1938   **1550.00**   **1700.00**

Hn 422
☐ Yellow and pink striped skirt, height 9", designer G. Lambert.   1920-1938   **1550.00**   **1700.00**

	Date	Price Range

HN 428
☐ Blue gown, shawl striped, height 9″, designer G. Lambert.   1921-1938   1550.00 1700.00

HN 429
☐ Multicolored gown, with green designed shawl, colored flowers, height 9″, designer G. Lambert.   1921-1938   1550.00 1700.00

HN 567
☐ Shaded design pink dress with white shawl with designs of red and green, colored flowers, height 9″, designer G. Lambert.   1923-1938   1550.00 1700.00

HN 794
☐ Blue shawl with red and green spots, height 9″, designer G. Lambert.   1926-1938   1550.00 1700.00

BOY FROM WILLIAMSBURG
HN 2183
☐ Dark blue trousers and coat with gold trim, red long vest, white cravat, black hat, holding brown and white object, brown stamp behind figure, height 5½″, designer M. Davies.   1969-1983   75.00 115.00

BOY ON A CROCODILE
HN 373
☐ Small white figure seated on crocodile, height 5″, designer C. J. Noke. . .   1920-1938   4000.00 4500.00

BOY ON PIG
HN 1369
☐ Small white figure seated on multicolored pig, height 4″, designer C. J. Noke.   1930-1938   900.00 1000.00

BOY WITH TURBAN
HN 586
☐ Small seated Arab figure with blue and green costume, height 3¾″, designer L. Harradine.   1923-1938   550.00 650.00

HN 587
☐ Green trousers and red shirt, height 3¾″, designer L. Harradine.   1923-1938   550.00 650.00

HN 661
☐ Blue costume, height 3¾″, designer L. Harradine.   1924-1938   500.00 600.00

	Date	Price Range	

HN 662

☐ Costume of black and white checks, height 3¾", designer L. Harradine. .. 1924-1938 — 500.00 — 600.00

HN 1210

☐ Black and red turban, white pants with large red dots, height 3¾", designer L. Harradine. .... 1926-1938 — 500.00 — 600.00

HN 1212

☐ Blue and green trousers, multicolored turban and shirt, height 3¾", designer L. Harradine. .... 1926-1938 — 550.00 — 650.00

HN 1213

☐ White costume with black squares, height 3¾", designer L. Harradine. .. 1926-1938 — 500.00 — 600.00

HN 1214

☐ White costume with black and green markings, height 3¾", designer L. Harradine. .... 1926-1938 — 500.00 — 650.00

HN 1225

☐ Yellow trousers with blue spots, height 3¾", designer L. Harradine. .. 1927-1938 — 500.00 — 650.00

BRIDE

HN 1588

☐ White bridal gown and veil, holding lilies in arm (1st version), height 8¾", designer L. Harradine. .... 1933-1938 — 750.00 — 850.00

HN 1600

☐ Flowers are roses (1st version), height 8¾", designer L. Harradine. .... 1933-1949 — 650.00 — 750.00

HN 1762

☐ Cream dress (1st version), height 8¾", designer L. Harradine. .... 1936-1949 — 700.00 — 800.00

HN 1841

☐ Blue dress (1st version), height 9½", designer L. Harradine. .... 1938-1949 — 800.00 — 900.00

HN 2166

☐ Full bridal gown, holding flower bouquet in hand (2nd version), height 8", designer M. Davies. .... 1956-1976 — 175.00 — 225.00

HN 2873

☐ Empire style gown of white trimmed in gold, holding single flower (4th version), height 8", designer M. Davies. . 1980- — 170.00

	Date	Price Range	

BRIDESMAID, The LITTLE

HN 1433

☐ Multicolored tiered gown, holding bouquet with green ribbon, flowered band in hair (1st version), height 5¼", designer L. Harradine. 1930-1951   175.00   225.00

HN 1434

☐ Green and yellow gown, blue band in hair (1st version), height 5", designer L. Harradine. 1930-1949   225.00   275.00

HN 1530

☐ Yellow and green dress, height 5", designer L. Harradine. 1932-1938   200.00   250.00

☐ **M 11** Made as a miniature, pink and lilac dress, height 3¾", designer L. Harradine. 1932-1938   325.00   375.00

☐ **M 12** Multicolored gown, height 3¾", designer L. Harradine. 1932-1945   200.00   275.00

☐ **M 30** Red and lavender gown, height 3¾", designer L. Harradine. 1932-1945   200.00   275.00

HN 2148

☐ Off white full gown with blue sash, holding flowers in right arm (2nd version), height 5½", designer M. Davies. 1955-1959   175.00   225.00

HN 2196

☐ Full skirted light blue gown with raised design of white, small red ribbons on white collar, small brimmed head piece, holding small flowers in hand (3rd version), height 5¼", designer M. Davies. 1960-1976   100.00   125.00

HN 2874

☐ White gown and cap trimmed in gold, holding very small bouquet in hand (4th version), height 5¼", designer M. Davies. 1980-   100.00

BRIDGET

HN 2070

☐ Older lady, green dress with yellow design, orange shawl and hand bag, black hat with red ribbon, height 8¾", designer M. Davies. 1951-1973   250.00   325.00

BROKEN LANCE, The	Date	Price Range	

HN 2041

☐ Green base with design, horse is white with blue cloth cover that has darker blue and yellow designs, red lining, gray suit of armor, red and dark blue headdress, red and gold shield, brown and light red lance, height 8¾″, designer M. Davies. 1949-1975 500.00 600.00

Broken Lance,
HN2041,
500.00 – 600.00

BUDDIES
HN 2546

☐ Black and green base, seated boy in brown shorts, blue shirt, brown and black dog, matt finish, height 6″, designer E. J. Griffiths. 1973-1976 200.00 250.00

	Date	Price Range

BUMBLE
Issued only as a miniature

☐ **M 76** Red vest, black pants, green cape with yellow trim, black tri-cornered hat with yellow trim, black stand, height 4″, designer L. Harradine. 1939-1982   29.95

BUNNY
HN 2214

☐ Small girl, green and pink gown, holding bunny, height 5″, designer M. Davies. 1960-1975   125.00   175.00

BUTTERCUP
HN 2309

☐ Gown of shaded yellow, green bodice, hand on green hat, height 7″, designer M. Davies. 1964-   145.00

HN 2399

☐ Gown and hat scarlet, sleeves and bow of gown lemon yellow, height 7½″, designer M. Davies 1983-   145.00

BUTTERFLY
HN 719

☐ Butterfly costumed figure on black pedestal type base, wings are multicolored, pink and black dress, height 6½″, designer L. Harradine. 1925-1938   900.00   1050.00

HN 720

☐ Red wings, white dress with black checks, height 6½″, designer L. Harradine. 1925-1938   900.00   1050.00

HN 730

☐ Yellow dress, blue and black wings, height 6½″, designer L. Harradine. . . 1925-1938   1000.00   1100.00

HN 1203

☐ Gold wings, height 6½″, designer L. Harradine. 1926-1938   1100.00   1250.00

HN 1456

☐ Wings in shades of lavender and pink, dress shades of green, height 6½″, designer L. Harradine. 1931-1938   1000.00   1100.00

Butterfly,
HN720,
900.00 – 1050.00

	Date	Price Range	
BUZ FUZ			
HN 538			
☐ A character from Dicken's "Pickwick Papers," height 3¾", designer L. Harradine.	1922-	45.00	60.00
☐ **M 53** Renumbered as a miniature, height 4", designer L. Harradine.	1932-1983	20.00	30.00
'CALLED LOVE, A LITTLE BOY . . .'			
HN 1545			
☐ Small naked child crouching on base, holding red and blue bucket, height 3½", designer unknown.	1933-1949	325.00	375.00
CALUMET			
HN 1428			
☐ Base is multicolored striped blanket, Indian costume is light brown, robe is stripes of green, yellow, red and tan, bowl on base has red and green stripe, height 6", designer C. J. Noke.	1930-1949	1000.00	1100.00

	Date	Price Range	

HN 1689

☐ Base is green blanket with patch of blue, red and green, Indian costume is darker brown, robe is green with yellow, blue bowl, height 6½", designer C. J. Noke.   1935-1949   800.00   900.00

HN 2068

☐ HN 1689 with minor glaze differences, height 6¼", designer C. J. Noke.   1950-1953   625.00   725.00

CAMELLIA

HN 2222

☐ Pink gown with very light blue scarf and bow in hair, height 7¾", designer M. Davies.   1960-1971   200.00   275.00

CAMILLA

HN 1710

☐ 18th century style gown of red and white with red lines, dark hair with green bow, on light colored base, height 7", designer L. Harradine.   1935-1949   700.00   800.00

HN 1711

☐ Light hair, light red gown with darker red design, green overdress with white designs, height 7", designer L. Harradine.   1935-1949   700.00   800.00

CAMILLE

HN 1586

☐ 18th century style gown of very light red with overdress of darker red, black hat with light red trim, holding mirror, height 6½", designer L. Harradine.   1933-1949   650.00   700.00

HN 1648

☐ Light red gown with overdress of cream skirt with red flower design, green bodice with red bows, green hat with red trim, height 6½", designer L. Harradine.   1934-1949   600.00   675.00

HN 1736

☐ Red and white costume, height 6½", designer L. Harradine.   1935-1949   700.00   800.00

	Date	Price Range	
CAPTAIN			

HN 778

☐ Black pedestal style base, red long coat with gold trim, white trousers and long vest with gold buttons, black boots, black hat with white and gold trim, white cravat, black strap holding sword (1st version), height 7″, designer L. Harradine.   1926-1938   1250.00   1400.00

HN 2260

☐ White trousers and stockings, black shoes with gold trim, black coat and hat with white and gold trim, hand on map lies on brown stand, book and paper on bottom of stand (2nd version), height 9½″, designer M. Nicoll.   1965-1982   ⁻ 175.00   225.00

CAPTAIN COOK

HN 2889

☐ Navy uniform of white trousers, black coat with yellow trim and white buttons, seated on stool with base of light brown, maps in drawer on base, map on lap, black bag leaning against yellow pedestal, height 8″, designer W. K. Harper.   1980-   365.00

CAPTAIN CUTTLE
Issued only as a miniature

☐ **M 77** Yellow vest, light yellow pants, red tie, black coat, light brown hat with black band, black stand, height 4″, designer L. Harradine.   1939-   29.95

CAPTAIN MAC HEATH

HN 464

☐ A character of "The Beggar's Opera," red coated figure on black material, height 7″, designer L. Harradine.   1921-1949   750.00   850.00

HN 590

☐ Yellow cravat only difference, height 7″, designer L. Harradine.   1924-1949   750.00   850.00

HN 1256

☐ Earthenware, height 7″, designer L. Harradine.   1927-1949   700.00   800.00

	Date	Price Range

CARMEN

HN 1267

☐ Dark haired figure with red dress, red and black shawl, red shoes, on base, holding tambourine (1st version), height 7″, designer L. Harradine. 1928-1938   600.00   725.00

HN 1300

☐ Blue and yellow gown, green shoes, green base (1st version), height 7″, designer L..Harradine. 1928-1938   750.00   850.00

HN 2545

☐ Tall figure with black hair, blue and black gown, light blue bodice (2nd version), height 11½″, designer E. J. Griffiths 1974-1979   200.00   250.00

CARNIVAL

HN 1260

☐ Half nude figure with pink tights on black base, height 8¼″, designer L. Harradine. 1927-1938   1500.00   1650.00

HN 1278

☐ Half nude figure with blue tights, black and gold waist band, holding long cloth behind head which is yellow and purple, on black base, height 8½″, designer L. Harradine. 1928-1938   1400.00   1550.00

CAROLYN

HN 2112

☐ White gown with flowers, green cummerbund and gloves, holding black hat and white handkerchief, height 7″, designer L. Harradine. 1953-1959   350.00   400.00

HN 2974

☐ Two tone green gown, frilled white cuffs and trim. Low neckline accented by yellow rose, (2nd version), height 5½″, designer A. Hughes. 1983-   155.00

CARPET SELLER, The

HN 1464

☐ Blue robed figure with black and multicolored rug on black base, hand open, height 9″, designer L. Harradine. 1931-1969   300.00   375.00

	Date	Price Range	

HN 1464A
☐ Same figure with same coloring except hand closed, height 9¼", designer L. Harradine. . . . . | 1931-? | 275.00 | 350.00

CARPET VENDOR, The
HN 38
☐ Kneeling figure on green base, holding one end of unrolled blue striped carpet, costume of blue trousers, yellow and red shirt trimmed in white, dark blue and red turban (1st version), height unknown, designer C. J. Noke. | 1914-1938 | 2750.00 | 3000.00

HN 38A
☐ Persian style carpet (1st version), height unknown, designer C. J. Noke. | 1914-1938 | 2750.00 | 3000.00

HN 76
☐ Kneeling figure on blue and black checked cushion, blue costume with orange trim, turban green, orange rug in front of figure (2nd version), height 5½", designer C. J. Noke. . . . . | 1917-1938 | 3000.00 | 3500.00

HN 348
☐ Blue and green costume with checkered base (1st version), height unknown, designer C. J. Noke. . . . . . . | 1919-1938 | 1750.00 | 2000.00

HN 350
☐ Blue costume, green and brown floral carpet (1st version), height 5½", designer C. J. Noke. . . . . | 1919-1938 | 3000.00 | 3500.00

CARRIE (Kate Greenaway)
HN 2800
☐ Small girl with blue coat, white hat with blue and red ribbons, holding single flower in one hand, on white base, height 6", designer M. Davies. . | 1976-1981 | 65.00 | 100.00

CASSIM
HN 1231
☐ Small seated Arab figure, with blue trousers, multicolored vest and blue cone shaped hat (1st version), height 3", designer L. Harradine. . . . . | 1927-1938 | 550.00 | 600.00

	Date	Price Range	

HN 1232
☐ White and orange striped trousers, dark colored vest with red hat (1st version), height 3″, designer L. Harradine.   1927-1938   550.00   600.00

HN 1311
☐ HN 1231 mounted on lidded pink bowl (2nd version), height 3¾″, designer L. Harradine.   1929-1938   700.00   800.00

HN 1312
☐ Mounted on blue bowl (2nd version), height 3¾″, designer L. Harradine. . .   1929-1938   700.00   800.00

CAVALIER

HN 369
☐ Blue trousers, white stockings, black shoes with blue bows, dark blue coat, light green waistcoat with white collar, yellow feather on hat, base (1st version), height unknown, designer unknown.   1920-1938   2100.00   2400.00

HN 2716
☐ Black trousers, boots, vest and hat, white shirt, dark cape with red lining (2nd version), height 9¾″, designer E. J. Griffiths.   1976-1982   200.00

CELESTE

HN 2237
☐ Gown of shaded greens with dark ribbon at waist, sleeves and shoulder, height 6¾″, designer M. Davies   1959-1971   200.00   250.00

CELIA

HN 1726
☐ Tall figure with pale pink night gown, height 11½″, designer L. Harradine. .   1935-1949   750.00   850.00

HN 1727
☐ Pale green night gown, height 11½″, designer L. Harradine.   1935-1949   750.00   850.00

CELLIST, The

HN 2226
☐ Black suit, white shirt, black bow tie, playing brown cello seated on brown stool, blue and purple books under cello, height 8″, designer M. Davies. .   1960-1967   450.00   500.00

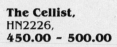

The Cellist,
HN2226,
450.00 - 500.00

	Date	Price Range	
CENTURION, The			
HN 2726			
☐ Depicts a warrior perhaps from the old Roman Empire in his armor, sword in hand and shield of light and dark brown standing at his feet. Figure on gray base, height 9½ ", designer W. K. Harper.	1982-	250.00	
CERISE			
HN 1607			
☐ Small figure in light red figured gown with darker sash, holding fruit basket, height 5¼ ", designer L. Harradine. . .	1933-1949	300.00	375.00
CHARLOTTE			
HN 2421			
☐ Purple gown with gold design at hem line, holding small light tan dog, seated on yellow chair, height 6½ ", designer J. Bromley.	1972-	185.00	

CHARMIAN	Date	Price Range	
HN 1568			
☐ White gown with shaded red over-dress, holding small dark fan, height 6½″, designer L. Harradine.	1933-1938	**650.00**	**750.00**
HN 1569			
☐ Green gown with red and blue over-dress, height 6½″, designer L. Harradine.	1933-1938	**650.00**	**750.00**
HN 1651			
☐ Red bodice, green skirt, height 6½″, designer L. Harradine.	1934-1938	**800.00**	**900.00**

CHARLEY'S AUNT

	Date	Price Range	
HN 35			
☐ Black and white gowned figure on base which has the inscription 'W. S. Penley as Charley's Aunt' (1st version), height 7″, designer A. Toft.	1914-1938	**700.00**	**800.00**
HN 640			
☐ Green dress, mauve spotted (1st version), height 7″, designer A. Toft.	1924-1938	**900.00**	**1000.00**
HN 1411			
☐ Seated figure with dark dress and white lace shawl (2nd version), height 8″, designer H. Fenton.	1930-1938	**1375.00**	**1425.00**
HN 1554			
☐ Purple dress (2nd version), height 8″, designer H. Fenton.	1933-1938	**1200.00**	**1350.00**
HN 1703			
☐ Not mounted on base, lilac and white dress with dark ribbons on bonnet (3rd version), height 6″, designer A. Toft.	1935-1938	**800.00**	**900.00**

CHELSEA PAIR (Female)

	Date	Price Range	
HN 577			
☐ 18th century styled figure seated on tree on green base, white gown with blue flower design, red bonnet with blue ribbons, height 6″, designer L. Harradine.	1923-1938	**700.00**	**800.00**
HN 578			
☐ Red blouse, height 6″, designer L. Harradine.	1923-1938	**700.00**	**800.00**

	Date	Price Range	
CHELSEA PAIR (Male)			

HN 579

☐ 18th century style figure seated on tree, reddish-brown coat, black trousers, black hat, green base, height 6″, designer L. Harradine.   1923-1938   725.00   800.00

HN 580

☐ Blue flowers instead of white, height 6″, designer L. Harradine.   1923-1938   725.00   800.00

CHELSEA PENSIONER

HN 689

☐ Red coated seated figure with black trousers, hat, cane and pipe on brown base, height 5¾″, designer L. Harradine.   1924-1938   1250.00   1400.00

CHERIE

HN 2341

☐ Small figure wearing blue gown with white cuffs holding yellow gloves in hands, blue hat with light blue feather and yellow ribbon bow, height 5½″, designer M. Davies.   1966-   100.00

CHIEF, The

HN 2892

☐ Seated figure on green and brown base, light brown costume with blue trim on front, green cloth with design of red, blue and orange on lap, blue, black and white feathered headdress, band of blue with yellow design, mocassins of white tops with brown and blue design, brown peace pipe in hands, height 7″, designer W. K. Harper.   1979-   200.00

CHILD FROM WILLIAMSBURG

HN 2154

☐ Small girl figure in blue gown, holding flower, height 5¾″, designer M. Davies   1964-1983   75.00   115.00

CHILD AND CRAB

HN 32

☐ Green and brown crab, child wears pale blue robe, height 5¼″, designer C. J. Noke.   1913-1938   1750.00   2000.00

	Date	Price Range	

CHILD'S GRACE, A

HN 62

☐ HN 62A except there is additional black patterning over the green coat, height 6¾", designer L. Perugini..... 1916-1938   **1400.00 1600.00**

HN 62A

☐ Small girl figure with hands clasped on pedestal which contains printed poem, green dress with orange underlay, height 6¾", designer L. Perugini. 1916-1938   **1500.00 1700.00**

HN 510

☐ Checkered dress, green base, height 6¾", designer L. Perugini. 1921-1938   **1650.00 1800.00**

CHILD STUDY

HN 603A

☐ White child's nude figure seated on rock with base which has flowers, height 4¾", designer L. Harradine. .. 1924-1938   **275.00 325.00**

HN 603B

☐ Kingcup flowers around base, height 4¾", designer L. Harradine. 1924-1938   **300.00 350.00**

HN 604A

☐ HN 604B except primroses around base are primroses, height 5¾", designer L. Harradine. 1924-1938   **300.00 350.00**

HN 604B

☐ White nude lady figure kneeling on pedestal which is on a base with flowers, height 5¾", designer L. Harradine. 1924-1938   **300.00 350.00**

HN 605A

☐ Standing white nude child's figure on pedestal and base covered with flowers, height 5¾", designer L. Harradine. 1924-1938   **300.00 350.00**

HN 605B

☐ Different flowers, height 5¾", designer L. Harradine. 1924-1938   **300.00 350.00**

HN 606A

☐ White nude child's figure standing on rock bending over to look at flowers on base, height 5", designer L. Harradine. 1924-1938   **300.00 350.00**

HN 606B

☐ Kingcups on base, height 5", designer L. Harradine. 1924-1938   **300.00 350.00**

	Date	Price Range	

HN 1441

☐ Seated white nude child's figure with blonde hair, multicolored rock, with applied flowers on base, height 5″, designer L. Harradine. 1931-1938   350.00   400.00

HN 1442

☐ Standing white nude child's figure with blonde hair, multicolored rock, with applied flowers on base, height 6¼″, designer L. Harradine. 1931-1938   350.00   400.00

HN 1443

☐ Figure 1540, with applied flowers on base, height 5″, designer L. Harradine. 1931-1938   350.00   400.00

CHINA REPAIRER, The

HN 2943

☐ Man seated at his work bench working on a broken horse. Gray hair, blue shirt, white apron, height 6¾″, designer R. Tabbenor. 1983-   185.00

The China Repairer,
HN2943,
185.00

	Date	Price Range	

CHLOE
HN 1470
☐ Red and cream tiered gown, blue bonnet with ribbons, height 5¾", designer L. Harradine. 1931-1949 275.00 325.00
☐ **M 29** Made as a miniature, height 3", designer L. Harradine. 1932-1945 250.00 300.00

HN 1476
☐ Blue gown with pink bonnet with ribbons, height 5¾", designer L. Harradine. 1931-1938 275.00 325.00

HN 1479
☐ Blue gown with red bonnet and ribbons, height 5¾", designer L. Harradine. 1931-1949 250.00 300.00

HN 1498
☐ Yellow and green, height 5¾", designer L. Harradine. 1932-1938 300.00 350.00

HN 1765
☐ Blue gown with blue ribbon on bonnet, height 6", designer L. Harradine. 1936-1950 250.00 300.00
☐ **M 10** Made as a miniature, height 3", designer L. Harradine. 1932-1945 250.00 300.00

HN 1956
☐ HN 1470 except red skirt and green ribbon, height 6", designer L. Harradine. 1940-1949 400.00 450.00
☐ **M 9** Made as a miniature, height 3", designer L. Harradine. 1932-1945 250.00 300.00

CHOICE, The
HN 1959
☐ Red gowned lady trying on bonnet, with box at foot, height 7", designer L. Harradine. 1941-1949 850.00 950.00

HN 1960
☐ Red and blue gown, height 7", designer L. Harradine. 1941-1949 850.00 950.00

CHOIR BOY
HN 2141
☐ Red and white choir robe, height 4⅞", designer M. Davies. 1954-1975 75.00 125.00

CHORUS GIRL
HN 1401
☐ Red, yellow and black costume, figure on pedestal, height and designer unknown. 1930-1938 1650.00 1800.00

	Date	Price Range	

CHRISTINE
HN 1839
☐ Lilac tiered dress with blue shawl, bonnet trimmed with flowers (1st version), height 7¾", designer L. Harradine. 1938-1949   650.00   750.00

HN 1840
☐ Red dress with blue figured shawl (1st version), height 7¾", designer L. Harradine. 1938-1949   650.00   750.00

HN 2792
☐ Light cream gown with shades of very light red and yellow, with multicolored flowers over skirt (2nd version), height 7⅞", designer M. Davies.   1978-   250.00

CHRISTMAS MORN
HN 1992
☐ Red coat with jacket trimmed in white fur, with muff, height 7¼", designer M. Davies. 1947-   155.00

CHRISTMAS PARCELS
HN 2851
☐ Dark green cloak with yellow trim, figure holding one Christmas parcel of purple and red, many parcels around foot, small basket, green Christmas tree, height 8⅝", designer W. K. Harper. 1978-1982   165.00   200.00

CHRISTMAS TIME
HN 2110
☐ Red cloak trimmed with white around bottom, holding small parcels in hand, black bonnet, height 6⅞", designer M. Davies. 1953-1967   350.00   400.00

CICELY
HN 1516
☐ Light blue skirt with darker blue jacket figure seated on small couch, height 5½", designer L. Harradine. . . 1932-1949   1100.00   1200.00

	Date	Price Range	
CIRCE			
HN 1249			
☐ White nude figure of woman on base, with multicolored robe hanging from one arm, height 7½ ", designer L. Harradine.	1927-1938	1200.00	1400.00
HN 1250			
☐ Orange and black robe, height 7½ ", designer L. Harradine.	1927-1938	1200.00	1400.00
HN 1254			
☐ Orange and red robe, height 7½ ", designer L. Harradine.	1927-1938	1200.00	1400.00
HN 1255			
☐ Blue robe, height 7½ ", designer L. Harradine.	1927-1938	1200.00	1400.00
CISSIE			
HN 1808			
☐ Small figure with green dress, holding basket of flowers on arm, height 5", designer L. Harradine.	1937-1951	225.00	275.00
HN 1809			
☐ Shaded red dress with blue bonnet and green ribbons, height 5", designer L. Harradine.	1937-	100.00	
CLARE			
HN 2793			
☐ Shaded blue gown with multicolored flower design, yellow shawl and bonnet with red ribbon, height 7½ ", designer M. Davies.	1980-	250.00	
CLARIBEL			
HN 1950			
☐ Small figure with blue skirt, white cap with green ribbon, height 4¾ ", designer L. Harradine.	1940-1949	350.00	400.00
HN 1951			
☐ Red and shaded blue dress, blue ribbon on cap, height 4¾ ", designer L. Harradine.	1940-1949	325.00	375.00

	Date	Price Range	

CLARINDA
HN 2724
☐ Blue and green gown with light blue designs, darker blue and green overdress, figure on green base with blue and white bird on green pedestal at side, height 8½", designer W. K. Harper. 1975-1980   175.00   225.00

CLARISSA
HN 1525
☐ Green gown with red shawl, holding open parasol (1st version), height 10", designer L. Harradine. 1932-1938   625.00   700.00

HN 1687
☐ Pale blue gown, green shawl (1st version), height 10", designer L. Harradine. 1935-1949   675.00   750.00

HN 2345
☐ Green gown with white sleeves, figure holding basket with two hands (2nd version), height 8", designer M. Davies. 1968-1981   125.00   175.00

CLEMENCY
HN 1633
☐ White, two tiered dress with flower design, blue jacket, green bonnet with red ribbons, height 7", designer L. Harradine. 1934-1938   650.00   750.00

HN 1634
☐ White dress trimmed in red, multicolored jacket, height 7", designer L. Harradine. 1934-1949   650.00   750.00

HN 1643
☐ White gown trimmed in green, red jacket, height 7", designer L. Harradine. 1934-1938   650.00   750.00

CLOCKMAKER, The
HN 2279
☐ Character figure in green coat, green shirt, ligher green apron, blue shirt, brown tie, black shoes, looking at clock piece, clock is brown and green setting on dark stand, height 7¼", designer M. Nicoll. 1961-1975   300.00   350.00

	Date	Price Range	
CLOTHILDE			

HN 1598
☐ Pale pink gown with red robe, height 7¼ ", designer L. Harradine. 1933-1949 550.00 650.00

HN 1599
☐ Pale blue gown with multi-flowered top and sleeves with blue robe with red lining, height 7¼ ", designer L. Harradine. 1933-1949 550.00 650.00

CLOUD, The

HN 1831
☐ Flowing white robed figure with long golden hair, height 23", designer R. Garbe. 1937-1949 4000.00 4500.00

CLOWN, The

HN 2890
☐ Clown on brown and yellow base, blue trousers, gold coat, spotted yellow tie, dark hat with flower, gray bucket also on base, height 8¾ ", designer W. K. Harper. 1979- 295.00

COACHMAN, The

HN 2282
☐ Character figure seated in brown chair, long purple coat, green coat and trousers, purple coat has blue lining, black tall hat with green trim, holding blue tankard, height 7", designer M. Nicoll. 1963-1971 475.00 550.00

COBBLER, The

HN 542
☐ Green costumed, round turban, seated on brown base (1st version), height 7½ ", designer C. J. Noke. 1922-1939 1100.00 1200.00

HN 543
☐ Specially fired (1st version), height 7½ ", designer C. J. Noke. 1922-1938 1200.00 1300.00

HN 681
☐ Larger figure on black base, with green costume, red shirt and cone shaped turban (2nd version), height 8½ ", designer C. J. Noke. 1924-1938 600.00 700.00

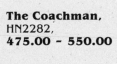

The Coachman,
HN2282,
475.00 - 550.00

	Date	Price Range	
HN 682			
☐ Red shirt with green robe (1st version), height 7½″, designer C. J. Noke.	1924-1938	700.00	800.00
HN 1251			
☐ Black trousers and red shirt, height 8½″, designer C. J. Noke.	1927-1938	600.00	700.00
HN 1283			
☐ Green costume with yellow and red shirt (2nd version), height 8½″, designer C. J. Noke.	1928-1949	600.00	700.00
HN 1705			
☐ Multicolored costume with blue shirt on colored base (3rd version), height 8″, designer C. J. Noke.	1935-1949	550.00	600.00
HN 1706			
☐ Brown costume with green striped shirt (3rd version), height 8″, designer C. J. Noke.	1935-1969	275.00	325.00

COLLINETTE	Date	Price Range	
HN 1998			
☐ White gown with long blue cloak, height 7¼ ", designer L. Harradine. ..	1947-1969	450.00	500.00
HN 1999			
☐ Red cloak, height 7¼ ", designer L. Harradine....................	1947-1949	425.00	475.00

COLUMBINE

HN 1296			
☐ A tutu style costume on figure seated on cream colored pedestal, red and blue striped costume (1st version), height 6", designer L. Harradine.	1928-1938	700.00	800.00
HN 1297			
☐ Costume not striped, white base (1st version), height 6", designer L. Harradine..........................	1928-1938	700.00	800.00
HN 1439			
☐ Costume multicolored floral design, light green base (1st version), height 6", designer L. Harradine.	1930-1938	700.00	800.00
HN 2185			
☐ Standing figure on white base, light pink dress with blue design, small crown on head, holding tambourine (2nd version), height 7", designer M. Davies............................	1957-1969	225.00	275.00

COMING OF SPRING, The

HN 1722			
☐ Pink costume on barefoot figure, flower ringed base, holding light colored robe above head, height 12½ ", designer L. Harradine.	1935-1949	1250.00	1400.00
HN 1723			
☐ Light green costume, height 12½ ", designer L. Harradine.	1935-1949	1250.00	1400.00

CONSTANCE

HN 1510			
☐ Purple and yellow four tiered gown, holding small purse, height unknown, designer L. Harradine.	1932-1938	1500.00	1700.00
HN 1511			
☐ Pale pink gown, holding red handbag, height unknown, designer L. Harradine............................	1932-1938	1500.00	1700.00

	Date	Price Range	

CONTENTMENT

HN 395

☐ Woman seated in chair with small child in arms, yellow skirt with pink stripes, blue patterned blouse, height 7¼", designer L. Harradine. 1920-1938 **1850.00 2000.00**

HN 396

☐ Yellow and pink striped chair, height 7¼", designer L. Harradine. 1920-1938 **1850.00 2000.00**

HN 421

☐ Gown of light blue patterned with darker blue, light yellow blouse with colored circle pattern, height 7¼", designer L. Harradine. 1920-1938 **1500.00 1700.00**

HN 468

☐ Green spotted dress, height 7¼", designer L. Harradine. 1921-1938 **1750.00 2000.00**

HN 572

☐ Spotted cream skirt with spotted pink blouse, height 7¼", designer L. Harradine. 1923-1938 **1750.00 2000.00**

HN 685

☐ Black and white floral dress, height 7¼", designer L. Harradine. 1923-1938 **1900.00 2000.00**

HN 686

☐ Black and white striped chair, height 7¼", designer L. Harradine. 1924-1938 **1900.00 2000.00**

HN 1323

☐ Shades of blue and red skirt, with red blouse, blue chair, height 7¼", designer L. Harradine. 1929-1938 **1550.00 1700.00**

COOKIE

HN 2218

☐ Small figure, red dress, white apron, holding a small object in each hand, height 4¾", designer M. Davies. 1958-1975 **125.00 175.00**

COPPELIA

HN 2115

☐ Ballet figure, red, blue, white costume, standing on toes on base that has books on it, height 7¼", designer M. Davies. 1953-1959 **600.00 700.00**

COQUETTE, The

HN 20

	Date	Price Range	
☐ Red haired, bare footed figure on base, green gown, holding fan, height 9¼″, designer W. White.	1913-1938	2500.00	3000.00

HN 37

☐ Green costume with flower sprays, height 9¼″, designer W. White.	1914-1938	2500.00	3000.00

CORALIE

HN 2307

☐ Yellow gown with white and brown dots under gown and cuffs, height 7⅛″, designer M. Davies.	1964-	155.00

**Coralie,
HN2307,
155.00**

	Date	Price Range

CORINTHIAN, The

HN 1973

☐ Male figure on base, cream trousers, blue coat, white vest with multicolored design, black cloak with red lining, black hat, holding cane, height 7¾", designer H. Fenton.   1941-1949   950.00   1050.00

COUNTRY LASS

HN 1991

☐ Figure on base, blue dress, white apron, white kerchief on head, goose in arm, basket on the other arm, brown shawl. Also see Market Day, height 7⅜", designer L. Harradine. . . .   1975-1981   125.00   175.00

COURTIER, The

HN 1338

☐ Male figure seated in red and gold chair on base, red and white costume, black base, height 4½", designer L. Harradine.   1929-1938   1200.00   1350.00

COURT SHOEMAKER, The

HN 1755

☐ Two figures, 18th century style, costume of man is red, woman's gown is shaded blue, trying on red shoes, height 6¾", designer L. Harradine. . .   1936-1949   1500.00   1700.00

COVENT GARDEN

HN 1339

☐ Figure wearing green dress with shaded red and blue apron, green hat, holding basket on head and carrying basket in other hand, height 9", designer L. Harradine.   1929-1938   1000.00   1200.00

CRADLE SONG

HN 2246

☐ Seated lady rocking cradle, green dress, dark hair, baby in brown cradle, height 5½", designer M. Davies.   1959-1962   400.00   450.00

	Date	Price Range	
CRAFTSMAN, The			

HN 2284

☐ Character figure on one knee, in blue shirt, tan apron, black shoes, white stockings, tools in pocket, working on brown and cream colored chair, height 6", designer M. Nicoll. 1961-1965 475.00 525.00

CRINOLINE, The

HN 8

☐ Figure is wearing a wide hooped gown of shaded blue, flowers at neck and in hand, height 6¼", designer G. Lambert. 1913-1938 1300.00 1450.00

HN 9

☐ Pale green skirt with flower sprays, height 6¼", designer G. Lambert. . . . 1913-1938 1300.00 1450.00

HN 9A

☐ No flower sprays on skirt, height 6¼", designer G. Lambert. 1913-1938 1300.00 1450.00

HN 21

☐ Yellow skirt with rosebuds, height 6¼", designer G. Lambert. 1913-1938 1300.00 1450.00

HN 21A

☐ No rosebuds on skirt, height 6¼", designer G. Lambert. 1913-1938 1250.00 1400.00

HN 413

☐ Cream skirt with blue trim, blue ribbons on flowers, height 6¼", designer G. Lambert. 1920-1938 1700.00 1950.00

HN 566

☐ Cream skirt with green spots, green blouse, height 6¼", designer G. Lambert. 1923-1938 1250.00 1400.00

HN 628

☐ Bodice of yellow and blue checks, height 6¼", designer G. Lambert. . . . 1924-1938 1350.00 1500.00

CRINOLINE LADY (Miniature)

HN 650

☐ Small 18th century style figure with wide hooped gown, white with red rosebuds trim, light green overlay, green bodice, height 3", designer unknown. 1924-1938 550.00 650.00

HN 651

☐ White gown with orange trim and green design, black bodice, height 3", designer unknown. 1924-1938 550.00 650.00

	Date	Price Range	

HN 652
☐ Purple dress, height 3", designer unknown 1924-1938   550.00   650.00

HN 653
☐ Gray and white striped dress, height 3", designer unknown. 1924-1938   550.00   650.00

HN 654
☐ Orange and green mottled dress, height 3", designer unknown. 1924-1938   550.00   650.00

HN 655
☐ Blue dress, height 3", designer unknown......................... 1924-1938   550.00   650.00

CROUCHING NUDE

HN 457
☐ Crouching white figure on green base, height 5½", designer unknown. 1921-1938   1100.00   1300.00

CUP OF TEA, The

HN 2322
☐ Older lady figure seated in chair, feet on stool holding cup and saucer, black dress, gray sweater, height 7½", designer M. Nicoll. 1964-1983   115.00   150.00

CURLY LOCKS

HN 2049
☐ Small female figure seated on base, red dress with blue designs, golden curly locks, height 4½", designer M. Davies. 1949-1953   250.00   300.00

CURLY KNOB

HN 1627
☐ Seated figure on box style base holding baby in arms, blue costume with red and blue striped shawl, basket of flowers in front of figure, height 6¼", designer L. Harradine. 1934-1938   525.00   575.00

CURTSEY, The

HN 57
☐ Figure making curtsy, orange lustre dress, height 11", designer E. W. Light. 1916-1938   1500.00   1750.00

	Date	Price Range
HN 57B		
☐ Lilac dress, height 11″, designer E. W. Light.	1916-1938	1500.00 1750.00
HN 66A		
☐ Lilac dress, this could possibly be renumbered version of 57B, height 11″, designer E. W. Light.	1916-1938	1550.00 1700.00
HN 327		
☐ Dark blue dress, height 11″, designer E. W. Light.	1918-1938	1550.00 1700.00
HN 334		
☐ Lilac dress with brown design and green trim, height 11″, designer E. W. Light.	1918-1938	1450.00 1600.00
HN 363		
☐ Lilac and peach costume, height 11″, designer E. W. Light.	1919-1938	1600.00 1700.00
HN 371		
☐ Yellow dress, height 11″, designer E. W. Light.	1920-1938	1650.00 1800.00
HN 518		
☐ Lilac skirt with orange spots, height 11″, designer E. W. Light.	1921-1938	1650.00 1800.00
HN 547		
☐ Blue bodice, green and yellow skirt, height 11″, designer E. W. Light.	1922-1938	1450.00 1600.00
HN 629		
☐ Green dress with black trimmings, height 11″, designer E. W. Light.	1924-1938	1650.00 1800.00
HN 670		
☐ Pink and yellow spotted dress, height 11″, designer E. W. Light.	1924-1938	1450.00 1600.00

CYNTHIA

	Date	Price Range
HN 1685		
☐ Seated figure with pink and blue gown, holding flowers, height 5¾″, designer L. Harradine.	1935-1949	500.00 600.00
HN 1686		
☐ Red gown with multicolored cloak, green ribbons on bonnet, height 5¾″, designer L. Harradine.	1935-1949	500.00 600.00

	Date	Price Range	

HN 2440
☐ Dressed in swirling gown of green and white, dark haired figure with her head held high and her hands lifting her gown as if she were ready to dance, height unknown, designer M. Davies............................. 1984- **125.00**

DAFFY DOWN DILLY

HN 1712
☐ Green gown and bonnet, height 8″, designer L. Harradine.............. 1935-1975 **225.00 300.00**

HN 1713
☐ Shaded blue gown with white apron, bonnet with red trim, holding flat baskets of flowers under each arm, height 8″, designer L. Harradine. 1935-1949 **425.00 500.00**

DAINTY MAY

HN 1639
☐ 18th century figure with ball red and green gown, small green hat, holding small bouquet, height 6″, designer L. Harradine....................... 1934-1949 **400.00 450.00**

HN 1656
☐ Blue and white gown with flowers, small blue hat, height 6″, designer L. Harradine....................... 1934-1949 **300.00 350.00**
☐ **M 67** Made as a miniature, blue and white gown, dark hat, height 4″, designer L. Harradine.............. 1935-1949 **325.00 375.00**
☐ **M 73** Red and green gown, green hat, height 4″, designer L. Harradine. 1935-1949 **325.00 375.00**

DAISY

HN 1575
☐ Small figure with blue gown, white floral design, height 3½″, designer L. Harradine....................... 1933-1949 **250.00 300.00**

HN 1961
☐ Pink dress, height 3½″, designer L. Harradine...................... 1941-1949 **275.00 325.00**

Daisy, HN1575, **250.00 – 300.00**

	Date	Price Range	
DAMARIS			
HN 2079			
☐ Blue and white gown, long red and blue cloak trimmed with white fur, white and dark blue head piece, height 7½″, designer M. Davies.	1951-1952	800.00	950.00
'DANCING EYES AND SUNNY HAIR'			
HN 1543			
☐ Small dark haired white female seated on shaded blue rock, height 5″, designer unknown..............	1933-1949	225.00	300.00
DANCING FIGURE			
HN 311			
☐ Pink flowing gown, holding tambourine in hand, height 17¾″, designer unknown	1918-1938	3500.00	4000.00

	Date	Price Range

DANCING YEARS

HN 2235

☐ Blue and pink costume, blue ribbon in hair, figure in deep curtsy position, height 7", designer M. Davies.   1965-1971   375.00   425.00

DANDY, The

HN 753

☐ 18th century style costume of male, white trousers, black boots, red coat, red and black hat, leaning against tree, height 6¾", designer L. Harradine.   1925-1938   1100.00   1250.00

The Dandy,
HN753,
1100.00 – 1250.00

DAPHNE

HN 2268

☐ Pink gowned figure on white base, height 8½", designer M. Davies.   1963-1975   210.00   260.00

	Date	Price Range	

DARBY

HN 1427

☐ Gray haired male seated in high backed blue-green chair, black trousers, blue jacket, red patterned long coat, black shoes, white stockings, height 5½ ", designer L. Harradine. . . 1930-1949 325.00 400.00

HN 2024

☐ Minor glaze differences, height 5½ ", designer L. Harradine. . . . . , ... 1949-1959 300.00 375.00

DARLING

HN 1

☐ Blonde haired figure in white nightshirt, on white base (1st version), height 7½ ", designer C. Vyse. 1913-1928 1000.00 1150.00

HN 1319

☐ Black base (1st version), height 7½ ", designer C. Vyse. 1929-1959 150.00 200.00

HN 1371

☐ Green nightshirt (1st version), height 7½ ", designer C. Vyse. 1930-1938 275.00 325.00

HN 1372

☐ Pink nightshirt (2nd version), height 7½ ", designer C. Vyse. 1930-1938 275.00 325.00

HN 1985

☐ Small figure in white nightshirt on black base (2nd version), height 5¼ ", designer C. Vyse. 1946- 55.00

DAVID COPPERFIELD

Issued only as a miniature.

☐ **M 88** White collar, yellow vest, tan pants, brown hat in hand, black jacket and black stand, height 4¼ ", designer L. Harradine. 1949-1983 20.00 30.00

DAWN

HN 1858

☐ White nude figure on blue base, holding blue material down front. Earlier version of this figure had a headdress making it 10¼ " in height without figure is approximately 9¾ ", designer L. Harradine. 1938-1949 1350.00 1500.00

☐ With headdress 1000.00 1250.00

	Date	Price Range	
DAYDREAMS			

HN 1731
☐ Figure seated on bench, cream gown with red bodice and blue trim, light red bonnet, holding small bouquet, height 5½″, designer L. Harradine. .. 1935-   155.00

HN 1732
☐ Pale blue dress with pink trim, height 5½″, designer L. Harradine. 1935-1949   300.00   350.00

HN 1944
☐ Red dress with white trim, figure holding larger bouquet, height 5½″, designer L. Harradine. 1940-1949   350.00   400.00

DEBBIE

HN 2385
☐ Small figure in dark blue over gown, white with green design under gown, height 5¾″, designer M. Davies. 1969-1982   115.00   135.00

Debbie,
HN2385,
115.00 - 135.00

	Date	Price Range	

HN 2400
☐ Yellow gown, rose overdress with frilled sleeves of half length. Blonde hair, height 6″, designer M. Davies. 1983- 75.00

DEBUTANTE
HN 2210
☐ Bowing figure in blue dress with high blue headdress, height 5″, designer M. Davies. 1963-1967 375.00 425.00

DEIDRE
HN 2020
☐ Blue and red gown, blue bonnet with red lining, height 7″, designer L. Harradine. 1949-1955 350.00 400.00

DELICIA
HN 1662
☐ Pink, shaded blue and white gown, small ribbon tied hat has small bouquet on wrist, height 5¾″, designer L. Harradine. 1934-1938 550.00 650.00
HN 1663
☐ Flowered purple, green and yellow skirt, height 5¾″, designer L. Harradine. 1934-1938 550.00 650.00
HN 1681
☐ Green and purple dress, height 5¾″, designer L. Harradine. 1935-1938 600.00 700.00

DELIGHT
HN 1772
☐ Red gowned figure on black base, small white cap, trimmed with blue ribbons, height 6¾″, designer L. Harradine. 1936-1967 150.00 200.00
HN 1773
☐ Blue gown with red bow, height 6¾″, designer L. Harradine. 1936-1949 375.00 425.00

DELPHINE
HN 2136
☐ Light lavender gown with blue coat that has cream lining, fur stole, bonnet with flower trim, height 7¼″, designer M. Davies. 1954-1967 275.00 325.00

	Date	Price Range	

DENISE

HN 2273

☐ Red gown with white trim, bonnet with blue ribbons, height 7¼″, designer M. Davies.   1964-1971   275.00   325.00

☐ **M 34** Made as a miniature, pale green dress, rose overskirt, blue bodice and cap, height 4½″, designer unknown. .   1933-1945   350.00   400.00

☐ **M 35** No color detail available, height 4½″, designer unknown.   1933-1945   350.00   400.00

DERRICK

HN 1398

☐ Dutch boy on base, blue trousers, white and light blue shirt, yellow buttons, red hat, height 8″, designer L. Harradine.   1930-1938   650.00   750.00

DESPAIR

HN 596

☐ Small figure all wrapped in cobalt blue cape, features are light blue, height 4½″, designer unknown.   1924-1938   1400.00   1650.00

DETECTIVE, The

HN 2359

☐ Green and black base, character figure in long brown coat with cape, double billed brown cap, white shirt, black tie, brown trousers, black shoes, holding magnifying glass and white object, height 9¼″, designer E. J. Griffiths.   1977-1983   125.00   165.00

DIANA

HN 1716

☐ Small figure in blue skirt, pink blouse, holding small bouquet, height 5¾″, designer L. Harradine.   1935-1949   300.00   375.00

HN 1717

☐ Green and white dress, white gloves, dark ribbons, height 5¾″, designer L. Harradine.   1935-1949   300.00   375.00

HN 1986

☐ Shaded red dress, red bonnet, height 5¾″, designer L. Harradine.   1946-1975   125.00   175.00

	Date	Price Range	

DICK SWIVELLER
Issued only as a miniature.

☐ **M 90** Brown hat, yellow vest and pants, dark brown coat, cane and stand, height 4 ¼ ", designer unknown — 1949- — 29.95

DIGGER (New Zealand)
HN 321

☐ Green mottled figure of soldier on base, height 11 ¼ ", designer E. W. Light. . . . . — 1918-1938 — 1250.00 1500.00

DIGGER (Australian)
HN 322

☐ Brown soldier figure on base, height 11 ¼ ", designer E. W. Light. . . . . — 1918-1938 — 1250.00 1500.00

HN 353

☐ This figure painted naturalistically, height 11 ¾ ", designer E. W. Light. . . . — 1919-1938 — 1350.00 1600.00

DILIGENT SCHOLAR, The
HN 26

☐ Seated figure on green base, green trousers, light shirt, multicolored coat, holding slate, height 7 ", designer W. White. . . . . — 1913-1938 — 1750.00 2000.00

DIMITY
HN 2169

☐ Two tiered white gown with lavender and green flowers, green bodice, lavender sleeves, height 5 ¾ ", designer L. Harradine. — 1956-1959 — 300.00 350.00

DINKY DOO
HN 1678

☐ Small figure in shaded blue gown, white cap, height 4 ¾ ", designer L. Harradine. . . . . — 1934- — 65.00

HN 2120

☐ Figure is in curtsy position. Gown has red bodice with shades of pink in her skirt. (2nd Version), height 4 ¾ ", designer L. Harradine. . . . . — 1983- — 65.00

	Date	Price Range
DOCTOR, The		

HN 2858
☐ Black coat, blue trouser and vest, seated in chair with doctor's bag at side, height 7½", designer W. K. Harper.   1979-   225.00

DOLLY

HN 355
☐ Figure in shaded blue and white gown, holding doll, height 7¼", designer C. J. Noke.   1919-1938   1250.00   1500.00

DOLLY VARDON

HN 1514
☐ White gown with floral flower figures, red patterned cloak with light lining, white muff, green basket at feet, height 8½", designer L. Harradine. . .   1932-1938   700.00   800.00

HN 1515
☐ White and shaded blue gown, multicolored cloak with light green lining, brown basket at feet, height 8½", designer L. Harradine.   1932-1949   800.00   900.00

DORCAS

HN 1490
☐ Light colored gown with darker over blouse, Dutch style bonnet with dark ribbons, holding bowl of flowers, height 7", designer L. Harradine.   1932-1938   450.00   500.00

HN 1491
☐ Shaded green gown with darker blouse, height 7", designer L. Harradine.   1932-1938   450.00   500.00

HN 1558
☐ Shaded red gown with designed red over blouse, height 7", designer L. Harradine.   1933-1952   350.00   400.00

DOREEN

HN 1363
☐ Figure in curtsy position wearing pink gown, height 5¼", designer L. Harradine.   1929-1938   900.00   1000.00

	Date	Price Range	

HN 1389
☐ Green gown trimmed in white, dark
haired figure, height 5¼", designer
L. Harradine. 1930-1938 **600.00 700.00**

HN 1390
☐ Shaded blue gown with white trim,
light haired, height 5¼", designer
L. Harradine. 1929-1938 **600.00 700.00**

DORIS KEENE as Cavallini

HN 90
☐ Black hair, black full gown with silver
jewelry (1st version), height 11",
designer C. J. Noke. 1918-1936 **2000.00 2250.00**

HN 96
☐ Black gown, white fur coat and muff,
small hat (2nd version), height 10½",
designer C. J. Noke. 1918-1932 **2250.00 2500.00**

HN 345
☐ Dark fur collar, striped muff (2nd ver-
sion), height 10½", designer C. J.
Noke. 1919-1949, **2750.00 3000.00**

HN 467
☐ Gold jewelry (1st version), height 11",
designer C. J. Noke. 1921-1936 **2000.00 2200.00**

'DO YOU WONDER . . .'

HN 1544
☐ Small blonde figure wearing blue sun
suit on light base, height 5", designer
unknown. 1933-1949 **300.00 350.00**

DOUBLE JESTER

HN 365
☐ Multicolored Jester costume, standing
on base, holds pole which has two
faced bust, height unknown, designer
C. J. Noke. 1920-1938 **2750.00 3250.00**

DREAMLAND

HN 1473
☐ Figure lying on multicolored sofa,
costume of several colors, throw on
back of couch is also multicoloured,
height 4¾", designer L. Harradine. . . 1931-1938 **1850.00 2000.00**

	Date	Price Range

HN 1481
□ Darker sofa, yellow and red costume, height 4¾″, designer L. Harradine. .. 1931-1938 1350.00 1500.00

DREAMWEAVER
HN 2283
□ Bearded figure seated on base which contains small animals playing pipes, green trousers, dark blue shirt, wearing sandals, this figure has matt finish, height 8¾″, designer M. Nicoll... 1972-1976 250.00 300.00

DRUMMER BOY
HN 2679
□ Brown base, soldier uniform of blue trousers, red and white jacket, black tall hat with white and gold trim, gray knapsack, black boots, sitting on drum of red, white and blue, height 8½″, designer M. Nicoll. 1976-1981 325.00 375.00

DRYAD OF THE PINES
HN 1869
□ White nude figure with flowing gold hair, standing on gold colored rock on base, height 23″, designer R. Garbe ... 1938-1949 2750.00 3000.00

DULCIE
HN 2305
□ Full white skirt, white bodice with red, yellow and white designs, trimmed in blue, royal blue overshirt, height 7¼″, designer M. Davies. 1981- 185.00

DULCINEA
HN 1343
□ Figure seated on multicolored chaise lounge, of red and black costume, black Spanish style hat, height 5¼″, designer L. Harradine. 1929-1938 900.00 1050.00
HN 1419
□ Red and pink dress with green shoes, height 5¼″, designer L. Harradine. .. 1930-1938 1000.00 1150.00

	Date	Price Range	

DUNCE

HN 6
☐ Cloaked figure on base wearing dunce cap, height 10½", designer C. J. Noke. . . . . 1913-1938 — 2750.00 3000.00

HN 310
☐ Black and white patterned costume, green base, height 10½", designer C. J. Noke. . . . . 1918-1938 — 2750.00 3000.00

HN 357
☐ Gray costume with black pattern, height 10½", designer C. J. Noke. . . . 1919-1938 — 2750.00 3000.00

EASTER DAY

HN 1976
☐ Full skirted pale lavender flowered gown, dark bodice, height 7½", designer M. Davies. . . . . 1945-1951 — 425.00 475.00

HN 2039
☐ Gown with multicolored flowers around bottom, black bonnet with blue ribbons and green lining, height 7½", designer M. Davies. . . . . 1949-1969 — 275.00 325.00

EDITH

HN 2957
☐ One of the charming Kate Greenaway collection. Small figure with green dress, white underskirt, white apron held up containing red flowers, blonde hair, white bonnet, height 5¾", designer P. Parsons. . . . . 1982- — 75.00

ELAINE

HN 2791
☐ Blue ball gown, holding fan, height 7½", designer M. Davies. . . . . 1980- — 185.00

ELEANORE

HN 1753
☐ Figure leaning against post, green and pink skirt with blue bodice, wearing small bonnet on side of head, height 7", designer L. Harradine. . . . . 1936-1949 — 700.00 850.00

	Date	Price Range	

HN 1754
☐ White gown with blue and red flowers, shaded red bodice, blue bonnet
with blue ribbons, height 7″, designer
L. Harradine. 1936-1949   700.00   850.00

ELEANOR OF PROVENCE
HN 2009
☐ Queen figure, dark blue and red gown,
red cloak, and white covering on
head, height 9½″, designer M. Davies   1948-1953   600.00   700.00

ELEGANCE
HN 2264
☐ Shaded green gown trimmed in white
and green, green cloak, blue ribbon in
hair, height 7½″, designer M. Davies.   1961-   155.00

ELFREDA
HN 2078
☐ Patterned red and blue ball gown, carrying white fan, feathers trimmed in
black, height 7¼″, designer L. Har-
radine.   1951-1955   600.00   700.00

ELIZA
HN 2543
☐ Tall figure (11¾″), brown costume,
black flat hat, carrying basket of flowers on arm, holding bouquet in hand,
designer E. J. Griffiths.   1974-1979   175.00   225.00

ELIZABETH
HN 2946
☐ A regal lady in her gown of shaded
green with gold ruffle showing layers
of white skirt underneath. Gold shawl
adorns her shoulders. Carrying a very
light green parasol. Red hair underneath a bonnet of yellow, height 8″,
designer B. Franks.   1982-   225.00

ELIZABETH FRY
HN   2
☐ Shaded light blue costume, head covering in same color, on light green
base, height 17″, designer C. Vyse. . .   1913-1938   4000.00   4500.00

	Date	Price Range

HN 2A

☐ Blue base, height 17″, designer
C. Vyse.   1913-1938   **4000.00 4500.00**

ELLEN

HN 639

☐ Child sitting on a floor cushion rocking
her doll, dressed in a white pinafore
with puffed sleeves and wearing a
white cap, height unknown, designer
unknown.   1984-   **75.00**

Ellen, HN3020, **75.00**

ELLEN TERRY as Queen Catherine

HN 379

☐ Shaded blue gown trimmed in black,
white and green on black base, head
gear of blue, yellow and white, height
12½ ″, designer C. J. Noke.   1920-1949   **2750.00 3000.00**

	Date	Price Range

ELSIE MAYNARD

HN 639

☐ Multicolored costume, white stockings, black shoes on black base, holding tambourine in hand above head, height 7″, designer C. J. Noke. .   1924-1949   800.00   900.00

ELYSE

HN 2429

☐ Seated figure, blue gown, flowers in hair, holding white hat with red ribbons, height 6¾″, designer M. Davies   1972-   185.00

EMBROIDERING

HN 2855

☐ Older figure seated in chair, blue gown, green apron, with embroidery on lap, sewing basket at side, height 7¼″, designer W. K. Harper.   1980-   225.00

EMIR

HN 1604

☐ Cream colored robe with red and green patterned scarf, height 7½″, designer C. J. Noke.   1933-1949   900.00   1000.00

HN 1605

☐ Cream robe with shades of yellow, multicolored striped scarf, height 7½″, designer C. J. Noke.   1933-1949   900.00   1000.00

EMMA (Kate Greenaway)

HN 2834

☐ Small figure, red dress, white apron trimmed with red flowers, holding green flowers in hands on white base, height 5¾″, designer M. Davies.   1977-1981   65.00   100.00

ENCHANTMENT

HN 2178

☐ Shaded blue gown with white and yellow sleeves, gown has dark blue designs, height 7¾″, designer M. Davies .   1957-1982   125.00   175.00

	Date	Price Range	

ERMINE COAT, The
HN 1981
☐ Red gown with white fur coat and muff, red stole with light blue and green designs, height 6¾", designer L. Harradine. 1945-1967   200.00   275.00

ERMINIE
Issued only as a miniature.
☐ **M 40** Pink skirt with white cape, pink shoes on white stand, height 4", designer unknown. 1933-1945   400.00   500.00

ESMERALDA
HN 2168
☐ Cream gown with blue design, red shawl, dark blue parasol, holding small bird on hand, height 5¼", designer M. Davies. 1956-1959   350.00   400.00

ESTELLE
HN 1566
☐ Light colored gown with shaded blues, blue bonnet, blue muff, blue shoes, height 8", designer L. Harradine. 1933-1938   800.00   900.00
HN 1802
☐ Pink dress, height 8", designer L. Harradine. 1937-1949   700.00   800.00

EUGENE
HN 1520
☐ Seated figure in shaded green and pink gown, holding fan, height 5¾", designer L. Harradine. 1932-1938   575.00   675.00
HN 1521
☐ Shaded red and white gown, height 5¾", designer L. Harradine. 1932-1938   575.00   675.00

EUROPA AND THE BULL
HN 95
☐ Lady seated on bull, naturalistically painted, height 9¾", designer H. Tittensor. 1918-1938   3000.00   3500.00

	Date	Price Range	

EVELYN
HN 1622
☐ Cream coloured gown with red bodice, red bonnet with shaded blue feathers, holding parasol across lap, height 6″, designer L. Harradine. 1934-1949 **700.00 850.00**

HN 1637
☐ Blue bodice, green hat, red parasol, height 6″, designer L. Harradine. 1934-1938 **850.00 950.00**

EVENTIDE
HN 2814
☐ Seated old lady figure in blue dress with white apron, patchwork quilt on lap, height 7¾″, designer W. K. Harper. 1977- **165.00**

FAGIN
HN 534
☐ A character from Dicken's "Oliver Twist," height 4″, designer L. Harradine. 1922- **45.00 60.00**

☐ **M 49** Renumbered as a miniature, height 4″, designer L. Harradine. 1932-1983 **20.00 30.00**

FAIR LADY
HN 2193
☐ Green gown, yellow sleeves, bonnet hanging on arm, height 7¾″, designer M. Davies. 1963- **155.00**

HN 2832
☐ Red gown, green sleeves, dark hair, height 7¾″, designer M. Davies. 1977- **155.00**

HN 2835
☐ Orange gown with multicolored designs on white sleeves, height 7¾″, designer M. Davies. 1977- **155.00**

FAIR MAIDEN
HN 2211
☐ Small figure, green dress, yellow sleeves, bonnet handing on right wrist, height 5¼″, designer M. Davies 1967- **100.00**

Fair Lady,
HN2193,
155.00

	Date	Price Range	
HN 2434			
☐ Scarlet gown with green puffed sleeves and a multi-layered petticoat. Green hat trimmed in gold, gold coif in her dark brown hair, height 5¼″, designer M. Davies.	1983-	95.00	
FAIRY			
HN 1324			
☐ Nude white child figure seated on pedestal style base with multicolored wings, height unknown, designer L. Harradine	1929-1938	850.00	950.00
HN 1374			
☐ Nude white figure seated on toad stool, which is on green base surrounded by yellow flowers, height 4″, designer L. Harradine.	1930-1938	850.00	950.00
HN 1375			
☐ Fairy type figure lying on base covered with flowers, height 3″, designer L. Harradine.	1930-1938	750.00	850.00

	Date	Price Range	

HN 1376
☐ No mushroom, height 2½ ", designer
L. Harradine.   1930-1938   **650.00   750.00**

HN 1378
☐ Small white kneeling figure on green
base with orange flowers, height
2½ ", designer L. Harradine.   1930-1938   **550.00   650.00**

HN 1379
☐ Small white kneeling figure on green
base, has blue and white flowers
around figure, height 2½ ", designer
L. Harradine.   1930-1938   **550.00   650.00**

HN 1380
☐ Dark mottled mushroom, height 4",
designer L. Harradine.   1930-1938   **850.00 · 950.00**

HN 1393
☐ Small white figure seated on green
base covered with yellow flowers and
green leaves, height 2½ ", designer
L. Harradine.   1930-1938   **650.00   750.00**

HN 1394
☐ Yellow flowers, height 2½ ", designer
L. Harradine.   1930-1938   **550.00   650.00**

HN 1395
☐ Blue flowers, height 3", designer
L. Harradine.   1930-1938   **750.00   850.00**

HN 1396
☐ Small white kneeling figure on green
base with blue and white flowers on
base and on arm, height 2½ ",
designer L. Harradine.   1930-1938   **550.00   650.00**

HN 1532
☐ Nude white figure seated on toad
stool, which is on green base sur-
rounded by multicolored flowers,
height 4", designer L. Harradine.   1932-1938   **550.00   650.00**

HN 1533
☐ Multicolored flowers, height 3",
designer L. Harradine.   1932-1938   **550.00   650.00**

HN 1534
☐ Large yellow flowers, height 2½ ",
designer L. Harradine.   1932-1938   **550.00   650.00**

HN 1535
☐ Yellow and blue flowers, height 2½ ",
designer L. Harradine.   1932-1938   **550.00   650.00**

HN 1536
☐ Light green base, height 2½ ", designer
L. Harradine   1932-1938   **550.00   650.00**

FALSTAFF	Date	Price Range	
HN 571			
☐ Rotund figure in shades of brown costume on base, base has wicker stand covered with green and black striped cover, dark hat with orange feather (1st version), height 7″, designer C. J. Noke.	1923-1938	**700.00**	**800.00**
HN 575			
☐ Brown coat, yellow spotted cloth over base (1st version), height 7″, designer C. J. Noke.	1923-1938	**700.00**	**800.00**
HN 608			
☐ Red coat with red cloth over base (1st version), height 7″, designer C. J. Noke.	1924-1938	**700.00**	**800.00**
HN 609			
☐ Green coat with green cloth over base (1st version), height 7″, designer C. J. Noke.	1924-1938	**700.00**	**800.00**
HN 618			
☐ Black color, spotted lilac cloth on green base (2nd version), height 7″, designer C. J. Noke.	1924-1938	**700.00**	**800.00**
HN 619			
☐ Brown coat with green collar, yellow cloth over base (1st version), height 7″, designer C. J. Noke.	1924-1938	**700.00**	**800.00**
HN 638			
☐ Red coat, spotted cream cloth over base (1st version), height 7″, designer C. J. Noke.	1924-1938	**700.00**	**800.00**
HN 1216			
☐ With multicolored costume (1st version), height 7″, designer C. J. Noke. .	1926-1949	**700.00**	**800.00**
HN 1606			
☐ Red costume, brown boots, black hat with red feathers, green cloth with red design on base (1st version), height 7″, designer C. J. Noke.	1933-1949	**700.00**	**800.00**
HN 2054			
☐ Red jacket, brown boots, gloves and collar, no hat, cream colored cloth on orange colored base (2nd version), height 7″, designer C. J. Noke.	1950-	**150.00**	

Falstaff,
HN2054,
150.00

	Date	Price Range	
FAMILY ALBUM			
HN 2321			
☐ Older lady seated in chair with album in lap, blue skirt, lavender blouse and cap, blue and black striped shawl, height 6¼″, designer M. Nicoll.	1966-1973	350.00	400.00
FARAWAY			
HN 2133			
☐ Girl figure lying on tummy on pillow, reading book, white dress, blue bodice and shoes, height 2½″, designer M. Davies.	1958-1962	300.00	350.00
FARMER'S BOY, The			
HN 2520			
☐ Farmer figure seated on large horse, mounted on base, height 8¾″, designer W. M. Chance.	1938-1960	1000.00	1250.00

FARMER'S WIFE
HN 2069

	Date	Price Range	
☐ Green skirt, red blouse with green collar, white bonnet, skirt has chicken feed in it, base has two chickens on it, height 9″, designer L. Harradine. . .	1951-1955	400.00	500.00

The Farmer's Wife,
HN2069,
400.00 ~ 500.00

FAT BOY, The
HN 530

	Date	Price Range	
☐ A character from Dicken's "Pickwick" Papers" (1st version), height 3½″, designer L. Harradine.	1922-	45.00	60.00
☐ **M 44** Renumbered as a miniature, height 4¼″, designer L. Harradine. . .	1932-1983	20.00	30.00

HN 555

☐ Larger version of character, white trousers, blue coat with white buttons, white neck scarf and cloth over hand, on same base (2nd version), height 7″, designer L. Harradine.	1923-1952	400.00	500.00

HN 1893

☐ Very minor color changes (2nd version), height 7″, designer L. Harradine.	1938-1952	325.00	375.00

	Date	Price Range

HN 2096
☐ White trousers, blue coat, yellow and black dotted scarf, white cloth with red trim on arm, on dark green base (3rd version), height 7¼", designer L. Harradine.   1952-1967   300.00   350.00

Fat Boy,
HN555,
400.00 - 500.00

FAVORITE, The

HN 2249
☐ Older lady figure with cream pitcher and saucer in hands, blue gown with white apron, brown cat at feet, height 7¼", designer M. Nicoll.   1960-   165.00

FIDDLER, The

HN 2171
☐ 18th century figure, dancing and playing fiddle on brown base, light yellow trouser, jacket has yellow and green stripes, black hat with feather, height 8¾", designer M. Nicoll.   1956-1962   650.00   800.00

	Date	Price Range	

FIONA

HN 1924

☐ Shaded red gown with purple jacket trimmed in black and white, small black bonnet, seated on green couch with multicolored design (1st version), height 5¾″, designer L. Harradine. 1940-1949 550.00 650.00

HN 1925

☐ Green skirt (1st version), height 5¾″, designer L. Harradine. 1940-1949 550.00 650.00

HN 1933

☐ Multicolored gown, red hat, shaded blue couch (1st version), height 5¾″, designer L. Harradine. 1940-1949 650.00 750.00

HN 2694

☐ Standing figure with blue and red skirt, white bodice and sleeves with small lavender designs (2nd version), height 7½″, designer M. Davies. 1974-1980 95.00 150.00

FISHERWOMAN

HN 80

☐ Three figures on brown base, first figure with green shawl, height unknown, designer unknown 1917-1938 3000.00 3500.00

HN 349

☐ Central figure has yellow shawl, height unknown, designer unknown. . 1919-1968 2750.00 3000.00

HN 359

☐ Central figure has red with black stripes in shawl, height unknown, designer unknown. 1919-1938 3000.00 3500.00

HN 631

☐ Central figure has green shawl, height unknown, designer unknown. . 1924-1938 3000.00 3500.00

FIRST DANCE

HN 2803

☐ White gown with flower trim, green bodice, holding multi-flowered fan, height 7¼″, designer M. Davies. 1977- 170.00

	Date	Price Range

FIRST STEPS
HN 2242
☐ Blue gown with beige sleeves and white collar, figure holding hands of small figure, wearing blue trousers with beige skirt, height 6¾″, designer M. Davies.   1959-1965   **500.00   550.00**

FIRST WALTZ
HN 2862
☐ Ball gown of red with blue and green designs, light blue sleeves, holding large white feather fan, height 7½″, designer M. Davies.   1979-1983   **165.00   225.00**

MRS. FITZHERBERT
HN 2007
☐ Yellow and white gown, blue and white bonnet, holding blue and white fan, height 9″, designer M. Davies. . . .   1948-1953   **700.00   800.00**

FLEUR
HN 2368
☐ Green gown with gold design at hemline, darker green jacket with gold dots, holding single flower in upraised hand, light green drape from top of bodice back, height 7½″, designer J. Bromley.   1968-   **185.00**

HN 2369
☐ Orange dress, pale blue jacket trimmed in white, height 7½″, designer John Bromley.   1984-   **185.00**

FLEURETTE
HN 1587
☐ White gown with red designs, red overlay, holding fan, height 6½″, designer L. Harradine.   1933-1949   **625.00   700.00**

FLORA
HN 2349
☐ Older lady figure in dark brown dress with white apron, flowers in pot and under stool, height 7¾″, designer M. Nicoll.   1966-1973   **175.00   225.00**

Fleur,
HN2368,
185.00

FLOUNCED SKIRT, The

	Date	Price Range	
HN 57A			
☐ Many tiered orange dress, figure wearing jewelry, height 9¾", designer E. W. Light.	1916-1938	1650.00	1800.00
HN 66			
☐ Lilac dress, height 9¾", designer E. W. Light.	1916-1938	1650.00	1800.00
HN 77			
☐ Lemon yellow dress with black trimmings, height 9¾", designer E. W. Light.	1917-1938	1650.00	1800.00
HN 78			
☐ Flowered yellow dress, height 9¾", designer E. W. Light.	1917-1938	1650.00	1800.00
HN 333			
☐ Mottled brown tone dress, height 9¾", designer E. W. Light.	1918-1938	1550.00	1700.00

	Date	Price Range	

FLOWER SELLER, The

HN 789

☐ Yellow dress with green designs, red blouse, green shawl, green feathers on black hat, holding wrapped baby in one arm and a basket of flowers on other arm, height 8¾″, designer L. Harradine.   1926-1938   600.00   700.00

FLOWER SELLER'S CHILDREN, The

HN 525

☐ Boy and girl seated on stone bench with basket of flowers, green costume on boy, blue costume on girl, height 8¼″, designer L. Harradine. . .   1921-1949   650.00   750.00

HN 551

☐ Costume of boy blue, girl's checkered orange and yellow, height 8¼″, designer L. Harradine.   1922-1949   500.00   600.00

HN 1206

☐ Costume of girl multicolored, boy's in shaded blues, cloth of dark blue, most flowers dark blue, height 8¼″, designer L. Harradine.   1926-1949   450.00   500.00

HN 1342

☐ Boy's costume shades of blue and red, girl's red with black design, robe shades of red and blue, height 8¼″, designer L. Harradine.   1929-   395.00

HN 1406

☐ Yellow costume, dark blue cloth over basket, height 8¼″, designer L. Harradine.   1930-1938   550.00   600.00

FOAMING QUART, The

HN 2162

☐ Rotund figure seated in dark gray and white chair, purple trousers, purple and red tunic with yellow collar, green gloves and long boots, purple hat with beige trim, blue and gray beard and hair, light blue tankard, height 5¾″, designer M. Davies.   1955-   165.00

	Date	Price Range	

FOLLY
HN 1335
☐ Short red costume, green collar, dark blue sash, light green dunce type hat, holding several small round objects of red, yellow and white, height 9″, designer L. Harradine. 1929-1938 1600.00 1750.00

HN 1750
☐ Earthenware, with brown hat, white muff, dark dress, height 9½″, designer L. Harradine 1936-1949 1100.00 1250.00

FORGET-ME-NOT
HN 1812
☐ Red haired figure seated on bench style base, pink dress, green ribbons, holding small round purse, height 6″, designer L. Harradine. 1937-1949 550.00 650.00

HN 1813
☐ Red dress, dark blue bonnet with ribbons, height 6″, designer L. Harradine. 1937-1949 550.00 650.00

FORTUNE TELLER
HN 2159
☐ Gypsy figure seated on wicker stand, at small table with green and black cover, crystal ball and cards on table, red dress with green shawl, height 6½″, designer L. Harradine. 1955-1967 425.00 475.00

FORTY WINKS
HN 1974
☐ Elderly lady seated in tall backed red and yellow chair, dark skirt, white apron, red blouse, dark shawl, cat at feet, height 6¾″, designer H. Fenton. 1945-1973 165.00 250.00

FOUR O'CLOCK
HN 1760
☐ Shaded blue gown with white trim, multicolored bonnet, holding tea cup and saucer, height 6″, designer L. Harradine. 1936-1949 475.00 575.00

	Date	Price Range

FRAGRANCE
HN 2334
☐ Blue gown with white circular designs and white trim, height 7⅜", designer M. Davies. 1966- 170.00

FRANCINE
HN 2422
☐ Small dark haired figure with green dress and yellow sleeves, blue waist ribbon, holding brown bird on arm, height 5¼", designer J. Bromley..... 1972-1980 50.00 100.00

FRANGCON
HN 1720
☐ Multicolored flowered gown with black hat and shoes, on base trimmed in black, height 7½", designer L. Harradine. 1935-1949 650.00 750.00

HN 1721
☐ Green dress, green hat and shoes, base trimmed in brown, height 7½", designer L. Harradine. 1935-1949 650.00 750.00

FRENCH PEASANT
HN 2075
☐ Light red skirt with red designs, shaded blue blouse, white headdress with red ribbons, on multicolored base, height 9½", designer L. Harradine. 1951-1955 600.00 700.00

FRIAR TUCK
HN 2143
☐ Brown monk's robe, holding sword and shield, on brown base, height 7½", designer M. Davies. 1954-1965 500.00 600.00

FRUIT GATHERING
HN 449
☐ Blue striped blouse, blue skirt, figure holding basket, has dog on base with figure, height 7¾", designer L. Harradine. 1921-1938 2750.00 3000.00

HN 476
☐ Green check blouse, blue check skirt, height 7¾", designer L. Harradine. ... 1921-1938 2650.00 2800.00

	Date	Price Range

HN 503
☐ Brown and blue checkered dress, height 7¾", designer L. Harradine. .. 1921-1938 2500.00 3000.00

HN 561
☐ Yellow designed skirt, green blouse, bonnet same as skirt, height 7¾", designer L. Harradine. 1923-1938 2500.00 3000.00

HN 562
☐ Pink blouse with spotted skirt, height 7¾", designer L. Harradine. 1923-1938 2500.00 3000.00

HN 706
☐ Purple blouse with yellow skirt, height 7¾", designer L. Harradine. .. 1925-1938 2500.00 3000.00

HN 707
☐ Red blouse, spotted skirt, height 7¾", designer L. Harradine. 1925-1938 3000.00 3500.00

GAFFER, The

HN 2053
☐ Elderly male figure with white beard on base, green trousers, dark coat, red vest, brown hat, holding staff and red and white dotted kerchief, height 7¾", designer L. Harradine. 1950-1959 350.00 400.00

GAINESBOROUGH HAT, The

HN 46
☐ Lilac dress, wearing huge black and white hat, height 8¾", designer H. Tittensor. 1915-1938 1200.00 1350.00

HN 46A
☐ Black patterned collar was added to costume, height 8¾", designer H. Tittensor. 1915-1938 1200.00 1350.00

HN 47
☐ Green dress, height 8¾", designer H. Tittensor. 1915-1938 1200.00 1350.00

HN 329
☐ Patterned blue dress, height 8¾", designer H. Tittensor. 1918-1938 1200.00 1350.00

HN 352
☐ Yellow dress and purple hat, height 8¾", designer H. Tittensor. 1919-1938 1750.00 2000.00

HN 383
☐ Striped dress, height 8¾", designer H. Tittensor. 1920-1938 1150.00 1300.00

	Date	Price Range

HN 453
☐ Red, blue and green costume, height 8¾", designer H. Tittensor. 1921-1938   **1250.00 1400.00**

HN 675
☐ Cream gown with red and yellow design, black hat, height 8¾", designer H. Tittensor. 1924-1938   **1350.00 1500.00**

HN 705
☐ Shaded blue gown with red and yellow designs, height 8¾", designer H. Tittensor. 1925-1938   **1200.00 1350.00**

GAMEKEEPER, THE

HN 2879
☐ Figure kneeling on ground (base) dressed in gray colored trousers, dark green jacket, cream colored polo neck sweater, dog sitting beside him is black, gamekeeper is holding a gun, height unknown, designer Eric Griffiths. 1984-   **125.00**

The Gamekeeper,
HN2879,
125.00

	Date	Price Range	
GAY MORNING			
HN 2135			
☐ Cream colored skirt, with very light red bodice, large white sleeves trimmed in blue, blue and red scarf in hand, height 7″, designer M. Davies. .	1954-1967	225.00	300.00
GEISHA, A			
HN 354			
☐ Japanese style figure, yellow kimono, pink cuffs, blue flowered waistband, holding fan (1st version), height 10¾″, designer H. Tittensor.	1919-1938	2250.00	2500.00
HN 376			
☐ Blue and yellow mottled kimono (1st version), height 10¾″, designer H. Tittensor.	1920-1938	2300.00	2500.00
HN 387			
☐ Blue kimono, yellow cuffs (1st version), height 10¾″, designer H. Tittensor.	1920-1938	2250.00	2500.00
HN 634			
☐ Black and white kimono (1st version), height 10¾″, designer H. Tittensor. . .	1924-1938	2250.00	2500.00
HN 741			
☐ Dark multicolored kimono, black trim (1st version), height 10¾″, designer H. Tittensor.	1925-1938	2250.00	2500.00
HN 779			
☐ Red kimono with black spots (1st version), height 10¾″, designer H. Tittensor.	1926-1938	2250.00	2500.00
HN 1223			
☐ Seated Japanese style figure playing instrument on base, red and black striped costume, flowers in hair (2nd version), height 6¾″, designer C. J. Noke.	1927-1938	900.00	1000.00
HN 1234			
☐ Multicolored costume (2nd version), height 6¾″, designer C. J. Noke.	1927-1938	900.00	1000.00
HN 1292			
☐ Orange kimono, blue and green collar (2nd version), height 6¾″, designer C. J. Noke.	1928-1938	900.00	1000.00
HN 1310			
☐ Multicolored spotted kimono (2nd version), height 6¾″, designer C. J. Noke.	1929-1938	800.00	900.00

	Date	Price Range

HN 1321
☐ HN 779 with green kimono (1st version), height 10¾", designer H. Tittensor.   1929-1938   **2250.00 2500.00**

HN 1322
☐ Pink kimono, with blue markings (1st version), height 10¾", designer H. Tittensor.   1929-1938   **2250.00 2500.00**

GENEVIEVE

HN 1962
☐ Full red gown with blue and pink ribbons, white muff, black ribbon on dark blue hat with green lining, height 7", designer L. Harradine.   1941-1975   **160.00   225.00**

GENIE, The

HN 2989
☐ Rising from a lamp this figure has a dark blue cloak around his bare torso. Head bald except for a black topknot. Arms are folded, height 9¾", designer R. Tabbenor.   1983-   **95.00**

GENTLEMEN FROM WILLIAMSBURG

HN 2227
☐ Green costume, white stockings, black shoes, black hat, seated figure on wooden bench, height 6¼", designer M. Davies.   1960-1983   **100.00   175.00**

GENTLEWOMAN, A

HN 1632
☐ Older woman in lavender gown holding green parasol and bonnet, height 7½", designer L. Harradine.   1934-1949   **675.00   775.00**

GEORGIANA

HN 2093
☐ 18th century ball gown in red, blue and pale yellow, headdress of red and blues, height 8¼", designer M. Davies   1952-1955   **600.00   700.00**

The Genie,
HN2989,
95.00

	Date	Price Range	
GEORGINA (Kate Greenaway)			
HN 2377			
☐ White base, shaded yellow gown, red cloak, white bonnet with blue ribbons, holding hoop and stick, height 5¾″, designer M. Davies.	1981-	75.00	
GERALDINE			
HN 2348			
☐ Brown gown with white flowers on bottom edge, white collar, brown ribbon in hair, matte finish, height 7½″, designer M. Davies.	1972-1976	125.00	175.00
GILLIAN			
HN 1670			
☐ Shaded red gown, green bonnet and ribbons, white shawl with multicolored design, height 7¾″, designer L. Harradine.	1934-1949	700.00	800.00

	Date	Price Range

GIRL WITH YELLOW FROCK

HN 588
☐ Young girl in yellow frock on green base, height 6¼″, designer unknown.   1923-1938   1350.00 1500.00

GISELLE

HN 2139
☐ Seated ballet dancer on wooden bench on shaded green base, light blue costume with white trim, blue headdress, height 6¼″, designer M. Davies.   1954-1969   300.00   350.00

GISELLE, THE FOREST GLADE

HN 2140
☐ Ballet figure standing on toes on base of shaded greens, white costume, holding blue cloth by one hand, height 7¼″, designer M. Davies.   1954-1965   300.00   375.00

GLADYS

HN 1740
☐ Figure only of head, shoulders and arms leaning on green base, green gown, height 5″, designer L. Harradine.   1935-1949   550.00   600.00

HN 1741
☐ Pink dress, height 5″, designer L. Harradine.   1935-1938   575.00   625.00

GLORIA

HN 1488
☐ Shaded blue gown and cloak, fur trimmed sleeves, blue hat with red feather, red purse, height 7″, designer L. Harradine.   1932-1938   900.00 1000.00

HN 1700
☐ Light green skirt, green blouse with black designs, black jacket, cloak multicolored, black hat, height 7″, designer L. Harradine.   1935-1938   1000.00 1100.00

GNOME, A

HN 319
☐ Seated elf type figure with pale blue costume, height 6¼″, designer H. Tittensor.   1918-1938   1000.00 1200.00

	Date	Price Range	

HN 380
☐ Purple costume, height 6¼ ″, designer
H. Tittensor.   1920-1938   1000.00 1200.00
HN 381
☐ Purple and green costume, green
face, hands and arms green, height
6¼ ″, designer H. Tittensor.   1920-1938   1000.00 1200.00

GOLDEN DAYS

HN 2274
☐ Small girl and dog on dark brown and
green base, yellow gown with blue
trim, white and brown dog, height 4″,
designer M. Davies.   1964-1973   125.00   175.00

GOLLYWOG

HN 1979
☐ Small boy figure in white coveralls
with animal designs, on base, holding
doll, height 5¼ ″, designer L. Har-
radine.   1945-1959   300.00   350.00
HN 2040
☐ Light blue coveralls, green hat, height
5¼ ″, designer L. Harradine.   1949-1959   225.00   275.00

GOOD CATCH, A

HN 2258
☐ Man in dark brown suit, on base with
fish in hand, net and hamper on base,
height 7″, designer M. Nicoll.   1966-   165.00

GOOD KING WENCESLAS

HN 2118
☐ Costume of shaded oranges, dark
cloak, holding lantern in one hand, on
light brown base, height 9″, designer
M. Davies.   1953-1976   250.00   300.00

GOOD MORNING

HN 2671
☐ Lady feeding birds, bird house on tree
stump, gown white with floral design
edge, light red blouse, matt finish,
height 8″, designer M. Nicoll.   1974-1976   325.00   375.00

Good King Wenceslas,
HN2118,
250.00 - 300.00

GOODY TWO SHOES	Date	Price Range	
HN 1889			
☐ Small figure in green dress with white trim, white cap, height 4¾", designer L. Harradine.	1938-1949	250.00	300.00
HN 1905			
☐ Pink skirt with red overdress, height 4¾", designer L. Harradine.	1939-1949	225.00	275.00
HN 2037			
☐ Red dress with white trim, red shoes, white cap, height 5¼", designer L. Harradine.	1949-	100.00	
☐ **M-80** Made as a miniature, blue skirt, height 4", designer L. Harradine.	1939-1949	400.00	450.00
☐ **M-81** Cream skirt with mottled overlay, height 4", designer L. Harradine.	1939-1949	350.00	400.00

	Date	Price Range	

GOOSEGIRL, The

HN 425
☐ Figure on dark base with goose, blue skirt, striped blue blouse, holding basket, height unknown, designer L. Harradine...................... 1921-1938   2750.00   3000.00

HN 436
☐ Green skirt with blue spots, spotted blouse, height unknown, designer L. Harradine........................ 1921-1938   2500.00   3000.00

HN 437
☐ Checkered brown and blue dress, height unknown, designer L. Harradine   1921-1938   2500.00   3000.00

HN 448
☐ Blue striped blouse, blue hat, height unknown, designer L. Harradine. 1921-1938   2750.00   3000.00

HN 559
☐ Spotted pink dress, height unknown, designer L. Harradine.............. 1923-1938   2750.00   3000.00

HN 560
☐ Red striped skirt, red blouse, white apron, white with designed rings head kerchief, height unknown, designer L. Harradine................ 1923-1938   2750.00   3000.00

GOSSIPS, The

HN 1426
☐ Two ladies seated on brown sofa, one costume of shaded blues, with blue ribbon on bonnet, other costume of white with shaded reds, dark hair with small hat, height 5¾", designer L. Harradine...................... 1930-1949   500.00   750.00

HN 1429
☐ Red sofa, one gown of red with bonnet, other is white with floral design, small red hat, height 5¾", designer L. Harradine...................... 1930-1949   525.00   575.00

HN 2025
☐ Minor glaze differences, height 5¾", designer L. Harradine.............. 1949-1967   350.00   400.00

GRACE

HN 2318
☐ Green skirt, dark green jacket with fur trim, small fur hat and muff, figure is skating, height 7⅞", designer M. Nicoll. 1966-1980   110.00   155.00

	Date	Price Range

GRADUATE
HN 3016
☐ Young lady wearing the classic black gown and hat, height unknown, designer unknown. 1984-   100.00

HN 3017
☐ Young man wearing a black gown over a gray pin stripped suit and cap, height unknown, designer unknown. . 1984-   100.00

GRANDMA
HN 2052
☐ White skirt, red jacket, multicolored, carrying basket on arm, walking stick in other hand. There are some known color variations of this number, height 6¾", designer L. Harradine. . . 1950-1959   325.00   400.00

GRAND MANNER
HN 2723
☐ Yellow, blue and red gown with white flower design, with hat to match, dark green ribbon on dress, height 7¾", designer W. K. Harper. 1975-1981   250.00   300.00

GRANNY
HN 1804
☐ Seated figure on chair, gray dress, purple and brown checkered shawl, small tea table at side, height 7", designer L. Harradine. 1937-1949   850.00   950.00

HN 1832
☐ Yellow dress with green trim on edge, red and blue shawl, height 7", designer L. Harradine. 1937-1949   850.00   950.00

GRANNY'S HERITAGE
HN 1873
☐ Seated older lady with child in front, flower baskets on each side, red flowered shawl on granny, green dress on child, height 6¼", designer L. Harradine. 1938-1949   450.00   500.00

HN 1874
☐ Granny in blue shawl, green skirt, height 6¼", designer L. Harradine. . . 1938-1949   450.00   500.00

	Date	Price Range	

HN 2031
☐ Granny in green skirt with mottled blue shawl, child in shaded blue dress, height 6¼", designer L. Harradine. 1949-1969   400.00   450.00

GRANNY'S SHAWL

HN 1642
☐ White dress, blue cloak with red ribbons, bonnet with green ribbons, holding basket of flowers, height 6", designer L. Harradine. 1934-1949   400.00   500.00

HN 1647
☐ White dress, red cloak, bonnet with dark green ribbons, height 6", designer L. Harradine. 1934-1949   350.00   400.00

GRETA

HN 1485
☐ Small figure on base, white gown with blue tinge, red scarf, holding basket in front of her with both hands, height 5½", designer L. Harradine. 1931-1953   300.00   350.00

GRETCHEN

HN 1397
☐ Dutch girl on base, blue gown with white apron, white bonnet with green trim, holding jug, height 7¾", designer L. Harradine. 1930-1938   650.00   700.00

HN 1562
☐ Dark hair, multicolored skirt, red blouse, height 7¾", designer L. Harradine. 1933-1938   700.00   800.00

GRIEF

HN 595
☐ Small seated figure wrapped completely in blue robe, dark hair, has only toes peeking from robe, height 2", designer unknown. 1924-1938   900.00   1000.00

	Date	Price Range

GRIZEL

HN 1629

☐ Pink tiered skirt with multicolored blouse, green hat and green shoes, small bit of pantalettes showing, height 6¾″, designer L. Harradine. ... 1934-1938   550.00   650.00

GRISELDA

HN 1993

☐ Cream coloured gown with lavender overlay, trimmed in white, green bonnet with red ribbons, height 5¾″, designer L. Harradine. 1947-1953   500.00   600.00

GROSSMITH'S 'TSANG IHANG' PERFUME OF TIBET

HN 582

☐ Chinese lady on black base with printing, yellow costume with red flowers, trimmed in blue, wearing white jewelry (See classification Tibetian Lady), height 11½″, designer unknown   1923-Unknown   650.00   700.00

GUY FAWKES

HN 98

☐ Black costume covered with red cloak, black hat, carrying lantern, height 10½″, designer C. J. Noke. ... 1918-1949   1300.00   1500.00

HN 347

☐ Brown cloak, height 10½″, designer C. J. Noke. 1919-1938   1250.00   1400.00

HN 445

☐ Green cloak, height 10½″, designer C. J. Noke. 1921-1938   1250.00   1400.00

GWENDOLEN

HN 1494

☐ Seated dark haired figure, tiered green and pink gown, green shoes, holding small floral bouquet on lap, height 6″, designer L. Harradine. 1932-1938   775.00   850.00

HN 1503

☐ Shaded yellow and orange gown, height 6″, designer L. Harradine. 1932-1949   700.00   800.00

HN 1570

☐ Pink gown, height 6″, designer L. Harradine. 1933-1949   675.00   750.00

	Date	Price Range	

GWYNNETH

HN 1980

☐ Red gown trimmed with white, small white head cap, height 7″, designer L. Harradine.   1945-1952   250.00   325.00

GYPSY DANCE, A

HN 2157

☐ White and shaded blue gown, bare footed, free hand not attached to dress (1st version), height 7″, designer M. Davies.   1955-1957   350.00   400.00

HN 2230

☐ White and shaded purple gown, hand is attached to gown (2nd version), height 7″, designer M. Davies.   1959-1971   200.00   275.00

GYPSY WOMAN WITH CHILD

HN 1301

☐ Blue skirt, red blouse, green shawl, holding wrapped baby in one arm, red tied scarf in other hand, height unknown, designer unknown.   1928-1938   2250.00   2400.00

GYPSY GIRL WITH FLOWERS

HN 1302

☐ Striped green skirt, red blouse, holding flowers, height unknown, designer unknown.   1928-1938   2250.00   2400.00

'HAPPY JOY, BABY BOY'

HN 1541

☐ Small white figure standing on multicolored rock, holding small very light green robe, height 6¼″, designer unknown.   1933-1949   300.00   350.00

HARLEQUIN

HN 2186

☐ Light blue trousers with darker blue design, blue jacket with darker blue and white checks, white stockings, blue hat with white trim, on base, height 7¼″, designer M. Davies.   1957-1969   225.00   275.00

	Date	Price Range

HARLEQUINADE

HN 585

☐ Costume of black, yellow, green, purple checks, trimmed in white, black hat, black shoes, dark stockings, standing on pedestal style base, height 6½ ″, designer L. Harradine. .. **1923-1938   850.00   950.00**

HN 635

☐ Gold costume, height 6½ ″, designer L. Harradine. **1924-1938   1150.00 1300.00**

HN 711

☐ Black and white costume, height 6½ ″, designer L. Harradine. **1925-1938   850.00   950.00**

HN 780

☐ Pink dress with blue, black and orange markings, height 6½ ″, designer L. Harradine. **1926-1938   850.00   950.00**

HARLEQUINADE MASKED

HN 768

☐ Black, red and green checkered costume, figure standing on black pedestal style base, height 6½ ″, designer L. Harradine. **1925-1938   1350.00 1450.00**

HN 769

☐ Blue, red and yellow checkered costume, height 6½ ″, designer L. Harradine. **1925-1938   1350.00 1450.00**

HN 1274

☐ Red and black checkered costume with red hat, height 6½ ″, designer L. Harradine. **1928-1938   1350.00 1450.00**

HN 1304

☐ Spotted black costume, height 6½ ″, designer L. Harradine. **1928-1938   1350.00 1450.00**

HARMONY

HN 2824

☐ Figure holding small white bird in hand, blue and gray gown, height 8″, designer R. Jefferson. **1978-   170.00**

HAZEL

HN 1796

☐ Small figure in green tiered dress, green bonnet, holding small round purse, height 5¼ ″, designer L. Harradine. **1936-1949   350.00   400.00**

Harmony,
HN2824,
170.00

	Date	Price Range	

HN 1797
☐ Shaded red dress, trimmed with small floral design, blue and red shawl, small blue purse, height 5¼ ", designer L. Harradine. 1936-1949   300.00   350.00

HEART TO HEART

HN 2276
☐ Two figures each seated in yellow chairs, one dressed in lavender gown trimmed in white, the other in white with blue designs and blue shawl, the figures are facing each other, height 5½ ", designer M. Davies. 1961-1971   400.00   500.00

HELEN

HN 1508
☐ Green gown with red floral design trimmed in white, bonnet with red ribbons, black shoes on base, open parasol, height 8 ", designer L. Harradine. 1932-1938   650.00   800.00

	Date	Price Range	

HN 1509
□ White gown with red floral design, red shoes, height 8″, designer L. Harradine. 1932-1938   650.00   800.00

HN 1572
□ Red gown, shaded red bonnet with blue ribbons, height 8″, designer L. Harradine. 1933-1938   550.00   700.00

HELMSMAN

HN 2499
□ Foul weather costume, black hat, figure standing on base before helm with hands on wheel, height 8½″, designer M. Nicoll. 1974-   200.00

HE LOVES ME

HN 2046
□ Small blonde girl standing on yellow rock, red and blue sun dress, holding single flower in hands, height 5½″, designer L. Harradine. 1949-1962   175.00   225.00

HENRIETTA MARIA

HN 2005
□ Red and yellow gown with light blue designs, holding small round red and white fan, height 9½″, designer M. Davies. 1948-1953   550.00   650.00

HENRY VIII

HN 370
□ Purple, brown, yellow and green robes, standing on base (1st version), height unknown, designer C. J. Noke. 1920-1938   2350.00   2600.00

HN 673
□ Brown and lilac robes (1st version), height unknown, designer C. J. Noke. 1924-1938   2350.00   2600.00

HENRY IRVING AS CARDINAL WOLSEY

HN 344
□ Figure with red costume and red hat on black base, height 13¼″, designer C. J. Noke. 1919-1949   2000.00   2500.00

	Date	Price Range	

HENRY LYTTON AS JACK POINT
HN 610
☐ Figure in clown costume of blue with red and black stripes, green stockings and shoes, on black base, height 6½ ", designer C. J. Noke.   1924-1949   800.00   900.00

'HERE A LITTLE CHILD I STAND'
HN 1546
☐ Small child standing on multicolored rock, light blue gown, height 6¼ ", designer unknown.   1933-1949   300.00   350.00

HER LADYSHIP
HN 1977
☐ Light green gown with green floral design, paisley shawl, pale green bonnet with green ribbons, white fur muff, height 7¼ ", designer L. Harradine.   1945-1959   250.00   325.00

HERMINIA
HN 1644
☐ White gown and shawl with red and green floral design, light green bonnet with green ribbons, small red purse, height 6½ ", designer L. Harradine.   1934-1938   850.00   950.00
HN 1646
☐ Red dress, white stripes, height 6½ ", designer L. Harradine.   1934-1938   900.00   1000.00
HN 1704
☐ Red gown, mottled green shawl and purse, green bonnet with red ribbons, height 6½ ", designer L. Harradine. . .   1935-1938   850.00   950.00

HERMIONE
HN 2058
☐ Cream and shaded blue gown with red trim, large red hat with feathers and ribbons, black ribbon around neck, height 7½ ", designer M. Davies   1950-1952   600.00   700.00
☐ M40 Height 4¼ ", designer L. Harradine. 400.00   500.00

	Date	Price Range	

HIGHWAYMAN, The

HN 527

☐ A character from "The Beggar's Opera," red coat with dark overcoat, black hat with red trim, black stockings and shoes, drawing pistol, figure on black base, height 6½", designer L. Harradine.   1921-1949   700.00   800.00

HN 592

☐ Different glaze finish, height 6½", designer L. Harradine.   1924-1949   700.00   800.00

HN 1257

☐ Earthenware, height 6½", designer L. Harradine.   1927-1949   600.00   700.00

The Highwayman,
HN527,
700.00 – 800.00

HILARY

HN 2335

☐ Blue gown with white designs, trimmed in white and blue, holding yellow and white hat, height 7¼", designer unknown.   1967-1980   95.00   150.00

	Date	Price Range

HINGED PARASOL, The

HN 1578
☐ Tiered cream and red gown with large blue dots, green hat, shoes and parasol, height 6½", designer L. Harradine.   1933-1949   350.00   450.00

HN 1579
☐ Red and blue gown, red shoes, parasol and hat, height 6½", designer L. Harradine.   1933-1949   350.00   450.00

HIS HOLINESS POPE JOHN PAUL II

HN 2888
☐ Beautiful likeness of His Holiness inspired by his visit to the United Kingdom, height 10", designer E. J. Griffiths.   1982-   150.00

HOME AGAIN

HN 2167
☐ Small girl in red gown with white dog on base, small green hat, green shoes and ribbons, height 3½", designer M. Davies.   1956-   125.00

HONEY

HN 1909
☐ Pink dress with red jacket, blue shawl with white dots, blue bonnet with green ribbons, holding small round purse in one hand, small bouquet in other, height 7", designer L. Harradine.   1939-1949   350.00   400.00

HN 1910
☐ Blue dress with darker blue jacket, white shawl with blue designs, bonnet has black ribbons, holding larger bouquet of flowers, height 7", designer L. Harradine.   1939-1949   375.00   450.00

HN 1963
☐ Red and blue hat strings and shawl, height 7", designer L. Harradine.   1941-1949   400.00   450.00

	Date	Price Range

HORNPIPE, The
HN 2161
☐ Figure of sailor in dancing position on base, striped trousers, blue and white jacket, white shirt, black hat, height 9¼ ″, designer M. Nicoll. 1955-1962   750.00   850.00

HOSTESS OF WILLIAMSBURG
HN 2209
☐ Pink gown with trim of white and blue ribbons, holding closed fan in hand, height 7¼ ″, designer M. Davies. 1960-1983   135.00   200.00

HUNTING SQUIRE
HN 1409
☐ Figure seated on blue and white horse mounted on black base, red jacket, white trousers, black boots, black hat, height 9¾ ″, designer unknown........................ 1930-1938   2000.00   2500.00

HUNTS LADY
HN 1201
☐ Riding costume of white trousers, blue and gray coat, brown boots and hat, white shirt, standing on brown base, height 8¼ ″, designer L. Harradine. 1926-1938   1100.00   1200.00

HUNTSMAN, The
HN 1226
☐ Riding costume of red jacket, white trousers, black boots and hat, holding riding crop, standing on brown base (1st version), height 8¾ ″, designer L. Harradine. 1927-1938   1350.00   1500.00
HN 1815
☐ Seated figure on brown horse mounted on black base, red jacket, white trousers, black boots and hat, blowing horn, earthenware (2nd version), height 9½ ″, designer unknown. 1937-1949   2300.00   2500.00
HN 2492
☐ Seated figure on wooden bench with dog at side, yellow trousers, gray jacket, black riding cap, black boots with brown trim (3rd version), height 7½ ″, designer M. Nicoll. 1974-1980   135.00   200.00

	Date	Price Range

IBRAHIM
HN 2095
☐ Shaded light red robe with cream colored scarf, height 7¾", designer C. J. Noke. 1952-1955   **700.00**   **800.00**

IONA
HN 1346
☐ Lady and German Shepherd dog on black base, blue costume trimmed in purple, red and green, tall green hat with purple feather, height 7½", designer L. Harradine. 1929-1938   **2500.00**   **3000.00**

IN GRANDMA'S DAY
HN 339
☐ See classification "LILAC SHAWL, A", height 8¾", designer C. J. Noke. 1919-1938   **1250.00**   **1500.00**
HN 340
☐ See classification "LILAC SHAWL, A", height 8¾", designer C. J. Noke. 1919-1938   **1250.00**   **1500.00**
HN 362
☐ See classification "LILAC SHAWL, A", height 8¾", designer C. J. Noke. 1919-1938   **1550.00**   **1700.00**
HN 388
☐ See classification "LILAC SHAWL, A", height 8¾", designer C. J. Noke. 1920-1938   **1650.00**   **1800.00**
HN 442
☐ See classification "LILAC SHAWL, A", height 8¾", designer C. J. Noke. .*. . . 1921-1938   **1650.00**   **1800.00**

IN THE STOCKS
HN 1474
☐ This figure also known as LOVE IN THE STOCKS and LOVE LOCKED IN — Small white angel in stocks, girl seated beside stocks in red dress, holding bonnet by ribbons (1st version), height 5¼", designer L. Harradine. 1931-1938   **1300.00**   **1500.00**
HN 1475
☐ Green gown and green slippers, blue ribbons (1st version), height 5¼", designer L. Harradine. 1931-1938   **1000.00**   **1250.00**
HN 2163
☐ Character figure in brown stocks on brown base, red costume with black hat (2nd version), height 5", designer M. Nicoll. 1955-1959   **600.00**   **700.00**

In The Stocks, HN2163, **600.00 ~ 700.00**

	Date	Price Range	
INNOCENCE			
HN 2842			
☐ Dark haired figure in red gown with black ribbon straps, height 7½″, designer E. J. Griffiths.	1979-1983	**110.00**	**150.00**
INVITATION			
HN 2170			
☐ Pink gown with shoulder trim of blue ribbon and white flowers, holding open fan of blue, red and white, height 5½″, designer M. Davies.	1956-1975	**110.00**	**150.00**
IRENE			
HN 1621			
☐ Tiered light yellow gown, with red bodice, light red bonnet with green ribbon, holding small flower, height varies from 6½ to 7″, designer L. Harradine.	1934-1951	**350.00**	**400.00**
HN 1697			
☐ Red gown, green bonnet, bouquet of yellow roses, height varies from 6½ to 7″, designer L. Harradine.	1935-1949	**400.00**	**475.00**

	Date	Price Range	

HN 1952
☐ Red and blue gown, blue bonnet, multicolor flowers in bouquet, height varies from 6½ to 7″, designer L. Harradine. 1940-1950   500.00   600.00

IRISH COLLEEN

HN 766
☐ Figure standing on black base, short black skirt with white stipes, red jacket, black vest, tall black hat with red floral trim, height 6½″, designer L. Harradine. 1925-1938   1650.00   1800.00

HN 767
☐ Black, red and green stripe skirt, black jacket, red vest, red shoes, height 6½″, designer L. Harradine. 1925-1938   1650.00   1800.00

IRISHMAN, AN

HN 1307
☐ Figure standing on shaded blue base, green coat, red vest, brown striped trousers, green hat, height 6¾″, designer H. Fenton. 1928-1938   1150.00   1250.00

IVY

HN 1768
☐ Small figure in blue gown, red bonnet with white feather and green ribbon, holding small round purse, white pantalettes showing slightly, height 4¾″, designer L. Harradine. 1936-1979   50.00   75.00

HN 1769
☐ Color details not recorded, made for a brief period, height 4¾″, designer L. Harradine. 1938-   350.00   400.00

JACK

HN 2060
☐ Small boy figure on green and yellow base, holding pail, black trousers, blue coat, white shirt, red sash, black shoes, height 5½″, designer L. Harradine. 1950-1971   125.00   175.00

	Date	Price Range

JACK POINT

HN 85

☐ Jester type figure standing on green base, red checkered costume, holding small pouch, hand under chin, height 16¼", designer C. J. Noke. ... 1918-1938 **2000.00 3200.00**

HN 91

☐ Green, black and purple checkered costume, very light colored base, height 16¼", designer C. J. Noke. ... 1918-1938 **2000.00 2250.00**

HN 99

☐ Heraldic tunic, height 16¼", designer C. J. Noke. ... 1918-1938 **2000.00 2250.00**

JACQUELINE

HN 2000

☐ Blue and gray gown with white apron, flower trimmed sleeves, height 7½", designer L. Harradine. ... 1947-1951 **400.00 450.00**

HN 2001

☐ Red gown with white apron, darker flowers on sleeves, height 7½", designer L. Harradine. ... 1947-1951 **425.00 475.00**

HN 2333

☐ Light gray gown with yellow band and flower at the waist, height 7½", designer M. Davies. ... 1983- **145.00**

JAMES

HN 3013

☐ Young male figure in gray knee length breeches, wearing a white smock, black shoes, wide hat with black bow, reddish brown hair, holding a puppy, height 6", designer P. Parsons. ... 1983- **75.00**

JANE

HN 2014

☐ Red skirt, red overlay with blue dots, trimmed in white, white cap with blue ribbons, holding water jug and glass in hands, height 6¼", designer L. Harradine. ... 1948-1951 **600.00 700.00**

	Date	Price Range

JANE
HN 2806
☐ Pastel yellow gown, black ribbon at the waist, holding an umbrella reflecting many colors, blonde hair, height 8″, designer M. Davies. 1983-   135.00

JANET
HN 1537
☐ Red and white gown, white bonnet with green ribbons, carrying flat basket of flowers (1st version), height 6½″, designer L. Harradine. 1932-   125.00

HN 1538
☐ Red and blue gown, white bonnet with green ribbon (1st version), height 6½″, designer L. Harradine. 1932-1949   275.00   325.00

HN 1652
☐ Pink skirt with floral pattern, red bodice (1st version), height 6½″, designer L. Harradine. 1934-1949   300.00   350.00

HN 1737
☐ Green gown, red shoe (1st version), height 6½″, designer L. Harradine. .. 1935-1949   300.00   350.00

HN 1916
☐ Small figure with red skirt, blue bodice, red shoes (2nd version), height 5¼″, designer L. Harradine. .. 1939-1949   350.00   400.00

HN 1964
☐ Pink dress (2nd version), height 5¼″, designer L. Harradine. 1936-1949   350.00   400.00

☐ **M69** Made as a miniature, green dress, height 4″, designer L. Harradine. 1936-1949   300.00   350.00

☐ **M75** Red and blue dress, height 4″, designer L. Harradine. 1936-1949   300.00   350.00

JANICE
HN 2022
☐ Green and orange Regal gown, small green headdress, jewels at neck, holding small book in hand, height 7¼″, designer M. Davies. 1949-1955   450.00   500.00

HN 2165
☐ Dark green and white gown, blonde hair, height 7¼″, designer M. Davies. 1955-1965   450.00   500.00

Janice,
HN2165,
450.00 - 500.00

	Date	Price Range	
JANINE			
HN 2461			
☐ Green and white gown with green designs, height 7⅞″, designer J. Bromley.	1971-	**170.00**	
JAPANESE FAN			
HN 399			
☐ Japanese lady seated, gown of purple with multicolored jacket, holding round fan, also made as a lidded bowl, height 4¾″, designer H. Tittensor.	1920-1938	**1450.00**	**1600.00**
HN 405			
☐ Pale yellow costume, height 4¾″, designer H. Tittensor.	1920-1938	**1250.00**	**1500.00**
HN 439			
☐ Blue costume, green spots, height 4¼″, designer H. Tittensor	1921-1938	**1500.00**	**1600.00**
HN 440			
☐ Yellow costume, orange spots, height 4¼″, designer H. Tittensor.	1921-1938	**1500.00**	**1600.00**

	Date	Price Range	
JASMINE			
HN 1862			
☐ Green gown with multicolored, flowered jacket, strand of long beads on front, head covering of same material as jacket, height 7½ ", designer L. Harradine.....................	1938-1949	625.00	675.00
HN 1863			
☐ White gown with multicolored, flowered jacket, beige with green border on jacket, light colored beads, head covering is flowered to match jacket, height 7½ ", designer L. Harradine. ..	1938-1949	625.00	675.00
HN 1876			
☐ Flowered blue coat with pink trim, height 7½ ", designer L. Harradine. ..	1938-1949	650.00	675.00
JEAN			
HN 1877			
☐ Shaded light red gown with blue cloak with ribbon of green, holding basket of flowers on one arm; height 7½ ", designer L. Harradine.	1938-1949	475.00	525.00
HN 1878			
☐ Green dress with red shawl, height 7½ ", designer L. Harradine.	1938-1949	375.00	450.00
HN 2032			
☐ Green dress with accents of darker green, red cloak with black ribbons, flowers yellow in basket, height 7½ ", designer L. Harradine.	1949-1959	225.00	300.00
JENNIFER			
HN 1484			
☐ Light yellow gown with yellow flower design, multi-yellow flowered jacket, dark blue cloak, green bonnet, height 6½ ", designer L. Harradine.	1931-1949	400.00	500.00
HN 2392			
☐ Beautiful figure of young girl in blue gown with yellow sash, cream sleeves, long blonde hair, height 7", designer M. Davies.	1982-	155.00	

	Date	Price Range	

JERSEY MILKMAID, The

HN 2057

☐ Green skirt, brown blouse, blue and white apron trimmed in brown, blue and white farm bonnet, carrying brown jug. In 1975 re-issued same number titled "THE MILKMAID," see proper classification, there are known color variations of this number dress and jug, height 6½ ", designer L. Harradine.................... 1950-1959   275.00   325.00

JESTER, A

HN   45

☐ Figure seated on light pedestal base, black and white checkered costume, holding one leg (1st version), height 10 ", designer C. J. Noke. 1915-1938   1250.00 1500.00

HN   45A

☐ Costume of green and white checks, legs crossed, one hand to face (2nd version), height 10 ", designer C. J. Noke.......................... 1915-1938   1250.00 1500.00

HN   45B

☐ Brown and white checkered costume (2nd version), height 10 ", designer C. J. Noke...................... 1915-1938   1250.00 1500.00

HN   55

☐ Black and lilac costume (2nd version), height 10 ", designer C. J. Noke. 1916-1938   1300.00 1500.00

HN   71

☐ Black and green costume with black and green checks and orange balls (1st version), height 10 ", designer C. J. Noke....................... 1917-1938   1250.00 1500.00

HN 71A

☐ No color details available (1st version), height 10 ", designer C. J. Noke. 1917-1938   1250.00 1500.00

HN 308

☐ A note below HN 308 in the figure design book says, 'same as 55' (2nd version), height 10 ", designer C. J. Noke. 1918-1938   1250.00 1500.00

HN 320

☐ HN 45, green and black costume (1st version), height 10 ", designer C. J. Noke. 1918-1938   1250.00 1500.00

	Date	Price Range	

HN 367
☐ Green and shaded red costume, seated on black pedestal (1st version), height 10″, designer C. J. Noke. 1920-1938 1400.00 1500.00

HN 412
☐ Green and red striped tights (1st version), height 10″, designer C. J. Noke. 1920-1938 1350.00 1500.00

HN 426
☐ Costume of pink markings, black tights (1st version), height 10″, designer C. J. Noke. 1921-1938 1250.00 1500.00

HN 446
☐ Green sleeves, blue pedestal (1st version), height 10″, designer C. J. Noke. 1921-1938 1350.00 1500.00

HN 552
☐ Black and red costume (1st version), height 10″, designer C. J. Noke. 1922-1938 1350.00 1500.00

HN 616
☐ Quartered heraldic tunic (1st version), height 10″, designer C. J. Noke. 1924-1938 1350.00 1500.00

HN 627
☐ Brown checkered costume (1st version), height 10″, designer C. J. Noke. 1924-1938 1350.00 1500.00

HN 630
☐ HN 45A, brown striped tights (2nd version), height 10″, designer C. J. Noke. 1924-1938 1350.00 1500.00

HN 1295
☐ Brown costume, brown and orange stripes, seated on black pedestal (1st version), height 10″, designer C. J. Noke. 1928-1949 900.00 1000.00

HN 1333
☐ Blue tunic with yellow and black stripes (2nd version), height 10″, designer C. J. Noke. 1929-1949 1350.00 1500.00

HN 1702
☐ HN 2016, with minor variations (1st version), height 10″, designer C. J. Noke. 1935-1949 900.00 1000.00

HN 2016
☐ Shaded brown costume, one leg with darker stripes, costume trimmed in orange with orange balls, pedestal is gray with darker base (1st version), height 10″, designer C. J. Noke. 1949- 200.00

A Jester,
HN45,
1250.00 - 1500.00

	Date	Price Range	
JILL			
HN 2061			
☐ Small girl figure on yellow and green base, red dress with white apron, white bonnet with green ribbons, height 5½ ″, designer L. Harradine. ..	1950-1971	150.00	200.00
JOAN			
HN 1422			
☐ Older lady figure seated in blue and green back chair, blue dress, black shawl, holding red yarn in hands, small foot stool, height 5½ ″, designer L. Harradine.	1930-1949	450.00	550.00
HN 2023			
☐ Minor glaze differences, height 5¾ ″, designer L. Harradine.	1949-1959	350.00	400.00

	Date	Price Range	

JOHN PEEL
HN 1408
☐ Figure seated on brown horse mounted on black base, red coat, white trousers, black hat and boots, blowing horn. Later re-issued with the new title, THE HUNTSMAN, height 9¼", designer unknown................ 1930-1937   **2750.00 3000.00**

JOLLY SAILOR
HN 2172
☐ Seated character figure of sailor, black trousers, white and blue striped shirt, straw colored hat, playing instrument, height 6½", designer M. Nicoll......................... 1956-1965   **600.00 700.00**

JOVIAL MONK, The
HN 2144
☐ Brown robe with rope style belt, carrying basket in one hand, height 7¾", designer M. Davies................ 1954-1976   **175.00 225.00**

JUDGE, The
HN 2443
☐ Red and white costume, seated in brown high back chair, white wig, black shoes, holding papers in hand, height 6½", designer M. Nicoll...... 1972-   **175.00**
In 1976 this figure was changed from a matte to a glazed finish, height 6½", designer M. Nicoll............ Matte Finish   **175.00 225.00**

JUDGE AND JURY
HN 1264
☐ Judge figure in red and white costume, little dog chained to chair, three small children in witness stand, another child outside of stand, all on black base, height 6", designer J. G. Hughes.......................... 1927-1938   **3000.00 3500.00**

JUDITH
HN 2089
☐ Red dress with blue vest which has a darker blue design and blue trim on sleeves, blue shoes, height 6⅞", designer L. Harradine............. 1952-1959   **225.00 300.00**

	Date	Price Range

JULIA

HN 2705

☐ Brown gown with white trim, brown hat with yellow ribbons, carrying yellow parasol, height 7⅝", designer M. Davies. ... 1975- 155.00

JUNE

HN 1690

☐ Green and white gown, green bonnet with black ribbons, carrying flowers in one arm, holding parasol in other, height 7½", designer L. Harradine. .. 1935-1949 450.00 500.00

HN 1691

☐ Cream gown with light shades of green and yellow, front panel has flower designs, red bonnet, parasol has green trim, shawl black, height 7½", designer L. Harradine. 1935-1949 350.00 400.00

HN 1947

☐ Shaded red and blue gown trimmed with white, bonnet same trimmed with blue ribbons, parasol dark, height 7½", designer L. Harradine. .. 1940-1949 450.00 500.00

HN 2027

☐ Minor glaze changes, height 7½", designer L. Harradine. 1949-1952 325.00 375.00

☐ **M-65** Made as a miniature figure, shaded red gown with dark trim, height 4", designer L. Harradine. 1935-1949 325.00 375.00

☐ **M-71** Shaded blue gown with red trim, height 4", designer L. Harradine. 1936-1949 325.00 375.00

KAREN

HN 1994

☐ Figure in Edwardian riding costume of red and white, green hat with feather, holding riding crop, on brown base, height 8", designer L. Harradine. 1947-1955 350.00 400.00

HN 2388

☐ Red gown with white bodice, black waistband, dark hair (2nd version), height 8", designer M. Davies. 1982- 185.00

	Date	Price Range

KATE
HN 2789
☐ White gown with multicolored flower design around bottom, white headband, height 7½ ", designer M. Davies . 1978-   155.00

KATE HARDCASTLE
HN 1718
☐ 18th century style pink and green gown, pink bonnet with green ribbons, green gloves, leaning on light colored pedestal on base, height 8", designer L. Harradine. 1935-1949   475.00   575.00

HN 1719
☐ Red and green gown, green bonnet with red ribbons, red gloves, leaning on dark pedestal with light base, height 8¼ ", designer L. Harradine. . . 1935-1949   475.00   575.00

HN 1734
☐ Green and white gown with green designs, light yellow bonnet with green ribbons, green gloves, dark pedestal on light base, height 8¼ ", designer L. Harradine. 1935-1949   500.00   600.00

HN 1861
☐ Red gown with shaded blue and green overlay, black bonnet with blue ribbons, red gloves, green colored pedestal on light base, height 8¼ ", designer L. Harradine. 1938-1949   500.00   600.00

HN 1919
☐ Red overskirt, green dress, black base, height 8¼ ", designer L. Harradine. 1939-1949   800.00   900.00

HN 2028
☐ HN 1719, with minor glaze difference, height 8¼ ", designer L. Harradine. . . 1949-1952   500.00   600.00

KATHERINE
HN 61
☐ Full covering gown of green with white collar, green hat with white brim, height 5¾ ", designer C. J. Noke. 1916-1938   1500.00   1700.00

HN 74
☐ Pale blue dress with green spots, height 5¾ ", designer C. J. Noke. 1917-1938   1650.00   1800.00

	Date	Price Range	

HN 341
☐ Red gown, height 5¾", designer C. J. Noke. 1919-1938 1250.00 1500.00

HN 471
☐ Spotted blouse and dress, height 5¾", designer C. J. Noke. 1921-1938 2000.00 2500.00

HN 615
☐ Pink skirt with green spots, height 5¾", designer C. J. Noke. 1924-1938 1650.00 1800.00

HN 793
☐ Lilac dress with green spots, height 5¾", designer C. J. Noke. 1926-1938 1650.00 1800.00

KATHLEEN

HN 1252
☐ Shaded blue skirt, red jacket, red and blue shawl, black ribbon in hair, holding black bonnet in one hand, height 7½", designer L. Harradine. . . 1927-1938 800.00 850.00

HN 1253
☐ Red skirt, multicolored jacket, dark blue and black shawl, height 7½", designer L. Harradine. 1927-1938 800.00 850.00

HN 1275
☐ HN 1252, Flowered black shawl, height 7½", designer L. Harradine. . . 1928-1938 800.00 850.00

HN 1279
☐ Mottled red skirt and jacket, red shawl, height 7½", designer L. Harradine. 1928-1938 800.00 850.00

HN 1291
☐ Red shawl with mottled yellow dress, height 7½", designer L. Harradine. . . 1928-1938 850.00 950.00

HN 1357
☐ Pink, orange and yellow mottled skirt, height 7½", designer L. Harradine. . . 1929-1938 800.00 850.00

HN 1512
☐ Pale lilac dress, blue hat, height 7½", designer L. Harradine. 1932-1938 700.00 800.00

HN 2933
☐ This figure is seated, multicolored gown, she is wearing a dark green large hat, holding an artist palette leaning forward as if to paint, height unknown, designer Sharon Keenan. . . 1984- 195.00

	Date	Price Range
KATHY (Kate Greenaway)		
HN 2346		
☐ This figure is seated on green stool, wearing white gown with red sash, white bonnet with light blue ribbon, red shoes, holding small light blue flower in one hand, height 4¾″, designer M. Davies.	1981-	75.00
KATRINA		
HN 2327		
☐ Red gown trimmed with white collar, high comb in hair, both hands on head, height 7½″, designer M. Davies	1965-1969	250.00	300.00
KING CHARLES		
HN 404		
☐ Deep navy blue costume, deep navy blue cloak, navy blue with light blue feather hat, deep navy stockings, black shoes, black walking stick on pink base, height 16¾″, designers C. J. Noke and H. Tittensor.	1920-1951	1750.00	2000.00
KIRSTY		
HN 2381		
☐ Yellow gown with shades of brown with design around rim of skirt, white trim on sleeves, white collar with ribbon, height 7¾″, designer M. Davies.	1971-	185.00
KITTY		
HN 1367		
☐ Lady seated with foot on footstool, white gown and yellow with darker thin stripes of blue, holding dark kitten in hands, has small white cap with red ribbon on head, height 4″, designer unknown.	1930-1938	1000.00	1100.00
KO-KO		
HN 1266		
☐ Japanese figure with black and yellow costume, standing on green and yellow base, holding fan, height 5″, designer L. Harradine.	1928-1949	650.00	750.00

	Date	Price Range

HN 1286

☐ Red and blue costume standing on dark base, height 5″, designer L. Harradine.   1938-1949   650.00   750.00

HN 2898

☐ Japanese figure with black hair on light brown base, orange, blue, green, black and red costume, holding scroll, with large ax-like weapon on stand (2nd version), height 11½″, designer W. K. Harper.   1980-   750.00

LADY ANNE, The

HN   83

☐ Yellow gown with dark trim, one foot on stool, has high head covering of net and flowers, height unknown, designer E. W. Light.   1918-1938   2750.00   3000.00

HN   87

☐ Green gown, red shoes, height unknown, designer E. W. Light   1918-1938   2750.00   3000.00

HN   93

☐ Blue gown, height unknown, designer E. W. Light. . . . ,.   1918-1938   2750.00   3000.00

LADY ANNE NEVILL, The

HN 2006

☐ Purple gown with white fur trim, gold belt and jewels, very high and wide head covering of white, height 9¾″, designer M. Davies.   1948-1953   800.00   900.00

LADY APRIL

HN 1958

☐ Red gown, purple, blue and red cloak with green straps, red bonnet with red and black trim, holding small bouquet in one arm, green gloves, height 7″, designer L. Harradine.   1940-1959   250.00   300.00

HN 1965

☐ Green dress, height 7″, designer L. Harradine. . . . . :. . . .   1941-1949   300.00   350.00

	Date	Price Range

LADY BETTY
HN 1967

☐ Red gown with blue ruffle trim collar, blue bonnet with cream feather and black ribbons, holding flower basket, height 6½ ", designer L. Harradine. ...   1941-1951   **250.00**   **325.00**

LADYBIRD
HN 1638

☐ Young girl in pink ballet costume, standing on toes on base, spray of flowers in hair, height 7¾ ", designer L. Harradine.   1924-1949   **900.00**   **1000.00**

HN 1640

☐ Light blue costume and ballet shoes, height 7¾ ", designer L. Harradine. ..   1934-1938   **900.00**   **1000.00**

LADY AND BLACKAMOOR
HN 374

☐ Large full skirted gown of blue and green patterns with blue bodice, holding fan in one hand, high hair style with small black figure behind her, with blue costume and yellow turban (1st version), height unknown, designer H. Tittensor.   1920-1938   **2500.00**   **2700.00**

HN 375

☐ Light colored skirt with designs of flowers and leaves with purple trim, black bodice trimmed in pink (2nd version), height unknown, design H. Tittensor.   1920-1938   **2500.00**   **2700.00**

HN 377

☐ Pink and green dress (2nd version), height unknown, designer H. Tittensor.   1920-1938   **2500.00**   **2700.00**

HN 470

☐ Green and lilac dress (2nd version), height unknown, design H. Tittensor.   1921-1938   **2500.00**   **2700.00**

LADY CHARMIAN
HN 1948

☐ Green gown, mottled red shawl, green bonnet, holding single flower in one hand and basket of flowers with other, height 8", designer L. Harradine.   1940-1973   **275.00**   **325.00**

	Date	Price Range	

HN 1949

☐ Red gown, green shawl, red bonnet with black ribbons, height 8″, designer L. Harradine. . . . . :. — 1940-1975 — **275.00** — **325.00**

LADY CLARE

HN 1465

☐ Red and blue tiered gown with blue and red shawl holding small purse and parasol, light bonnet with red ribbons, height 7¾″, designer L. Harradine. . . . . — 1931-1938 — **700.00** — **800.00**

LADY CLOWN

HN 717

☐ White costume with red and green stripes and black blocks, dunce style hat, red shoes, standing on one foot on black base, height 7½″, designer L. Harradine. — 1925-1938 — **1300.00** — **1450.00**

HN 718

☐ White costume, red stripes, black spots, height 7½″, designer L. Harradine. . . . . — 1925-1938 — **1300.00** — **1450.00**

HN 738

☐ Black and white trousers, red spots, height 7½″, designer L. Harradine. . . — 1925-1938 — **1300.00** — **1450.00**

HN 770

☐ Costume painted with green masks and streamers, height 7½″, designer L. Harradine. . . . . — 1925-1938 — **1300.00** — **1450.00**

HN 1263

☐ Multicolored trousers, one leg blue, the other one with red stripes, height 7½″, designer L. Harradine. . . . . — 1927-1938 — **1300.00** — **1450.00**

LADY ERMINE

HN 54

☐ Light green gown, blue coat with fur trim, muff of fur, green hat with yellow ribbon and feather, height 8½″, designer C. J. Noke. . . . . — 1916-1938 — **1250.00** — **1500.00**

HN 332

☐ Red coat and hat, green and yellow patterned skirt, height 8½″, designer C. J. Noke. . . . . : — 1918-1938 — **1450.00** — **1750.00**

	Date	Price Range	

HN 671
☐ Green coat, yellow skirt, height 8½ ″,
designer C. J. Noke.   1924-1938   **1650.00 1800.00**

LADY FAYRE
HN 1265
☐ Blue and red gown and bodice,
blonde hair, red shoes, in curtsy posi-
tion, height 5¾ ″, designer L. Har-
radine.   1928-1938   **550.00   650.00**
HN 1557
☐ Pink gown, height 5¾ ″, designer L.
Harradine.   1933-1938   **750.00   850.00**

LADY FROM WILLIAMSBURG
HN 2228
☐ Figure seated on bench, green gown
with yellow ribbon trim, small white
covering on head, holding bonnet in
hands, height 6 ″, designer M. Davies.   1960-1983   **110.00   200.00**

LADY JESTER
HN 1221
☐ Costume of checkered pink and black
skirt, standing on pedestal style base
(1st version), height 7 ″, designer L.
Harradine.   1927-1938   **1350.00 1500.00**
HN 1222
☐ Checkered black and white costume
with shoes (1st version), height 7 ″, de-
signer L. Harradine.   1927-1938   **1350.00 1500.00**
HN 1284
☐ Seated figure with legs crossed, costume of red tights, dark blue vest with
checkered red and black sleeves,
holding jester doll with black and
white costume (2nd version), height
4¼ ″, designer L. Harradine.   1928-1938   **750.00   850.00**
HN 1285
☐ Blue costume with red stripes on
tights, red vest with very light red
sleeves, holds jester doll in white,
black and blue costume (2nd version),
height 4¼ ″, designer L. Harradine. . .   1928-1938   **750.00   850.00**
HN 1332
☐ Red costume, blue and black scal-
loped pattern on skirt (1st version),
height 7 ″, designer L. Harradine.   1929-1938   **1250.00 1300.00**

Lady Jester,
HN1284,
750.00 – 850.00

LADY OF THE ELIZABETHAN PERIOD	Date	Price Range	
HN 40			
☐ Very full gown of brown and patterned orange, high wide white collar, headdress dark and has a long hanging cloth (1st version), height 9½″, designer E. W. Light.	1914-1938	1750.00	2000.00
HN 40A			
☐ No pattern on dress (1st version), height 9½″, designer E. W. Light.	1914-1938	1750.00	2000.00
HN 73			
☐ Dark blue-green costume (1st version), height 9½″, designer E. W. Light.	1917-1938	1800.00	2000.00
HN 309			
☐ Green patterned costume, with white patterned and raised green dots, gown trimmed in blue, headdress dark (2nd version), height 9½″, designer E. W. Light.	1918-1938	1750.00	2000.00

	Date	Price Range

HN 411

☐ Costume of purple patterned with mottled colors in sleeves and under-skirt, wide white collar (1st version), height 9½″, designer E. W. Light..... 1920-1938   2000.00 2250.00

LADY OF THE FAN

HN 48

☐ Lilac dress, black shoes, feather in hair, holding fan, figure in bowing position, height 9½″, designer E. W. Light............................ 1916-1938   1650.00 1800.00

HN 52

☐ Shaded yellow gown, height 9½″, designer E. W. Light................. 1916-1938   1650.00 1800.00

HN 53

☐ Dark blue dress, height 9½″, designer E. W. Light...................... 1916-1938   1650.00 1800.00

HN 53A

☐ Green and blue dress, height 9½″, designer E. W. Light. 1916-1938   1650.00 1800.00

HN 335

☐ Blue dress with brown patterning, height 9½″, designer E. W. Light..... 1919-1938   1650.00 1800.00

HN 509

☐ Green lilac and blue spotted dress, height 9½″, designer E. W. Light..... 1921-1938   1650.00 1800.00

LADY OF THE GEORGIAN PERIOD

HN 41

☐ Red and white gown which has shaded blue and dark bows, has large white turban style headdress trimmed with dark blue ribbons, height 10¼″, designer E. W. Light................. 1914-1938   2000.00 2300.00

HN 331

☐ Patterned brown and yellow gown, dark brown headdress with red ribbons, height 10¼″, designer E. W. Light. 1918-1938   1650.00 1800.00

HN 444

☐ Green-blue spotted dress, height 10¼″, designer E. W. Light.......... 1921-1938   2100.00 2300.00

HN 690

☐ Color design not available, height 10¼″, designer E. W. Light.......... 1925-1938   2150.00 2300.00

	Date	Price Range

HN 702
☐ Striped pink skirt, green overdress, height 10¼ ″, designer E. W. Light.... 1925-1938 2150.00 2300.00

LADY OF THE SNOWS

HN 1780
☐ No further information available, height unknown, designer R. Garbe. . 1933- 3500.00 4000.00

HN 1830
☐ Tinted model, height unknown, designer R. Garbe. 1937-1949 3500.00 4000.00

LADY OF THE TIME OF HENRY VI

HN 43
☐ Yellow gown with green overdress trimmed in fur, green head covering, height 9¼ ″, designer E. W. Light..... 1914-1938 2750.00 3250.00

LADY PAMELA

HN 2718
☐ Lavender gown with lighter lavender overlay, dark lavender bonnet with still darker ribbon trim, holding mirror, height 8 ″, designer D. V. Tootle. . . 1974-1980 150.00 200.00

LADY WITH ROSE

HN 48A
☐ White gown with dark ribbon style trim on ruffles and orange lining, black waistband, holding red rose, height 9½ ″, designer E. W. Light..... 1916-1938 1650.00 1800.00

HN 52A
☐ Yellow dress, height 9½ ″, designer E. W. Light. 1916-1938 1650.00 1800.00

HN 68
☐ Green and yellow dress, height 9½ ″, designer E. W. Light. 1916-1938 1650.00 1800.00

HN 304
☐ Gray-lilac dress with brown patterning, height 9½ ″, designer E. W. Light. 1918-1938 1650.00 1800.00

HN 336
☐ Multicolored dress with brown patterning, height 9½ ″, designer E. W. Light. 1919-1938 1700.00 1800.00

HN 515
☐ Striped lilac and green dress, height 9½ ″, designer E. W. Light.......... 1921-1938 1700.00 1800.00

	Date	Price Range

HN 517
☐ Lilac dress with orange spots, height
9½", designer E. W. Light........... 1921-1938 1650.00 1800.00

HN 584
☐ Green and pink dress, height 9½",
designer E. W. Light. 1923-1938 1650.00 1800.00

HN 624
☐ Green-blue skirt, pink and black cuffs,
height 9½", designer E. W. Light..... 1924-1938 1650.00 1800.00

LADY WITHOUT BOUQUET

HN 393
☐ Light red gown with blue and white
ring designs, blue bodice with gold
trim, large blue stole with purple lining with blue and white ring design,
height 9", designer G. Lambert. 1920-1938 2000.00 2500.00

HN 394
☐ Blue and yellow costume, height 9",
designer G. Lambert. 1920-1938 2000.00 2500.00

LADY WITH SHAWL

HN 447
☐ Figure on mottled blue base, white
and blue striped gown, dark blue
waistband with white round designs,
white shawl with blue and gold ring
designs, height 13¼", designer L.
Harradine....................... 1921-1938 3250.00 3500.00

HN 458
☐ Multicolored shawl, pink dress,
height 13¼", designer L. Harradine. . 1921-1938 3000.00 3500.00

HN 626
☐ Yellow shawl with pink spots, white
dress with green spots, height 13¼",
designer L. Harradine. 1924-1938 3000.00 3500.00

HN 678
☐ Black and white shawl, yellow and
white dress, height 13¼", designer
L. Harradine..................... 1924-1938 3250.00 3500.00

HN 679
☐ Black, yellow and blue shawl, black
and white dress, height 13¼", de-
signer L. Harradine. 1924-1938 3250.00 3500.00

	Date	Price Range

LAIRD, The
HN 2361
☐ Character figure in Scottish costume, green and black striped skirt, dark green and beige jacket, brown tam, brown shoes and green stockings, holding staff, greenish tan shawl over shoulder, height 8⅛″, designer M. Nicoll. 1969-   **175.00**

LAMBETH WALK, The
HN 1880
☐ Blue dress, height 10″, designer L. Harradine. 1938-1949   **1300.00   1400.00**
HN 1881
☐ Shaded red dress with red flower design on bottom, large blue hat with red trim, red shoe, light colored base, height 10″, designer L. Harradine. . . . 1938-1949   **1300.00   1400.00**

LAMBING TIME
HN 1890
☐ Character figure on brown base, brown trousers with long yellow and brown coat, brown hat and small scarf, holding a lamp under each arm, height 8½″, designer L. Harradine. . . 1938-1980   **100.00   150.00**

LAND OF NOD, The
HN   56
☐ HN 56A, ivory nightshirt, height 9¾″, designer H. Tittensor. 1916-1938   **1750.00   2000.00**
HN   56A
☐ Small figure in very light blue nightshirt, holding candle with brown and white owl on light base with printing, height 9¾″, designer H. Tittensor. . . . 1916-1938   **2000.00   2300.00**
HN   56B
☐ Pale gray nightshirt and red candlestick, height 9¾″, designer H. Tittensor. 1916-1938   **1750.00   2000.00**

LAST WALTZ
HN 2315
☐ White gown with gold designs, dark yellow overlay trimmed in green, holding dance program book and pencil, height 8″, designer M. Davies. . . . 1967-   **185.00**

	Date	Price Range	

LA SYLPHIDE
HN 2138

☐ White gown with light blue trim, ribbon around head, hands crossed, light blue ballet slippers on green and yellow base, height 7¼", designer M. Davies. 1956-1965 325.00 400.00

LAURA
HN 2960

☐ Seated figure with blue and white gown decorated on the bodice and overskirt with orange flowers, blonde hair, height 7¼", designer P. Parsons. 1983- 145.00

LAURIANNE
HN 2719

☐ Seated lady with blue and white gown, dark blue overdress, with book on lap, height 6½", designer D. V. Tootle. 1974-1979 150.00 200.00

LAVENDER WOMAN, The
HN 22

☐ Light blue dress and shawl, holding wrapped infant in one arm and brown basket with flowers in other arm, on light blue base, height 8¼", designer P. Stabler. 1913-1938 1750.00 2000.00

HN 23

☐ Green dress, height 8¼", designer P. Stabler. 1913-1938 1750.00 2000.00

HN 23A

☐ Blue and green dress, height 8¼", designer P. Stabler. 1913-1938 1750.00 2000.00

HN 342

☐ Patterned dress and lilac shawl, height 8¼", designer P. Stabler. 1919-1938 1750.00 2000.00

HN 569

☐ Blue gown with large red spots, red shawl with shaded blue stripes, on brown base, height 8¼", designer P. Stabler. 1924-1938 1150.00 1300.00

HN 744

☐ Spotted dress and striped shawl, height 8¼", designer P. Stabler. 1925-1938 1750.00 2000.00

	Date	Price Range

LAVINIA

HN 1955

☐ Small figure with red gown trimmed with white, white ruffled cap with blue ribbon trim, carrying basket on arm and small object in other hand, height 5″, designer L. Harradine. 1940-1978   85.00   125.00

LEADING LADY

HN 2269

☐ Pale yellow gown with lavender over-dress, red bow on bodice, yellow ribbon in hair, lavender shoe, holding brown and white object in uplifted hand, height 7¾″, designer M. Davies   1965-1976   150.00   225.00

LEISURE HOUR, The

HN 2055

☐ Lady seated in very high backed brown chair on brown base, gown of pale orange with overdress of patterned green and white with red trim, holding large red backed open book on lap, height 6¾″, designer M. Davies   1950-1965   400.00   500.00

LIDO LADY

HN 1220

☐ Pajama clad figure seated on pedestal style base, holding very small brown dog, blue costume with red and dark blue designa, height 6¾″, designer L. Harradine.   1927-1938   1000.00   1100.00

HN 1229

☐ Flowered pink costume, height 6¾″, designer L. Harradine.   1927-1938   1100.00   1200.00

LIGHTS OUT

HN 2262

☐ Small boy figure in pajama costume, blue trousers, white top with gold dots, white pillow with red stripes on white base, height 5″, designer M. Davies............................   1965-1969   225.00   275.00

LILAC SHAWL, A	Date	Price Range	
HN 44 ☐ Cream colored tiered gown with dark ribbon trim, lilac shawl with red rose figure design, light colored bonnet with yellow ribbons, height 8¾″, designer C. J. Noke.	1915-1938	1250.00	1500.00
HN 44A ☐ Roses on shawl replaced by printed pattern, height 8¾″, designer C. J. Noke.	1915-1938	1250.00	1500.00
HN 339 ☐ This figure is now called IN GRANDMA'S DAY. Yellow gown with brown trim, dark patterned brown shawl, dark bonnet with red rose trim and with blue ribbon with darker dots and fringe, height 8¾″, designer C. J. Noke.	1919-1938	1250.00	1500.00
HN 340 ☐ Yellow and lilac costume, height 8¾″, designer C. J. Noke.	1919-1938	1250.00	1500.00
HN 362 ☐ Green, red, yellow striped skirt, height 8¾″, designer C. J. Noke.	1919-1938	1550.00	1700.00
HN 388 ☐ Patterned blue costume, height 8¾″, designer C. J. Noke.	1920-1938	1650.00	1800.00
HN 442 ☐ White spotted skirt, green shawl, height 8¾″, designer C. J. Noke.	1921-1938	1650.00	1800.00
HN 612 ☐ This figure is now called THE POKE BONNET. Dark yellow gown with dark blue circle design, blue and green patterned shawl, dark blue bonnet with red flower trim, red ribbons with blue and white stripes and small dark dots, height 8¾″, designer C. J. Noke.	1924-1938	1350.00	1500.00
HN 765 ☐ Mottled dark green, blue and purple skirt, height 8¾″, designer C. J. Noke.	1925-1938	1500.00	1600.00

	Date	Price Range	

LILAC TIME

HN 2137
□ Red costume with hat which has lilac trim, figure holding bouquet of lilacs in arm, height 7½ ″, designer M. Davies — 1954-1969 — 250.00 — 300.00

LILY

HN 1798
□ Small figure with shaded red gown, white shawl with red and blue designs, cream bonnet with blue ribbons, pantalettes showing slightly, height 5″, designer L. Harradine. .... — 1936-1949 — 100.00 — 150.00

HN 1799
□ Blue shawl, with green dress, height 5″, designer L. Harradine. .... — 1936-1949 — 100.00 — 150.00

LINDA

HN 2106
□ Small figure seated on white bench, red cloak, with blue ribbon trim, basket on bench also, height 4¾″, designer L. Harradine. .... — 1953-1976 — 120.00 — 150.00

LISA

HN 2310
□ Dark blue skirt with large white trim at bottom, white bodice and sleeves with small dark blue dots, matte-finish, height 7½″, designer M. Davies .... — 1969-1982 — 200.00 — 225.00

HN 2394
□ Pink and blue gown, lilac slippers, dark hair (2nd version), height 7½″, designer M. Davies. .... — 1983- — 125.00

LISETTE

HN 1523
□ Small figure with cream tiered skirt, red bodice, holding open fan, red ribbon in hair, height 5¼″, designer L. Harradine. .... — 1932-1938 — 900.00 — 1000.00

HN 1524
□ Red and blue gown with blue bows as trim, height 5¼″, designer L. Harradine. .... — 1932-1938 — 900.00 — 1000.00

	Date	Price Range

HN 1684
☐ Pink dress with green trim, height
5¼ ", designer L. Harradine.   1935-1938   **900.00 1000.00**

LITTLE BOY BLUE

HN 2062
☐ Small boy figure on yellow and green
base, light blue trousers, long dark
coat with white collar and red bow,
black shoes, horn strapped over
shoulder, height 5½ ", designer L. Har-
radine.   1950-1973   **115.00   175.00**

'LITTLE CHILD SO RARE AND SWEET'

HN 1540
☐ Small white nude blonde haired figure on multicolored rock, figure is
bending as if looking for something,
height 5", designer unknown.   1933-1949   **425.00   475.00**

HN 1542
☐ Small white nude figure seated on
shaded blue rock, figure has dark
hair, height 5", designer unknown. . . .   1933-1949   **375.00   425.00**

LITTLE JACK HORNER

HN 2063
☐ Small figure seated on bench style
base of shaded blue and yellows, red
jacket with black buttons, holding pie
on lap, has plum in hand at mouth,
height 4½ ", designer L. Harradine. . .   1950-1953   **225.00   275.00**

LITTLE LADY MAKE BELIEVE

HN 1870
☐ Small figure seated on bench style
base, blue dress, red cloak with blue,
green bonnet with blue ribbons,
holding small parasol in both hands,
height 6", designer L. Harradine.   1938-1949   **500.00   550.00**

LITTLE LAND, The

HN   63
☐ Green and yellow costume, height
7½ ", designer H. Tittensor.   1916-1938   **2000.00 2500.00**

	Date	Price Range	

HN   67
☐ Light colored gray gown with a black trim and small round raised white dots, seated on green base which contains little fairies and elfs, height 7½ ", designer H. Tittensor.   1916-1938   **1750.00   2000.00**

LITTLE MISTRESS, The

HN 1449
☐ Light green gown, shawl of shaded blue with green trim and red stripes and darker blue fringe, red bonnet with red ribbons, carrying basket, height 6 ", designer L. Harradine.   1931-1949   **500.00   550.00**

LITTLE MOTHER, The

HN   389
☐ Figure in pink nightdress, standing on brown pillow, holding small black animal, fair hair (1st version), height unknown, designer H. Tittensor.   1920-1938   **2500.00   2700.00**

HN   390
☐ Dark hair (1st version), height unknown, designer H. Tittensor.   1920-1938   **2500.00   2700.00**

HN   469
☐ Cream nightdress, brown hair (1st version), height unknown, designer H. Tittensor.   1921-1938   **1750.00   2000.00**

HN 1418
☐ Young girl and small boy seated on block, girl's costume of mottled dark blue, red and light blues, multicolored shawl, boy's costume striped red and blue, girl holding bouquet of flowers and large brown basket with flowers in front of figures (2nd version), height unknown, designer H. Tittensor.   1930-1938   **1100.00   1200.00**

HN 1641
☐ Green shawl, pale skirt and basket is of a lighter color (2nd version), height unknown, designer H. Tittensor.   1934-1949   **900.00   1000.00**

LITTLE NELL

HN   540
☐ A character from Dicken's "The Old Curiosity Shop," height 4 ", designer L. Harradine.   1922-   **45.00   60.00**

	Date	Price Range	

☐ **M 51** Renumbered as a miniature, height 4¼ ", designer L. Harradine. . .   1932-1983   **20.00**   **30.00**

LIZANA
HN 1756
☐ Shaded red gown, shawl of multicolored flowers, second shawl is very long and patterned greens, Spanish comb in hair, height 8½ ", designer L. Harradine.   1936-1949   **650.00**   **750.00**

HN 1761
☐ Green dress, leopard-skin cloak, height 8½ ", designer L. Harradine. . .   1936-1938   **650.00**   **750.00**

LOBSTER MAN, The
HN 2317
☐ Character figure seated on green base, with brown lobster basket, brown trousers, dark blue sweater, black cap, black boots with white tops, has lobster in hand, pipe in mouth, height 6⅞ ", designer M. Nicoll. .   1964-   **165.00**

LONDON CRY, STRAWBERRIES
HN 749
☐ Lady and small girl figures on brown base, lady's skirt is red, white apron, red belt, white bonnet, girl's skirt is dark color, red blouse, white bonnet, each is carrying basket of light colour, with large basket on base at their feet, height 6¾ ", designer L. Harradine.   1925-1938   **900.00**   **1000.00**

HN 772
☐ Both gowns are multicolored, baskets are of darker brown, base is of a lighter brown, height 6¾ ", designer L. Harradine.   1925-1938   **900.00**   **1000.00**

	Date	Price Range

LONDON CRY, TURNIPS AND CARROTS

HN 752

☐ Lady and small boy figures on brown base, lady's skirt purple and red with lightly colored apron, boy's brown trousers, jacket and hat, with light shirt, both are holding vegetables with basket on base, height 6¾", designer L. Harradine.   1925-1938   **900.00 1000.00**

HN 771

☐ Lady's dress of shaded blues and reds, boy's lighter brown suit and hat, basket on base is darker brown, cream base, height 6¾", designer L. Harradine.   1925-1938   **900.00 1000.00**

LONG JOHN SILVER

HN 2204

☐ Black, gold and white Pirate costume, on red and green base, parrot is green, red and light brown, height 9", designer M. Nicoll.   1957-1965   **425.00   500.00**

LORETTA

HN 2337

☐ Purple gown with yellow shawl, green and white feathers in hair, height 7¾", designer M. Davies.   1966-1980   **100.00   150.00**

LORI (Kate Greenaway)

HN 2801

☐ Small girl on white base, white gown with red sash and red flowers around bottom, large brim hat of white with red ribbon trim, holding single flower, height 5⅞", designer M. Davies.   1976-   **75.00**

LORNA

HN 2311

☐ Green gown trimmed in yellow, yellow stole, holding small blue and white fan, long blue gloves, height 8⅜", designer M. Davies.   1965-   **125.00**

Loretta,
HN2337,
100.00 - 150.00

	Date	Price Range	

LOUISE (Kate Greenaway)

HN 2869

☐ Small figure, brown gown with white crossed collar, black bonnet with yellow ribbon, single flower in both hands, height 6″, designer M. Davies. — 1979- — 75.00

LOVE LETTER

HN 2149

☐ Two figures seated on couch with small red table at side, one gown is red and white with gold design, black shoes, small white head covering, other gown is shaded blues with black trim, light blue pillow on couch, one figure holding small white paper, height 5″, designer M. Davies. ...... — 1958-1976 — 250.00   300.00

	Date	Price Range
LUCY (Kate Greenaway)		

HN 2863
☐ Small figure on white base, holding single flower in hands, skirt of light blue and white, vest of dark blue, white and blue blouse, tall blue hat with white and blue ribbon, height 6″, designer M. Davies. 1980- 75.00

LUCY ANN

HN 1502
☐ Shaded red gown with blue ribbon, holding skirt up which is filled with flowers, height 5¼″, designer L. Harradine. 1932-1951 300.00 350.00

HN 1565
☐ Pale green dress, height 5¼″, designer L. Harradine. 1933-1938 325.00 375.00

LUCY LOCKETT

HN 485
☐ Very wide skirted green gown with red gloves and small red purse, long strand of dark beads, on black base, has hands crossed. A character from "The Beggar's Opera" (1st version), height 6″, designer L. Harradine. 1921-1949 800.00 900.00

HN 524
☐ HN 695, yellow dress, wine gloves and purse (2nd version), height 6″, designer L. Harradine. 1921-1949 850.00 950.00

HN 695
☐ Orange gown with red gloves and purse, also beads, this figure has one hand in waist and one hand in front (2nd version), height 6″, designer L. Harradine. 1925-1949 650.00 750.00

HN 696
☐ Powder blue costume (2nd version), height 6″, designer L. Harradine. 1925-1949 650.00 750.00

	Date	Price Range

LUNCHTIME
HN 2485
☐ Male figure seated on brown bench on base, one squirrel also on base and bench, green suit with light brown overcoat, hat and scarf same color as suit, holding open paperbag, feeding one squirrel, height 8″, designer M. Nicoll. 1973-1980   150.00   200.00

LYDIA
HN 1906
☐ Figure seated with flowers in back on each side, gown of orange and pink overdress, pale pink flowered underskirt, holding open book in one hand, height 4¼″, designer L. Harradine. . . 1939-1949   300.00   350.00

HN 1907
☐ Green gown, green bonnet with black ribbon, height 4¼″, designer L. Harradine. 1939-1949   300.00   350.00

HN 1908
☐ Red gown and bonnet, height 4⅛″, designer L. Harradine. 1939-   125.00

LYNNE
HN 2329
☐ Yellow and green gown with white designs on bottom, yellow and green ribbon in hair, height 7″, designer M. Davies. 1971-   170.00

MADONNA OF THE SQUARE
HN 10
☐ Lilac costume, height 7″, designer P. Stabler. 1913-1938   1450.00   1600.00

HN 10A
☐ Seated lady, blue costume which covers her entirely, only face and hand shows, infant in lap also wrapped in blue, small basket at feet filled with multicolored flowers, height 7″, designer P. Stabler. 1913-1938   1350.00   1500.00

HN 11
☐ Gray costume, height 7″, designer P. Stabler. 1913-1938   1450.00   1700.00

	Date	Price Range	

HN 14
☐ Renumbered version of HN 10A, height 7″, designer P. Stabler.   1913-1938   **1450.00   1700.00**

HN 27
☐ Mottled green and blue costume, height 7″, designer P. Stabler.   1913-1938   **1650.00   1800.00**

HN 326
☐ Gray and blue costume, earthenware, height 7″, designer P. Stabler.   1918-1938   **1650.00   1800.00**

HN 573
☐ Orange skirt and cubist-style shawl, height 7″, designer P. Stabler.   1913-1938   **1650.00   1800.00**

HN 576
☐ Green skirt and patterned black shawl, height 7″, designer P. Stabler.   1923-1938   **1650.00   1800.00**

HN 594
☐ Green skirt and patterned brown shawl, height 7″, designer P. Stabler.   1924-1938   **1650.00   1800.00**

HN 613
☐ Striped pink skirt and spotted orange shawl, height 7″, designer P. Stabler.   1924-1938   **1650.00   1800.00**

HN 764
☐ Blue and purple striped shawl, yellow skirt, height 7″, designer P. Stabler. ...   1925-1938   **1650.00   1800.00**

HN 1968
☐ Pale green costume, height 7″, designer P. Stabler.   1941-1949   **850.00   950.00**

HN 1969
☐ Lilac costume, height 7″, designer P. Stabler.   1941-1949   **850.00   950.00**

HN 2034
☐ Shaded green and blue costume, height 7″, designer P. Stabler.   1949-1951   **800.00   900.00**

MAISIE

HN 1618
☐ Tiered pale green skirt, shaded blue blouse, red bonnet, white pantalettes showing, on base, height 6¼″, designer L. Harradine.   1934-1949   **475.00   525.00**

HN 1619
☐ Shaded red gown, dark hair, dark base, height 6¼″, designer L. Harradine.   1934-1949   **475.00   525.00**

	Date	Price Range

MAKE BELIEVE
HN 2225
☐ Small figure in very light blue gown, holding very large yellow hat with flower trim, green shoes on one side, red purse on other side, height 5¾", designer M. Nicoll.   1962-   100.00

MAM'SELLE
HN 658
☐ Black and white costume with black triangular hat, black shoes, standing on black pedestal style base, height 7", designer L. Harradine.   1924-1938   850.00   950.00
HN 659
☐ Dark blue and red costume, hat matches costume, height 7", designer L. Harradine.   1924-1938   900.00 1000.00
HN 724
☐ Red hat, yellow trimmed dress, height 7", designer L. Harradine.   1925-1938   900.00 1000.00
HN 786
☐ Red skirt with black squares, top is black with gold stripe, height 7", designer L. Harradine.   1926-1938   900.00 1000.00

MANDARIN, A
HN 84
☐ HN 318, mauve shirt, green cloak (1st version), height 10¼", designer C. J. Noke. 1918-1938 2250.00 2500.00
HN 316
☐ Rotund Chinese figure, black and gold costume, yellow tunic with green dragon and gold flower design (1st version), height 10¼", designer C. J. Noke. 1918-1938 2250.00 2500.00
HN 318
☐ Rotund Chinese figure with black costume with gold designs, gold tunic with raised pattern design of dragon and other designs (1st version), height 10¼", designer C. J. Noke. 1918-1938 2250.00 2500.00
HN 366
☐ Small seated Chinese male on a pedestal, yellow and blue costume (2nd version), height 8¼", designer C. J. Noke. 1920-1938 1400.00 1550.00

	Date	Price Range	

HN 382
☐ Blue and yellow costume (1st version), height 10¼", designer C. J. Noke. 1920-1938 **2250.00 2500.00**

HN 450
☐ Red costume with black designs in circle of deeper red trimmed in green, also has red and black design, red, black and green cap (3rd version), height unknown, designer C. J. Noke. 1921-1938 **1500.00 1750.00**

HN 455
☐ Green costume (2nd version), height 8¼", designer C. J. Noke. 1921-1938 **1750.00 2000.00**

HN 460
☐ Blue costume (3rd version), height unknown, designer C. J. Noke. 1921-1938 **2250.00 2500.00**

HN 461
☐ Red costume (3rd version), height unknown, designer C. J. Noke. 1921-1938 **2250.00 2500.00**

HN 601
☐ Blue costume (3rd version), height unknown, designer C. J. Noke. 1924-1938 **2250.00 2500.00**

HN 611
☐ Yellow patterned tunic (3rd version), height 10¼", designer C. J. Noke. . . . 1924-1938 **2000.00 2500.00**

HN 641
☐ HN 366, onyx style coloring (2nd version), height 8¼", designer C. J. Noke. 1924-1938 **1100.00 1200.00**

HN 746
☐ Black costume with green dragons (1st version), height 10¼", designer C. J. Noke. 1925-1938 **2250.00 2500.00**

HN 787
☐ Pink and orange tunic decorated with black flowers (1st version), height 10¼", designer C. J. Noke. 1926-1938 **2250.00 2500.00**

HN 791
☐ Yellow tunic with green and red markings (1st version), height 10¼", designer C. J. Noke. 1926-1938 **2250.00 2500.00**

	Date	Price Range

MANDY

HN 2476

☐ Young girl in a cream colored off the shoulder gown with short bouffant sleeves, dark hair, holding a yellow lantern, height 4½″, designer M. Davies......................... 1982-   65.00

MAN IN TUDOR COSTUME

HN 563

☐ Gold, green and purple costume on black base, height 3¾, designer unknown......................... 1923-1938   1400.00 1750.00

MANTILLA

HN 2712

☐ Tall figure in red spanish style costume with black and red shawl, high comb in hair, height 11¾″, designer E. J. Griffiths. 1974-1979   300.00   350.00

MARGARET

HN 1989

☐ Green gown with mottled red, blue and yellow overdress, green hat with red ribbon, height 7¼″, designer L. Harradine....................... 1947-1959   350.00   400.00

MARGARET OF ANJOU

HN 2012

☐ Mottled green and yellow gown trimmed in white with wide and high bluish white head covering, height 9¼″, designer M. Davies. 1948-1953   500.00   600.00

MARGERY

HN 1413

☐ Red and patterned black gown trimmed in white with various colors, green bonnet with black ribbons, height 10¾″, designer L. Harradine. 1930-1949   350.00   400.00

	Date	Price Range	

MARGOT
HN 1628
☐ Full skirted gown of shaded blues, large brim blue hat with red ribbons, carrying small basket of flowers, height 5¾″, designer L. Harradine. .. 1934-1938 · 700.00 · 800.00

HN 1636
☐ Red bodice, pink and yellow skirt, height 5¾″, designer L. Harradine. .. 1934-1938 · 700.00 · 800.00

HN 1653
☐ White skirt with blue flower design, red bodice, red hat, height 5¾″, designer L. Harradine. . . . . 1934-1938 · 700.00 · 800.00

MARGUERITE
HN 1928
☐ HN 1946, pink dress, height 8″, designer L. Harradine. . . . . 1940-1959 · 300.00 · 350.00

HN 1929
☐ Pink fading to yellow at bottom of dress, height 8″, designer L. Harradine 1940-1949 · 500.00 · 600.00

HN 1930
☐ Blue dress with purple stripes, height 8″, designer L. Harradine. . . . . 1940-1949 · 550.00 · 650.00

HN 1946
☐ Red gown with white and green trim on bodice, black bonnet with green lining and green feather trim, holding small bouquet of flowers to face, height 8″, designer L. Harradine. . . . . 1940-1949 · 400.00 · 500.00

MARIANNE
HN 2074
☐ Red skirt with darker red jacket trimmed in white, black hat trimmed in white, holding riding crop, height 7¼″, designer L. Harradine. . . . . 1951-1953 · 475.00 · 550.00

MARIE
HN 401
☐ White skirt with purple designs trimmed in gold, purple and pink overlay, pink bodice trimmed with white (1st version), height unknown, designer L. Harradine. . . . . 1920-1938 · 2250.00 · 2500.00

HN 434
☐ Yellow skirt with orange stripes (1st version), height unknown, designer L. Harradine. 1921-1938 · 2250.00 · 2500.00

	Date	Price Range	

HN 502
☐ White dress, red and blue bodice (1st version), height unknown, designer L. Harradine. 1921-1938 2250.00 2500.00

HN 504
☐ Green and blue dress, red spots (1st version), height unknown, designer L. Harradine. 1921-1938 2250.00 2500.00

HN 505
☐ Spotted blue bodice, green and lilac skirt (1st version), height unknown, designer L. Harradine. 1921-1938 2250.00 2500.00

HN 506
☐ Blue and green striped bodice, spotted lilac skirt (1st version), height unknown, designer L. Harradine. 1921-1938 2250.00 2500.00

HN 1370
☐ Small figure in full shaded purple gown (2nd version), height 4½", designer L. Harradine. 1930- 65.00

HN 1388
☐ Red and blue flowered dress (2nd version), height 4½", designer L. Harradine. 1930-1938 250.00 300.00

HN 1417
☐ Orange dress (2nd version), height 4½", designer L. Harradine. 1930-1949 250.00 300.00

HN 1489
☐ Shaded green dress (2nd version), height 4½", designer L. Harradine. . . 1932-1949 250.00 300.00

HN 1531
☐ Yellow and green dress (2nd version), height 4½", designer L. Harradine. . . 1932-1938 250.00 300.00

HN 1635
☐ Flowered pink skirt (2nd version), height 4½", designer L. Harradine. . . 1934-1949 250.00 300.00

HN 1655
☐ Pink bodice, flower white shirt (2nd version), height 4½", designer L. Harradine. 1934-1938 250.00 300.00

MARIETTA

HN 1341
☐ Stylish bat costume of black and red on red base, height 8", designer L. Harradine. 1929-1949 700.00 800.00

Marietta,
HN1341,
700.00 – 800.00

	Date	Price Range	
HN 1446			
☐ Shaded blue and red costume, green cloak with green lining, height 8″, designer L. Harradine.	1931-1949	700.00	800.00
HN 1699			
☐ Green costume, red cloak with blue lining, height 8″, designer L. Harradine.	1935-1949	700.00	800.00
MARIGOLD			
HN 1447			
☐ Shaded blue gown, green bonnet with green ribbons, height 6″, designer L. Harradine.	1931-1949	450.00	500.00
HN 1451			
☐ Yellow dress, height 6″, designer L. Harradine.	1931-1938	450.00	500.00

	Date	Price Range	

HN 1555

☐ Costume is red skirt with light blue jacket, blue bonnet with darker blue ribbons, height 6″, designer L. Harradine. 1931-1951 450.00 500.00

MARION

HN 1582

☐ Green bonnet, pink skirt, height 6½″, designer L. Harradine. 1933-1938 700.00 800.00

HN 1583

☐ Figure seated in cream chair, blue skirt, dark blue blouse, multicolored shawl, shaded blue and red bonnet with red ribbons, height 6½″, designer L. Harradine. 1933-1938 700.00 800.00

MARIQUITA

HN 1837

☐ Red and shaded blue skirt, bodice and sleeves red trimmed with white, blue hat, holding open fan in one hand, height 8″, designer L. Harradine. 1938-1949 1400.00 1750.00

MARJORIE

HN 2788

☐ Figure in seated position, white gown with blue trim, blue bodice, height 5¼″, designer M. Davies. 1980- 185.00

MARKET DAY

HN 1991

☐ Blue skirt, white apron, shaded blue and red shawl, white head covering, goose under one arm and basket of flowers under other. Reissued as Country Lass, height 7¼″, designer L. Harradine. 1947-1955 275.00 325.00

MARY HAD A LITTLE LAMB

HN 2048

☐ Small figure in seated position in shaded blue and red gown trimmed in white, blue ribbon in hair, small lamb on lap with blue ribbon, height 3⅝″, designer M. Davies. 1949- 100.00

	Date	Price Range	

MARY JANE

HN 1990

☐ Light red dress with flower design, shaded blue apron, small white cap with black ribbon, height 7½″, designer L. Harradine.   1947-1959   375.00   425.00

MARY MARY

HN 2044

☐ Small girl figure on yellow-green base, pink skirt, red blouse, blue sash, holds watering can, height 5″, designer L. Harradine.   1949-1973   125.00   175.00

MASK, The

HN 656

☐ Blue and purple costume, height 6¾″, designer L. Harradine.   1924-1938   850.00   950.00

HN 657

☐ White costume with black trim and black spots, on black base, holding mask, small black cap, height 6¾″, designer L. Harradine.   1924-1938   850.00   950.00

HN 729

☐ Red costume with black squares and black collar, height 6¾″, designer L. Harradine.   1925-1938   850.00   950.00

HN 733

☐ White costume with black squares, height 6¾″, designer L. Harradine. . .   1925-1938   850.00   950.00

HN 785

☐ Blue costume, pink striped skirt, height 6¾″, designer L. Harradine. . .   1926-1938   850.00   950.00

HN 1271

☐ Black and red costume with spots of blue, green, and yellow, height 6¾″, designer L. Harradine.   1928-1938   850.00   950.00

MASK SELLER

HN 1361

☐ Character figure in black cloak, red hat with green feather, green stockings and shoes on gray and green base, holds white masks on red carrier, holds flute in hands, height 8⅜″, designer L. Harradine.   1929-1938   650.00   750.00

	Date	Price Range	

HN 2103
☐ Green cloak, black hat, brown stockings and shoes on brown base, masks of different colors, flute is larger, lantern panes are colored, height 8⅜", designer L. Harradine. . . .   1953-   175.00

MASQUE
HN 2554
☐ Dark blue with black shadings, cloak covers figure, has mask on long handle. Note: Second figure has hand up to mask with dark blue cloak, discontinued, height 8⅞", designer D. V. Tootle.   1973-1982   170.00

MASQUERADE
HN 599
☐ Male figure standing on brown base with brown bush, 18th century style costume of red coat, brown trousers, white stockings, brown shoes and hat (1st version), height 6¾", designer L. Harradine.   1924-1949   750.00   800.00

HN 600
☐ Female figure standing on brown base with bush, holding basket of fruit, white 18th century style costume with red designs, white hair (1st version), height varies from 6" to 6¾", designer L. Harradine.   1924-1949   750.00   800.00

HN 636
☐ Male, gold costume (1st version), height 6¾", designer L. Harradine. . .   1924-1938   1000.00   1250.00

HN 637
☐ Female, everything gold (1st version), height varies from 6" to 6¾", designer L. Harradine.   1924-1938   1000.00   1250.00

HN 674
☐ Female, orange and yellow checkered dress (1st version), height varies from 6" to 6¾", designer L. Harradine.   1924-1938   700.00   800.00

HN 683
☐ Male, green coat (1st version), height 6¾", designer L. Harradine.   1924-1938   700.00   800.00

Masquerade Man,
HN599,
750.00 - 800.00

	Date	Price Range	

HN 2251

☐ 18th century style figure on white base, blue and white costume with green designs, tiny blue head cap (2nd version), height 8½″, designer M. Davies. 1960-1965   350.00   400.00

HN 2259

☐ Red dress with white, no gold design (2nd version), height 8½″, designer M. Davies. 1960-1965   300.00   350.00

MASTER, The

HN 2325

☐ Character figure seated on rock with dog and staff, brown trousers and shoes, green coat, light tan hat lying beside figure, height 5⅝″, designer M. Davies. 1967-   165.00

MASTER SWEEP	Date	Price Range

HN 2205
☐ Boy figure with black trousers, dark green coat, black hat and shoes, orange scarf, standing on dark base, has brown bag in one hand, chimney brush in other, height 8½ ″, designer M. Nicoll. 1957-1962   600.00   700.00

MATILDA

HN 2011
☐ Purple and red gown, long red cloak, gold rope belt, holding open book, dark braided hair, height 9¼ ″, designer M. Davies. 1948-1953   600.00   700.00

MAUREEN

HN 1770
☐ Light red gown, black gloves, black hat with white and black tip feathers, holding black riding crop, height 7½ ″, designer L. Harradine. 1936-1959   250.00   325.00

HN 1771
☐ Shaded blue dress, green bonnet with white feather, green gloves, holding brown riding crop, height 8 ″, designer L. Harradine. 1936-1959   600.00   700.00
☐ **M 84** Made as a miniature, shaded orange gown, height 4 ″, designer L. Harradine. 1939-1949   350.00   400.00
☐ **M 85** Light blue skirt, red and blue jacket, height 4 ″, designer L. Harradine 1939-1949   350.00   450.00

MAYOR, The

HN 2280
☐ Red and white costume, black hat with white trim, black shoes with buckle trim, gold chain around chest, height 8¼ ″, designer M. Nicoll. 1963-1971   400.00   500.00

MAYTIME

HN 2113
☐ Shaded red gown, light blue and green scarf, bonnet with red ribbons, dark hair, height 6¾ ″, designer L. Harradine. 1953-1967   225.00   300.00

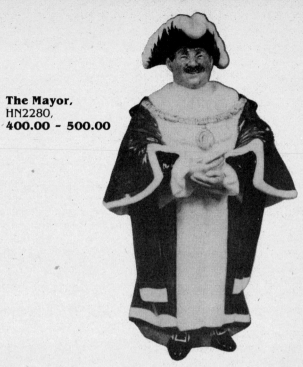

The Mayor,
HN2280,
400.00 - 500.00

	Date	Price Range	
MEDITATION			
HN 2330			
☐ Lady seated at skirted writing table of white with shaded green which contains yellow candleholder, yellow ink bottle and open book, brown gown with cream which contains orange designs, white hair, height 5¾", designer M. Davies.	1971-1983	225.00	300.00
MELANIE			
HN 2271			
☐ Blue gown with yellow collar, hair tied with pink ribbon, holding small wrapped bouquet in hand, height 7⅞", designer M. Davies.	1965-1980	125.00	175.00

	Date	Price Range

MELISSA

HN 2467

☐ White undergown and cuffs, shaded red and purple overdress, one hand raised to blonde hair, height 6¾", designer M. Davies. 1981- 170.00

MELODY

HN 2202

☐ Lady seated, gown of light orange, skirt with green bodice trimmed in white, playing white instrument held on lap, height 6¼", designer M. Davies. 1957-1962 200.00 275.00

MEMORIES

HN 1855

☐ Green bodice and hat, red skirt, height 6", designer L. Harradine. 1938-1949 450.00 500.00

HN 1856

☐ Lady seated leaning against brown tree stump, pale blue gown with darker blue designs, blue bodice trimmed in white, bonnet with black ribbons, holding green open book on knee, height 6", designer L. Harradine. 1938-1949 450.00 500.00

HN 1857

☐ Red bodice with red and lilac skirt, height 6", designer L. Harradine. 1938-1949 450.00 500.00

HN 2030

☐ Shaded red skirt, green bodice, bonnet with green ribbons, height 6", designer L. Harradine. 1949-1959 400.00 450.00

MENDICANT, The

HN 1355

☐ Shaded brown, black and green costume, orange, green and brown turban, seated on base of reddish bricks with multicolored cloth, holding tambourine, height 8¼", designer L. Harradine. 1929-1938 350.00 400.00

HN 1365

☐ Minor glaze differences, height 8¼", designer L. Harradine. 1929-1969 300.00 350.00

	Date	Price Range

MEPHISTO

HN 722
☐ Black blouse, height 6½", designer L. Harradine. 1925-1938 1350.00 1500.00

HN 723
☐ Masquerade type costume of red with black stripes on skirt, red jacket, red cap with black lining, wide white collar, small triangular hat of red and black, on black pedestal style base, height 6½", designer L. Harradine. . . 1925-1938 1500.00 1600.00

MEPHISTOPHELES AND MARGUERITE

HN 755
☐ Two-sided figure with black base, one side lady in orange dress, purple cloak, other side male figure in red outfit with red cloak, height 7¾", designer C. J. Noke. 1925-1949 1350.00 1500.00

HN 775
☐ Two figures on black base, the lady in white costume with gold designs, red cloak with white lining, red shoes, reverse side is male figure in red with black stripes and red cloak with black lining, height 7¾", designer C. J. Noke. 1925-1949 1350.00 1500.00

MERIEL

HN 1931
☐ Pink gown with wide white collar, bonnet with trim of black, seated on bench, height 7¼", designer L. Harradine. 1940-1949 850.00 950.00

HN 1932
☐ Green gown, height 7¼", designer L. Harradine. 1940-1949 850.00 950.00

MERMAID, The

HN 97
☐ Mermaid seated on brown and yellow rock, green and blue fish tail, upper torso white, red beads and red decoration in hair, height 7", designer H. Tittensor. 1918-1936 650.00 750.00

HN 300
☐ Red berries in hair, with darker base, height 7", designer H. Tittensor. 1918-1936 850.00 1000.00

	Date	Price Range

MERYLL
HN 1917
☐ Red jacket and green skirt. This figure was renamed shortly after its introduction, height 6¾ ", designer L. Harradine. 1939-1940   **1200.00 1350.00**

MICHELLE
HN 2234
☐ Gown of green with white design on edge, undergown of light red, also sleeves of light red, height 6⅞", designer M. Davies. 1967-   **155.00**

MIDINETTE
HN 1289
☐ Short skirt of light red with flower design, mottled red jacket, red shoes on light base, carrying two hat boxes, one is white with yellow stripes and yellow and brown dots, the other is yellow, dark blue, black and white stripes (1st version), height 9", designer L. Harradine. 1928-1938   **1500.00 1600.00**

HN 1306
☐ Green skirt, red jacket, black base, one hat box is white with green and gold stripes, the other is white with red and green stripes (1st version), height 9", designer L. Harradine. 1928-1938   **1500.00 1600.00**

HN 2090
☐ Light blue skirt and jacket, hat with red feather, white hat box with blue design and red ribbon, full length skirt, this figure is not on a base (2nd version), height 7¼ ", designer L. Harradine. 1952-1965   **225.00 300.00**

MIDSUMMER NOON
HN 1899
☐ Figure seated on bench, beige skirt, red, white and blue bodice, on bench is basket of flowers and shawl with green border, height 4½ ", designer L. Harradine. 1939-1949   **550.00 600.00**

HN 1900
☐ Blue dress, height 4½ ", designer L. Harradine. 1939-1949   **550.00 600.00**

	Date	Price Range	

HN 2033
☐ Only minor color differences, height 4½ ″, designer L. Harradine.   1949-1955   **475.00   525.00**

MILADY

HN 1970
☐ Shaded red gown with white collar with black ribbon, black gloves, black hat with feather trim, holding riding crop, height 6½ ″, designer L. Harradine.   1941-1949   **900.00   950.00**

MILKING TIME

HN   3
☐ Light blue gown with white apron, standing on round base with brown and white goat, figure holding jug on arm, height unknown, designer P. Stabler.   1913-1938   **3000.00   3500.00**

HN   306
☐ Pale costume with black printed markings, height unknown, designer P. Stabler.   1913-1938   **2750.00   3000.00**

MILKMAID, The

HN 2057
☐ Green skirt, brown blouse, blue and white apron trimmed in brown, white farm bonnet, carrying brown jug, height 6½ ″, designer L. Harradine. . .   1975-1981   **135.00   185.00**

MILLICENT

HN 1714
☐ Red and white gown with blue designs and stripes, red shawl, blue bonnet with green ribbons, holding small round purse, height 8″, designer L. Harradine.   1935-1949   **1050.00   1150.00**

HN 1715
☐ Flowered shawl and purple dress, height 8″, designer L. Harradine.   1935-1949   **1050.00   1150.00**

HN 1860
☐ No details of color available, height 8″, designer L. Harradine.   1938-1949   **1050.00   1150.00**

	Date	Price Range	

MINUET

HN 2019

☐ White gown with blue and gold designs, light blue shoes, height 7¼ ", designer M. Davies.   1949-1971   225.00   275.00

HN 2066

☐ Red and blue gown, height 7¼ ", designer M. Davies.   1950-1955   225.00   275.00

MIRABEL

HN 1743

☐ Cream and shaded blue gown and cloak, cloak has red edge trim, green hat, red open parasol, height 7¾ ", designer L. Harradine.   1935-1949   750.00   850.00

HN 1744

☐ Shaded red gown with red flowers and cream colored stripes, red cloak, light green bonnet, open parasol, height 7¾ ", designer L. Harradine. . .   1935-1949   750.00   800.00

☐ **M 68** Introduced as a miniature, red gown with green cloak, black bonnet, green parasol, height 4 ", designer L. Harradine.   1936-1949   300.00   350.00

☐ **M 74** Green dress, height 4 ", designer L. Harradine.   1936-1949   300.00   350.00

MIRANDA

HN 1818

☐ Red skirt, with blue mottled bodice and overskirt, trimmed with green, small wrapped head covering of green with black ribbon, holding open fan in one hand, on black base, height 8½ ", designer L. Harradine.   1937-1949   750.00   850.00

HN 1819

☐ Green skirt, height 8½ ", designer L. Harradine.   1937-1949   750.00   850.00

MIRROR, The

HN 1852

☐ Slender figure in red and blue gown with white collar that has blue and red flowers, holding small mirror, height 7½ ", designer L. Harradine. . .   1938-1949   800.00   1000.00

HN 1853

☐ Blue costume, height 7½ ", designer L. Harradine. . . . . , ...   1938-1949   800.00   1000.00

	Date	Price Range	
MISS DEMURE			
HN 1402			
☐ Pink gown with blue shawl that has yellow and green stripe, light green bonnet with darker green ribbons, open red parasol with white fringe, height 7″, designer L. Harradine.	1930-1975	250.00	300.00
HN 1440			
☐ Blue gown with dark blue shawl, blue bonnet with darker blue ribbons, open red parasol with reddish white trim, height 7″, designer L. Harradine.	1930-1949	350.00	400.00
HN 1463			
☐ Green dress, height 7″, designer L. Harradine.	1931-1949	350.00	400.00
HN 1499			
☐ Yellow bonnet, pink dress, height 7″, designer L. Harradine.	1932-1938	400.00	450.00
HN 1560			
☐ Cream and shaded blue gown, shaded red and blue shawl, red bonnet with dark blue ribbons, open multicolored parasol, height 7″, designer L. Harradine.	1933-1949	350.00	400.00
MISS 1926			
HN 1205			
☐ Figure standing on brown pedestal style base, with dark fur coat with white fur trim, height 7¼″, designer L. Harradine.	1926-1938	2050.00	2200.00
HN 1207			
☐ Black fur collar, height 7¼″, designer L. Harradine.	1926-1938	2050.00	2200.00
MISS FORTUNE			
HN 1897			
☐ Red skirt, shawl of white with blue and green designs, blue bonnet with red ribbons, on base which has basket of flowers and single yellow flower on it, height 5¾″, designer L. Harradine.	1938-1949	450.00	500.00
HN 1898			
☐ Green and yellow shawl, mauve dress, height 5¾″, designer L. Harradine.	1938-1949	450.00	500.00

	Date	Price Range	

MISS MUFFET

HN 1936

☐ Small figure in white gown, red long coat with white fur trim, white fur muff, white open parasol, red cap with black ribbons, height 5½″, designer L. Harradine. 1940-1967   150.00   200.00

HN 1937

☐ Very light red gown, green long coat with white fur trim, green cap with red ribbons, parasol, height 5½″, designer L. Harradine. 1940-1952   300.00   350.00

MISS WINSOME

HN 1665

☐ Shaded purple gown, white shawl with red flower design, green bonnet, small green round purse, height 6¾″, designer L. Harradine. 1934-1949   600.00   700.00

HN 1666

☐ Green gown, shawl multicolored, red bonnet with green ribbons, small red purse, height 6¾″, designer L. Harradine. 1934-1938   650.00   750.00

M'LADY'S MAID

HN 1795

☐ Red gown with very small white apron, white trim on sleeves, small white cap with ribbon trim, gold rope with key attached, carrying small tray with objects on it, height 9″, designer L. Harradine. 1936-1949   1150.00   1300.00

HN 1822

☐ Multicolored dress, height 9″, designer L. Harradine. 1937-1949   1150.00   1300.00

MODENA

HN 1845

☐ Blue dress, height 7¼″, designer L. Harradine. 1938-1949   750.00   850.00

HN 1846

☐ Full red skirt with green bows, green bodice with red rose trim, white shawl with green and red design, shawl covers comb in hair, red rose in hair, height 7¼″, designer L. Harradine. . . 1938-1949   750.00   850.00

	Date	Price Range	

MODERN PIPER, The
HN 756
☐ Costume of pink tights with blue diamond design and gold jacket mottled red and blue, green and blue cloak, gold pipe on green and yellow base with four tiny figures, height 8½ ", designer L. Harradine. 1925-1938 **1650.00 1800.00**

MOIRA
HN 1347
☐ Figure of lady with dog on pedestal style base, woman's costume of blue, green, yellow, and black, vest also multicolored, green and blue striped hat, green gloves, dark brown and white dog, height 6½ ", designer L. Harradine. 1929-1938 **2750.00 3000.00**

MOLLY MALONE
HN 1455
☐ Skirt with white apron with blue tint, overdress is of red and darker blue, dark bodice with multicolored collar, multicolored kerchief on head , the base contains figure, brown wheel barrow and basket, height 7", designer L. Harradine. 1931-1938 **1350.00 1500.00**

MONICA
HN 1458
☐ Small seated figure, white gown with multicolored flower designs, black bonnet with green ribbons, holds red basket of flowers, height 4", designer L. Harradine. 1931-1949 **200.00 250.00**
HN 1459
☐ Lilac dress, height 4", designer L. Harradine. 1931-Unknown **200.00 250.00**
HN 1467
☐ White and shaded blue gown with a very faint flower design, red bodice, red and blue sleeves, red bonnet with blue ribbon, basket is light color, red flowers, height 4", designer L. Harradine. 1931- **100.00**
☐ **M 66** Introduced as a miniature, height 3", designer L. Harradine. 1935-1949 **300.00 350.00**

	Date	Price Range	

☐ **M 72** White gown with large blue spots, blue bodice, pink bonnet with black ribbons, basket has yellow and red flowers, height 3″, designer L. Harradine.   1936-1949   300.00   350.00

MOOR, The
HN 1308
☐ Patterned blue costume with mottled red cloak, height 16½″, designer C. J. Noke.   1929-1938   1500.00   1750.00

HN 1366
☐ Red costume with multicolored patterning, height 16½″, designer C. J. Noke.   1930-1949   1500.00   1750.00

HN 1425
☐ Dark multicolored costume, height 16½″, designer C. J. Noke.   1930-1949   1500.00   1750.00

HN 1657
☐ Striped waistband, black cloak, height 16½″, designer C. J. Noke. . . .   1934-1949   1500.00   1750.00

MOORISH MINSTREL
HN 34
☐ Brown figure on brown pedestal, dark blue costume, small brown hat and shoes, holding brown instrument, height 13½″, designer C. J. Noke. . . .   1913-1938   2000.00   2200.00

HN 364
☐ Blue, green and orange striped costume, height 13½″, designer C. J. Noke.   1920-1938   2750.00   3000.00

HN 415
☐ Green and yellow striped costume, height 13½″, designer C. J. Noke. . . .   1920-1938   2750.00   3000.00

HN 797
☐ Purple costume, height 13½″, designer C. J. Noke.   1926-1949   2150.00   2300.00

MOORISH PIPER MINSTREL
HN 301
☐ Dark figure on dark brown base, purple costume with orange scarf around neck, dunce shaped orange and brown hat, light colored pipe, height 13½″, designer C. J. Noke.   1918-1938   2750.00   3000.00

	Date	Price Range	

HN 328
☐ Green and brown striped robe, height 13½ ", designer C. J. Noke.   1918-1938   2750.00   3000.00

HN 416
☐ Green and yellow striped robe, height 13½ ", designer C. J. Noke.   1920-1938   2750.00   3000.00

MOTHERHOOD

HN 28
☐ Gray costume, height unknown, designer P. Stabler.   1913-1938   1750.00   2000.00

HN 30
☐ Figure seated on bench which is on base, white gown with blue designs and dots, white apron with blue designs and blue trim, holding small nude child figure, height unknown, designer P. Stabler.   1913-1938   2250.00   2500.00

HN 303
☐ White dress with black patterning, height unknown, designer P. Stabler. .   1918-1938   2250.00   2500.00

MOTHER'S HELP

HN 2151
☐ Small figure in brown gown with white bib apron, white sleeves and collar, white head covering, height 5 ", designer M. Davies.   1962-1969   175.00   225.00

MR. MICAWBER

HN 532
☐ Character from Dicken's "David Copperfield" (1st version), height 3½ ", designer L. Harradine.   1922-   45.00   60.00
☐ **M 42** Renumbered as a miniature, height 4 ", designer L. Harradine.   1932-1983   20.00   30.00

HN 557
☐ Larger figure standing on brown base with green bush, black trousers, brown coat, yellow vest, white shirt with black bow tie (2nd version), height 7 ", designer L. Harradine.   1923-1939   400.00   500.00

HN 1895
☐ Very minor color changes (2nd version), height 7 ", designer L. Harradine. .   1938-1952   400.00   450.00

Mr. Micawber,
HN557,
400.00 – 500.00

	Date	Price Range	

HN 2097

☐ Figure standing on small black base, light brown trousers, black coat, brown and yellow vest, white shirt, red bow tie (3rd version), height 7½″, designer L. Harradine. 1952-1967   **325.00**   **375.00**

MR. PICKWICK

HN 529

☐ Character from Dicken's "Pickwick Papers" (1st version), height 3¾″, designer L. Harradine. 1922-   **45.00**   **60.00**

☐ **M 41** Renumbered as a miniature, height 4″, designer L. Harradine. 1932-1983   **20.00**   **30.00**

HN 556

☐ Figure standing on brown base with bush, yellow trousers, blue coat, tan vest, white cravat, black hat in hand, black boots (2nd version), height 7″, designer L. Harradine. 1923-1939   **400.00**   **500.00**

	Date	Price Range	

HN 1894
☐ Very minor color changes (2nd version), height 7″, designer L. Harradine. 1938-1942 400.00 450.00

HN 2099
☐ Figure on green base, light brown trousers, black coat, brown and orange vest, white cravat, brown hat, yellow spats (3rd version), height 7½″, designer L. Harradine. 1952-1967 325.00 375.00

MRS. BARDELL
Issued only as a miniature

☐ **M 86** White dress, white hood with black trim, very light pink shawl, black stand, height 4¼″, designer L. Harradine. 1949- 29.95

MRS. FITZHERBERT
HN 2007
☐ White gown with blue bow trim, mottled yellow, blue and orange overdress, red bodice, head covering of white with blue ribbon trim, holding red and white open fan, height 9″, designer M. Davies. 1948-1953 600.00 700.00

MY LOVE
HN 2339
☐ White gown with gold trim and gold design in part of gown, gold shoes, holding single red rose, dark hair, height 6¼″, designer M. Davies. 1969- 185.00

MY PET
HN 2238
☐ Small figure seated on cushion, blue and white skirt, blouse with blue trim, holding small brown dog in one arm and open book in other, brown shoes, height 3″, designer M. Davies. 1962-1975 100.00 150.00

	Date	Price Range	

MY PRETTY MAID
HN 2064
☐ Small figure on yellow and green base, shaded blue gown with white collar, dark blue waistband with red trim, holding milking stool, bucket on base, height 5½″, designer L. Harradine. 1950-1954   250.00   300.00

MY TEDDY
HN 2177
☐ Small figure seated on white base, shaded green gown with white collar, holding brown teddy bear and small mirror, height 3¼″, designer M. Davies. 1962-1967   250.00   300.00

NADINE
HN 1885
☐ Light blue gown with green sash, multicolor shawl, green bonnet, blue shoes, height 7¾″, designer L. Harradine. 1938-1949   650.00   750.00
HN 1886
☐ Orange and red gown with blue sash, red shawl with blue and green trim, blue bonnet, height 7¾″, designer L. Harradine. 1938-1949   650.00   750.00

NANA
HN 1766
☐ Small figure in light red and white gown, tiny hat on side of head is blue with red trim, open fan in hand, height 4¾″, designer L. Harradine. 1936-1949   275.00   325.00
HN 1767
☐ Shaded blue and green gown, green hat with red trim, height 4¾″, designer L. Harradine. 1936-1949   275.00   325.00

NANNY
HN 2221
☐ Older figure seated in gray rocker with brown teddy bear on lap, blue and green gown with white apron and headcap, toys on base, also basket, height 5⅝″, designer M. Davies. 1958-   175.00

	Date	Price Range	
NEGLIGEE			

HN 1219
☐ Figure kneeling on brown and orange cushion base, short gown of shaded blues, blue ribbon in hair, height 5″, designer L. Harradine. . . . . — 1927-1938 — 1100.00 — 1200.00

HN 1228
☐ Red, blue, and black cushion, blue gown, red ribbon in hair, height 5″, designer L. Harradine. . . . . — 1927-1938 — 1100.00 — 1200.00

HN 1272
☐ Mottled red and yellow negligee, height 5″, designer L. Harradine. . . . . — 1928-1938 — 1100.00 — 1200.00

HN 1273
☐ White negligee, height 5″, designer L. Harradine. . . . . — 1928-1938 — 1100.00 — 1200.00

HN 1454
☐ Red cushion with multicolored design, shaded pink gown, pink ribbon in hair, height 5″, designer L. Harradine. . . . . — 1931-1938 — 1100.00 — 1200.00

NELL

HN 3014
☐ Seated figure in white pinafore over a pink dress. Seated in blue cart, bright yellow wheels. Light brown hair, height 4″, designer P. Parsons. . . . . — 1983- — 75.00

NELL GWYNN

HN 1882
☐ Blue skirt, red overlay, red bodice, white shawl, white apron, white sleeves with blue trim, green bonnet with red feather and red ribbons, blue shoes, standing on base which is shaded blue, pedestal has white cloth with basket, height 6¾″, designer L. Harradine. . . . . — 1938-1949 — 600.00 — 700.00

HN 1887
☐ Red skirt, green bodice and overlay, red bonnet with blue feather and ribbons, black shoes, base cream, height 6¾″, designer L. Harradine. . . . . — 1938-1949 — 600.00 — 700.00

NEW BONNET, The	Date	Price Range	

HN 1728

☐ Red full gown with very wide white collar, red shoes, small white cap on head, holding green bonnet with yellow rose trim and red ribbons, standing on base of light green, height 7″, designer L. Harradine. 1935-1949 **525.00 575.00**

HN 1957

☐ Red gown with shaded blues at hemline, white collar, red and white cap, green bonnet with black ribbon trim and red flower, blue shoes, black base, height 7″, designer L. Harradine. 1940-1949 **500.00 550.00**

NEW COMPANION

HN 2770

☐ Gray and black skirt, white apron, blue shawl, black hat with pink ribbons, black and white puppy in beige basket, height 7¾″, designer W. K. Harper. 1982- **185.00**

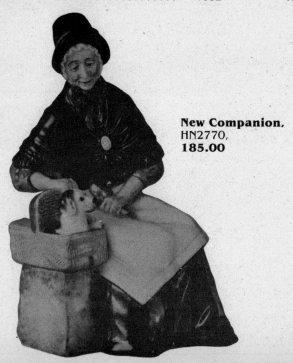

New Companion,
HN2770,
185.00

	Date	Price Range

NEWHAVEN FISHWIFE

HN 1480

☐ Skirt of red and white stripes, black and white striped apron, white blouse with red and blue designs, brown cloak, white head-covering with design, carrying brown basket with strap around head, on base of light brown with another basket, height 7¾", designer H. Fenton. 1931-1938   1350.00   1500.00

NEWSBOY

HN 2244

☐ Boy figure on green base, brown trousers, black coat, green scarf, black and green striped cap, holding newspaper placard and folded newspapers — Note: A limited edition of 250 was also produced for Stoke-on-Trent's local paper, The Evening Sentinel; figure had the word Sentinel printed on newsboy's placard, height 8½", designer M. Davies. 1959-1965   525.00   625.00

News Boy,
HN2244,
525.00 – 625.00

Nicola,
HN2839,
250.00

NICOLA	Date	Price Range	
HN 2839			
☐ Shaded blue and red gown with white, yellow and green flower design, white trim, dark bow on hair curls, holding bird in hand, height 7⅛″, designer M. Davies...........................	1978-	250.00	
NINA			
HN 2347			
☐ Blue gown with white design at hemline, white collar, with white ribbon in hair, this figure has a matt finish, height 7½″, designer M. Davies.	1969-1976	125.00	175.00
NINETTE			
HN 2379			
☐ Yellow gown with white trim and golden design, flower in hair, height 8″, designer M. Davies.	1971-	185.00	

Noelle,
HN2179,
350.00 - 400.00

NOELLE	Date	Price Range	
HN 2179			
☐ White gown with black stripes, long red jacket with hood trimmed in white fur, white muff, height 6¾ ", designer M. Davies.	1957-1967	350.00	400.00
NORMA			
Issued only as a miniature			
☐ **M 36** No color details available, height 4½ ", designer unknown.	1933-1945	375.00	425.00
☐ **M 37** Red and blue print dress, blue sleeves, green and blue shawl, green and red hat, height 4½ ", designer unknown.	1933-1945	375.00	425.00
NUDE ON ROCK			
HN 593			
☐ White nude figure lying on blue and white rock, height unknown, designer unknown.	1924-1938	950.00	1000.00

Odds And Ends,
HN1844,
800.00 – 900.00

ODDS AND ENDS	Date	Price Range	
HN 1844			
☐ Green skirt with black, red and yellow stripes, yellow bibbed apron, red blouse, green shawl, black hat with colored feathers, holding potted plants in one arm, height 7¾", designer L. Harradine.	1938-1938	800.00	900.00
OFFICER OF THE LINE			
HN 2733			
☐ Depicts a soldier of the Napoleon era. High boots, light waistcoat and pants, coat red with matching sash, hair powdered white to gray, black tricorn hat, height 9", designer W. K. Harper.	1983-	195.00	

	Date	Price Range

OLD BALLOON SELLER

HN 1315

□ Older figure seated holding many different colored balloons, green skirt, white apron, red blouse, green shawl with red fringe, hat multicolored, basket at side, height 7″, designer L. Harradine.................... 1929-   185.00

OLD BALLOON SELLER AND BULLDOG

HN 1791

□ Same figure as Old Balloon Seller with the addition of bulldog, all mounted on mahogany stand, height 7″, designer L. Harradine.......... 1932-1938   1250.00 1500.00

HN 1912

□ No details available, height 7″, designer L. Harradine............. 1939-1949   1350.00 1500.00

OLD HUNTSMAN, The

HN 1403

□ Not issued......................

OLD KING, An

HN 358

□ HN 2134, green shirt, purple robe, height 9¾″, designer C. J. Noke..... 1919-1938   1150.00 1300.00

HN 623

□ Gray, red and green robes, height 9¾″, designer C. J. Noke.......... 1924-1938   1300.00 1500.00

HN 1801

□ No detail available, height 9¾″, designer C. J. Noke................. 1937-1954   950.00 1150.00

HN 2134

□ Figure seated in brown chair on brown base, green robe, with purple overrobe trimmed in a green design, red scarf, gold crown, holding sword, height 10¾″, designer C. J. Noke.... 1954-   475.00

OLD KING COLE

HN 2217

□ Figure seated in light colored chair, brown and beige costume with robe trimmed in white fur, brown and gold crown, small stool at feet, holding goblet, height 6¾″, designer M. Davies.......................... 1963-1967   750.00   850.00

Old Lavender Seller, HN1492, **600.00 - 700.00**

OLD LAVENDER SELLER	Date	Price Range	
HN 1492			
☐ Older figure seated, very dark green gown with white apron, red and yellow striped shawl with green squares, basket on one arm and small basket at side, black hat with flowers, height 6″, designer L. Harradine.	1932-1949	**600.00**	**700.00**
HN 1571			
☐ Patterned orange cap, height 6″, designer L. Harradine.	1933-1949	**600.00**	**700.00**
OLD MAN, An			
HN 451			
☐ A seated figure covered completely by blue, green and brown robe, height unknown, designer unknown.	1921-1938	**2250.00**	**2500.00**

	Date	Price Range	

OLD MEG
HN 2494
☐ Blue and gray gown, white and blue apron, shawl of patterned purple, green hat with blue and white scarf, red shoes, base looks like stones with brown basket, height 8″, designer M. Nicoll.   1974-1976   325.00   375.00

OLD MOTHER HUBBARD
HN 2314
☐ Dark green gown with lighter green trim, white apron with dark green dots, green headcap, holds bone in hand for brown and white dog, height 8″, designer M. Nicoll.   1964-1975   300.00   350.00

OLGA
HN 2463
☐ Yellow underskirt with blue overgown, holds single red rose, yellow ribbon in light brown hair, height 8¼″, designer J. Bromley.   1972-1975   175.00   225.00

OLIVER TWIST
Issued only as a miniature
☐ **M 89** White shirt, red tie, black jacket, tan pants, black stand, height 4¼″, designer L. Harradine.   1949-1983   20.00   30.00

OLIVIA
HN 1995
☐ Light green gown with cape of red with blue trim, holding white lilies in one arm, height 7½″, designer L. Harradine.   1947-1951   300.00   400.00

OMAR KHAYYAM AND THE BELOVED
HN 407
☐ Colors were unrecorded, height 10″, designer C. J. Noke.   1920-1938   3500.00   4000.00

	Date	Price Range	

HN 419

☐ Two figures standing together, blue costume with dark blue robe with green dot trim, green and blue turban, her costume is gown of shaded blues with yellow dots, robe and head trim have orange designs and orange dots, she holds jug, height 10″, designer C. J. Noke. 1920-1938 3500.00 4000.00

HN 459

☐ Multicolored costumes, height 10″, designer C. J. Noke. 1921-1938 3500.00 4000.00

HN 598

☐ Lady has striped pink cloak, striped blue dress, height 10″, designer C. J. Noke. 1924-1938 3500.00 4000.00

OMAR KHAYYAM

HN 408

☐ Seated figure, blue and black robes with brown (1st version), height 6″, designer C. J. Noke. 1920-1938 2250.00 3000.00

HN 409

☐ Black robe, yellow trousers (1st version), height 6″, designer C. J. Noke. . 2250.00 3000.00

HN 2247

☐ Brown costume with robe of orange and brown, orange turban, holding gray jug and red open book (2nd version), height 6¼″, designer M. Nicoll. 1965-1983 115.00 165.00

ONCE UPON A TIME

HN 2047

☐ Small figure of little girl seated on tan bench, on a yellow-green base, red dress with white dots and blue trim, blue shoes, open book on bench, height 4¼″, designer L. Harradine. . . 1949-1955 200.00 250.00

ONE OF THE FORTY

All of the "One of the Forty" models were designed by H. Tittensor, their height ranging from 2¾″ to 7″.

HN 417

☐ HN 528, green and blue robes (1st version), height 5″, designer H. Tittensor. 1920-1938 1100.00 1200.00

	Date	Price Range	
HN 418 ☐ HN 494, striped green robes (2nd version)	1920-1938	1100.00	1200.00
HN 423 ☐ These figures were very small and produced in a variety of colour finishes (3rd version)	1921-1938	450.00	500.00
HN 427 ☐ Brown costume, brown and green turban, holding green bag in one arm (9th version)	1921-1938	1100.00	1200.00
HN 480 ☐ Yellow trousers with black stripes, mottled dark green robe, high blue hat, mottled green bag (10th version), height 7″.........................	1921-1938	800.00	900.00
HN 481 ☐ HN 491, dark spotted robes (11th version).............................	1921-1938	1100.00	1200.00
HN 482 ☐ HN 492, spotted waistband (12th version).............................	1921-1938	1100.00	1200.00
HN 483 ☐ HN 491, brown hat, green striped robes (11th version)	1921-1938	1100.00	1200.00
HN 484 ☐ HN 492, mottled green robes (12th version)	1921-1938	1100.00	1200.00
HN 490 ☐ HN 528, blue and brown checkered coat (1st version), height 5″.........	1921-1938	1100.00	1200.00
HN 491 ☐ Blue costume with white robe, blue hat, white bag which he holds under one arm and holds closed with other hand (11th version)	1921-1938	1100.00	1200.00
HN 492 ☐ White costume with yellow band and yellow turban, white bag he holds with one hand, bag is open (12th version).............................	1921-1938	1100.00	1200.00
HN 493 ☐ HN 480, blue hat and waistband (10th version)	1921-1938	1100.00	1200.00
HN 494 ☐ White costume with blue waistband and blue turban, holds white bag over shoulder with one hand, white bag at feet also (2nd version)	1921-1938	1100.00	1200.00

	Date	Price Range	

HN 495

☐ HN 528, blue hat and waistband (1st version), height 5″   1921-1938   **1100.00   1200.00**

HN 496

☐ HN 665, yellow hat and vase (13th version)   1921-1938   **1100.00   1200.00**

HN 497

☐ HN 480, brown hat, checkered trousers (10th version)   1921-1938   **1100.00   1200.00**

HN 498

☐ HN 494, dark striped coat, pale striped trousers (2nd version)   1921-1938   **1100.00   1200.00**

HN 499

☐ HN 480, cream costume, green hat (10th version)   1921-1938   **1100.00   1200.00**

HN 500

☐ HN 665, checkered coat and red hat (13th version)   1921-1938   **1100.00   1200.00**

HN 501

☐ HN 528, green striped coat (1st version), height 5″   1921-1938   **1100.00   1200.00**

HN 528

☐ Brown costume, brown and purple robe, green waistband with red and yellow dots, green turban with red and yellow squares, one hand on open bag at feet, other hand holds necklace, second bag open in front of him (1st version)   1921-1938   **1100.00   1200.00**

HN 645

☐ HN 492, blue, black and white robes (12th version)   1924-1938   **1100.00   1200.00**

HN 646

☐ HN 491, blue, black and white robes (2nd version)   1924-1938   **1100.00   1200.00**

HN 647

☐ HN 494, blue, black and white robes (2nd version)   1924-1938   **1100.00   1200.00**

HN 648

☐ HN 528, blue, black and white robes (1st version)   1924-1938   **1100.00   1200.00**

HN 649

☐ HN 665, blue, black and white robes (13th version)   1924-1938   **1100.00   1200.00**

HN 663

☐ HN 492, checkered red robes (12th version)   1924-1938   **1100.00   1200.00**

	Date	Price Range	

HN 664
☐ HN 480, patterned yellow robes (10th version) 1924-1938 **1100.00 1200.00**

HN 665
☐ Orange robe with red and black stripes and black and green dots, turban of same colour, holding black bag and green jug or bottle (13th version) 1924-1938 **1100.00 1200.00**

HN 666
☐ HN 494, checkered yellow robes (2nd version) 1924-1938 **1100.00 1200.00**

HN 667
☐ HN 491, checkered yellow robes (11th version) 1924-1938 **1100.00 1200.00**

HN 677
☐ HN 528, orange, green and red striped coat (1st version) 1924-1938 **1100.00 1200.00**

HN 704
☐ HN 494, checkered red robe (2nd version) 1925-1938 **1100.00 1200.00**

HN 712
☐ HN 491, checkered red robes (11th version) 1925-1938 **1100.00 1200.00**

HN 713
☐ HN 492, checkered red robes (12th version) 1925-1938 **1100.00 1200.00**

HN 714
☐ HN 480, patterned red robes (10th version) 1925-1938 **1100.00 1200.00**

HN 1336
☐ HN 491, mottled red, orange and blue robes (11th version) 1929-1938 **1100.00 1200.00**

HN 1350
☐ HN 491, multicolored robes (11th version) 1929-1949 **1100.00 1200.00**

HN 1351
☐ HN 528, no color detail available (1st version) 1929-1949 **1100.00 1200.00**

HN 1352
☐ HN 528, multicolored robes (1st version) 1929-1949 **1100.00 1200.00**

HN 1353
☐ HN 494, multicolored robes (2nd version) 1929-1949 **1100.00 1200.00**

HN 1354
☐ HN 665, multicolored robes (13th version) 1929-1949 **1100.00 1200.00**

	Date	Price Range	

ONE THAT GOT AWAY, The
HN 2153
☐ Fisherman's costume of brown coat, green trousers, brown hat, black boots, on base of yellow and green, fishing basket of brown also on base, height 6¼ ″, designer M. Davies. 1955-1959   250.00   300.00

ORANGE LADY, The
HN 1759
☐ Older lady in gown of pink, with shawl of black and red, black hat with red trim, two brown baskets with oranges, height 8¾ ″, designer L. Harradine. 1936-1975   250.00   300.00
HN 1953
☐ Light green gown, black and green shawl, height 8¾ ″, designer L. Harradine. 1940-1975   200.00   250.00

ORANGE SELLER, The
HN 1325
☐ Shaded green and blue gown, shaded red and blue blouse and apron, green head covering with red trim, holding brown basket of oranges, height 7″, designer L. Harradine. 1929-1949   900.00   1000.00

ORANGE VENDOR, AN
HN 72
☐ Light green costume, dark green robe and hood, face and hands are lighter color, smaller brown basket of oranges, earthenware, height 6¼ ″, designer C. J. Noke. 1941-1949   700.00   800.00
HN 508
☐ Purple coat, height 6¼ ″, designer C. J. Noke. 1921-1938   1000.00   1100.00
HN 521
☐ Pale blue costume, black collar, purple hood, height 6¼ ″, designer C. J. Noke. 1921-1938   1000.00   1100.00
HN 1966
☐ Dark seated male figure in shaded red and blue costume, darker blue and red robe, shaded blue and red hood, large basket of oranges in front of figure, height 6¼ ″, designer C. J. Noke. 1917-1938   950.00   1100.00

	Date	Price Range	

ORGAN GRINDER, The
HN 2173
☐ Yellow and brown trousers, green coat, blue and red scarf, brown hat, on brown base, brown organ grinder instrument, monkey in red coat with yellow trim, blue trousers, height 8¾ ″, designer M. Nicoll.   1956-1965   650.00   700.00

OUT FOR A WALK
HN   86
☐ Pink and grey dress, height unknown, designer H. Tittensor.   1918-1936   2250.00   2500.00

HN   443
☐ Checkered skirt, green coat with white fur trim, white muff, green hat with feather trim, height unknown, designer H. Tittensor.   1921-1936   2250.00   2500.00

HN   748
☐ Dark multicolored dress, white muff, height unknown, designer H. Tittensor.   1925-1936   2350.00   2500.00

OWD WILLUM
HN 2042
☐ Character figure seated on green and gray stones, dark green trousers, brown leg coverings, green coat, brown hat with darker brown band, very light tan vest, red tie, large white and blue mug in one hand, red bag with white dots also on base, height 6¾ ″, designer L. Harradine.   1949-1959   175.00   250.00

PAISLEY SHAWL
HN 1392
☐ White gown with shaded green and yellow flower designs, red paisley design shawl, light red bonnet with darker red lining with feather trim, carrying parasol (1st version), height 9 ″, designer L. Harradine.   1930-1949   570.00   670.00

HN 1460
☐ Light green gown, darker green shawl with pink trim, dark green bonnet with red feather and ribbon trim, light red parasol (1st version), height 9 ″, designer L. Harradine.   1931-1949   400.00   450.00

	Date	Price Range	

HN 1707
☐ HN 1392, purple shawl, green hat (1st version), height 9″, designer L. Harradine.   1935-1949   525.00   575.00

HN 1739
☐ Shaded green gown, red shawl with paisley designs of darker green and black, bonnet has green feather and ribbons as trim, dark blue parasol (1st version), height 9″, designer L. Harradine.   1935-1949   400.00   450.00

HN 1914
☐ Small figure, green gown, red paisley design shawl, green bonnet with black trim and blue ribbons, white feather, white parasol with black, green, and red trim (2nd version), height 9″, designer L. Harradine.   1939-1949   300.00   350.00

HN 1987
☐ Light cream colored gown, black on red paisley design shawl, black bonnet with red lining, blue feather and ribbons, blue parasol (1st version), height 8½″, designer L. Harradine. . .   250.00   300.00

HN 1988
☐ HN 1914, cream and light red skirt, black bonnet (2nd version), height 6¼″, designer L. Harradine.   1946-1975   150.00   225.00
☐ M 3 Made as a miniature, blue gown, mottled blue shawl, light blue bonnet and parasol, height 4″, designer L. Harradine.   1932-1938   275.00   325.00
☐ M 4 Green gown, dark green shawl, black bonnet with red feather and ribbons, height 4″, designer L. Harradine.   1932-1945   300.00   350.00
☐ M-26 Cream and green gown, red shawl, black and red bonnet, red parasol, height 4″, designer L. Harradine.   1932-1945   275.00   325.00

PAMELA

HN 1468
☐ Dark blue tiered gown with red sash, holding long stemmed flowers in one arm, height 8″, designer L. Harradine.   1931-1938   750.00   850.00

	Date	Price Range	

HN 1469
☐ Shaded cream, red, and green tiered gown with red sash, height 8″, designer L. Harradine. 1931-1938 650.00 750.00

HN 1564
☐ Cream and red tiered gown, red and blue sash, height 8″, designer L. Harradine. 1933-1938 650.00 750.00

PAN ON ROCK

HN 621
☐ White nude figure of Pan seated on dark brown base, height unknown, designer unknown. 1924-1938 1100.00 1200.00

HN 622
☐ Black base, height unknown, designer unknown. 1924-1938 1100.00 1200.00

PANTALETTES

HN 1362
☐ Green skirt with reddish blue jacket, white pantalettes, light green bonnet with red trim and ribbons, black shoes, 7¾″, designer L. Harradine. 1929-1938 350.00 400.00

HN 1412
☐ Pink skirt, blue jacket trimmed in yellow and green, light green bonnet with darker green trim and ribbons, white pantalettes, red and black shoes, height 7¾″, designer L. Harradine. 1930-1949 350.00 400.00

HN 1507
☐ HN 1362, yellow dress, height 7¾″, designer L. Harradine. 1932-1949 450.00 500.00

HN 1709
☐ Red gown, red bonnet with very light blue trim and ribbons, red shoes, white pantalettes, height 7¾″, designer L. Harradine. 1935-1938 500.00 600.00

☐ **M 15** Made as a miniature, light blue skirt, darker blue bodice, red bonnet with blue trim, height 3¾″, designer L. Harradine. 1932-1945 250.00 300.00

☐ **M 16** Light red skirt, darker red bodice, black bonnet with red trim, height 3¾″, designer L. Harradine. . . 1932-1945 250.00 350.00

	Date	Price Range	

☐ **M 31** Green skirt with darker green bodice, light bonnet with red trim, height 3¾″, designer L. Harradine. . . 1932-1945 — 250.00 300.00

PARISIAN
HN 2445
☐ Gray trousers, blue jacket, brown shoes, brown tam, holding newspaper in hand, with brown fox at feet, height 8″, designer M. Nicoll. . . . . 1972-1975 — 130.00 200.00

PARSON'S DAUGHTER
HN 337
☐ HN 564, lilac dress with brown floral pattern, height 10″, designer H. Tittensor. . . . . 1919-1938 — 800.00 900.00
HN 338
☐ Patterned blue dress, red bonnet and shawl, height 10″, designer H. Tittensor. . . . . 1919-1938 — 800.00 900.00
HN 441
☐ Yellow dress with orange spots, height 10″, designer H. Tittensor. . . . . 1921-1938 — 850.00 950.00
HN 564
☐ This figure is 10″ in height, yellow skirt with red, blue, green and black blocks, red shawl and bonnet with black ribbon trim, large yellow sleeves, designer H. Tittensor. . . . . 1923-1949 — 350.00 400.00
HN 790
☐ Patchwork skirt, dark multicolored shawl, height 10″, designer H. Tittensor. . . . . 1926-1938 — 550.00 600.00
HN 1242
☐ Patchwork skirt, lilac shawl with yellow lining, height 10″, designer H. Tittensor. . . . . 1927-1938 — 550.00 600.00
HN 1356
☐ White skirt with stripes of red, blue and black at hemline, upper portion has orange spots, large green sleeves, red shawl and bonnet with black ribbon trim, large yellow sleeves, height 9¼″, designer H. Tittensor. . . . . 1929-1938 — 475.00 550.00

	Date	Price Range	

HN 2018
☐ Darker patchwork skirt, purple hat and cloak, height 9¾ ", designer H. Tittensor. 1949-1953   250.00   300.00

PAST GLORY
HN 2484
☐ Older male figure seated on brown and gray trunk, black trousers, red long coat, black cap with yellow trim, holding yellow bugle, height 7½ ", designer M. Nicoll. 1973-1979   200.00   250.00

PATCHWORK QUILT, The
HN 1984
☐ Seated figure in brown skirt, green blouse, white scarf and head covering, holding multicolored quilt on lap, height 6 ", designer L. Harradine. 1945-1959   450.00   500.00

PATRICIA
HN 1414
☐ Yellow gown with green sleeves and belt, black bonnet with green trim and ribbons with black tassels, height 8½ ", designer L. Harradine. 1930-1949   550.00   650.00

HN 1431
☐ Shaded blue and red gown, blue sleeves, black belt, light colored bonnet with dark blue ribbons and yellow tassels, height 8½ ", designer L. Harradine. 1930-1949   550.00   650.00

HN 1462
☐ Green gown with darker green top, shaded blue and green sleeves, pink bonnet with blue trim and ribbons and tassels, blue belt, height 8½ ", designer L. Harradine. 1931-1938   550.00   650.00

HN 1567
☐ Red gown with light green belt, shaded red and blue bonnet, height 8½ ", designer L. Harradine. 1933-1949   650.00   750.00

☐ M 7 Made as a miniature, cream and light green gown, red bodice and sleeves, light green bonnet, height 4 ", designer L. Harradine. 1932-1945   300.00   350.00

	Date	Price Range	
☐ **M 8** Green, yellow, and red gown, black bonnet and ribbons, height 4″, designer L. Harradine.	1932-1938	300.00	350.00
☐ **M 28** Shaded blue gown with dark blue sleeves, light bonnet with black trim, height 4″, designer L. Harradine.	1932-1945	325.00	375.00

PAULA
HN 2906
☐ Yellow gown with green trim, green shoes, holding small brown box in one hand, height 7″, designer P. Parsons. 1980-   185.00

PAULINE
HN 1444
☐ Mottled blue gown with green ribbon at bodice, green bonnet with darker green trim, height 6″, designer L. Harradine. 1931-1938   400.00   450.00

HN 2441
☐ This figure is relaxing on a couch with her elbow on the arm of the couch, her gown is tiered in shades of blue, pink and ochre which drapes to the floor with the tip of her shoe peeking out under the gown, height unknown, designer M. Davies. 1984-   155.00

PAVLOVA
HN 487
☐ Small figure in ballet position on brown base, white ballet costume with very light coloring, white headdress, height 4¼″, designer C. J. Noke. 1921-1938   1500.00   1700.00

HN 676
☐ Green base, height 4¼″, designer C. J. Noke. 1924-1938   1500.00   1700.00

Pearly Boy,
HN1482,
350.00 – 400.00

PEARLY BOY

	Date	Price Range	
HN 1482			
☐ Small figure of boy on cream colored base, brown trousers, brown coat, red vest, green scarf with black dots, black cap with white trim (1st version), height 5½″, designer L. Harradine.	1931-1949	350.00	400.00
HN 1547			
☐ Green jacket, purple trousers (1st version), height 5½″, designer L. Harradine.	1933-1949	400.00	450.00
HN 2035			
☐ Brown and red trousers, red and brown jacket, red vest, neck scarf with black dots, black hat with white trim, standing on reddish tint base (2nd version), height 5½″, designer L. Harradine.	1949-1959	150.00	225.00

Pearly Girl,
HN1483,
350.00 – 400.00

PEARLY GIRL	Date	Price Range	
HN 1483			
☐ Small girl on light colored base with pedestal, red and green skirt, brown, red and green jacket, large brown hat with red and green feathers (1st version), height 5½", designer L. Harradine.	1931-1949	350.00	400.00
HN 1548			
☐ Purple bodice, green skirt (1st version), height 5½", designer L. Harradine.	1933-1949	375.00	425.00
HN 2036			
☐ Red and brown skirt, red, brown and green jacket, green scarf with black dots, dark hat with red and green feathers, black shoes, white stockings, on light colored base (2nd version), height 5½", designer L. Harradine.	1949-1959	150.00	225.00

	Date	Price Range	

PECKSNIFF

HN 535

☐ A character of Dicken's "Martin Chuzzlewit" (1st version), height 3¾", designer L. Harradine. . . . . 1922- | 45.00 | 60.00

☐ **M 43** Renumbered as a miniature, height 4¼", designer L. Harradine. . . 1932- | 29.95

HN 553

☐ Black trousers, long black coat, yellow vest, white cravat, brown base with green bush (2nd version), height 7", designer L. Harradine. . . . . 1923-1939 | 400.00 | 500.00

HN 1891

☐ Very minor color changes (2nd version), height 7", designer L. Harradine. . . . . 1938-1952 | 400.00 | 450.00

HN 2098

☐ Green base, brown trousers, black coat, orange vest, white cravat with blue tint, gold watch with chain (3rd version), height 7", designer L. Harradine. . . . . 1952-1967 | 300.00 | 350.00

PEDLAR WOLF

HN 7

☐ Figure of wolf completely covered by gray and white robe, height 5½", designer C. J. Noke. . . . . 1913-1938 | 2000.00 | 2500.00

PEGGY

HN 1941

☐ HN 2038, minor glaze differences, height 5", designer L. Harradine. . . . . 1940-1949 | 150.00 | 200.00

HN 2038

☐ Red gown, darker red overdress trimmed in white, white head covering with ribbon, height 5", designer L. Harradine. . . . . 1949-1979 | 75.00 | 125.00

PENELOPE

HN 1901

☐ Figure seated on multicolored bench, red gown with blue bows, trimmed in white, white head covering with blue ribbon, small basket on bench, holding embroidering hoop etc. in one hand, height 7", designer L. Harradine. . . . . 1939-1975 | 300.00 | 350.00

Peggy,
HN2038,
75.00 - 125.00

	Date	Price Range	
HN 1902			
☐ Green petticoat, blue bodice, mauve and blue striped skirt, height 7″, designer L. Harradine.............	1939-1949	550.00	600.00
PENNY			
HN 2338			
☐ Small figure in white gown with green overdress, height 4½″, designer M. Davies...........................	1968-	65.00	
HN 2424			
☐ Beautiful blond figure with delicate yellow undergown, rich yelllow bodice and overgown, gown has layered frilled sleeves (2nd version), height 4¾″, designer M. Davies.....	1983-	65.00	

Penny,
HN2338,
65.00

	Date	Price Range	
PENSIVE MOMENTS			
HN 2704			
☐ Figure seated with large open parasol behind, blue gown with white and black designs on hemline, light colored hat with black ribbon trim and white flower lying on skirt, lavender and yellow parasol, height 4⅞″, designer M. Davies.	1975-1981	150.00	200.00
PERFECT PAIR, The			
HN 581			
☐ Two 18th century figures on single brown base, man's costume is black pants, long red coat trimmed in black, black shoes, white stockings, lady's costume is pink gown trimmed in lavender, red shoes, height 7″, designer L. Harradine.	1923-1938	1000.00	1100.00

	Date	Price Range	
PHILIPPA OF HAINAULT			
HN 2008			
☐ Mottled red and blue gown, red sleeves with white fur trim, green belt with red designs, height 9¾″, designer M. Davies.	1948-1953	650.00	725.00
PHYLLIS			
HN 1420			
☐ 18th century style gown of shaded reds and greens, white overlay with red and green designs, lavender shawl with spots of darker purples, light colored hat with floral trim, single red flower in hand, basket of flowers on light colored base, height 9″, designer L. Harradine.	1930-1949	570.00	670.00
HN 1430			
☐ Dark blue shawl, striped pink skirt, height 9″, designer L. Harradine.	1930-1938	700.00	800.00
HN 1486			
☐ Blue shawl, spotted pink overskirt, pink base, height 9″, designer L. Harradine.	1931-1949	650.00	750.00
HN 1698			
☐ Blue and green gown with darker green overskirt, white shawl with red and black floral designs, green hat with red flower trim, green and brown flower basket, light green base, height 9″, designer L. Harradine.	1935-1949	750.00	850.00
PICARDY PEASANT (Female)			
HN 4			
☐ HN 351, white hat and blue skirt, height 9½″, designer P. Stabler.	1913-1938	1500.00	2000.00
HN 5			
☐ Dove gray costume, height 9½″, designer P. Stabler.	1913-1938	1500.00	2000.00
HN 17A			
☐ Green hat and green costume, height 9½″, designer P. Stabler.	1913-1938	1850.00	2000.00
HN 351			
☐ Blue striped skirt, lighter blue blouse with trim of blue and pink, white apron with blue stripes, light blue hat with darker blue dots, seated on light pedestal type base, height 9½″, designer P. Stabler.	1919-1938	3000.00	3250.00

	Date	Price Range

HN 513
☐ Blue blouse, spotted skirt, height 9½ ", designer P. Stabler.   1921-1938   **1750.00 2000.00**

PICARDY PEASANT (Male)

HN 13
☐ Blue costume with lighter blue apron, white cap, seated on blue pedestal style base, height 9½ ", designer P. Stabler.   1913-1938   **1950.00 2000.00**

HN 17
☐ Green hat and green trousers, height 9½ ", designer P. Stabler.   1912-1939   **1850.00 2000.00**

HN 19
☐ Green costume, height 9½ ", designer P. Stabler.   1913-1938   **1600.00 1850.00**

PIED PIPER, The

HN 1215
☐ Dark brown base, costume of red leggings, red cloak with yellow lining, red hat, black costume, height 8¾ ", designer L. Harradine.   1926-1938   **800.00 900.00**

HN 2102
☐ Light brown base, beige costume, black cloak with red lining, blue hat and shoes, height 8½ ", designer L. Harradine.   1953-1976   **250.00 300.00**

PIERRETTE

HN 642
☐ Blue dress (1st version), height 7¼ ", designer L. Harradine.   1924-1938   **900.00 1000.00**

HN 643
☐ Black pedestal style base, red tights, black costume with white and red squares, black bodice, red sleeves, white and red collar, white hat with black balls (1st version), height 7¼ ", designer L. Harradine.   1924-1938   **900.00 1000.00**

HN 644
☐ White tights, white costume with a few black squares, collar with black trim, white hat with black balls (1st version), height 7¼ ", designer L. Harradine.   1924-1938   **800.00 900.00**

	Date	Price Range	
HN 691			
☐ HN 643, gold costume (1st version), height 7¼", designer L. Harradine. . .	1925-1938	**1250.00**	**1500.00**
HN 721			
☐ Black and white striped skirt (1st version), height 7¼", designer L. Harradine.	1925-1938	**900.00**	**1000.00**
HN 731			
☐ Spotted black and white skirt (1st version), height 7¼", designer L. Harradine.	1925-1938	**900.00**	**1000.00**
HN 732			
☐ Black and white dress with petalled border (1st version), height 7¼", designer L. Harradine.	1925-1938	**900.00**	**1000.00**
HN 784			
☐ Jazzy markings on pink costume with black muff (1st version), height 7¼", designer L. Harradine.	1926-1938	**900.00**	**1000.00**
HN 795			
☐ This figure is a miniature — pink roses on skirt, also made in color schemes not recorded in pattern books (2nd version), height 3½", designer L. Harradine.	1926-1938	**650.00**	**750.00**
HN 796			
☐ Also miniature — white skirt with silver spots (2nd version), height 3½", designer L. Harradine.	1926-1938	**650.00**	**750.00**
HN 1391			
☐ Black pedestal style base, red costume with tiny black, green and yellow blocks, white collar with red and green trim, black hat with yellow balls, this figure is holding a black half mask (3rd version), height 8½", designer L. Harradine.	1930-1938	**1000.00**	**1100.00**
HN 1749			
☐ HN 643, pink and blue costume with playing card patterns (3rd version), height 8½", designer L. Harradine. . .	1936-1949	**1000.00**	**1100.00**

	Date	Price Range

PICNIC

HN 2308

☐ Small female figure seated on green and yellow base, yellow gown with white trim, blue scarf, brown shoes, brown basket, white cloth and white cups on base, height 3¾", designer M. Davies. 1965-   100.00

PILLOW FIGHT

HN 2270

☐ Small girl figure in pink nightgown with tiny design and white collar, holding white pillow over shoulder, height 5¼", designer M. Davies. 1965-1969   200.00   250.00

PINKIE

HN 1552

☐ Small figure on light pedestal style base, shaded red with tiered blue gown and red sash, white pantalettes, white hat with blue ribbon trim, holding small bouquet of blue flowers, height 5", designer L. Harradine. 1933-1938   450.00   500.00

HN 1553

☐ Yellow and blue dress, height 5", designer L. Harradine. 1933-1938   450.00   500.00

PIPER, The

HN 2907

☐ Scottish figure seated on green stone-like base, blue skirt with black stripes, white shirt, brown vest, dark blue tam, green stockings, brown shoes, brown, black and white bagpipe, height 8", designer M. Abberley 1980-   250.00

PIRATE KING, The

HN 2901

☐ Character seated on black and white pirate flag on light tan base, costume of green shirt, white lace ruff, blue boots and blue braided jacket with plumed captain's hat, his belt holds dagger and pistol, height 10", designer W. K. Harper. 1981-   750.00

Pirouette, HN2216, **200.00 ‒ 250.00**

	Date	Price Range	
PIROUETTE			
HN 2216			
☐ Cream gown with blue tint, red trim at waist and shoulder, height 5¾ ″, designer M. Davies.	1959-1967	**200.00**	**250.00**
POACHER, The			
HN 2043			
☐ Character figure kneeling on one knee, brown trousers, blue and black coat, brown and orange vest and hat, red scarf with white dots, height 6″, designer L. Harradine.	1949-1959	**250.00**	**325.00**
POKE BONNET			
HN 612			
☐ See classification "LILAC SHAWL, A," height 9½ ″, designer C. J. Noke. .	1924-1938	**1350.00**	**1500.00**
HN 765			
☐ See classification "LILAC SHAWL, A," height 9½ ″, designer C. J. Noke. .	1925-1938	**1500.00**	**1600.00**

	Date	Price Range	
POLKA, The			
HN 2156			
☐ Pink gown with white trim and yellow rose, height 7½ ", designer M. Davies.	1955-1969	250.00	300.00
POLLY PEACHUM			
HN 463			
☐ Character from "The Beggar's Opera," black base, white gown with blue ribbon trim, white cap with blue ribbon (1st version), height 6¼ ", designer L. Harradine.	1921-1949	600.00	700.00
HN 465			
☐ Red dress (1st version), height 6½ ", designer L. Harradine.	1921-1949	500.00	600.00
HN 489			
☐ Figure in curtsy position, light green gown with white cap and green ribbon trim (2nd version), height 4¼ ", designer L. Harradine.	1921-1938	400.00	500.00
HN 549			
☐ Red gown (2nd version), height 4¼ ", designer L. Harradine.	1922-1949	450.00	500.00
HN 550			
☐ Pink gown (1st version), height 6½ ", designer L. Harradine.	1922-1949	500.00	600.00
HN 589			
☐ HN 463, pink dress, yellow underskirt (1st version), height 6½ ", designer L. Harradine.	1924-1949	500.00	600.00
HN 614			
☐ Pale pink dress, blue bows (1st version), height 6½ ", designer L. Harradine.	1924-1949	600.00	700.00
HN 620			
☐ HN 489, Rose dress, cream underskirt (2nd version), height 4¼ ", designer L. Harradine.	1924-1938	450.00	500.00
HN 680			
☐ HN 463, White dress with black, yellow and blue spots (1st version), height 6½ ", designer L. Harradine. . .	1924-1949	600.00	700.00
HN 693			
☐ Deep rose pink dress with green bows (1st version), height 6½ ", designer L. Harradine.	1925-1949	600.00	700.00

	Date	Price Range	

HN 694

☐ HN 489, deep rose pink dress, green bows (2nd version), height 4¼", designer L. Harradine. . . . . 1925-1949 — 400.00 — 500.00

HN 698

☐ Figure is miniature in curtsy position, pink gown (3rd version), height 2¼", designer L. Harradine. . . . . 1925-1949 — 400.00 — 500.00

HN 699

☐ Blue dress (3rd version), height 2¼", designer L. Harradine. . . . . 1925-1949 — 400.00 — 500.00

HN 734

☐ HN 489, black bodice, white skirt, black spots (2nd version), height 4¼", designer L. Harradine. . . . . 1925-1949 — 450.00 — 500.00

HN 757

☐ HN 698, red bodice, spotted skirt, holding colored streamers (3rd version), height 2¼", designer L. Harradine. . . . . 1925-1949 — 350.00 — 400.00

HN 758

☐ Pink skirt with orange stripes (3rd version), height 2¼", designer L. Harradine. . . . . 1925-1949 — 350.00 — 400.00

HN 759

☐ Yellow and white skirt with black spots (3rd version), height 2¼", designer L. Harradine. . . . . 1925-1949 — 350.00 — 400.00

HN 760

☐ Mottled multicolored skirt (3rd version), height 2¼", designer L. Harradine. . . . . 1925-1949 — 350.00 — 400.00

HN 761

☐ Blue and purple skirt (3rd version), height 2¼", designer L. Harradine. . . 1925-1949 — 350.00 — 400.00

HN 762

☐ Pink roses on skirt (3rd version), height 2¼", designer L. Harradine. . . 1925-1949 — 350.00 — 400.00

☐ **M 21** Miniature figures in curtsy position, deep red gown, height 2¼", designer L. Harradine. . . . . 1932-1945 — 325.00 — 375.00

☐ **M 22** Blue spotted gown, height 2¼", designer L. Harradine. . . . . 1932-1938 — 325.00 — 375.00

☐ **M 23** White gown with red and green stripes with red overlay with red and blue dots, height 2¼", designer L. Harradine. . . . . 1932-1938 — 325.00 — 375.00

	Date	Price Range	
POTTER, The			
HN 1493			
☐ Character figure seated on purple rug on brown base, dark brown and red robe and hood, multicolored jugs and jars on base, height 7″, designer C. J. Noke.	1932-	325.00	
HN 1518			
☐ Green cloak, height 7″, designer C. J. Noke.	1932-1949	425.00	475.00
HN 1522			
☐ Dark blue and green cloak, height 7″, designer C. J. Noke.	1932-1949	425.00	475.00
PREMIERE			
HN 2343			
☐ Blue and white gown, dark green cloak with white design on edge and yellow lining, black opera glasses, height 7½″, designer M. Davies.	1969-1979	175.00	225.00
PRETTY LADY			
HN 69			
☐ HN 70, flowered blue dress, height 9½″, designer H. Tittensor.	1916-1938	1250.00	1500.00
HN 70			
☐ Pale gray gown with raised white dots, height 9½″, designer H. Tittensor.	1916-1938	1250.00	1500.00
HN 302			
☐ Patterned lilac dress, height 9½″, designer H. Tittensor.	1918-1938	1350.00	1600.00
HN 330			
☐ Patterned blue dress, height 9½″, designer H. Tittensor.	1918-1938	1450.00	1600.00
HN 361			
☐ Blue and green dress, height 9½″, designer H. Tittensor.	1919-1938	1450.00	1600.00
HN 384			
☐ Red dress with striped skirt, height 9½″, designer H. Tittensor.	1920-1938	1450.00	1600.00
HN 565			
☐ Orange dress, white sleeves with green spots, height 9½″, designer H. Tittensor.	1923-1938	1450.00	1600.00
HN 700			
☐ Yellow dress with black spots, height 9½″, designer H. Tittensor.	1925-1938	1500.00	1750.00

	Date	Price Range

HN 763

☐ Orange gown with blue sleeves and black design, white waistband with red spots and stripes, orange ribbon in hair, height 9½", designer H. Tittensor. 1925-1938 **1450.00 1600.00**

HN 783

☐ HN 70, blue dress, height 9½", designer H. Tittensor. 1926-1938 **1450.00 1600.00**

PRETTY POLLY

HN 2768

☐ Deep pink dress over which is draped a gray cloth, she is shelling peas, turning she offers one to a colorful parrot perched on her chair, height 6", designer Bill Harper. 1984- **100.00**

Pretty Polly,
HN2768,
100.00

PRIMROSES

HN 1617

☐ Character figure seated with brown basket at her side, red dress, white apron, dark mottled shawl with orange fringe, black hat with floral trim and black ribbons, height 6½", designer L. Harradine. 1935-1949 **525.00 575.00**

	Date	Price Range	

PRINCE OF WALES, The

HN 1217

☐ Riding costume of white trousers, black and red boots, red jacket, yellow vest, white cravat, black hat, dark brown base, height 7½", designe L. Harradine. 1926-1938 1450.00 1600.00

PRINCESS, A

HN 391

☐ Purple skirt with green and yellow designs, green blouse, green cloak with orange round designs, has yellow lining, black rope belt, height unknown, designer unknown. 1920-1938 2750.00 3000.00

HN 392

☐ Multicolored costume, striped skirt, height unknown, designer unknown. . 1920-1938 2750.00 3000.00

HN 420

☐ Pink and green striped skirt, blue cloak, height unknown, designer unknown. 1920-1938 2750.00 3000.00

HN 430

☐ Green floral dress, blue and green striped cloak, height unknown, designer unknown. 1921-1938 2750.00 3000.00

HN 431

☐ Pink dress, blue-green cloak, height unknown, designer unknown. 1921-1938 2750.00 3000.00

HN 633

☐ Black and white dress, height unknown, designer unknown. 1924-1938 2750.00 3000.00

PRISCILLA

HN 1337

☐ Tiered gown of shaded reds, yellows, and blues, pantalettes and parasol of same color, darker mottled hat and jacket, black base, height 8", designer L. Harradine. 1929-1938 500.00 600.00

HN 1340

☐ Red tiered gown with dark blue collar, blue bonnet and parasol with dark blue trim, red shoes, black base, height 8", designer L. Harradine. 1929-1949 325.00 375.00

	Date	Price Range	

HN 1495
☐ Shaded blue gown with pink collar, green bonnet and parasol, white pantalettes, height 8″, designer L. Harradine. 1932-1949 500.00 600.00

HN 1501
☐ Shaded yellow gown, green bonnet and parasol, light red shoes, black base, height 8″, designer L. Harradine. 1932-1938 500.00 600.00

HN 1559
☐ HN 1337, pink and yellow skirt, height 8″, designer L. Harradine. 1932-1949 400.00 500.00
☐ **M 13** Made as a miniature, green and yellow gown, height 3¾″, designer L. Harradine. 1932-1938 400.00 500.00
☐ **M 14** Shaded blue gown,, height 3¾″, designer L. Harradine. 1932-1945 275.00 325.00
☐ **M 24** Red gown with green bonnet, height 3¾″, designer L. Harradine. . . 1932-1945 300.00 350.00

PROFESSOR, The

HN 2281
☐ Character figure seated on brown chair, brown suit, black robe with wine lining, white shirt with black bow tie, holding open book, books stacked beside chair, glasses on head and also on knee, height 7¼″, designer M. Nicoll. 1965-1980 150.00 200.00

PROMENADE

HN 2076
☐ Two figures on black base, lady has shaded red skirt with blue overskirt trimmed in black, high head piece of white and blue, male has red shoes, white stockings, long white coat with red, blue and black designs, multicolored long vest, red sash, black curly hair; height 8″, designer M. Davies. . . 1951-1953 1150.00 1350.00

	Date	Price Range
PROPOSAL (Lady)		

HN 715

☐ Lady seated in brown and cream love-seat on black base, red gown with shades of black, white cap with red and black ribbon, height 5¾″, designer unknown.   1925-1938   **950.00**   **1000.00**

HN 716

☐ White gown with a few black squares, white cap with black, height 5¾″, designer unknown.   1925-1938   **950.00**   **1000.00**

HN 788

☐ Pink gown, height 5¾″, designer unknown.   1926-1938   **900.00**   **1000.00**

PROPOSAL (Male)

HN 725

☐ Male on knee on black base, black shoes, white stockings, black trousers, black and white checkered long vest, red coat with black and white trim, white with black trim at wrist and neck, holding black hat with red feathers, dark curly hair, height 5½″, designer unknown.   1925-1938   **950.00**   **1000.00**

HN 1209

☐ Blue coat, flowered pink waistcoat, height 5½″, designer unknown.   1926-1938   **900.00**   **1000.00**

PRUDENCE

HN 1883

☐ Seated figure in shaded blue gown with lining of dark blue with red design, white collar and small white close bonnet, height 6¾″, designer L. Harradine.   1938-1949   **750.00**   **800.00**

HN 1884

☐ Shaded red gown with lining of white with blue designs, height 6¾″, designer L. Harradine.   1938-1949   **750.00**   **800.00**

PRUE

HN 1996

☐ Red gown with white apron and collar, dark red waistband, white cap with blue ribbon, carrying basket with fruit, height 6¾″, designer L. Harradine.   1947-1955   **275.00**   **325.00**

	Date	Price Range	

PUFF AND POWDER

HN 397
☐ HN 398, yellow skirt, brown bodice, height unknown, designer L. Harradine. 1920-1938 2000.00 2200.00

HN 398
☐ Lavender gown with black and white designs, purple bodice, yellow overskirt with black and white designs, height unknown, designer L. Harradine. 1920-1938 2000.00 2200.00

HN 400
☐ Green and blue bodice, yellow skirt, height unknown, designer L. Harradine. 1920-1938 2000.00 2200.00

HN 432
☐ Lilac skirt with orange spots, height unknown, designer L. Harradine. 1921-1938 2000.00 2200.00

HN 433
☐ Yellow skirt with blue spots, height unknown, designer L. Harradine. 1921-1938 2000.00 2200.00

PUNCH AND JUDY MAN

HN 2765
☐ Light tan base, of elderly man in yellow trousers, green sweater, black shoes, puppets are male with red, yellow and black costumes, lady's costume blue dress, green shawl and white hat, height 9", designer W. K. Harper. 1981- 295.00

PUPPETMAKER, The

HN 2253
☐ Brown trousers, green vest, white shirt, small cap of brown and tan, boy puppet costume of red and green and girl puppet dress of green with overdress of light and dark blue, height 8", designer M. Nicoll. 1962-1973 400.00 475.00

PUSSY

HN 18
☐ Barefooted girl seated holding black cat in lap, light blue gown, height 7½", designer F. C. Stone. 1913-1938 2400.00 2600.00

HN 325
☐ White dress with black patterning, height 7½", designer F. C. Stone. . . . 1918-1938 2450.00 2650.00

	Date	Price Range

HN 507
☐ Spotted blue dress, height 7½ ″, designer F. C. Stone.   1921-1938   **2400.00 2600.00**

Pyjams,
HN1942,
325.00 – 375.00

PYJAMS
HN 1942
☐ Small figure on white base wearing light red pajamas trimmed in white and blue stripe, holding blue ball, height 5¼ ″, designer L. Harradine. . .   1940-1949   **325.00   375.00**

QUALITY STREET
HN 1211
☐ Red gown with long blue and red scarf, light colored bonnet with red feathers and red ribbons, height 7¼ ″, designer unknown.   1926-1938   **1100.00 1200.00**

	Date	Price Range
RACHEL		
HN 2919		
☐ Green gown, yellow ochre hooded coat trimmed with brown fur, height 7½ ″, designer P. Gee.	1981-	185.00
RAG DOLL		
HN 2142		
☐ Small figure in blue gown with bibbed white apron, white cap, holding doll wrapped in red, height 4¾ ″, designer M. Davies.	1954-	75.00
RAG DOLL SELLER		
HN 2944		
☐ Old lady sitting on a light brown basket selling her rag dolls, light gray skirt, light blue blouse covered with a green shawl, her gray hair is covered with a white bonnet trimmed in black, height 7¼ ″, designer Robert Tabbenor.	1983-	150.00
REBECCA		
HN 2805		
☐ Pink gown with floral design at hemline, blue overskirt with dark blue trim, pink ribbon in hair, holding single red flower, height 7¼ ″, designer M. Davies.	1980-	325.00
REFLECTIONS		
HN 1820		
☐ HN 1821, red dress, lilac sofa, height 5 ″, designer L. Harradine.	1937-1938	1000.00 1100.00
HN 1821		
☐ Orange and green sofa, green gown with white trim, large white cap with red trim, multicolored pillow on sofa, height 5 ″, designer L. Harradine.	1937-1938	1000.00 1100.00
HN 1847		
☐ Green sofa, shaded red gown with white trim, red bonnet with blue ribbons, blue shoes, light green pillow on sofa, height 5 ″, designer L. Harradine.	1938-1949	1000.00 1100.00

	Date	Price Range	

HN 1848
☐ Green skirt, height 5″, designer L. Harradine.   1938-1949   1000.00   1100.00

REGAL LADY

HN 2709
☐ Cream skirt with yellow shadings, gold trim on hemline, dark blue overdress, height 7⅝″, designer M. Davies.   1975-1983   115.00   170.00

REGENCY

HN 1752
☐ Shaded green skirt with red, green and purple stripes at hemline, long purple jacket with green and red trim, white cravat, green triangular hat with red trim, holding white and brown riding crop, height 8″, designer L. Harradine.   1936-1949   600.00   700.00

REGENCY BEAU

HN 1972
☐ 18th century costume of red with black buttons, green cloak, black triangular hat, black shoes, white with black trim at wrist and neck, white stockings, on light colored base, height 8″, designer H. Fenton. .   1941-1949   850.00   950.00

RENDEZVOUS

HN 2212
☐ Light green gown with shaded red overdress, figure standing beside white pedestal with red roses on top, height 7¼″, designer M. Davies.   1962-1971   350.00   400.00

REPOSE

HN 2272
☐ Green and brown chaise lounge, barefoot figure in rose gown with blue trim, green ribbon in hair, holding small book, height 5¼″, designer M. Davies.   1972-1979   150.00   200.00

	Date	Price Range

REST AWHILE
HN 2728
☐ Older lady figure seated on brown stile on green base, gray and blue gown with white apron, purple jacket, gray and blue bonnet with red flowers and gray and blue ribbons, holding brown basket with a green and white striped cover, height 8″, designer W. K. Harper.   1981-   200.00

RETURN OF PERSEPHONE, The
HN 31
☐ Large, two figures on one base (16″), one costumed in gray robes, second in cream colored gown, green base with bush on one end, height 16″, designer C. Vyse.   1913-1938   4000.00 5000.00

REVERIE
HN 2306
☐ Figure seated on brown and white chaise lounge, peach and yellow gown with white trim, holding open book on lap, one gray and one purple pillow, height 6½″, designer M. Davies.   1964-1981   225.00   275.00

RHAPSODY
HN 2267
☐ Blue and green gown, long yellow scarf, small white fan in one hand, height 6¾″, designer M. Davies   1961-1973   135.00   200.00

RHODA
HN 1573
☐ Muted yellow and blue skirt, red bodice, shawl with colors of green, yellow and red trimmed in dark red and blue, green bonnet with green feather and purple ribbons, height 10¼″, designer L. Harradine.   1933-1949   575.00   650.00
HN 1574
☐ Purple gown with red bow trim, red shawl with shaded greens, green bonnet with light green feather and purple ribbons, height 10¼″, designer L. Harradine.   1933-1938   500.00   550.00

Rhoda,
HN1573,
575.00 ~ 650.00

	Date	Price Range	
HN 1688			
☐ Orange gown with purple bodice, red shawl with large green and black flower design with green fringe, black bonnet with green feather and dark ribbons, height 10¼″, designer L. Harradine.	1935-1949	550.00	650.00
RHYTHM			
HN 1903			
☐ HN 1904, pink dress, height 6¾″, designer L. Harradine.	1939-1949	575.00	625.00
HN 1904			
☐ Blue gown, blue overskirt with dark blue and gold floral designs, height 6¾″, designer L. Harradine.	1939-1949	575.00	625.00

	Date	Price Range	

RITA
HN 1448
☐ HN 1450, yellow and pink dress, height 7", designer L. Harradine. 1931-1938 600.00 700.00

HN 1450
☐ Blue patterned tiered gown with brown shawl, brown bonnet with green ribbons, green, white and yellow parasol, height 7", designer L. Harradine. 1931-1938 600.00 700.00

RIVER BOY
HN 2128
☐ Small figure of boy kneeling on green base, dark blue trousers, very light green shirt, cream colored hat, holding black frying pan over fire, height 4", designer M. Davies. 1962-1975 150.00 200.00

ROBERT BURNS
HN   42
☐ Scottish figure on black base, brown trousers, green coat, orange vest, white cravat, brown tam with green ball trim, yellow scarf with brown stripes, height 18", designer E. W. Light. 1914-1938 3000.00 3500.00

ROBIN
Girl on hands and knees
Issued only as a miniature

☐ **M 38** Red shirt with blue collar, blue shorts on green stand, height 2½", designer unknown. 1933-1945 300.00 350.00
☐ **M 39** Blue shirt with red collar, green shorts on tan stand, height 2½", designer unknown. 1933-1945 300.00 350.00

ROCKING HORSE, The
HN 2072
☐ Rocking horse on brown base, light blue-gray horse with red cloth and red straps, cream rocking base with red and yellow trim, boy figure in blue pants, lighter blue shirt, black shoes, height 7", designer L. Harradine. 1951-1953 1450.00 1750.00

Rocking Horse,
HN2072,
1450.00 - 1750.00

	Date	Price Range	
ROMANCE			
HN 2430			
☐ Figure seated in green chair, yellow gown with brown trim at hemline, black shoe, holding open book on lap, height 5¼ ″, designer M. Davies.	1972-1979	90.00	150.00
ROMANY SUE			
HN 1757			
☐ Green gown with pink and white striped apron, red and blue shawl with green fringe, black hat with blue and red feather, carrying basket of vegetables and flowers on each arm, height 9½ ″, designer L. Harradine. ..	1936-1949	700.00	800.00
HN 1758			
☐ Lavender gown with apron, also lavender with darker stripe, cream colored shawl with blue designs and green fringe, dark green hat with blue and red feather, two darker brown baskets, height 9½ ″, designer L. Harradine.	1936-1949	700.00	800.00

	Date	Price Range

ROSABELL

HN 1620

☐ Seated figure with muted blue and red skirt, red bodice, red hat with blue and red feather, multicolored shawl, height 6¾", designer L. Harradine. . .   1934-1938   900.00   1000.00

ROSALIND

HN 2393

☐ Dark blue gown with white floral design and large white cuffs, dark hair, holding white fan in one hand, flower in other, height 5½", designer M. Davies.   1970-1975   150.00   200.00

ROSAMUND

HN 1320

☐ Shaded green skirt, light red jacket, long purple-white, green and red scarf, tall green crown hat with black feather and red band (1st version), height 7½", designer L. Harradine. . .   1929-1938   1500.00   2000.00

HN 1497

☐ Red full skirted gown with lighter red trim, green hat, long necklace with cross, small bouquet of flowers in hand (2nd version), height 8½", designer L. Harradine.   1932-1938   800.00   1000.00

HN 1551

☐ Blue gown trimmed in lighter blue, shaded red and blue hat, white necklace and cross, height 8½", designer L. Harradine.   1932-1938   450.00   500.00

☐ **M 32** Made as a miniature, shaded yellow and blue gown and hat, height 4¼", designer L. Harradine.   1932-1945   250.00   375.00

☐ **M 33** Shaded red and blue gown, red hat, height 4¼", designer L. Harradine.   1932-1945   325.00   375.00

ROSE

HN 1368

☐ Small figure in tiered red gown, height 4⅝", designer L. Harradine. . . .   1930-   65.00

HN 1387

☐ Flowered blue and pink dress, orange roses, height 4½", designer L. Harradine.   1930-1938   250.00   300.00

	Date	Price Range	

HN 1416
☐ Tiered shaded blue gown, height 4½ ", designer L. Harradine. 1930-1949   150.00   200.00

HN 1506
☐ Yellow dress, height 4½ ", designer L. Harradine. 1932-1938   250.00   300.00

HN 1654
☐ Green bodice, floral skirt, height 4½ ", designer L. Harradine. 1934-1938   250.00   300.00

HN 2123
☐ Mauve gown with layers of flounces, height 4½ ", designer L. Harradine. . . 1983-   65.00

ROSEANNA

HN 1921
☐ HN 1926, green dress, height 8", designer L. Harradine. 1940-1949   400.00   450.00

HN 1926
☐ Shaded red gown with blue and red hemline, blue and green bow trim on bodice, dark bows in hairs, standing with hands on bowl of flowers on pedestal, height 8", designer L. Harradine. 1940-1959   275.00   325.00

ROSEBUD

HN 1580
☐ Very small figure, seated, in wide ruffled and pleated gown of pink (1st version), height 3", designer L. Harradine. 1933-1938   600.00   700.00

HN 1581
☐ Pale dress with flower sprays (1st version), height 3", designer L. Harradine. 1933-1938   600.00   700.00

HN 1983
☐ This is larger figure, shaded red gown with light green cross design as trim, darker red shawl, green bonnet with white trim, carrying small basket of flowers with flowers in other arm (2nd version), height 7½ ", designer L. Harradine. 1945-1952   450.00   500.00

	Date	Price Range	

ROSEMARY
HN 2091
☐ Red gown with blue shawl and red designs, dark blue bonnet with white scarf, carrying basket of flowers, height 7″, designer L. Harradine. 1952-1959   350.00   450.00

ROSINA ·
HN 1358
☐ Seated figure, red gown and red cape with white fur trim, red bonnet with purple ribbons, height 5½″, designer L. Harradine. 1929-1938   750.00   850.00
HN 1364
☐ Purple gown and cape with wide red stripe and dark dots as trim, red bonnet with purple trim and red ribbons, height 5½″, designer L. Harradine. 1929-1938   750.00   850.00
HN 1556
☐ Cream gown with shaded blues and reds, shaded red and blue bonnet with red trim and ribbons, height 5½″, designer L. Harradine. 1933-1938   500.00   600.00

ROWENA
HN 2077
☐ Shaded green and red underskirt, red overskirt, dark red overlay with blue and black designs, brown muff, green bonnet with shaded blue ribbons, height 7½″, designer L. Harradine. .. 1951-1955   550.00   650.00

ROYAL GOVERNOR'S COOK
HN 2233
☐ Seated colored figure, dark blue gown with white apron and crossed white scarf, white head covering, holding pink bowl on lap, height 6″, designer M. Davies. 1960-1983   115.00   200.00

RUBY
HN 1724
☐ Shaded red and white tiered gown, dark flowers on blue ribbons in hair, holding small bouquet in hand, height 5¼″, designer L. Harradine. 1935-1949   300.00   350.00

Rowena,
HN2077,
550.00 - 650.00

	Date	Price Range	

HN 1725
☐ Shaded blue tiered gown, red flowers on red ribbon in hair, height 5¼ ″, designer L. Harradine. . . . . | 1935-1949 | 300.00 | 350.00 |

RUSTIC SWAIN, The

HN 1745
☐ Two figures on brown couch, lady's white gown with red and blue floral design, green overlay, green bonnet and shoes, man's costume of brown and white, dark brown hat, brown shoes, red and white striped pillow on couch, height 5¼ ″, designer L. Harradine. . . . . | 1935-1949 | 1750.00 | 2250.00 |

HN 1746
☐ Man's costume of green, height 5¼ ″, designer L. Harradine. . . . . | 1935-1949 | 1850.00 | 2350.00 |

	Date	Price Range	

RUTH (Kate Greenaway)
HN 2799
☐ Green gown with red and yellow flowers at hemline, white waistband and collar, large white cap with red ribbon, holding single flower in one hand, on white base, height 6⅛″, designer M. Davies.   1976-1982   65.00   100.00

RUTH THE PIRATE MAID
HN 2900
☐ Costume of brown striped skirt, blue blouse with gold and black trim, white apron, black captain's hat with gold trim and white skull and cross bones, on mottled brown base, height 11¾″, designer W. K. Harper.   1981-   750.00

SABBATH MORN
HN 1982
☐ Red gown, mottled green and yellow shawl and parasol, red bonnet with green and white trim and blue ribbons, height 7¼″, designer L. Harradine.   1945-1959   265.00   325.00

SAILOR'S HOLIDAY
HN 2442
☐ Kneeling character figure on dark brown and purple base, purple trousers, yellow coat, green sweater, black cap, black tie, light purple shirt, holding small blue, tan and white sailboat, height 6¼″, designer M. Nicoll.   1972-1979   175.00   225.00

SAIREY GAMP
HN 533
☐ This figure is miniature — A character from Dicken's "Martin Chuzzlewit" (1st version), height 4″, designer L. Harradine.   1922-   45.00   60.00
☐ **M 46** Renumbered as a miniature. Light green gown, black cloak, white and pink head cap with black ribbons, red small round cloth with black dots in one hand, height 4″, designer L. Harradine.   1932-1983   20.00   30.00

	Date	Price Range	

HN 558
☐ Larger figure, dressed in black on black base, black bonnet with white trim, blue round cloth bag with white dots, green and blue umbrella (2nd version), height 7″, designer L. Harradine. 1923-1939   400.00   500.00

HN 1896
☐ Very minor color changes (2nd version), height 7″, designer L. Harradine. 1938-1952   325.00   375.00

HN 2100
☐ Light green gown, dark green cloak, black bonnet with white trim, red round cloth bag with white dots, black umbrella, black shoes, on black base (3rd version), height 7¼″, designer L. Harradine. 1952-1967   275.00   325.00

SALOME

HN 1828
☐ Tinted finish, height unknown, designer R. Garbe. 1937-1949   4500.00   5000.00

SAM WELLER

HN 531
☐ A character in Dicken's "Pickwick Papers" (1st version), height 4″, designer L. Harradine. 1922-   45.00   60.00
☐ **M 48** Renumbered as a miniature, brown trousers, yellow vest with red stripes, red neck scarf, black hat, seated on black base, height 4″, designer L. Harradine. 1932-1983   20.00   30.00

SANDRA

HN 2275
☐ Tan gown, white trim and petticoat with brown dots, brown hat to match gown, height 7¾″, designer M. Davies. 1969-   155.00

HN 2401
☐ Apple-green dress, white petticoat showing, deep green hat, height 7¾″, designer M. Davies. 1984-   155.00

Santa Claus,
HN2725,
195.00

SANTA CLAUS	Date	Price Range
HN 2725		
☐ Character figure in brilliant red suit with white fur, black boots, holding aloft a teddy bear in one hand and a sack of toys in the other, height 9½″, designer W. K. Harper..............	1982-	195.00
SARA		
HN 2265		
☐ White gown with red bodice and over-skirt, white collar with blue floral design, height 7½″, designer M. Davies..........................	1981-	215.00
SAUCY NYMPH, A		
HN 1539		
☐ Small white nude figure seated on mottled green, red, brown base, height 4½″, designer unknown.	1933-1949	275.00 325.00

	Date	Price Range

SCHOOLMARM
HN 2223
☐ Character figure seated at brown bench type desk, gray gown, purple shawl, white headcap with black ribbon, desk has red and gray inkwell, white dunce hat beside desk, white, black, orange and brown world globe under desk, height 6¾", designer M. Davies.............................. 1958-1980   110.00   175.00

SCOTCH GIRL
HN 1269
☐ Red costume with dark brown and black stripes, dark brown jacket with white trim, red stockings with black stripes, on black pedestal style base, height 7½", designer L. Harradine. .. 1928-1938   1350.00 1500.00

SCOTTIES
HN 1281
☐ Figure seated on cream colored bench, red dress, red shoes, one black scottie on bench, the other at side of bench, height 5¼", designer L. Harradine...................... 1928-1938   1100.00 1200.00
HN 1349
☐ Pale multicolored costume, white dogs, height 5¼", designer L. Harradine............................ 1929-1949   1500.00 1600.00

SCRIBE, A
HN 305
☐ Figure seated on blue and gold cushion, green robes, yellow costume, blue turban, light purple shoes, height 6", designer C. J. Noke. 1918-1936   1100.00 1200.00
HN 324
☐ Dark green and orange cushion, shades of brown costume and robes, green and blue turban, green shoes, height 6", designer C. J. Noke. 1918-1938   1100.00 1200.00
HN 1235
☐ Brown coat, blue hat, height 6", designer C. J. Noke. 1927-1938   1100.00 1200.00

	Date	Price Range	

SCROOGE
Issued only as a miniature

☐ **M 87** White cap, brown coat, black money bag in hands, tan shoes, black stand, height 4", designer L. Harradine.............................. 1949- 29.95

SEAFARER, The
HN 2455

☐ Character figure seated on light blue pedestal on blue base, blue trousers, black boots with red trim, yellow zippered sweater, blue shirt, black cap, base has bird on it, height 8½", designer M. Nicoll................ 1972-1976 225.00 275.00

SEA HARVEST
HN 2257

☐ Blue coat, brown trousers, black boots, black rain hat, holding large brown net, height 7½", designer M. Nicoll......................... 1969-1976 150.00 200.00

SEASHORE
HN 2263

☐ Small boy figure in red swim trunks, on light brown base, height 3½", designer M. Davies. 1961-1965 250.00 300.00

SEA SPRITE
HN 1261

☐ Small white nude figure standing on black rock style base with long red and black scarf behind figure (1st version), height 5", designer L. Harradine. 1927-1938 600.00 650.00

HN 2191

☐ Barefooted figure in blue and white shell, pink gown (2nd version), height 7", designer M. Davies. 1958-1962 475.00 525.00

SECRET THOUGHTS
HN 2382

☐ Seated figure, shaded green and yellow gown, blue bow in hair, holding two pink roses, leaning on cream colored pedestal, height 6¼", designer M. Davies. 1971- 215.00

Secret Thoughts,
HN2382,
215.00

	Date	Price Range	
SENTIMENTAL PIERROT, The			
HN 36			
☐ HN 307, dove gray costume, height 13½ ″, designer C. J. Noke.	1914-1938	1750.00	1900.00
HN 307			
☐ Seated male figure in black and white costume, height 13½ ″, designer C. J. Noke.	1918-1938	1750.00	1900.00
SENTINEL			
HN 523			
☐ Figure in knight's costume on black base, gray and red costume, shield has three golden lion's heads, height 17½ ″, designer unknown.	1921-1938	4500.00	5000.00
SERENA			
HN 1868			
☐ Red gown with blue ruffle trim, light red undergown with design of red, yellow and blue, red shoes, height 11″, designer L. Harradine.	1938-1949	1100.00	1200.00

Sharon,
HN3047,
85.00

SHARON

	Date	Price Range

HN 3047
☐ Child figure dressed in light blue with pink sash, plum colored hat with ribbons tied under her chin, black fingerless gloves, height 4¾″, designer P. Parsons. .... 1984- · · · 85.00

SHE LOVES ME NOT

HN 2045
☐ Small boy figure on yellow and green base, blue suit with white straps, barefooted, red hair, height 5½″, designer L. Harradine. .... 1949-1962 · · · 150.00 · · · 200.00

SHEILA

HN 2742
☐ Light blue gown with floral bottomed skirt, four layers of petticoat showing, a pink rose in hands, touching hair, height unknown, designer Sharon Keenan. .... 1984- · · · 125.00

	Date	Price Range

SHEPHERD, A

HN 81
☐ Black base, blue and gray trousers, brown coat, brown hat with light colored scarf tied around it, holding lantern in one hand and small lamb in other arm, earthenware (1st version), height 13¼", designer C. J. Noke. ... 1918-1938 2250.00 2500.00

HN 617
☐ China body and purple-blue trousers and coat (1st version), height 13¼", designer C. J. Noke. 1924-1938 1750.00 2000.00

HN 632
☐ China body and white smock, blue trousers (1st version), height 13¼", designer C. J. Noke. 1924-1938 1750.00 2000.00

HN 709
☐ This is a miniature figure, green jacket, red cloak and black trousers (1st version), height 3½", designer unknown. 1925-1938 550.00 650.00

HN 751
☐ Yellow and brown base, costume of black trousers, green coat, red cloak, white shirt, black hat, black cane, single flower in hand (3rd version), height 7", designer unknown. 1925-1938 1500.00 1750.00

HN 1975
☐ Green base, brown trousers, long tan coat, red scarf, brown hat, carrying lantern and staff (4th version), height 8½", designer H. Fenton. 1945-1975 150.00 200.00

☐ **M 17** Made as a miniature, in the style of HN 751, brown trousers, blue coat, red cloak, height 3¾", designer unknown. 1932-1938 550.00 700.00

☐ **M 19** Brown trousers, blue coat and blue cloak, height 3¾", designer unknown. 1932-1938 550.00 700.00

SHEPHERDESS

HN 708
☐ This is a miniature, on yellow and brown base, red overskirt with yellow and pink striped skirt (1st version), height 3½", designer unknown. 1925-1948 650.00 750.00

☐ **M 18** Made as a miniature, green bodice, pink overskirt. height 3½", designer unknown. 1932-1938 600.00 700.00

	Date	Price Range	
☐ **M 20** Yellow bodice, flowered dress, height 3¾", designer unknown......	1932-1938	600.00	700.00

HN 735
☐ Yellow and green base, black shoes with red bows, multicolored skirt with purple overlay, yellow trim on sleeves, dark bow in hair (2nd version), height 7", designer unknown............... 1925-1938   1500.00 1750.00

HN 750
☐ Pink bodice, yellow skirt (2nd version), height 7", designer unknown... 1925-1938   1500.00 1750.00

SHORE LEAVE

HN 2254
☐ Character figure seated on gray stone-line wall, black suit, black cap, gray sweater, green parrot on shoulder, bag between feet, wicker basket at side, height 8", designer M. Nicoll. 1965-1979   200.00 250.00

SHY ANNE

HN 60
☐ HN 64, floral blue dress, height 7¾", designer L. Perugini.............. 1916-1938   1500.00 1600.00

HN 64
☐ Light colored base, girl figure in white dress with raised white design, large white bow in hair, says Shy Anne on base, height 7¾", designer L. Perugini...................... 1916-1938   1500.00 1600.00

HN 65
☐ Spotted blue dress with dark blue hem, height 7¾", designer Perugini. . 1916-1938   1550.00 1800.00

HN 568
☐ Black base, shaded green dress with darker dots, yellow ribbon around waist, dark blue bow with pink squares in hair, pink and dark blue striped stockings, height 7¾", designer L. Perugini.............. 1923-1938   1450.00 1600.00

SHYLOCK

HN 79
☐ HN 317, multicolored cloak, yellow sleeves, height unknown, designer C. J. Noke............................ 1917-1938   2500.00 2750.00

	Date	Price Range	

HN 317

☐ Shaded blue and purple robes, headcap of same, height unknown, de-
signer C. J. Noke. 1918-1938   **2500.00 2750.00**

SIBELL

HN 1668

☐ 18th century gown of light green with
blue bow trim, red overskirt with
white trim, black hat with red trim,
height 6½ ″, designer L. Harradine. . . 1934-1949   **600.00 700.00**

HN 1695

☐ Green gown with blue bows, orange
overskirt with multicolored designs,
height 6½ ″, designer L. Harradine. . . 1935-1949   **600.00 700.00**

HN 1735

☐ HN 1668, blue and green gown, height
6½ ″, designer L. Harradine. 1935-1949   **800.00 850.00**

SIESTA

HN 1305

☐ White nude figure lying on dark red
couch, shaded reds and blues in cloth
covering couch, height 4¾ ″, designer
L. Harradine. 1928-1938   **1350.00 1500.00**

SILK AND RIBBONS

HN 2017

☐ Character figure seated on wooden
bench, dark green dress, dark green
shawl with black stripes, black bonnet with red ribbons, box of different
colored ribbons on lap, white apron,
brown wicker basket, height 6″,
designer L. Harradine. 1949-   **150.00**

SILVERSMITH OF WILLIAMSBURG

HN 2208

☐ White base with brown pedestal
which contains gray object, brown
trousers, long blue vest, white shirt,
brown headcovering, black shoes,
white stockings, height 6¼ ″, de-
signer M. Davies. 1960-1983   **125.00 200.00**

	Date	Price Range

SIMONE

HN 2378

☐ Shaded green gown with white cuffs and black trim around top, blue and yellow ribbons in hair, holding small fan in one hand, height 7¼", designer M. Davies. 1971-1981   125.00   185.00

SIR THOMAS LOVELL

HN 356

☐ Brown base, brown and red costume, green sleeves with yellow and red design, brown hat with orange feather, brown stockings and black shoes, height 7¾", designer C. J. Noke. 1919-1938   1500.00   1700.00

SIR WALTER RALEIGH

HN 1742

☐ Black base, red stockings, red and white costume, purple vest, dark green cloak, black hat, height 10½", designer L. Harradine. 1935-1949   550.00   700.00

Sir Walter Raleigh,
HN2015,
750.00 – 850.00

	Date	Price Range	

HN 1751
☐ Earthenware model, with minor glaze differences, height 11½ ″, designer L. Harradine. 1936-1949 **1000.00 1100.00**

HN 2015
☐ Green base, brown stockings, orange costume with brown designs and stripes, black cloak with blue and red, black hat, height 11½ ″, designer L. Harradine. 1948-1955 **750.00 850.00**

SKATER, The
HN 2117
☐ Red skirt, white jacket with brown collar, brown sash, light yellow bonnet with blue ribbons, brown muff on cords, height 7¼ ″, designer M. Davies 1953-1971 **275.00 350.00**

SLEEPYHEAD
HN 2114
☐ Red, orange, yellow and blue over-stuffed chair, girl in white dress with black trim, brown teddy bear, black and white dunce style hat, blue cushion, height 5 ″, designer M. Davies. 1953-1955 **850.00 1000.00**

SLEEP
HN 24
☐ Light blue gown and hood, holding naked baby to shoulder on light blue base, height 8 ″, designer P. Stabler. . 1913-1938 **2000.00 2250.00**

HN 24A
☐ Dark blue dress, height 8 ″, designer P. Stabler. 1913-1938 **2200.00 2400.00**

HN 25
☐ Blue-green dress, height 8 ″, designer P. Stabler. 1913-1938 **2500.00 2800.00**

HN 25A
☐ Fewer firings, height 8 ″, designer P. Stabler. 1913-1938 **2500.00 2800.00**

HN 424
☐ HN 24, smaller figure with blue dress, height 8 ″, designer P. Stabler. 1921-1938 **2000.00 2200.00**

HN 692
☐ Smaller figure with gold dress, height 8 ″, designer P. Stabler. 1925-1938 **2050.00 2200.00**

	Date	Price Range

HN 710

☐ Smaller figure with matt vellum finish, height 8″, designer P. Stabler. . 1925-1938 2050.00 2200.00

SLEEPY SCHOLAR, The

HN 15

☐ HN 16, blue costume, height 6¾″, designer W. White. 1913-1938 1650.00 1800.00

HN 16

☐ Seated figure on blue and gray basket on light green base, shaded yellow and green dress with narrow green trim on hemline, black shoes with gold trim, height 6¾″, designer W. White. 1913-1938 1550.00 1700.00

HN 29

☐ Brown costume, height 6¾″, designer W. White. 1913-1938 1450.00 1600.00

SMILING BUDDHA, The

HN 454

☐ Rotund blue and green seated figure, patterned blue costume, very tiny Chinese figure on one knee, height 6¼″, designer C. J. Noke. 1921-1938 1250.00 1400.00

SNAKE CHARMER, The

HN 1317

☐ Seated figure on multicolored base which has small snake on it, black, green and red costume, brown figure, green turban with black and red, brown and red basket, yellow and brown pipe, height 4″, designer unknown. 1929-1938 900.00 1000.00

SOIREE

HN 2312

☐ White gown with gold design at hemline, green overskirt, holding small white fan in one hand, height 7½″, designer M. Davies. 1967- 170.00

	Date	Price Range

SOLITUDE

HN 2810

☐ Figure seated on brown and yellow chaise lounge, white gown mottled yellow, green, blue halfway up skirt, multicolored pillow, holding open book on pillow, height 5½ ″, designer M. Davies.   1977-1983   **165.00   215.00**

Song Of The Sea,
HN2729,
150.00

SONG OF THE SEA

HN 2729

☐ Depicts a weather-beaten man with blue turtleneck sweater, denim trousers, black boots with white socks. Man seated on fishbasket, holding shell in his hand. Boy at his feet has green short trousers, light blue shirt, height 7¼ ″, designer W. K. Harper. . .   1983-   **150.00**

	Date	Price Range	

SONIA
HN 1692
☐ Figure seated on arm of brown and green chair, white tiered gown with red bodice and sleeves, small red hat with white trim, red shoes, small black purse and flowers on chair, height 6¼ ", designer L. Harradine. .. 1935-1949 **650.00 750.00**

HN 1738
☐ Green dress, height 6½ ", designer L. Harradine. 1935-1949 **750.00 850.00**

SONNY
HN 1313
☐ Seated barefoot figure in red costume, top has white dots, height 3½ ", designer L. Harradine. 1929-1938 **600.00 700.00**

HN 1314
☐ Blue costume, height 3½ ", designer L. Harradine. 1929-1938 **600.00 700.00**

SOPHIE (Kate Greenaway)
HN 2833
☐ Small figure on white base, mauve coat with white fur trim, white fur muff, large light red bonnet, holding single flower, height 6", designer M. Davies. 1977- **75.00**

SOUTHERN BELLE
HN 2229
☐ Shaded yellow gown, red overskirt with blue bow, trim on sleeves, blue shoes, height 7½ ", designer M. Davies. 1958- **185.00**

HN 2425
☐ Light blue blouse and pink bodice over a white petticoat with slight shading of pink, white bodice with pink ribbons, gold brooch accents gown, height 7½ ", designer M. Davies. 1984- **185.00**

	Date	Price Range
SPANISH LADY		
HN 1262		
☐ Brown base, patterned purple gown with large red rose design, patterned purple bodice with small red design, brown, blue and black mantilla, dark gray necklace, height 8½″, designer L. Harradine.	1927-1938	900.00 1000.00
HN 1290		
☐ Yellow dress, height 8¼″, designer L. Harradine.	1928-1938	900.00 1000.00
HN 1293		
☐ Patterned purple skirt with large yellow rose design, small red design bodice, brown and blue mantilla, green necklace, height 8¼″, designer L. Harradine.	1928-1938	900.00 1000.00
HN 1294		
☐ Tiered red gown, brown, green and black mantilla, white necklace, light brown base, height 8¼″, designer L. Harradine.	1928-1938	900.00 1000.00
HN 1309		
☐ HN 1262, black bodice, multicolored skirt, height 8¼″, designer L. Harradine.	1929-1938	900.00 1000.00
SPIRIT OF THE WIND		
☐ Entire figure and base is green, beginning at the head a very light green, lower torso and gown a darker green, base and flowers of another green, height unknown, designer R. Garbe.	1937-1949	3500.00 4000.00
SPOOK, A		
HN 50		
☐ Figure wrapped entirely in blue robe, black cap, height 7″, designer H. Tittensor.	1916-1938	1100.00 1200.00
HN 51		
☐ Green robe with red cap, height 7″, designer H. Tittensor.	1916-1938	1250.00 1400.00
HN 51A		
☐ Black cap, height 7″, designer H. Tittensor.	1916-1938	1250.00 1400.00
HN 51B		
☐ Blue cloak, height 7″, designer H. Tittensor.	1916-1938	1250.00 1400.00

	Date	Price Range

HN 58
☐ Color not recorded, height 7″, designer H. Tittensor. 1916-1938   1250.00   1400.00

HN 512
☐ Spotted blue costume, height 7″, designer H. Tittensor. 1921-1938   1250.00   1400.00

HN 625
☐ Yellow robe, height 7″, designer H. Tittensor. 1924-1938   1250.00   1400.00

HN 1218
☐ Multicolored costume, blue cap, height 7″, designer H. Tittensor...... 1926-1938   1250.00   1400.00

SPOOKS

HN 88
☐ Two figures wrapped in shaded blue robes, dark blue caps, height 7″, designer H. Tittensor. 1918-1936   1400.00   1650.00

HN 89
☐ Red caps, height 7″, designer H. Tittensor............................ 1918-1936   1400.00   1650.00

HN 372
☐ Patterned green costume, brown caps, height 7″, designer H. Tittensor. 1920-1936   1400.00   1650.00

SPRING

HN 312
☐ Blue and gray base, long narrow yellow gown, holds small bird in hands (1st version), height 7½″, designer unknown.................... 1918-1938   1500.00   1800.00

HN 472
☐ Patterned robes (1st version), height 7½″, designer unknown............ 1921-1938   1500.00   1800.00

HN 1827
☐ White base, barefooted figure in very light yellow robe with gold flowers held with both hands (2nd version), height 21″, designer R. Garbe. 1937-1949   2500.00   3000.00

HN 2085
☐ Cream and green base, shaded blue and red gown, dark blue bodice, white blouse, tiny blue and red cap, small white lamb on base (3rd version), height 7¾″, designer M. Davies. 1952-1959   400.00   450.00

	Date	Price Range	

SPRING FLOWERS

HN 1807

☐ Light green gown, shaded blue overskirt, white apron and white collar,
blue bonnet with green lining and
dark ribbons, holding flower in one
hand and small basket of flowers in
other arm, light colored basket of
flowers on light colored base, height
7¼ ", designer L. Harradine. 1937-1959   275.00   350.00

HN 1945

☐ Green skirt, pink overskirt, height
7¼ ", designer L. Harradine. 1940-1949   500.00   550.00

SPRING MORNING

HN 1922

☐ Light blue gown, long pink coat, blue
and green scarf, bonnet has white
feather and dark blue ribbons, height
7½ ", designer L. Harradine. 1940-1973   175.00   225.00

HN 1923

☐ Green gown, long red coat, green and
yellow scarf, bonnet blue with white
feather and darker blue ribbons,
height 7½ ", designer L. Harradine. . . 1940-1949   275.00   325.00

SPRINGTIME

HN 1971

☐ Small girl figure in blue gown, peach
coat, green bonnet, hanging head,
green ribbons, holding single flower
in hand, height 6", designer L. Har-
radine. 1941-1949   900.00   950.00

SQUIRE, The

HN 1814

☐ Figure seated on blue and white
horse mounted on black base, red
jacket, white trousers, black boots,
black hat, earthware, height 9¾ ", de-
signer unknown. 1937-1949   2100.00   2600.00

ST GEORGE

HN 385

☐ HN 386, blue-green multicolored
costume (1st version), height 16",
designer S. Thorogood. 1920-1938   4500.00   5000.00

	Date	Price Range

HN 386

☐ dark colored horse and base, cloth over horse is white with dark blue, yellow and red designs, blue and gray armor, white shield with blue design, dark haired figure (1st version), height 16″, designer S. Thorogood. 1920-1938   4500.00 5000.00

HN 1800

☐ White horse with white robe, green overlay with crosses as a design. Knight has blue and gray armor, dark hair, red robe with gold lion and purple border, (1st version), height 16″, designer S. Thorogood. 1934-1950   3000.00 3500.00

HN 2051

☐ Yellow and green base, white horse with gold straps, figure has green and blue armor with white overskirt with red cross, green dragon also on base (2nd version), height 7½″, designer M. Davies. 1950-   475.00

HN 2067

☐ Multicolored base, light colored horse with cloth of purple with gold lions and red lining, figure has gray and blue armor with shield of white with red stripes, figure has blonde hair (1st version), height 15¾″, designer S. Torogood. 1950-1976   3750.00 4500.00

STAYED AT HOME

HN 2207

☐ Green gown with darker green collar, white apron, holding white pig in arms, green head ribbon, height 5″, designer M. Davies. 1958-1969   150.00 200.00

STEPHANIE

HN 2807

☐ Yellow gown with brown trim near hemline, white trim on sleeves, height 7¼″, designer M. Davies. 1977-1882   175.00 225.00

HN 2811

☐ Crimson red and off-white gown, dark brown hair, height 7½″, designer M. Davies. 1983-

	Date	Price Range	

STIGGINS
HN 536
☐ A character of Dicken's "Pickwick Papers," 3¾", designer L. Harradine. 1922- 45.00 60.00
☐ **M 50** Renumbered as a miniature, height 4", designer L. Harradine. 1932-1983 20.00 30.00

STITCH IN TIME, A
HN 2352
☐ Character figure seated in brown rocking chair, with brown and red footstool, dark gray gown, brown shawl, green suit for child on lap, colored threads on chair arm, height 6¼", designer M. Nicoll. 1966-1980 95.00 150.00

STOP PRESS
HN 2683
☐ Character figure seated on wooden box, blue trousers, brown coat, beige vest, light green hat with dark band, reading newspaper and eating roll, newspapers on stand next to figure, height 7½", designer M. Nicoll. 1977-1980 150.00 200.00

SUITOR, The
HN 2132
☐ Two figures, male kneeling has beige trousers, dark brown coat, yellow vest, white cravat, female has cream colored gown with overskirt of shaded blues, height 7¼", designer M. Davies.......................... 1962-1971 400.00 475.00

SUMMER
HN 313
☐ Long light green slender gown, bouquet of flowers in left arm, on blue and gray base (1st version), height 7½", designer unknown........... 1918-1938 1650.00 1800.00
HN 473
☐ Patterned gown (1st version), height 7½", designer unknown........... 1921-1938 1650.00 1800.00
HN 2086
☐ Green and yellow base with brown wooden fence, red gown with blue designs, blue waistband, blue shoes, white scarf (2nd version), height 7¼", designer M. Davies. 1952-1959 500.00 550.00

	Date	Price Range

SUMMER'S DAY

HN 2181

☐ Seated figure on white wicker trunk, white gown with gold designs, white bonnet with gold trim beside trunk, height 5¾", designer M. Davies   1957-1962   375.00   450.00

SUNDAY BEST

HN 2206

☐ Yellow gown with large white and red floral design in skirt, yellow bonnet with red ribbons and flowers, height 7½", designer M. Davies.   1979-   295.00

SUNDAY MORNING

HN 2184

☐ Red cloak, dark red yoke with yellow bow trim and sleeves, bonnet with dark red ribbons and black and white feather, height 7½", designer M. Davies.   1963-1969   265.00   325.00

SUNSHINE GIRL

HN 1344

☐ Green and yellow base with red and white towel, figure seated on towel wears green and black bathing suit, green bathing cap with black dots, black and red open parasol, height 5", designer L. Harradine.   1929-1938   1400.00   1500.00

HN 1348

☐ Black and orange costume, height 5", designer L. Harradine.   1929-1938   1400.00   1500.00

SUSAN

HN 2056

☐ Blue skirt , darker blue blouse with white collar, light red apron with small blue design, little white cap, height 7", designer L. Harradine.   1950-1959   300.00   350.00

HN 2952

☐ Young lady with blonde hair, gold gown with pale blue overdress, black jacket with blue belt, holding a white kitten aloft (2nd version), height 8½", designer P. Parsons.   1982-   175.00

	Date	Price Range

SUSANNA
HN 1233
☐ White nude figure on red colored base, long red robe hanging down back from hands, has white designs, height 6½ ", designer L. Harradine. .. 1927-1938 **1100.00 1200.00**

HN 1288
☐ Yellow and green base, white nude figure with red and blue robe hanging down back, height 6", designer L. Harradine. 1928-1938 **1100.00 1200.00**

HN 1299
☐ HN 1233, black, red and blue robe, height 6", designer L. Harradine. 1928-1938 **1100.00 1200.00**

SUZETTE
HN 1487
☐ Light green gown with patterned red overgown, solid blue and red bodice, green and blue headcap with green ribbons, blue and white apron, height 7½ ", designer L. Harradine. 1931-1950 **300.00 350.00**

HN 1577
☐ Light red gown with patterned blue overgown, blue and red bodice, white apron, light red headcap with red ribbons, height 7½ ", designer L. Harradine. 1933-1949 **500.00 550.00**

HN 1585
☐ HN 1487, green and yellow dress, height 7½ ", designer L. Harradine. .. 1933-1938 **500.00 600.00**

HN 1696
☐ Blue gown with small red floral designs, blue shoes, small blue headcap with dark blue ribbons, height 7½ ", designer L. Harradine. 1935-1949 **400.00 450.00**

HN 2026
☐ HN 1487, minor color differences, height 7¼ ", designer L. Harradine. .. 1949-1959 **300.00 350.00**

SWEET ANNE
HN 1318
☐ Shaded blue and green skirt, dark blue jacket with black trim, dark blue bonnet with dark red ribbons, height 7½ ", designer L. Harradine. 1929-1949 **200.00 250.00**

Sweet And Twenty,
HN1298,
200.00 ~ 275.00

	Date	Price Range	
HN 1330			
☐ Shaded red skirt, shaded blue and green jacket, red bonnet and ribbons, height 7¼″, designer L. Harradine. ..	1929-1949	325.00	375.00
HN 1331			
☐ Shaded yellow and blue skirt, red jacket with purple trim, red bonnet with purple ribbons, height 7¼″, designer L. Harradine.	1929-1949	300.00	350.00
HN 1453			
☐ Light green skirt, shaded blue jacket with darker blue trim, blue bonnet with purple ribbons, height 7″, designer L. Harradine.	1931-1949	325.00	375.00
HN 1496			
☐ Red skirt with patterned red jacket, shaded red and blue bonnet and ribbons, height 7″, designer L. Harradine.	1932-1967	225.00	275.00
HN 1631			
☐ HN 1318, green bonnet, red jacket, pink and yellow skirt, height 7″, designer L. Harradine.	1934-1938	300.00	400.00

	Date	Price Range	

HN 1701

☐ Floral yellow and pink dress, blue trim, height 7″, designer L. Harradine. — 1935-1938 — 300.00 — 400.00

☐ **M 5** Made as a miniature, cream gown with red shading, shaded red and blue jacket, bonnet same with dark ribbons, height 4″, designer L. Harradine. .... — 1932-1945 — 200.00 — 275.00

☐ **M-6** Light blue designed gown, dark blue jacket and bonnet, height 4″, designer L. Harradine. .... — 1932-1945 — 250.00 — 325.00

☐ **M-27** Cream gown with shaded blues, red jacket with blue trim, red bonnet with blue ribbons, height 4″, designer L. Harradine. .... — 1932-1945 — 200.00 — 275.00

SWEET AND FAIR

HN 1864

☐ HN 1865, blue shawl with pink dress, height 7½ ″, designer L. Harradine. .. — 1938-1949 — 650.00 — 700.00

HN 1865

☐ Figure is seated on brown chair, light green skirt, dark green bodice, sleeves have blue trim, white shawl draped on chair back with multicolored flowers, open book in hand, height 7¼ ″, designer L. Harradine. .. — 1938-1949 — 650.00 — 700.00

SWEET AND TWENTY

HN 1298

☐ Figure seated on small shaded blue couch, red gown, black bonnet with multicolored ribbons, holding open fan, height 5¾″, designer L. Harradine. .... — 1928-1969 — 200.00 — 275.00

HN 1360

☐ Blue couch, shaded red and blue gown, dark blue bonnet with shaded red and blue ribbons, height 6″, designer L. Harradine. .... — 1929-1938 — 450.00 — 500.00

HN 1437

☐ HN 1298, dark sofa, shaded red dress, height 6″, designer L. Harradine. ..... — 1930-1938 — 400.00 — 450.00

HN 1438

☐ Mottled multicolored dress, height 6″, designer L. Harradine. .... — 1930-1938 — 450.00 — 500.00

Sweet Anne, HN1496, **225.00 – 275.00**

	Date	Price Range	

HN 1549
☐ Light multicolored couch, gown is dark multicolored in skirt and lighter at waist and bodice, light multicolored bonnet, height 6″, designer L. Harradine. 1933-1949 350.00 400.00

HN 1563
☐ HN 1298, black sofa, pale pink dress, height 6″, designer L. Harradine. 1933-1938 450.00 500.00

HN 1589
☐ Small figure, light green couch, red and blue gown, blue and red bonnet with blue ribbon, height 6″, designer L. Harradine. 1933-1949 225.00 275.00

HN 1610
☐ Small figure, blue and green couch, red gown, black bonnet with yellow ribbon, height 3½″, designer L. Harradine. 1933-1938 275.00 325.00

	Date	Price Range	

HN 1649

☐ HN 1298, orange couch, white gown with small red designs, green bodice, green bonnet with shaded red ribbons, height 6″, designer L. Harradine. 1934-1949   450.00   500.00

SWEET APRIL

HN 2215

☐ Light red gown with blue and red collar, blue hat with green bow on top, height 7¼″, designer L. Harradine. . . 1965-1969   325.00   400.00

SWEET DREAMS

HN 2380

☐ Character figure seated in cream colored chair with green skirt, head on brown pillow, foot on purple stool, green gown with white bibbed apron with red design, green shoes, holding small child on lap in blue and red sleeper, height 5″, designer M. Davies. 1971-   150.00

SWEETING

HN 1935

☐ Red and shaded blue gown, blue bow in hair, height 6″, designer L. Harradine. 1940-1973   100.00   150.00

HN 1938

☐ Multicolored skirt, blue bodice, red bow in hair, height 6″, designer L. Harradine. 1940-1949   275.00   350.00

SWEET LAVENDER

HN 1373

☐ Black base, cream skirt with red stripes, green blouse, black red and light green shawl, green hat with black feather and trim, brown basket, small baby in arm is dressed in red, red necklace, lavender in basket, height 9″, designer L. Harradine. 1930-1949   650.00   750.00

	Date	Price Range	

SWEET MAID

HN 1504

☐ Blue gown, dark blue cape, shaded red and blue bonnet with red ribbons, small round red purse, height 8″, designer L. Harradine.   1932-1938   900.00   1000.00

HN 1505

☐ Shaded red and blue gown, dark red and blue cape, red bonnet with green ribbons, small green purse (1st version), height 8″, designer L. Harradine.   1932-1938   900.00   1000.00

HN 2092

☐ Light lavender gown, white headdress with white veil with small design and purple ribbons, holding small round bouquet of flowers in hands, height 7″, designer L. Harradine.   1952-1955   350.00   400.00

SWEET SEVENTEEN

HN 2734

☐ White gown with narrow gold trim, height 7½″, designer D. V. Tootle. . . .   1975-   185.00

SWEET SIXTEEN

HN 2231

☐ White base, light blue skirt, white blouse with small black design, black belt, black shoes, red bow in blonde hair, height 7¼″, designer M. Davies.   1958-1965   275.00   325.00

SWEET SUZY

HN 1918

☐ Light green gown, light red overdress with dark green trim, black bonnet with green ribbon trim, height 6½″, designer L. Harradine.   1939-1949   650.00   750.00

SWIMMER, The

HN 1270

☐ Black base, black swimsuit with red, green, and purple spots, red bathing shoes with spots, red robe with black design, height 7¼″, designer L. Harradine.   1928-1938   1100.00   1200.00

HN 1326

☐ Lilac and orange costume, height 7½″, designer L. Harradine.   1929-1938   1300.00   1400.00

Swimmer,
HN1270,
1100.00 – 1200.00

	Date	Price Range	
HN 1329			
☐ Pink costume, height 7½ ″, designer L. Harradine.	1929-1938	1300.00	1400.00
SYLVIA			
HN 1478			
☐ Mottled orange and brown gown, blue, gray and brown jacket, yellow bonnet with brown feather, shaded red and cream scarf, small round orange and brown purse, height 10½ ″, designer L. Harradine.	1931-1938	700.00	800.00
SYMPHONY			
HN 2287			
☐ Light green skirt, brown bodice with light green bow, holding brown, blue and gray mandolin type instrument on lap, height 5¼ ″, designer D. B. Lovegrove.	1961-1965	250.00	325.00

	Date	Price Range

TAILOR

HN 2174

☐ Seated character figure, red trousers, cream shirt, orange vest, purple coat with orange buttons, bolts of different colored cloth at side, height 5″, designer M. Nicoll.   1956-1959   600.00   700.00

TAKING THINGS EASY

HN 2677

☐ Male figure seated in brown wicker chair, white trousers and shoes, blue coat, gray hat with light trim, newspapers on lap, also black rimmed glasses, height 6¾″, designer M. Nicoll   1975-   125.00

TALL STORY

HN 2248

☐ Character figure seated on wooden bench, dark gray trousers, darker grey jacket, black cap with yellow trim, black boots with white cuff, tackle box beside bench, height 6½″, designer M. Nicoll.   1968-1975   150.00   200.00

TEATIME

HN 2255

☐ Brown gown with dark reddish-brown jacket, beige blouse, holding white teapot and cup and saucer with blue design, height 7¼″, designer M. Nicoll.   1972-   165.00

TEENAGER

HN 2203

☐ Slender white dress with red cape, height 7¼″, designer M. Davies.   1957-1962   225.00   275.00

TERESA

HN 1682

☐ Lady seated on brown and multicolor loveseat, red gown with red shoes and small white cap with green ribbon, the base is black with small brown table with flowers on table and base, height 5¾″, designer L. Harradine.   1935-1949   800.00   900.00

	Date	Price Range	

HN 1683
☐ Pale blue dress, height 5¾″, designer L. Harradine.   1935-1938   900.00   1000.00

TESS (Kate Greenaway)

HN 2865
☐ Small figure on white base, green gown with red floral trim at hemline, red waistband and single red flower in hand, height 5¾″, designer M. Davies .   1978-1983   65.00   100.00

TETE-A-TETE

HN 798
☐ HN 799, lady's gown is pink with shades of very light blue and white stripes, blue and red bows on bodice. Male costume is brownish-orange with a white and green cravat, black hat with orange design, purple and yellow designed couch with brown, bright blue pillow with dark red and gold design, all on black base (1st version), height 5¾″, designer L. Harradine. . .   1926-1938   1150.00   1300.00

HN 799
☐ Two figures on black base, brown couch, lady's gown is lavender with red pattern, purple overskirt, male has costume of red with white, black hat with red trim (1st version), height 5¾″, designer L. Harradine.   1926-1938   1150.00   1300.00

HN 1236
☐ Color and design same but in miniature size (2nd version), height 3″, designer C. J. Noke.   1927-1938   650.00   750.00

HN 1237
☐ Pink dress (2nd version), height 3″, designer C. J. Noke.   1927-1938   650.00   700.00

THANKS DOC

HN 2731
☐ Brown trousers, long white coat, white shirt, dark tie, brown and white dog sitting on brown stand, white towel on side, height 8¾″, designer W. K. Harper.   1975-   200.00

THANK YOU
HN 2732

	Date	Price Range
☐ Old lady standing at cottage gate waving goodbye to someone who has given her a bouquet of bluebells. Gray hair, long brown skirt, white blouse with pink flowers, wearing cameo brooch, height 8¼″, designer W. K. Harper.	1983-	145.00

THANKSGIVING
HN 2446

	Date	Price Range	
☐ Light brown base, character figure in blue overalls, red shirt, light colored hat, turkey also on base, matt finish, height 8″, designer M. Nicoll.	1972-1976	200.00	250.00

This Little Pig,
HN1793,
75.00

THIS LITTLE PIG
HN 1793

☐ Small seated figure wrapped completely in red robe with small design of blue, height 4″, designer L. Harradine.	1936-	75.00

	Date	Price Range	

HN 1794
☐ Small figure wrapped completely in blue with green robe, height 4″, designer L. Harradine. 1936-1949 300.00 350.00

TIBETIAN LADY

HN 582
☐ Formal name is "Grossmith's 'Tsang lhang' Perfume of Tibet, see that classification, height 11½″, designer unknown. 1923-Unknown 650.00 700.00

TILDY

HN 1576
☐ Seated figure in tiered shaded colored gown, red bodice trimmed with blue bows, shaded blue bonnet with darker blue ribbons, light blue shoes, white pantalettes, height 5″, designer L. Harradine. 1933-1938 700.00 800.00

HN 1859
☐ No details of color available, height 5½″, designer L. Harradine. 1938-1949 800.00 900.00

TINKLE BELL

HN 1677
☐ Small figure in shaded red gown with darker red bodice, small white cap with red ribbons, small light colored basket on one arm, height 4¾″, designer L. Harradine. 1935- 75.00

TINSMITH

HN 2146
☐ Character figure seated, brown trousers, mottled brown stockings, lighter brown shirt, green vest, white cravat, working on blue and gray material, tools in front of green and gray stump, height 6½″, designer M. Nicoll. 1962-1967 450.00 500.00

TINY TIM

HN 539
☐ A character from Dicken's "Christmas Carol," height 3½″, designer L. Harradine. 1922- 45.00 60.00

	Date	Price Range	
☐ **M 56** Renumbered as a miniature, height 3¾", designer L. Harradine. ..	1932-1983	20.00	30.00

TO BED
HN 1805
☐ Small figure on light blue colored base, pulling light green shirt over head, light green shorts, barefooted, height 6", designer L. Harradine. ....

	1937-1959	110.00	175.00

HN 1806
☐ Green base, light blue and red shirt and shorts, height 6", designer L. Harradine. ....

	1937-1949	150.00	200.00

TOINETTE
HN 1940
☐ Full tiered red gown with darker red jacket, black stole trimmed with white fur, green bonnet, open parasol in one hand, flowers in other, height 6¾", designer L. Harradine. ....

	1940-1949	1450.00	1750.00

TOM (Kate Greenaway)
HN 2864
☐ Small male figure on white base, blue trousers, cream colored shirt with red designs and white collar, holding single flower in one hand and white and yellow toy horse with other hand, height 5¾", designer M. Davies .....

	1978-1981	85.00	110.00

TONY WELLER
HN 346
☐ HN 684, green coat, blue rug, brown base (1st version), height 10½", designer C. J. Noke. ....

	1919-1938	1800.00	2000.00

HN 368
☐ Blue coat, brown blanket (1st version), height 10½", designer C. J. Noke. ....

	1920-1938	1800.00	2000.00

HN 544
☐ Miniature figure, green coat, dark brown suit, red vest, white shirt, yellow cravat with dark spots, black hat (2nd version), height 3½", designer L. Harradine. ....

	1922-	45.00	60.00

Tom,
HN2864,
85.00 – 110.00

	Date	Price Range	
☐ **M 47** Renumbered as a miniature, height 4″, designer L. Harradine.	1932-1983	20.00	30.00
HN 684			
☐ Black base, long green coat, orange undercoat with black buttons, red rug with black stripes, black hat, orange scarf with black dots (1st version), height 10½″, designer L. Harradine. .	1924-1938	1650.00	1800.00

TOOTLES

HN 1680
☐ Small figure, shaded red skirt with blue stripes, red bodice, green apron with green stripes, white bonnet with green ribbons, height 4¾″, designer L. Harradine. . . . . | 1935-1975 | 60.00 | 125.00

Top O' The Hill,
HN1833,
225.00 - 275.00

TOP O' THE HILL	Date	Price Range	
HN 1833			
☐ Green skirt, shaded blue jacket, dark blue large brim hat, blue and green scarf with red designs, height 7″, designer L. Harradine.	1937-1971	225.00	275.00
HN 1834			
☐ Red gown, red hat with light green lining, mottled yellow and green scarf, height 7″, designer L. Harradine.	1937-	170.00	
HN 1849			
☐ Dark pink gown, black hat with blue ribbon and lining, striped red and blue scarf, height 7¼″, designer L. Harradine.	1938-1975	175.00	225.00

	Date	Price Range

TOWN CRIER
HN 2119
☐ Brown base, yellow trousers, red coat trimmed in yellow, black cloak with red coloring, green patterned vest, black hat trimmed in yellow, black boots with red tops, ringing bell and holding white papers, height 8½″, designer M. Davies.   1953-1976   250.00   300.00

TOYMAKER, The
HN 2250
☐ Character figure seated in dark gray rocker holding red engine, brown trousers, blue and green shirt, gray vest, green shoes, tools and toys at sides of rocker, height 6″, designer M. Nicoll   1959-1973   425.00   475.00

TOYS
HN 1316
☐ Green skirt, white apron with blue stripes, red jacket, yellow scarf with green dots and red fringe, black hat with green feathers, holding small black tray with three male dolls, height unknown, designer L. Harradine.   1929-1938   1200.00   1500.00

TREASURE ISLAND
HN 2243
☐ Small barefooted boy seated on white base, purple shorts, light brown shirt, holding open book on lap, book shows printing, height 4¾″, designer M. Davies.   1962-1975   150.00   200.00

TROTTY VECK
Issued only as a miniature.

☐ **M 91** Orange vest, white apron, brown hat, black coat and stand, height 4¼″, designer L. Harradine.   1949-   29.95

TULIPS
HN 466
☐ HN 747, green dress, height 9½″, designer unknown.   1921-1938   1500.00   1700.00

	Date	Price Range	

HN 488
- ☐ Ivory dress, height 9½ ″, designer unknown. 1921-1938 1500.00 1700.00

HN 672
- ☐ Green shawl and cream dress, height 9½ ″, designer unknown. 1924-1938 1550.00 1700.00

HN 747
- ☐ Purple dress with small black designs, green shawl with red thin stripes, holding bouquet of flowers in one hand, height 9½ ″, designer unknown. 1925-1938 1550.00 1700.00

HN 1334
- ☐ Pink and blue shawl and green dress, height 9½ ″, designer unknown. 1929-1938 1550.00 1700.00

TUPPENCE A BAG

HN 2320
- ☐ Seated character figure on blue and green bricks, basket beside figure, green gown, blue shawl, black brimmed hat, one bird on shoulder and one on basket handle, height 5½ ″, designer M. Nicoll. 1968- 165.00

TWILIGHT

HN 2256
- ☐ Character figure seated in brown rocker with purple pad and purple foot stool, knitting with black kitten playing with yarn, dark green gown, black shawl, small white headcap, height 5″, designer M. Nicoll. 1971-1976 125.00 200.00

TWO-A-PENNY

HN 1359
- ☐ Green and yellow shaded skirt, red jacket with black collar and buttons, yellow shawl with green stripes, black hat with green and black feathers, white apron, holding black tray with green and black objects, height 8¼ ″, designer L. Harradine. 1929-1938 1200.00 1500.00

	Date	Price Range	

UNCLE NED
HN 2094
☐ Character figure seated in brown and beige chair, green trousers, long brown coat and leggings, yellow and green scarf, holding blue mug, black and white dog sitting at feet, height 6¾", designer H. Fenton. 1952-1965   400.00   450.00

UNDER THE GOOSEBERRY BUSH
HN 49
☐ Small nude child laying on bed of flowers with black, green and brown bush over figure, height 3½", designer C. J. Noke. 1916-1938   1250.00   1500.00

'UPON HER CHEEKS SHE WEPT'
HN 59
☐ Figure of young girl, shaded blue dress, green and white checkered headband, barefooted, standing on light colored base which has flowers, printing on front of base, height 9", designer L. Perugini. 1916-1938   1500.00   1600.00

HN 511
☐ Lilac dress with large spots, height 9", designer L. Perugini. 1921-1938   1500.00   1600.00

HN 522
☐ Lilac dress with small spots, height 9", designer L. Perugini. 1921-1938   1500.00   1600.00

URIAH HEEP
HN 545
☐ A character from Dicken's "David Copperfield" (1st version), height 4", designer L. Harradine. 1922-   45.00   60.00

☐ **M 45** Renumbered as a miniature, height 4", designer L. Harradine. 1932-1983   20.00   30.00

HN 554
☐ Black base, complete black suit with white cravat, a stack of books also on base, red hair (2nd version), height 7¼", designer L. Harradine. 1923-1939   400.00   500.00

HN 1892
☐ Very minor color changes (2nd version), height 7", designer L. Harradine. 1938-1952   275.00   325.00

	Date	Price Range	

HN 2101

☐ Green base, green trousers, black coat, yellow vest, white shirt, white and blue scarf with blue dots, red hair, books on base are browns and blacks (3rd version), height 7½″, designer L. Harradine. 1952-1967   300.00   350.00

Valerie,
HN2107,
100.00

VALERIE

HN 2107

☐ Small figure, light red gown with white apron, darker red overskirt, white headcap with blue ribbons, holding single yellow flower with green leaves, height 4¾″, designer M. Davies. 1953-   100.00

	Date	Price Range

VANESSA

HN 1836

☐ Green skirt, dark blue bodice with green and white trim, green bonnet with red ribbons, height 7½″, designer L. Harradine. . . . . | 1938-1949 | 600.00 700.00

HN 1838

☐ Red skirt with green bodice with red and white trim, green bonnet with red lining, height 7½″, designer L. Harradine. . . . . . : . . . . | 1938-1949 | 600.00 700.00

VANITY

HN 2475

☐ Small figure, red gown with white waistband, white bow in dark hair, holding small yellow mirror, height 5¼″, designer M. Davies. . . . . | 1973- | 100.00

VENETA

HN 2722

☐ White gown with yellow and black design, green overdress, holding small white bird in hands, height 8″, designer W. K. Harper. . . . . | 1974-1980 | 100.00 150.00

VERA

HN 1729

☐ Head and shoulders only on cream colored base, pink dress, height 4¼″, designer L. Harradine. . . . . | 1935-1938 | 500.00 600.00

HN 1730

☐ Green dress, height 4¼″, designer L. Harradine. . . . . | 1935-1938 | 500.00 600.00

VERENA

HN 1835

☐ Green gown, orange overdress with yellow floral design, white ruffles on sleeves, green hat with white and black feathers, height 8¼″, designer L. Harradine. | 1938-1949 | 750.00 850.00

HN 1854

☐ Green dress, height 8¼″, designer L. Harradine. . . . . | 1938-1949 | 750.00 850.00

Vera, HN1729, **500.00 – 600.00**

VERONICA	Date	Price Range	
HN 1517			
☐ Tiered gown of shaded red with green ribbon trim, dark red bodice with green ribbon trim, large shaded blue and red brim hat with feathers of green, white and shaded red (1st version), height 8″, designer L. Harradine.	1932-1951	**350.00**	**400.00**
HN 1519			
☐ Shaded blue and cream gown, shaded red hat with cream and red feathers (1st version), height 8″, designer L. Harradine.	1932-1938	**400.00**	**450.00**
HN 1650			
☐ HN 1517, green dress (1st version), height 8″, designer L. Harradine.	1934-1949	**500.00**	**550.00**

	Date	Price Range	

HN 1915
- ☐ Smaller version with shaded red gown and green ribbon trim, dark red bodice with blue ribbon trim, green hat with blue ribbon and blue and white feathers (2nd version), height 5¾", designer L. Harradine.   1939-1949   400.00   450.00
- ☐ **M 64** Made as a miniature, shaded red gown, dark red bodice with green ribbons, blue hat, height 4½", designer L. Harradine.   1934-1949   325.00   375.00
- ☐ **M • 70** Green gown, height 4¼", designer L. Harradine.   1936-1949   325.00   375.00

HN 1943
- ☐ Pink dress and blue hat (1st version), height 8", designer L. Harradine.   1940-1949   400.00   450.00

VICTORIA

HN 2471
- ☐ Large full red gown with white and green flower design, gown trimmed in white, holding open white fan, height 6½", designer M. Davies.   1973-   170.00

Veronica,
HN1517,
350.00 - 400.00

VICTORIAN LADY, A

	Date	Price Range	

HN 726
☐ Tiered patterned purple, cream, red and black gown, very dark plain color shawl, black bonnet with light lining and red ribbons and red feather trim, height 7½″, designer L. Harradine. ..   1925-1938   350.00   400.00

HN 727
☐ Shaded yellow gown, red shawl, black bonnet with light red lining and red feather with red ribbons, height 7½″, designer L. Harradine.   1925-1938   350.00   400.00

HN 728
☐ Shaded red gown, shaded blue and red shawl, blue and red bonnet with feather and ribbons to match, height 7¾″, designer L. Harradine.   1925-1952   300.00   350.00

HN 736
☐ Purple gown with patterned white trim, red shawl, black bonnet with red feather and ribbons, height 7¾″, designer L. Harradine.   1925-1938   450.00   500.00

HN 739
☐ HN 726, mottled red, blue and yellow skirt, yellow scarf, height 7¾″, designer L. Harradine.   1925-1938   650.00   750.00

HN 740
☐ Shaded red gown, red shawl with black, red and blue spots, black bonnet with red feather and ribbons, height 7¾″, designer L. Harradine. ..   1925-1938   450.00   500.00

HN 742
☐ HN 726, black with white checkered shawl, white dress with blue spots, height 7¾″, designer L. Harradine. ..   1925-1938   450.00   500.00

HN 745
☐ Patterned dress with pink roses, height 7¾″, designer L. Harradine. ..   1925-1938   450.00   500.00

HN 1208
☐ Cream and green gown, shaded dark red shawl, dark bonnet with red feather and dark ribbons, height 7¾″, designer L. Harradine.   1926-1938   450.00   500.00

HN 1258
☐ HN 726, mottled purple shawl, mottled blue dress, height 7¾″, designer L. Harradine.   1927-1938   450.00   500.00

	Date	Price Range	

HN 1276

☐ Cream and green gown with large red spots, solid red bodice, purple shawl, dark bonnet with red feather and red ribbons, height 7½", designer L. Harradine.   1928-1938   350.00   400.00

HN 1277

☐ HN 726, red shawl, yellow and blue tiered dress, height 7¾", designer L. Harradine.   1928-1938   350.00   400.00

HN 1345

☐ Shaded green and blue gown, shaded lavender and red shawl, dark bonnet with red feather and ribbons, height 7¾", designer L. Harradine.   1929-1949   250.00   300.00

HN 1452

☐ HN 726, green dress and shawl, height 7¾", designer L. Harradine. . .   1931-1949   250.00   300.00

HN 1529

☐ Shaded green and red gown, shaded green shawl, light colored bonnet with shaded red ribbons and feather, height 7¾", designer L. Harradine. . .   1932-1938   400.00   450.00

☐ **M 1** Made as a miniature, red and cream gown, green shawl, blue and red bonnet with feather and ribbons to match, height 3¾", designer L. Harradine.   1932-1945   300.00   325.00

☐ **M 2** Blue gown, purple shawl, green bonnet with red feather and ribbons, height 3¾", designer L. Harradine. . .   1932-1945   300.00   325.00

☐ **M 25** Shaded red gown, shaded blue and red shawl, shaded red and blue bonnet with dark ribbons and feather, height 3¾", designer L. Harradine. . .   1932-1945   300.00   325.00

VIKING, The

HN 2375

☐ Beige and light blue base, costume is blue shirt, brown fur-like color cape, red belt and red straps on legs, light green leggings, helmet of blue and gray with white and black horns, height 8¾", designer J. Bromley.   1973-1976   250.00   300.00

The Viking,
Bisque, HN2375,
250.00 – 300.00

	Date	Price Range	
VIRGINIA			
HN 1693			
☐ Light colored base, yellow gown with floral design and light red bows, red underskirt, red shoes, small red scarf around neck, height 7½", designer L. Harradine.	1935-1949	650.00	750.00
HN 1694			
☐ Green gown with small red bows on bodice, white undergown with green dots, green shoes, red scarf around neck and held by each hand, light colored base, height 7½", designer L. Harradine.	1935-1949	650.00	750.00
VIVIENNE			
HN 2073			
☐ Full red gown with white at sleeves, black hat with white and pink feathers with blue ribbons, height 7¾", designer L. Harradine.	1951-1967	200.00	300.00

	Date	Price Range	

VOTES FOR WOMEN

HN 2816

☐ White base, green gown, long brown coat, black hat tied with white scarf, holding white placard with black printing, height 9¾", designer W. K. Harper.   1978-1981   200.00   250.00

WANDERING MINSTREL, The

HN 1224

☐ Checkered black and red costume, black stockings, red shoes, jester type black, red and green hat, holding small black and shaded red instrument, also small head on stick, seated on green and white brick wall, height 7", designer L. Harradine.   1927-1938   1250.00   1400.00

WARDROBE MISTRESS

HN 2145

☐ Character figure seated, black gown and white overdress, beside her are black and yellow hats, blue and red gown, height 5¾", designer M. Davies.   1954-1967   475.00   525.00

WAYFARER, The

HN 2362

☐ Character figure seated on brown base, blue and gray trousers, green jacket, red vest, checkered black and white cap, holding white bottle and white pipe, height 5½", designer M. Nicoll.   1970-1976   200.00   250.00

WEDDING MORN

HN 1866

☐ HN 1867, cream dress, height 10½", designer L. Harradine.   1938-1949   1200.00   1300.00

HN 1867

☐ Red gown with white veil and long white train, holding white lilies, height 10½", designer L. Harradine. .   1938-1949   1200.00   1300.00

	Date	Price Range

WEE WILLIE WINKIE
HN 2050
☐ Small figure on light blue and red base, long blue nightshirt, carrying brown, red and yellow lantern, height 5¼", designer M. Davies. 1949-1953 **225.00 250.00**

WELSH GIRL, The
HN 39
☐ Light brown base with MYFANWY JONES printed on base, purple skirt with red floral design, red blouse with white tie collar, white apron, black cape with cram lining, broad brim black hat, height 12", designer E. W. Light. 1914-1938 **2500.00 2750.00**

HN 92
☐ Blue and gray costume, height 12", designer E. W. Light. 1918-1938 **2500.00 2750.00**

HN 456
☐ Green blouse and brown skirt, height 12", designer E. W. Light. 1921-1938 **2500.00 2700.00**

HN 514
☐ Green skirt, spotted apron, height 12", designer E. W. Light. 1921-1938 **2500.00 2700.00**

HN 516
☐ Checkered lilac dress, black spotted cloak, height 12", designer E. W. Light. 1921-1938 **2500.00 2700.00**

HN 519
☐ Blue skirt, checkered lilac skirt, height 12", designer E. W. Light. 1921-1938 **2500.00 2700.00**

HN 520
☐ Spotted lilac dress, height 12", designer E. W. Light. 1921-1938 **2500.00 2700.00**

HN 660
☐ Spotted white costume, blue-lined cloak, height 12", designer E. W. Light. 1924-1938 **2500.00 2750.00**

HN 668
☐ Checkered yellow costume, pink lined cloak, height 12", designer E. W. Light. 1924-1938 **2500.00 2700.00**

HN 669
☐ Spotted yellow costume, checkered green lined cloak, height 12", designer E. W. Light. 1924-1938 **2500.00 2700.00**

	Date	Price Range

HN 701
☐ Striped costume, checkered blue lined cloak, height 12″, designer E. W. Light. 1925-1938 2500.00 2700.00

HN 792
☐ Pink checkered costume, blue cloak, height 12″, designer E. W. Light. 1926-1938 2550.00 2700.00

WENDY

HN 2109
☐ Small figure in blue gown with shades of red, blue bonnet with dark pink ribbons, light-colored basket with flowers in one hand, height 5″, designer L. Harradine. 1953- 75.00

WEST WIND

HN 1826
☐ Tinted finish, height 14½″, designer R. Garbe. 1937-1949 4500.00 5000.00

WIGMAKER OF WILLIAMSBURG

HN 2239
☐ White base, has brown pedestal with head form on it, costume of brown trousers, white stockings, black shoes, cream colored coat with black trim, white shirt, height 7½″, designer M. Davies. 1960-1983 115.00 200.00

WILLY-WON'T HE

HN 1561
☐ HN 1584, blue jacket and pink trousers, height 6″, designer L. Harradine. 1933-1949 500.00 550.00

HN 1584
☐ Two figures, Dutch costumes, boy's blue and brown trousers, red shirt, blue cap, girl's costume, blue dress, white apron and collar, white Dutch cap, both wearing wooden shoes, height 6″, designer L. Harradine. 1933-1949 350.00 400.00

HN 2150
☐ Minor glaze changes, height 5½″, designer L. Harradine. 1955-1959 250.00 300.00

The Wigmaker Of Williamsburg,
HN2239,
115.00 ~ 200.00

WINDFLOWER	Date	Price Range	
HN 1763			
☐ Pale yellow skirt with red floral design, red blouse, shaded red and blue hat with black ribbon, on green base (1st version), height 7¼", designer L. Harradine.	1936-1949	350.00	400.00
HN 1764			
☐ White skirt with blue floral design, blue blouse, shaded blue and red hat with green ribbon, green base (1st version), height 7¼", designer L. Harradine.	1936-1949	425.00	475.00
HN 1920			
☐ Multicolored skirt, red bodice, black base (2nd version), height 11", designer L. Harradine.	1939-1949	500.00	550.00
HN 1939			
☐ Floral pink skirt, blue hat and gloves (2nd version), height 11", designer L. Harradine.	1940-1949	500.00	550.00

	Date	Price Range	
☐ **M 78** Made as a miniature, light colored base, white skirt with red floral designs, red blouse, blue hat, height 4″, designer L. Harradine.	1939-1949	400.00	450.00
☐ **M 79** Green skirt, height 4″, designer L. Harradine.	1939-1938	500.00	550.00

HN 2029

☐ Light red skirt with red floral designs, red blouse, green hat with black ribbon, base is blue and green (1st version), height 7¼″, designer L. Harradine.	1949-1952	400.00	450.00

WINDMILL LADY, The

HN 1400

☐ Character figure seated on brown base, green skirt, black jacket, checkered red, yellow and green shawl, black hat, dark brown basket with green cloth at side, brown and white dog on other side, holding a ring of multicolored toy windmills, height 8½″, designer L. Harradine. ..	1930-1938	1550.00	1700.00

WINNER, The

HN 1407

☐ Green base with white fence, gray and white horse, rider in white trousers, dark red jacket with purple and white sleeves, purple cap, height 6¾″, designer unknown.	1930-1938	3000.00	3500.00

WINSOME

HN 2220

☐ Red gown, holding white bonnet with white ribbons over one arm, height 8″, designer M. Davies.	1960-	155.00	

WINTER

HN 315

☐ Light colored base, figure completely wrapped in shaded blue robe (1st version), height 7½″, designer unknown.	1918-1938	1500.00	1800.00

HN 475

☐ Patterned robe (1st version), height 7½″, designer unknown.	1921-1938	1500.00	1800.00

	Date	Price Range	

HN 2088

☐ Blue and gray base, shaded blue skirt, shaded green jacket, dark green cloak with red lining, hood trimmed in brown fur, holding brown lantern (2nd version), height 6¼", designer M. Davies. 1952-1959 350.00 425.00

WISTFUL

HN 2396

☐ Cream gown with light yellow shading with red floral design at hemline, red overdress with shaded blue and green design, white sleeves with green and yellow shading, holding purple mask in one hand, height 6½", designer M. Davies. 1979- 325.00

WIZARD, The

HN 2877

☐ Blue robe with beige colored rope belt, black coned hat with white designs, open book in hand, black cat at feet, brown and white owl on shoulder, height 9¾", designer A. Maslankowski. 1979- 215.00

WOMAN HOLDING CHILD

HN 462

☐ Green dress, white apron and blanket, height 9¼", designer unknown. 1921-1938 2000.00 2200.00

HN 570

☐ Pink and green striped skirt, pink and red striped blanket, height 9¼", designer unknown. 1923-1938 2000.00 2200.00

HN 703

☐ Purple cloak, black and red checkered skirt, height 9¼", designer unknown. 1925-1938 2000.00 2200.00

HN 743

☐ Blue and yellow striped apron, height 9¼", designer unknown. 1925-1938 2050.00 2200.00

	Date	Price Range

WOOD NYMPH
HN 2192
☐ White base with gray stripes and leaf design, blue and green costume with white waist straps, same color ribbon in hair, barefooted figure, height 7¼", designer M. Davies.   1958-1962   300.00   350.00

YEOMAN OF THE GUARD, A
HN 688
☐ Brown and green base which has brown chest, figure seated, orange and red costume with stripes of gold and black, white ruffled collar, white design on front of jacket, black shoes with red and white trim, height 5¾", designer L. Harradine.   1924-1938   950.00   1050.00
HN 2122
☐ Very minor glaze differences, height 5¾", designer L. Harradine.   1954-1959   650.00   750.00

YOUNG KNIGHT, The
HN 94
☐ Young man kneeling, hands holding a scepter, purple to maroon color gown, dark brown robe, armor headdress at his knees. Figurine is on a black base, height 9½", designer C. J. Noke.   1918-1936   2750.00   3250.00

YOUNG LOVE
HN 2735
☐ Two figures on white base with gold trim, girl's gown is white with light shades of green, red floral design skirt, shaded green bodice, male's costume is gray trousers, white stockings, black shoes, purple long coat, blue vest, height 10", designer D. V. Tootle.   1975-   695.00

YOUNG MASTER
HN 2872
☐ Shaded green base, young man with blue trousers, purple jacket trimmed in black, white shirt, holding yellow and black violin, tan dog at his feet, a sheet of music and books also on base, height 7", designer M. Davies. .   1980-   325.00

	Date	Price Range	

YOUNG MISS NIGHTINGALE, The
HN 2010

☐ Yellow and green gown with green overdress, red long jacket, green and yellow hat with red feathers, carrying parasol and round bag, height 9¼", designer M. Davies. 1948-1953   700.00   800.00

YOUNG WIDOW, The
HN 1399

☐ Quickly withdrawn and renamed 'THE LITTLE MOTHER'. See that classification, height 8", designer L. Harradine. 1930-   1250.00   1500.00

YUM-YUM
HN 1268

☐ Chinese figure on yellow and green base, shaded red and cream costume, large black and red fan behind head, height 5", designer L. Harradine. 1928-1938   650.00   750.00

HN 1287

☐ Shaded brown base, shaded red, yellow and blue costume, large dark blue and red fan, height 5", designer L. Harradine. 1928-1939   650.00   750.00

HN 2899

☐ Round light colored base, green and yellow costume with blue and gold waistband, white flowers in black hair, holding white fan in one hand (2nd version), height 10¾", designer W. K. Harper. 1980-   750.00

COLLECTIONS FEATURING CHILDHOOD THEMES

CHARACTERS FROM CHILDREN'S LITERATURE

This exciting new series begun in 1982 features favorite characters from children's literature. Each figure has been designed from the storybook originals. Each is hand-made and hand-decorated, thus making no two exactly the same.

Huckleberry Finn,
HN2927,
50.00

	Date	Price Range
TOM SAWYER		
HN 2926		
☐ Height 5¼ ", designer D. Littleton. . . .	1982-	50.00
HUCKLEBERRY FINN		
HN 2927		
☐ Height 7 ", designer D. Littleton.	1982-	50.00
TOM BROWN		
HN 2941		
☐ Height 7 ", designer R. Tabbenor.	1983-	50.00
POLLYANNA		
HN 2965		
☐ Height 6¾ ", designer P. Parsons. . . .	1982-	50.00
LITTLE LORD FAUNTLEROY		
HN 2972		
☐ Height 6¼ ", designer A. Hughes.	1982-	50.00

HEIDI	Date	Price Range
HN 2975		
☐ Height 4½ ″, designer A. Hughes.....	1983-	**50.00**

CHILDHOOD DAYS SERIES

An exciting new figure collection introduced in 1982. As the title suggests these pieces capture the memorable moments of children. Handmade and hand-decorated.

I'm Nearly Ready,
HN2976,
75.00

IT WON'T HURT
HN 2963
☐ Little girl in nurse outfit tending to a dog which is sitting on top of a brown woven basket. Both characters on a white base. height 7½ ″, designer P. Parsons.   1982-   **75.00**

	Date	Price Range

DRESSING UP
HN 2964
☐ Young lady in Mother's dress which is white with blue trim, high heel black slippers, carrying gold purse, her light brown hair showing under a white hat trimmed in blue ribbons, height 7½", designer P. Parsons. 1982-   75.00

AND SO TO BED
HN 2966
☐ Little girl with black hair clad in night-gown, clutching her teddy bear, ready for bed, height 7½", designer P. Parsons. 1983-   75.00

SAVE SOME FOR ME
HN 2959
☐ Little girl mixing cake in bowl while cat at her feet watches patiently, height 7¼", designer P. Parsons..... 1983-   75.00

PLEASE KEEP STILL
HN 2967
☐ Little boy on his knees bathing his dog, dog is standing in a tub patiently waiting for the boy to finish, height 4½", designer A. Hughes. 1983-   75.00

AND ONE FOR YOU
HN 2970
☐ Teddy bear sitting on a table with lit-tle girl bent over trying to feed him from the bowl which sits alongside the teddy bear, height 6½", designer A. Hughes...................... 1982-   75.00

AS GOOD AS NEW
HN 2971
☐ Dog in doghouse sitting on a white base, little boy sitting on top of dog-house with paint brush and bucket in hand painting the doghouse to make it "look as good as new," height 6½", designer A. Hughes............... 1982-   75.00

	Date	Price Range

STICK 'EM UP
HN 2981
☐ Little boy in cowboy outfit, his hands on the twin holder at his hips, height 7″, designer A. Hughes............. 1984-   75.00

I'M NEARLY READY
HN 2976
☐ Smartly groomed young man in black pants and white shirt tuning the strings of his violin in preparation for his debut, height 7½″, designer A. Hughes......................... 1984-   75.00

JUST ONE MORE
HN 2980
☐ Little boy in bathing trunks building sandcastles, height 7″, designer A. Hughes......................... 1984-   75.00

NURSERY RHYME FIGURINES

A new collection of figures being introduced in 1984 are the Nursery Rhyme group of figures. Each figures is created from the century old rhymes.

Little Miss Muffet,
HN2727,
95.00

	Date	Price Range
LITTLE JACK HORNER		
HN 3034		
☐ Height 7″, designer A. Hughes.......	1984-	**95.00**
TOM, TOM THE PIPER'S SON		
HN 3032		
☐ Height 7″, designer A. Hughes.......	1984-	**95.00**
LITTLE BOY BLUE		
HN 3035		
☐ Height 7¾″, designer A. Hughes.....	1984-	**95.00**
LITTLE BO PEEP		
HN 3030		
☐ Height 8″, designer A. Hughes.......	1984-	**95.00**
WEE WILLIE WINKIE		
HN 3031		
☐ Height 7¾″, designer A. Hughes.....	1984-	**95.00**
LITTLE MISS MUFFET		
HN 2727		
☐ Height 6¼″, designer W. Harper.....	1984-	**95.00**
POLLY PUT THE KETTLE ON		
HN 3021		
☐ Height 8″, designer P. Parsons.	1984-	**95.00**

COLLECTIONS FEATURING SPECIAL THEMES

ENCHANTMENT COLLECTION

A new series of subjects all presented in the beautiful ivory bone china each trimmed with burnished gold. These were fashioned after the first figures ever made at Burslem in what was called at that time "vellum" figures.

The collection was introduced in 1983.

		Price
RUMPLESTILTSKIN		
☐ HN 3025 Designer Robert Jefferson, height 8″		125.00
APRIL SHOWER		
☐ HN 3024 Designer Robert Jefferson, height 4¾″		75.00
FAIRYSPELL		
☐ HN 2979 Designer Adrian Hughes, height 5¼″		65.00
MAGIC DRAGON		
☐ HN 2977 Designer Adrian Hughes, height 4¾″		75.00
MAGPIE RING		
☐ HN Designer Adrian Hughes, height 8″		95.00
QUEEN OF THE DAWN		
☐ HN 2437 Designer M. Davies, height 8½″		125.00
QUEEN OF THE ICE		
☐ HN 2435 Designer M. Davies, height 8″		125.00
LYRIC		
☐ HN 2757 Designer Eric Griffiths, height 6¼″		95.00
MUSICALE		
☐ HN 2756 Designer Eric Griffiths, height 9″		125.00
SERENADE		
☐ HN 2753 Designer Eric Griffiths, height 9″		95.00
SONATA		
☐ HN 2438 Designer M. Davies, height 6½″		95.00

GILBERT & SULLIVAN SERIES

	Date	Price Range	
KO-KO			
HN 2898			
☐ Japanese figure from "The Mikado." Black hair on light brown base, costume of orange, blue, green, black, red, holding scroll, with large ax-like weapon on stand (2nd version), height 11½″, designer W. K. Harper.	1980-	650.00	750.00
YUM-YUM			
HN 2899			
☐ Japanese figure from "The Mikado." Round light coloured base, costume of green and yellow with waistband of blue and gold, white flowers in black hair, holding white fan in one hand (2nd version), height 10¾″, designer W. K. Harper.	1980-	650.00	750.00

Koko,
HN2898,
650.00 – 750.00

	Date	Price
RUTH, THE PIRATE MAID		
HN 2900		
☐ Figure from "The Pirates of Penzance." Costume of brown, striped skirt, blue blouse with gold and black trim, white apron, black captain's hat with trim of gold and white skull and crossbones on mottled brown base, height 11¾", designer W. K. Harper.	1981-	750.00
THE PIRATE KING		
HN 2901		
☐ Figure from "The Pirates of Penzance." Character seated on black and white pirate flag on light tan base, costume of green shirt, white lace ruff, blue boots and blue braided jacket with plumed captain's hat, his belt hold dagger and pistol, height 10", designer W. K. Harper.	1981-	750.00

ELSIE MAYNARD	Date	Price Range

HN 2902

☐ Figure from "The Yeomen of the Guard." Dancing girl with flowing red hair topped with a cap of blue, green skirt with white blouse, holding a tambourine aloft, height 11¼", designer W. K. Harper. 1982- 750.00

COLONEL FAIRFAX

HN 2903

☐ Figure from "The Yeomen of the Guard." Man in traditional Beefeater uniform standing on base of mottled greys, height 11½", designer W. K. Harper. 1982- 750.00

IMAGES

This series of modernistic figures, a fresh step taken by Doulton in 1980, combines old and new. "Images" features designs that are unmistakably 20th century, but in a concept that dates to the 18th. In Georgian England, it was popular to exhibit black basalt or white marble busts and other sculptures in fashionable homes. The "Images" series recalls this tradition as each piece is available in both black basalt (matte finish) or white bone china, suggesting marble. Subjects are inspired by the works of sculptors Henry Moore and Barbara Hepworth.

	Price
AWAKENING	
☐ HN 2837 Black	50.00
☐ HN 2875 White	50.00
CONTEMPLATION	
☐ HN 2241 Black	75.00
☐ HN 2213 White	75.00
FAMILY	
☐ HN 2721 Black	95.00
☐ HN 2720 White	95.00
LOVERS	
☐ HN 2763 Black	95.00
☐ HN 2762 White	95.00
MOTHER AND DAUGHTER	
☐ HN 2843 Black	95.00
☐ HN 2841 White	95.00
PEACE	
☐ HN 2433 Black	50.00
☐ HN 2470 White	50.00

Sisters,
HN3018,
95.00

	Price
SYMPATHY	
☐ **HN 2838** Black	75.00
☐ **HN 2876** White	75.00
TENDERNESS	
☐ **HN 2714** Black	75.00
☐ **HN 2713** White	75.00
TRANQUILITY	
☐ **HN 2426** Black	75.00
☐ **HN 2469** White	75.00
YEARNING	
☐ **HN 2921** Black	75.00
☐ **HN 2920** White	75.00
SISTERS	
☐ **HN 3019** Black	75.00
☐ **HN 3018** White	75.00

MIDDLE EARTH FIGURINES (J. R. R. TOLKIEN SERIES)

Inspired by the great work of J. J. R. Tolkien's fiction "The Lord of the Rings" and created by the artists of Royal Doulton is this new series of figures featuring new lands and new creatures. All are created from the vivid characters envisioned in the mind of Tolkien and portrayed in this book.

The entire line of Middle Earth figurines discontinued as of March 31, 1984.

ARAGORN	Date	Price
☐ HN 2916		
Tan Costume	1980-1983	45.00

Barliman Butterbur,
HN2923,
45.00

BARLIMAN BUTTERBUR
☐ HN 2923	1982-1983	45.00

BILBO
☐ HN 2914		
Brown shorts, tan vest	1980-1983	35.00

BOROMIR
☐ HN 2918	1981-1983	50.00

	Date	Price
FRODO		
☐ **HN 2912**		
Dark blue shorts and vest	1980-1983	35.00
GALADRIAL		
☐ **HN 2915**		
Ivory dress.	1981-1983	45.00
GANDALF		
☐ **HN 2911**		
Blue cloak	1980-1983	50.00
GIMLI		
☐ **HN 2922**	1981-1983	45.00
GOLLUM		
☐ **HN 2913**		
Green.	1980-1983	35.00

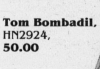

Samwise,
HN2925,
35.00

Tom Bombadil,
HN2924,
50.00

LEGOLAS	Date	Price
☐ HN 2917	1981-1983	**45.00**

SAMWISE		
☐ HN 2925	1982-1983	**35.00**

TOM BOMBADIL		
☐ HN 2924	1982-1983	**50.00**

PRESTIGE FIGURES

These are large-size figures, in some cases extremely large (Matador and Bull measures a huge 28″). While not actually limited editions, it is obvious that the Prestige Figures, because of their high retail prices, are produced in smaller edition sizes than the regular HN pieces. The concept for this series dates to 1952. Additions have been made to it only occasionally. Apparently the feeling, among directors of the factory, was that wealthy collectors might welcome deluxe figures. In general the series has been well received. It would be difficult to predict the prices that might be reached by Princess Badoura and Matador and Bull (the two most spectacular Prestige Figures) if they were taken out of production.

Columbine,
HN2738,
750.00

	Date	Price

COLUMBINE
HN 2738
☐ Subject from the famous "Commedia dell'Arte." Swirling gown of pink, floral bodice, on a rococo style base of white with gold trim, height 12½", designer D. Tootle.   1982-   **750.00**

ELEPHANT
HN 2640
☐ Fighting, 12" **1350.00**

FOX
HN 2634
☐ Sitting, 10⅜" **650.00**

HARLEQUIN
HN 2737
☐ Subject from the famous "Commedia dell'Arte." Brightly coloured chequered suit, on a rococo style base of white with gold trim, height 12½", designer D. Tootle.   1982-   **750.00**

JACK POINT
HN 2080
☐ Costume of red, purple, green with gold lion and leaf trim, has instrument slung over shoulder, base light beige   1952-   **1350.00**

KING CHARLES
HN 2084
☐ Figure is on light beige base, 17"   1952-   **1500.00**

LEOPARD ON ROCK
HN 2638
☐ 9" **1500.00**

LION ON ROCK
HN 2641
☐ 12" **1500.00**

	Date	Price

MATADOR AND BULL
HN 2324
☐ Bull is dark grey with brown shadings, matador costume of green and yellow, cape is blue/red with pale yellow lining, 28″   1964-   10500.00

THE MOOR
HN 2082
☐ Red with shaded greens costume with multicoloured waistband, deep brown cloak with shades of dark green, on dark brown base, 17½″   1952-   1350.00

PHEASANT
HN 2632
☐ (Cock) 495.00

PRINCESS BADOURA
HN 2081
☐ This is a 20″ figure, on black base, large elephant is dark grey with coverings of reds, blues, golds and brown, lady is seated in gold coloured chair with pink gown and gold head piece and necklace, male figure is seated on head of elephant costume of blue and gold with green trousers   1952-   14000.00 15000.00

ST. GEORGE AND THE DRAGON
HN 2856
☐ Blue/grey base with dragon head and brown treen trunk, horse is white with cloth of cream with gold designs, red lining, figure in blue/grey armor and helmet with white feather, 16″   1978-   6500.00

TIGER
HN 2646
☐ 850.00

TIGER ON ROCK
HN 2639
☐ 12″ 1500.00

ROYAL DOULTON INTERNATIONAL COLLECTORS CLUB

In 1979 the Royal Doulton International Collectors Club was created offering collectors of Royal Doulton items the opportunity of receiving newsletters from the company four times a year containing facts, articles on interesting items, new issues and announcements of shows and other special interest events. The club has offered each year special items available to club members only. The following is a listing of those items.

JOHN DOULTON CHARACTER JUG	Date	Price Range	
☐ Small.	1979-	50.00	

SLEEPY DARLING
HN 2953

☐	1981-	100.00	150.00

DOG OF FO

☐ Flambe piece.....................	1982-	50.00	200.00

PRIZED POSSESSION
HN 2942

☐	1982-	125.00	200.00

LOVING CUP
D 6696

☐ Pottery in the Past................	1983-	75.00	

SPRINGTIME
HN 3033

☐ Four Seasons, set of four.	1983-	125.00	200.00

VANITY FAIR SERIES

This collection of figurines was introduced in 1982, and is becoming extremely popular.

Vanity Fair ladies are individually hand-made and hand-decorated so each will be an original, each different from the other. Subtle matte skin tones are complemented by highly glazed white clothes, most with a small touch of color.

ANGELA	Date	Price
HN 2389		
☐ White gown, flowing skirt with elbow length sleeves, dark brown hair highlighted with golden colour, height 7⅜", designer M. Davies.	1982-	95.00

Mary,
HN2374,
95.00

	Date	Price

ANN
HN 2739
☐ Young lady dressed in a sleeveless white gown with wide skirt, white ribbon in her hair, height unknown, designer M. Davies. 1984-   95.00

BARBARA
HN 2962
☐ White gown, white hat hanging at the neckline tied in front with white ribbons, auburn hair, height 8″, designer P. Parsons. 1982-   95.00

CAROL
HN 2961
☐ Regal figure with white gown accented with pale pink, embroidering in hand with design on work of red flowers, green stems and leaves, reddish hair, height 7½″, designer P. Parsons. 1982-   95.00

	Date	Price

HEATHER

HN 2956

☐ Seated figure, white gown, white purse on arm, blonde hair, height 6″, designer P. Parsons.   1982-   **95.00**

JEAN

HN 2710

☐ Victorian lady in white gown putting the finishing touches to her hair, hair brush and ribbon lay on her gown, height unknown, designer M. Davies. .   1984-   **95.00**

JOANNE

HN 2373

☐ Seated figure with legs tucked up revealing ruffled petticoats, gown is white, hair blonde, height 5¼″ [6] designer E. J. Griffiths.   1982-   **95.00**

LINDA

HN 2758

☐ Young lady dressed in white ball gown, gown is close fitting draped to a bow in the back. Attractive frilled neckline, dark hair, height unknown, designer E. J. Griffiths.   1984-   **95.00**

MARGARET

HN 2397

☐ Gown is white accented at waistline with blue ribbon, hat is white with blue ribbon, dark hair, height 7½″, designer M. Davies.   1982-   **95.00**

MARY

HN 2374

☐ Blonde lady out for a walk in her white afternoon dress, her dress flares at the bottom revealing a tiered petticoat, her blonde tresses are covered by a perky white hat tied with a bow under her chin, height unknown, designer E. J. Griffiths.   1984-   **95.00**

	Date	Price

NANCY
HN 2955
☐ White gown, white flower in light brown hair, height 7½", designer P. Parsons. 1982- 95.00

PATRICIA
HN 2715
☐ Beautiful dark haired figure with ball gown of white satin, height 7½", designer J. Bromley. 1982- 95.00

SAMANTHA
HN 2954
☐ Beautiful blonde lady, white gown, white hat, height 7", designer P. Parsons. 1982- 95.00

TRACY
HN 2736
☐ Gown white with tight fitting bodice and plunging neckline with flowing skirt, rose in the folds of the skirt, blonde hair, height 7⅜", designer D. Tootle. 1983- 95.00

DOLLS
KATE GREENAWAY HEIRLOOM SERIES

LITTLE MODEL
☐ Gown is light beige with blue ribbon at waist, hat is blue matching ribbon on dress with deep maroon ties, cape is maroon. Limited edition of 5,000, height 12". 1981- 175.00

VERA
☐ Beautiful deep beige dress with matching color overdress, hat matches dress, light auburn hair, carrying basket of pink flowers. Limited edition of 5,000, height 12". 1981- 175.00

WINTER
☐ Costume is scarlet red trimmed with black fur, carrying fur muff, beautiful black hat showing underneath is her red hair, black shoes. Limited edition of 5,000, height 12". 1981- 175.00

**The Muff,
195.00**

BIG SISTER

☐ Beautiful white dress with lacey underskirt, royal blue ribbon at the waist, hat is white trimmed in same color blue, slippers white, carrying dark brown basket with white and red flowers. Limited edition of 5,000, height 12″......................

SMALL SISTER

☐ Small child has all white dress with white shoes tied with pink ribbons, bonnet is white with pink bows over dark blonde hair. Limited edition of 5,000, height 8″. ....

PINK RIBBON

☐ Dress is white taffeta line with pink underskirt, hat white with pink satin ribbon and white feathers, carrying a miniature bouquet of silk rosebuds. Limited edition of 5,000, height 12″...

	Date	Price
BIG SISTER	1981-	**175.00**
SMALL SISTER	1981-	**125.00**
PINK RIBBON	1982-	**195.00**

	Date	Price

WAITING

☐ Simple white gown of silk with frilled neckline and cuff. Wide sash of orange satin ribbon at waistline, matching the lining of her dark brown lace and feather hat, under the hat is a white linen cap trimmed in lace. Limited edition of 5,000, height 12″... 1982- **195.00**

THE MUFF

☐ Dressed in tailored full length coat with a fur cape collar and carrying a fur muff, the coat has a pink lining, dress is maroon satin, hat is plum colored and trimmed with chocolate and pink feathers, hair is auburn. Limited edition of 5,000, height 12″.......... 1982- **195.00**

SWANSDOWN

☐ Dressed in a white figured satin fur trimmed coat over a white satin dress, she carries a white fur muff and wears a lace trimmed hat over her blonde curly hair, decorated with Swansdown and yellow ribbons. Limited edition of 5,000, height 12″... 1982- **195.00**

PINK SASH

☐ Dressed in white taffeta over a pink underskirt, wearing white hat decorated with feathers and pink ribbon, over blonde hair, carrying a miniature bouquet of silk rosebuds. Limited edition of 5,000, height 10″. 1982- **150.00**

OTHER HEIRLOOM DOLLS

WEDDING DAY

☐ Bride wears a wedding dress of ivory silk which is almost entirely covered with ivory lace, the veil is matching lace and pink and cream flowers accentuate her brunette real hair, she carries a miniature bouquet of yellow, orange and white flowers, height 14″. 1982 **225.00**

	Date	Price

LITTLE BRIDESMAID

☐ Dressed in cream satin, trimmed with cream lace which matches the lace on the bride (Wedding Day), flowers are yellow, orange and white, hair is light auburn, and headdress is a ringlet of similar flowers. **175.00**

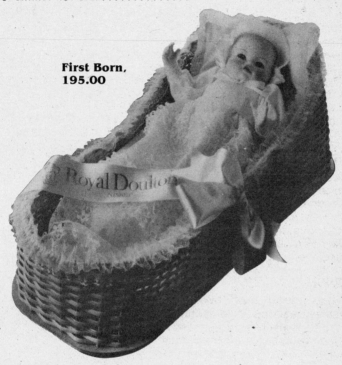

First Born, 195.00

ROYAL BABY DOLL

☐ To commemorate the birth of His Royal Highness Prince William of Wales, born June 21, 1982. Baby wears a dress and bonnet of cream lace and net over taffeta, underneath are cream cotton bloomers, Bonnet is cream trimmed in matching lace and ribbons, the canopied crib is draped with a white and cream figured cotton, trimmed with baby blue, the face, hands and feet are a delicate baby tone. Limited edition of 2,500.   1982-   **295.00**

	Date	Price

FIRSTBORN

☐ This baby doll is a beautiful blue-eyed infant in a basket crib trimmed in lace, the infant is dressed in a traditional christening robe of white figured cotton with a lace front panel, bonnet is of white satin and lace.   1982-   **195.00**

HRH PRINCE WILLIAM OF WALES

☐ Toddler doll dressed in a blue and white striped sailor suit trimmed with navy blue. Wearing a white cap with a navy blue bill, cap has embroidered in gold "H.R.H. Prince William." Baby is holding a light brown teddy bear. Limited edition of 2,500. . . . .   **175.00**

CHRISTMAS

☐ First in a series. Bright red costume trimmed in white fur, red hat trimmed in white fur. She is carrying a green box with Royal Doulton printed in gold on the box. It is a miniature of the green Heirloom doll box in which she is packaged. Limited edition of 3,500. . . . .   **195.00**

PRINCESS OF WALES

☐ The Princess is dressed in her wedding dress of ivory colored taffeta with puffed sleeves, ruffles and a long train, trimmed with white lace. Her bouquet is of cream colored flowers, her outfit is held in place by a tiara. Limited edition of 3,500. . . . .   **250.00**

EDWARDIAN SOCIAL SEASON DOLLS

(Limited edition of 3500)

PRESENTATION AT COURT

☐ A young debutante ready to be presented at court her gown is white, trimmed in embroidered yellow flowers, also trimmed with very pastel yellow flowers on her bodice and sleeves. **195.00**

ASCOT

Price

☐ Black and white striped satin gown with lace sleeves, beautiful black straw hat trimmed with violets. She carries a black and white lace parasol. 195.00

HENLEY REGATTA

☐ Dressed in blue, skirt, jacket and hat all matching. Crepe material with gold threads. Chiffon blouse trimmed with embroidery. 195.00

LORDS

☐ Light green gown with long sleeves, green wide brimmed hat trimmed with yellow roses. She carries a matching parasol. 195.00

**Monday's Child,
125.00**

VICTORIAN BIRTHDAY DOLLS

The well remembered nursery rhyme inspired this charming new collection. While each Day's child is represented by a boy and girl doll, each girl has a hairpiece while the boys hair is sculptured in the ceramic. Their costumes follow the 19th century tradition. This is a non-limited edition. Victorian Birthday dolls were discontinued as of January 1, 1984.

	Price
☐ **Monday's Child** is fair of face.	125.00
☐ **Tuesday's Child** is full of grace.	125.00
☐ **Wedneday's Child** is full of woe.	125.00
☐ **Thursday's Child** has far to go.	125.00
☐ **Friday's Child** is loving and giving. . .	125.00
☐ **Saturday's Child** works hard for a living.	125.00
☐ **Sunday's Child,** a child that is born on the Sabbath Day is bonny and blithe and good and gay.	125.00

LIMITED EDITIONS

The Doulton Company has on numerous occasions issued a series in a limited edition. Limited edition, of course, being a pre-determined number of a given item. Each piece, normally, is sequentially numbered and accompanied with a certificate of authenticity, and beautifully boxed.

DANCERS OF THE WORLD. This series, begun in 1977, was created by Royal Doulton's premier modeler of feminine figurines, Peggy Davies. The concept is to show folk dancers from various parts of the world, garbed in native costume. The series is noteworthy for the attention given to small detailing and coloration. As the costumes are "traditional," they cannot be assigned to any given time-period. Many other porcelain makers have attempted works of this kind, but the Doulton Dancers of the World is generally acknowledged to be the outstanding series of the type.

FEMME FATALE SERIES. A new series begun in 1979. Each figure is limited to 750 pieces. These are large and rather elaborate works. To date only two have been issued, both on historical themes, but it would seem as though the "femme fatale" concept could lend itself to inclusion of fictional or modern types as well — these may be added in the future.

HEIRLOOM DOLLS. In 1981 Royal Doulton combined with the talents of the House of Nisbet introduced their first limited edition dolls. The heads and hands are fine bone china each hand painted with each doll having a different face. The costumes are created to perfection through the skills of the House of Nisbet, whose dolls have long been collected throughout the world. Each carries the Royal Doulton stamp on the nape of the neck, the costumes have a sewn-in label bearing the wording "Royal Doulton and Nisbet".

LADY MUSICIANS. Instituted in 1970. Each has been limited to 750 pieces and at this writing all are entirely sold out (that is, obtainable now only from retail dealers — not obtainable from the factory). Each figure shows a female musician playing a different instrument. Some collectors like to group them together as a "band," in the spirit of early porcelain sets that were intended to be displayed in that manner (Staffordshire put out many "bands").

MISCELLANEOUS FIGURINES. These are individually issued Limited Editions, not part of any sub-series. All carry numbering in the standard HN prefix series for Fancy and Character figures. These very desirable works have all been completely sold out and have definite investment appeal. The variety in subject matter adds to their interest.

MYTHS AND MAIDENS. A new collection introduced in 1982 these fine bone china figures have been inspired by ancient myths and legends. Each figure will be limited to 300, and a subject will be offered each year until 1986.

SHIPS' FIGUREHEADS. This series, introduced in 1980, has limited figures of 950 each. These are ceramic reproductions of colorful ship figureheads, from the days of sailing vessels. The originals were made of sculptured wood, but porcelain faithfully captures their line and color.

SOLDIERS OF THE REVOLUTION. This limited edition series was issued in conjunction with the U.S. Bicentennial. Most of the figures were released in 1975 on the eve of the celebration, but an additional figure (George Washington at Prayer), appeared two years later.

AGE OF CHIVALRY

A set of three knights issued in a limited edition of 500.

	Date	Price
SIR EDWARD		
HN 2370		
☐ Blue and gold base, blue and gold shield. Red cloak trimmed in silver, height 10¾″, designer John Bromley.	1979-	**750.00**
SIR RALPH		
HN 2371		
☐ Red and gold base, red and blue shield, light blue cloak, silver armor, height 10½″, designer John Bromley.	1979-	**750.00**
SIR THOMAS		
HN 2372		
☐ Green and gold base, black armor, height 10¾″, designer John Bromley.	1979-	**750.00**

CARNIVAL OF CLOWNS

Created by the well-known artist Ben Black, this series of four figurines were introduced in 1983. This series is a limited edition of 3,500 worldwide.

	Price
☐ **FINAL TOUCHES**...............	100.00
☐ **BETWEEN ACTS.**	100.00
☐ **THREE RING PICNIC.**	100.00
☐ **BREATHTAKING** **PERFORMANCE.**	100.00

DANCERS OF THE WORLD

The Dancers of the World Series was fully subscribed and no longer available as of January 1, 1984.

Spanish Flemenco Dancer,
HN2831,
800.00 - 850.00

	Date	Price

BALINESE DANCER
HN 2808

☐ Delicate in her gown of green with gold design, overskirts of yellow and pink, sleeveless bodice of multicolours, highlighted with a beautiful black belt. Gold necklace, gold and jeweled crown. Limited edition of 750, height 8 ¾ ", designer M. Davies.   1982-   950.00

BRETON DANCER
HN 2410

☐ Cream coloured headdress in lace, black and green bodice over royal blue striped full dress, creamy pink apron, decoration on cuffs and skirt hem are as lace, matt finish. Limited edition of 750, height 8 ¾ ", designer M. Davies.   1981-   850.00

CHINESE DANCER
HN 2840

☐ Costume is of blue with over-blouse of orange and blue, green skirt, purple sash which is long and extending almost to feet, base is white, height 9", designer M. Davies.   1980-   750.00

INDIAN TEMPLE DANCER
HN 2830

☐ Costume of yellow with trim of green and gold design. Limited edition of 750, figure on white base, height 9 ¼ ", designer M. Davies.   1977-   800.00   850.00

KURDISH DANCER
HN 2867

☐ Base is light blue, costume is purple trousers, gown of dark blue with trim of white with black design and red and yellow dots, purple head covering trimmed with gold dots, gold necklace. Limited edition of 750, height 8 ¼ ", designer M. Davies.   1979-   550.00

	Date	Price	

MEXICAN DANCER
HN 2866
☐ Light brown base, group of orange with shaded browns, trimmed at hem line in designs of black on yellow, waistband of dark brown, hat light yellow with very light red/blue ribbons, long white cloth falls from under hat, figure base footed. Limited edition of 750, height 8¼ ", designer M. Davies. 1979-   **550.00**

NORTH AMERICAN INDIAN DANCER
HN 2809
☐ Beautiful young Indian maiden in traditional dress, holding a bouquet of wildflowers. Hair is raven black with headband of white with red design and white feather. Limited edition of 750, height 8¼ ", designer M. Davies. 1982-   **950.00**

PHILIPPINE DANCER
HN 2439
☐ Skirt of light blue with red shading with darker blue and yellow trim, blouse peach with leaf design of red and green, open fan of white in each hand, head-covering is yellow with white trim with long light blue cloth, red shoes, base is blue with cream. Limited edition of 750, height 9½ ", designer M. Davies. 1978-   **550.00**   **650.00**

POLISH DANCER
HN 2836
☐ Green base, red boots, skirt white with blue design and coloured flowers, white apron with red flowers, black and gold bodice, blue/white blouse, headdress of red, blue and yellow flowers, several strands of coloured beads, height 9½ ", designer M. Davies. 1980-   **750.00**

	Date	Price Range	

SCOTTISH HIGHLAND DANCER
HN 2436

☐ Green base, skirt of red with black stripes and squares, red vest trimmed in yellow, white blouse, red and white chequered stockings, black shoes. Limited edition of 750, height 9½ ", designer M. Davies.   1978-   600.00   650.00

SPANISH FLEMENCO DANCER
HN 2831

☐ Gown of red with large blue/white ruffles trimmed in black, single red flower in hair, red shoes on white/blue base. Limited edition of 750, height 9½ ", designer M. Davies.   1977-   800.00   850.00

WEST INDIAN DANCER
HN 2384

☐ Costume is a long sleeved dress of buttercup yellow decorated with a reddish design, a long white petticoat decorated around hem, figure is brown colour on multicoloured base, semi-matt finish. Limited edition of 750, height 9 ", designer M. Davies. . .   1981-   800.00   850.00

FEMME FATALE SERIES

CLEOPATRA & SLAVE
HN 2868

☐ Large light brown base, blue chair, gown of white with shaded blues and reds, necklace of blue, red, black and gold, head band gold and blue, mirror blue and gold, black slave holding gold and red bowl, fan is white feathers and red design with blue/red handle, chest of white and black, two bowls, one of gold and blue, the other gold and black. Limited edition of 750, height 7¼ ", designer M. Davies.   1979-   1100.00   1300.00

HELEN OF TROY

HN 2387

	Date	Price
☐ Figure is standing on base which contains a marble pillar which holds a peacock, his tail flows to base, costume of figure is pale pink dress and sage green cloak. Limited edition of 750, height 12″, designer M. Davies. .	1981-	**1250.00**

QUEEN OF SHEBA

HN 2328

	Date	Price
☐ Regal lady she is. Tall in stature, gown is gold and blue with yellow draping sash at waist, lilac cloak draped over her shoulder trimmed in gold, gold neckband, gold crown over her auburn hair. Cheetah at her side. Both figures on a green base, height 9″, designer M. Davies.	1982-	**1250.00**

Eve,
HN2466,
1250.00

TZ'U-HSI EMPRESS DOWAGER	Date	Price

HN 2391

☐ Beautiful figure sitting on a dragon throne green in color with a marble like effect. The Empress Dowager is cooling herself with a fan. Pekingese dog stands on a black laquered stool. Figure is dressed in red cloak with a deep blue dragon decorated cloak, height 8″, designer M. Davies. 1983-   1250.00

EVE

HN 2466

☐ Nude figure standing on a base with long golden blonde hair flowing almost to her knees. In her hand she is holding an apple. She is standing in front of an apple tree, tree has cloud like foliage with a serpent swirling up through the tree to the top of the tree as if to whisper in her ear, height 9¼″, designer M. Davies. 1984-   1250.00

LADY MUSICIANS

CELLO	Date	Price Range	

HN 2331

☐ Seated lady in gown of yellow with white bow trim, darker brown bodice, white ribbon in hair, playing brown cello. Limited edition of 750, now sold out, height 6″, designer M. Davies.... 1970-   750.00   800.00

CHITARRONE

HN 2700

☐ Standing figure in gown of dark blue and light blue with trim of roses on bodice, holding very long neck instrument. Limited edition of 750, now sold out, height 7½″, designer M. Davies........................... 1974-   650.00   700.00

CYMBALS

HN 2699

☐ Green and orange gown, standing figure holding cymbals. Limited edition of 750, now sold out, height 7½″, designer M. Davies. 1974-   650.00   700.00

Chitarrone,
HN2700,
650.00 ~ 700.00

DULCIMER	Date	Price Range	
HN 2798			
☐ Seated lady at table holding instrument, round box at side, gown of lavenders and white. Limited edition of 750, now sold out, height 6½″, designer M. Davies.	1975-	650.00	700.00
FLUTE			
HN 2483			
☐ Seated figure in red and white gown playing flute. Limited edition of 750, now sold out, height 6¼″, designer M. Davies.	1973-	750.00	800.00
FRENCH HORN			
HN 2795			
☐ Seated lady holding french horn, gown of light green with darker green design, overlay of purple with white design. Limited edition of 750, now sold out, height 6″, designer M. Davies...........................	1976-	650.00	700.00

	Date	Price Range	

HARP
HN 2482
☐ Lady seated in chair with hands on golden harp, blue gown with purple overlay. Limited edition of 750, now sold out, height 8¾", designer M. Davies......................... 1973- 1100.00 1200.00

HURDY GURDY
HN 2796
☐ Lady seated in chair with instrument on lap, white gown with blue overlay, roses as trim on skirt, red hair. Limited edition of 750, which are now sold out, height 6", designer M. Davies. 1975- 650.00 750.00

LUTE
HN 2431
☐ Figure seated before a marble top table, holding lute on table, gown of blue and white, white ribbon in hair, open book on table. Limited edition of 750, now sold out, height 6½", designer M. Davies. 1972- 750.00 800.00

VIOLA d'AMORE
HN 2797
☐ Seated figure on brown and green chair, gown of yellow with red roses around hemline, overdress is blue with flower designs of red and green, holding viola under chin (viola is brown). Limited edition of 750 which is now sold out, height 6", designer M. Davies. 1976- 650.00 700.00

VIOLIN
HN 2432
☐ Figure seated, gown of yellow with shaded brown overdress holding brown violin under chin. Limited edition of 750 which is now sold out, height 6½", designer M. Davies. 1972- 750.00 800.00

VIRGINALS	**Date**	**Price Range**
HN 2427		
☐ Figure seated at brown and white top table with instrument of brown colour, gown of yellow with white bows, overdress of green with white bows, open book on instrument top. Limited edition of 750 which is now sold out, height 6½″, designer M. Davies.	1971-	750.00 800.00

MISCELLANEOUS FIGURINES

BEETHOVEN		
HN 1778		
☐ Bust style of Beethoven with figures of women around what appears to be hair, matte ivory glaze. Limited edition of 25, sold out, height 22″, designer R. Garbe.	1933-1939	6000.00 6500.00

HENRY VIII		
HN 370		
☐ Robe of red, blue and black trimmed in fur, beige coloured stockings, red shoes, standing on small base which has his name on it. Limited edition of 200, sold out, height unknown, designer C. J. Noke.	1933-1939	1750.00 2000.00

HER MAJESTY QUEEN ELIZABETH II		
HN 2878		
☐ Designed as a tribute to Her Majesty, Queen of England to commemmorate her 30th Anniversary of the Coronation. Figure has gown of white over which is a blue and crimson robe, badge of order is worn on the left, chain has the initials of the order 22 kt. gold trimmed with white crosses, white ribbons on the shoulder. Limited edition of 2,500, height 10½″, designer E. J. Griffiths.	1983-	450.00

His Holiness Pope John Paul II,
HN2888,
150.00

	Date	Price
HIS HOLINESS POPE JOHN PAUL II		
HN 2888		
☐ Beautiful likeness of His Holiness inspired by his visit to the United Kingdom, height 10″, designer E.J. Griffiths.	1982-	**150.00**
H.R.H. THE PRINCE OF WALES		
HN 2883		
☐ Beautiful figure in black suit with red trim, cloak is purple and white with gold trim, gold sword in hand. Limited edition of 15,000, height 8″, designer E. J. Griffiths.	1982-	**750.00**

	Date	Price Range

INDIAN BRAVE
HN 2376

☐ Indian mounted on black and white horse, costume of beige, dark blue, red and white, holding lance and shield of light brown with darker brown figures, headdress has yellow feathers. Limited edition of 500, which are now sold out, height 15½ ", designer M. Davies. 1967- 4000.00 5000.00

LADY DIANA SPENCER
HN 2885

☐ Sleeveless gown of blue with white polka dots, white ruffle at bust line, white shawl over her bare shoulders, carrying beautiful bouquet of flowers, blonde hair. Limited edition of 1,500, height 7¾ ", designer E. J. Griffiths. . . 1982- 750.00

MARRIAGE OF ART AND INDUSTRY
HN 2261

☐ Two bronze coloured figures on base of bronze with tints of green, base has figures of birds, flowers, etc. Limited edition of 12 — was never put on sale, height 18", designer M. Davies. 1958- 7000.00 8000.00

PALIO, The
HN 2428

☐ Knight mounted on horse on walnut base, armor of dark blue and light blue with gold design, light brown footwear, horse costume of light blue with gold design, light blue with white design, black, gold and red stripes, dark brown color for animal. Limited edition of 500, height 18", designer M. Davies. 1971-1973

PRINCE PHILIP, DUKE OF EDINBURG
HN 2386

☐ Limited edition of 750, height 8¼ ", designer M. Davies. 1981- 750.00

	Date	Price Range

QUEEN ELIZABETH II
HN 2502
☐ Gown of light blue with blue designs, purple ribbon over shoulder and front. Limited edition of 750, now sold out, height 7¾ ", designer M. Davies. 1973-   2000.00   2500.00

QUEEN ELIZABETH, The QUEEN MOTHER
HN 2882
☐ Figure is mounted on dark wooden base, gown is pink with white designs, dark blue ribbons across shoulder down to waist, wearing crown and necklace, holding white gloves. Limited edition of 1500, height 11¾ ", designer unknown. 1980-   1250.00   1500.00

ROYAL CANADIAN MOUNTED POLICE
HN 2547
☐ Bust figure of a Royal Canadian Policeman showing red coat and brown hat mounted on a black base. Limited edition of 1,500, height 8", designer unknown. 1973-   150.00   200.00

SALOME
HN 1775
☐ Matt ivory finish. Limited edition of 100, sold out by 1939, height unknown, designer R. Garbe. 1933-   4500.00   5000.00

SPIRIT OF THE WIND
HN 1777
☐ HN 1825, matte ivory finish. Limited edition of 40, sold out in 1939, height 14½ ", designer R. Garbe. 1933-   3500.00   4000.00

SPRING
HN 1774
☐ As 1827 but with matte ivory finish. Limited edition of 100, sold out by 1939, height 21 ", designer R. Garbe. . 1933-   2500.00   3000.00

	Date	Price Range

WEST WIND
HN 1776

☐ Large figure (14½ ") of two, head and shoulders only, each has wings, matte ivory finish. Limited edition of 25 sold out in 1939, height 14½ ", designer R. Garbe.   1933-   4500.00 5000.00

MYTHS & MAIDENS

LADY AND THE UNICORN
HN 2825

☐ White Unicorn lying on a blue and gold base, lady's dress blue, gold flowers, red bodice with white ties, she is holding a gold mirror to reflect the unicorn to itself, beautiful fleurs de lis emphasis on the base, height 8¾ ", designer R. Jefferson.   1982-   2500.00

LEDA AND THE SWAN
HN 2826

☐ Seated figure within the wingspan of a white swan, barefooted, gown is pale and gold, trimming is black and white, dark brown hair with red headband, base is decorated in blues, greens and reds, banded in blue and gold, height 9¾ ", designer R. Jefferson.   1983-   2500.00

JUNO AND THE PEACOCK
HN 2827

☐ Juno, the wife of Jupiter greatest of the Roman gods, is beautiful in her soft yellow gown, with a soft lavender accentuated with purple draping over her gown. Standing at her side a beautiful peacock. Figures are on an aquamarine base with flowers, gold acorn leaves as trim, height 11 ", designer R. Jefferson.   1984-   2500.00

Juno,
HN2827,
2500.00

SHIPS FIGUREHEADS

All are Limited Editions of 950. Designed by Sharon Keenan. Ships Figure heads fully subscribed and no longer available as of January 1, 1984.

	Issue Date	Price
AJAX		
☐ HN 2908 1980		750.00
BENMORE		
☐ HN 2909 1980		750.00
CHIEFTAN		
☐ HN 2929 1982		950.00
HIBERNIA		
☐ HN 2932 1983		950.00
LALLA ROOKH		
☐ HN 2910 1981		950.00

Ajax,
HN2908,
750.00

Hibernia,
HN2932,
950.00

Mary Queen Of Scots,
HN2931,
950.00

MARY QUEEN OF SCOTS	Date	Price
☐ HN 2931 1983		950.00
NELSON		
☐ HN 2928 1981		950.00
POCAHONTAS		
☐ HN 2930 1982		950.00

SOLDIERS OF REVOLUTION

CAPTAIN, 2nd NEW YORK REGIMENT	Date	Price Range
HN 2755		
☐ Brown base, beige trousers, darker beige coat with blue trim, holding lance. Limited edition of 350	1975-1980	750.00
CORPORAL, 1st NEW HAMPSHIRE REGIMENT 1778		
HN 2780		
☐ Brown base, green trousers, lighter green coat with red trim, white cross straps, green vest, black hat, white stockings, brown shoes. Limited edition of 350	1975-1980	750.00
GEORGE WASHINGTON AT PRAYER		
HN 2861		
☐ George Washington in full uniform, kneeling on white base. Limited edition of 750, created by Laszlo Ispansky and available by subscription only from Limited Editions Collectors Society of America	1977-	1800.00 2000.00
MAJOR, 3rd NEW JERSEY REGIMENT 1776		
HN 2752		
☐ Brown base, seated on wooden fence, light blue costume with darker blue trim, hat black with white trim. Limited edition of 350	1975-1980	750.00

	Date	Price

PRIVATE, CONNECTICUT REGIMENT, 1777

HN 2845

☐ Yellow/green base, beige trousers, brown coat, white cross straps, red trim on coat, black hat with blue/white trim, small cannon on base. Limited edition of 350 1975-1980   **750.00**

PRIVATE, DELAWARE REGIMENT 1776

HN 2761

☐ Yellow/green base, beige trousers, coat dark blue with red and white trim, cross strap of white, hat dark blue with white trim, small black box at waist, white vest. Limited edition of 350 1975-1980   **750.00**

PRIVATE, 1st GEORGIA REGIMENT 1777

HN 2779

☐ Brown base, white leggings, brown long coat, white shirt, white cross straps, has a tomahawk attached to base. Limited edition of 350 1975-1980   **750.00**

PRIVATE, MASSACHUSETTS REGIMENT 1778

HN 2760

☐ Dark coloured figure in blue/white uniform, dark blue hat, cross straps of dark blue, base contains blue/black barrel, brown box and cream coloured box, base is yellow/green. Limited edition of 350 1975-1980   **750.00**

PRIVATE, PENNSYLVANIA RIFLE BATTALION, 1776

HN 2846

☐ Kneeling figure on yellow/green base, costume of blue/grey, large brimmed hat of same colour, powder horn, knife holder and small pouch of brown. Limited edition of 350 1975-1980   **750.00**

	Date	Price

PRIVATE, RHODE ISLAND REGIMENT 1781

HN 2759

☐ Costume of beige trousers, white stockings, black shoes, blue coat with red trim, white crossed straps, black hat with yellow trim, holding ram pole for cannon. Limited edition of 350 . . . . 1975-1980 **750.00**

PRIVATE, 2nd SOUTH CAROLINA REGIMENT 1781

HN 2717

☐ Brown base, light coloured trousers, blue coat with red lining, dark brown hat. Limited edition of 350 . . . . 1975-1980 **750.00**

PRIVATE, 3rd NORTH CAROLINA REGIMENT 1778

HN 2754

☐ Brown base, costume of beige with green rolled bundle around shoulder. Limited edition of 350 . . . . 1975-1980 **750.00**

SERGEANT, 6th MARYLAND REGIMENT 1777

HN 2815

☐ Brown base, blue trousers, lighter blue coat and vest trimmed in green, waistband blue with red trim, hat black with white trim. Limited edition of 350 . . . . 1975-1980 **750.00**

SERGEANT, VIRGINIA 1st REGIMENT CONTINENTAL LIGHT DRAGOON 1777

HN 2844

☐ Light yellow/green base which contains tree trunk with posted white sign, horse is brown and black, trappings on horse are green and yellow, costume of soldier is white trousers, brown coat with green trim, blue/white gloves, black hat with green ribbon trim. Limited edition of 350 . . . . 1975-1980 **1750.00**

MISCELLANEOUS LIMITED EDITIONS

Royal Doulton certainly ranks as one of the pace-setters in the Limited Editions field. It was experimenting — very successfully — with limited editions as long ago as the 1930's, to which decade the first issues in its Jugs and Loving Cups date. Since there was no plan to issue such items on a regular basis, they were not given serial numbers; and this practice, once adopted, was continued even after the issues became more profuse. The majority of issues have had very limited editions indeed, even including those of recent date which went into a greatly expanded market.

CHERUB BELLS. Royal Doulton instituted its still-young series of Cherub Bells in 1979. To date, one has been issued each year, in an edition limited to 5,000 specimens. The name derives from the fact that cherubs (youthful angels) are always included in the motif.

CIGARETTE LIGHTERS. This series was introduced in 1958, when 11 designs were placed on the market, some of which were manufactured in that year only. The last year in which new additions was made was 1964. Royal Doulton's cigarette lighters feature "character" portraits, similar to those on its jugs. A number of the types are drawn from Dickens' novels but Shakespeare is also represented (Falstaff) as well as the creation of an American author (Rip Van Winkle, a character of Washington Irving). The scarcest are Musketeer and Rip Van Winkle, made in 1958 only.

EGG SERIES. In 1980 the factory began issuing decorative porcelain eggs, in editions of 3,500. The tradition for decorative porcelain eggs is very old, as they were a favorite at European royal courts and especially at St. Petersburg in Russia more than 100 years ago.

GOBLET SERIES.

JUG SERIES. This series goes back to the 1930's and includes some highly sought-after items.

JUGS. These include the "Cliff Cornell Jugs," made in the 1950's for an American business executive as a special order. Royal Doulton has very seldom, in modern times, created "special order" items. Thus the Cliff Cornell jugs have a definite collector appeal.

LIQUOR CONTAINERS. Apparently made for a commercial liquor dealer.

LOVING CUPS. The company began issuing limited edition Loving Cups in 1933 and has added periodically to the series. Originally, loving cups were awarded as prizes in British sporting events, usually made of silver. The Royal Doulton versions are in porcelain with attractive enameling.

MUSICAL JUGS.

NAPKIN RINGS.

NATIVITY CUP AND SAUCER SERIES.

TABLE LAMPS. These have never been a really significant part of the factory line, but some are quite old (from the '30's) and very attractive. They probably suffered destruction at a heavier rate than figurines and may be scarcer than many collectors realize.

TANKARD SERIES. Begun in 1971, this consists of decorative tankards with motifs from Dickens' "A Christmas Carol." Editions have run from 13,000 to 15,000 pieces.

TEAPOTS.

TOBACCO JARS.

WALL MASKS. Porcelain portaits in small size, to mount on the wall.

"SPEECH OF ANGELS" CHERUB BELL SERIES (LIMITED EDITION)

	Number	Year	Edition Size	Issue Price
☐ Glad Tidings (Clarion)	No. 1	1979	5000	95.00
☐ Peace (Harp)	No. 2	1980	5000	95.00
☐ Joy (Cymbals)	No. 3	1981	5000	100.00
☐ Glory	No. 4	1982	5000	100.00

"TWELVE DAYS OF CHRISTMAS" GOBLET SERIES (LIMITED EDITION)

	Number	Year	Edition Size	Issue Price
☐ Partridge in a Pear Tree	No. 1	1980	10000	55.00
☐ Two Turtle Doves	No. 2	1981	10000	60.00
☐ Three French Hens	No. 3	1982	10000	60.00
☐ Four Colly Birds	No. 4	1983	10000	60.00
☐ Five Golden Rings	No. 5	1984	10000	

"JOY TO THE WORLD" NATIVITY CUP AND SAUCER SERIES (LIMITED EDITION)

	Number	Year	Edition Size	Issue Price
☐ The Annunciation	No. 1	1980	10000	55.00
☐ Journey to Bethlehem	No. 2	1981	10000	60.00
☐ Shepherds In The Fields	No. 3	1982	10000	60.00
☐ We Three Kings	No. 4	1983	10000	60.00
☐ The Adoration	No. 5	1984	10000	65.00

**Shepherds In The Fields,
60.00**

CIGARETTE LIGHTERS

Left to Right: **Bacchus**, 1964 – 1973, **100.00 – 125.00**
Lawyer, 1962 – 1973, **100.00 – 125.00**

	Date	Price Range	
☐ Bacchus	1964-1973	100.00	125.00
☐ Beefeater	1958-1973	75.00	100.00
☐ Buz Fuz	1958 only	155.00	175.00
☐ Captain Ahab	1964-1973	100.00	125.00
☐ Cap 'N Cuttle	1958 only	175.00	200.00
☐ Falstaff	1958-1973	75.00	100.00
☐ Lawyer	1962-1973	100.00	125.00
☐ Long John Silver	1958-1973	100.00	125.00
☐ Mr. Micawber	1958 only	155.00	175.00
☐ Mr. Pickwick	1958-1961	125.00	150.00
☐ Musketeer (Porthos)	1958 only	375.00	425.00
☐ Old Charley	1958 only	75.00	100.00
☐ Poacher	1958-1973	75.00	100.00
☐ Rip Van Winkle	1958 only	375.00	425.00

EGG SERIES

	Date	Edition Size	Issue Price
☐ Rouge Flambe Egg	1980	3500	100.00
☐ Royal Crown Derby Paradise Cobalt	1981	3500	175.00
☐ Minton 19th Century Egg	1979	3500	75.00
☐ Minton Emperors Garden Egg	1982	3500	95.00

JUGS

	Date	Edition Size	Price Range	
☐ Captain Cook Jug	1933	350	1500.00	1900.00
☐ Captain Phillip Jug	1938	350	2000.00	2500.00
☐ Charles Dickens Jug	1936	1000	600.00	675.00
☐ Dickens Dream Jug			700.00	800.00
☐ George Washington Jug	1932	-150	2500.00	3000.00
☐ Guy Fawkes Jug	1934	600	500.00	600.00

**The Emperor's Garden,
95.00**

**Master Of Fox Hounds,
500.00 – 600.00**

	Date	Edition Size	Price Range	
☐ Master of Fox Hounds MFH Presentation Jug	1930	500	500.00	600.00
☐ Pied Piper Jug	1934	600	550.00	650.00
☐ Regency Coach Jug	1931	500	500.00	600.00
☐ Sir Frances Drake Jug	1933	500	600.00	675.00
☐ Tower of London Jug	1933	500	500.00	575.00
☐ Treasure Island Jug	1934	600	450.00	550.00
☐ Village Blacksmith Jug	1936	600	500.00	600.00
☐ William Shakespeare Jug	1933	1000	600.00	675.00

JUGS (LIMITED EDITION)

	Date	Price Range	
CHARRINGTON TOBY			
☐ Made in the mid to late 1950's this jug which is about 9¼″ high was produced for Charrington, well known brewers, for advertising purposes. One version reads "Toby Ales", and the second version reads "One Toby Leads to Another."		250.00	300.00
☐ Toby Ale		200.00	250.00

CLIFF CORNELL

Special design produced in the late 1950's for Cliff Cornell, an American businessman for presentation to friends and as gifts. Jug depicts Mr. Cornell.

	Date	Price Range	
☐ Large size, 9″, brown suit		275.00	325.00
☐ Large size, 9″, blue suit		325.00	400.00
☐ Large size, 9″, tan suit		400.00	450.00
☐ Medium size, 5½″, brown suit		150.00	200.00
☐ Medium size, 5½″, blue suit	1939-	175.00	225.00
☐ Medium size, 5½″, tan suit		RARE	

	Price Range	
CHARLIE CHAPLIN		
☐ Seated Toby	3500.00	4500.00
GEORGE ROBEY		
☐ Seated Toby	2500.00	3500.00

LIQUOR CONTAINERS

	Price Range	
☐ Falstaff	85.00	100.00
☐ Poacher	85.00	100.00
☐ Rip Van Winkle	85.00	100.00

Charlie Chaplin,
3500.00 – 4500.00

LOVING CUPS

	Date	Edition Size	Price Range	
☐ Admiral Lord Nelson	1935	600	700.00	850.00
☐ The Apothecary	1934	600	450.00	550.00
☐ Captain Cook	1933	350	1700.00	2000.00
☐ Captain Cook (Black Basalt)	1970	500	250.00	300.00
☐ Charles Dickens	1970	500	250.00	350.00
☐ Queen Elizabeth II Coronation	1953	1000	500.00	600.00
☐ Jan Van Riebeeck.................	1935	300	1500.00	1750.00
☐ John Peel	1933	500	650.00	750.00
☐ King Edward VIII Coronation (large) ..	1937	1080	475.00	550.00
☐ King Edward VIII Coronation (small) .	1937	464	475.00	550.00
☐ King George VI and Queen Elizabeth Coronation (large)	1937	2000	425.00	475.00
☐ King George VI and Queen Elizabeth Coronation (small)	1937	2000	425.00	475.00
☐ King George and Queen Mary Silver Wedding	1935	1000	475.00	550.00
☐ Mayflower (Black Basalt)..........	1970	500	250.00	350.00
☐ Queen Elizabeth II Silver Jubilee	1977	250	700.00	800.00

	Date	Edition Size	Price Range	
☐ **Robin Hood**	1938	600	550.00	650.00
☐ **The Wandering Minstrel**	1934	600	500.00	600.00
☐ **Three Musketeers**	1936	600	550.00	650.00
☐ **Wm. Wordsworth,** unlimited but rare			500.00	600.00

MUSICAL JUGS

	Price Range	
☐ **Paddy**	400.00	500.00
☐ **Auld Mac**	400.00	500.00
☐ **Tony Weller**	400.00	500.00
☐ **Old Charley**	400.00	500.00
☐ **Old King Cole**	700.00	800.00

NAPKIN RINGS

	Price Range	
☐ **Mr. Pickwick M 57**	400.00	500.00
☐ **Mr. Micawber M 58**	400.00	500.00
☐ **Fat Boy M 59**	400.00	500.00
☐ **Tony Weller M 60**	400.00	500.00
☐ **Sam Weller M 61**	400.00	500.00
☐ **Sairey Gamp M 62**	400.00	500.00
☐ **Set of six with original box**	2800.00	3600.00

These came in a set and were given numbers for record purposes, however, it does not always appear on the napkin rings. Introduced about 1939 and withdrawn in 1960.

TABLE LAMPS

	Price Range	
☐ **Arabian Horse**	450.00	500.00
☐ **Autumn Breezes**	600.00	700.00
☐ **Alice**	250.00	300.00
☐ **Balloon Man**	250.00	300.00
☐ **Barnaby**	375.00	425.00
☐ **Captain, The**	300.00	350.00
☐ **Carmen**	200.00	250.00
☐ **Celeste**	250.00	300.00
☐ **Clotilde**	575.00	650.00
☐ **Fair Lady**	250.00	300.00
☐ **Falstaff**	400.00	450.00
☐ **Foaming Quart**	300.00	350.00
☐ **Friar Tuck**	700.00	750.00
☐ **Gay Morning**	225.00	275.00
☐ **Good Catch**	250.00	300.00
☐ **Huntsman Fox**	200.00	250.00
☐ **Immortal (The),** sitting green mandarin, 12″	900.00	1000.00

	Price Range	
☐ Jemima Puddleduck	250.00	300.00
☐ Judge, The	500.00	600.00
☐ Old Balloon Seller	250.00	300.00
☐ Peter Rabbit	250.00	300.00
☐ Polly Peachum	275.00	325.00
☐ Top Of The Hill	250.00	300.00
☐ Town Crier	300.00	400.00
☐ Uriah Heep	375.00	425.00
☐ Winston Churchill	250.00	300.00

"BESWICK" CHRISTMAS TANKARDS SERIES

	Issue Date	Edition Size	Price
☐ Bob Crachit and Scrooge	1971	13000	50.00
☐ Christmas Carolers at Scrooge's Door	1972	13000	40.00
☐ Ghost of Christmas Future	1979	15000	60.00
☐ Marley's Ghost Visits Scrooge	1974	15000	45.00
☐ Scrooge is Asked to Aid the Poor	1973	13000	40.00
☐ Scrooge is Visited by Ghost of Christmas Past	1975	15000	50.00
☐ Scrooge is Visited by Ghost of Christmas Present	1976	15000	60.00
☐ Scrooge with Ghost of Christmas Present	1977	15000	50.00
☐ Scrooge with Ghost of Christmas Present	1978	15000	55.00
☐ Scrooge Going to Church	1981	15000	70.00
☐ Scrooge Visits His Own Grave	1980	15000	65.00
☐ Christmas at Bob Crachits	1982	15000	

TOBACCO JARS

	Price Range	
☐ Paddy	450.00	500.00
☐ Old Charley	450.00	500.00
☐ Dogs (5 or 6 encircling jar)	200.00	300.00

TEAPOTS

	Price Range	
☐ Sairey Gamp	450.00	500.00
☐ Old Charley	450.00	500.00
☐ Tony Weller	450.00	500.00
☐ Polar Bears on blue or green band, circling pot	75.00	125.00

WALL MASKS

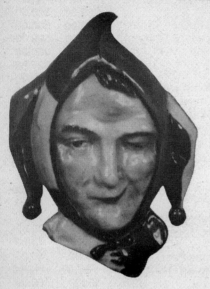 

Jesters, 300.00 - 450.00

	Price Range	
☐ **Baby**	450.00	550.00
☐ **Blue Lady,** mini	300.00	350.00
☐ **Fate**	1000.00	1200.00
☐ **Friar Of Orders**	800.00	900.00
☐ **Green Lady,** mini	300.00	350.00
☐ **Greta Garbo**	700.00	800.00
☐ **Jester,** large	300.00	375.00
☐ **Jester,** small	375.00	450.00
☐ **Jester,** mini	375.00	450.00
☐ **Marlene Dietrich**	700.00	800.00
☐ **Pink Lady,** mini	300.00	350.00
☐ **Pompadour,** large	850.00	1000.00
☐ **Pompadour,** small	550.00	650.00
☐ **St. Agnes**	1000.00	1200.00
☐ **Sweet Anne,** pink	450.00	550.00
☐ **Sweet Anne,** green	600.00	700.00
☐ **Sweet Anne,** blue	600.00	700.00

WALL POCKETS

	Price Range	
☐ **Jester**	650.00	750.00
☐ **Old Charley**	500.00	600.00

NUMERICAL LISTINGS OF "D" MODEL NUMBERS

The following is a NUMERICAL listing of all Royal Doulton products bearing the prefix letter D. Mostly these are Character or Toby Jugs, for which the D prefix was instituted. However, over the years the factory has occasionally issued other items bearing the D prefix. In all cases, these non-jug articles with D prefix are directly associated with the company's jugs, as the motifs they carry are adapted *from* Character or Toby Jugs. Since this is a NUMERICAL listing, all objects bearing the same motif are not necessarily grouped together. Missing numbers were, mostly, used for miscellaneous items bearing jug-type motifs. See next section.

	Date	Price Range	
D 5327			
☐ John Barleycorn, large.............	1934-1960	150.00	170.00
D 5327			
☐ John Barleycorn, large.............	1978-	110.00	140.00
D 5420			
☐ Old Charley, large................	1934-1983	75.00	
D 5451			
☐ Sairey Gamp, large................	1935-	75.00	
D 5486			
☐ Parson Brown, large...............	1935-1960	95.00	115.00
D 5495			
☐ Dick Turpin (1st version), large	1935-1960	100.00	125.00
D 5504			
☐ Simon the Cellarer, large...........	1935-1960	125.00	150.00
D 5521			
☐ Granny, large	1935-1983	60.00	75.00
D 5527			
☐ Old Charley, small	1935-1983	39.95	
D 5528			
☐ Sairey Gamp, small	1935-	39.95	
D 5529			
☐ Parson Brown, small	1935-1960	60.00	70.00
D 5530			
☐ Tony Weller, small	1936-1960	50.00	60.00
D 5531			
☐ Tony Weller, large	1936-1960	125.00	150.00
D 5556			
☐ Jester, small	1936-	75.00	115.00
D 5584			
☐ Old Curiosity Shop Jug (Miscellaneous, Dickens Jug)	1935-1960	125.00	175.00
D 5599			
☐ Old Charley (Ash Tray)	1936-1960	100.00	125.00
D 5600			
☐ Parson Brown (Ash Tray)	1936-1960	85.00	125.00
D 5601			
☐ Dick Turpin (Ash Tray)	1936-1960	100.00	125.00

	Date	Price Range	
D 5602			
☐ John Barleycorn (Ash Tray)	1936-1960	85.00	125.00
D 5610			
☐ Clown, red hair	1937-1942	5500.00	6500.00
D 5612			
☐ John Peel, large	1936-1960	110.00	125.00
D 5613			
☐ Touchstone, large	1936-1960	225.00	300.00
D 5614			
☐ Cardinal, large	1936-1960	110.00	135.00
D 5615			
☐ The Vicar of Bray, large	1936-1960	175.00	200.00
D 5616			
☐ Simon the Cellarer, small	1936-1960	75.00	100.00
D 5617			
☐ Oliver Twist Jug (Miscellaneous Dickens Jugs)	1937-1960	125.00	175.00
D 5618			
☐ Dick Turpin (1st version), small	1935-1960	55.00	70.00
D 5731			
☐ John Peel, small	1937-1960	60.00	70.00
D 5735			
☐ John Barleycorn, small	1937-1960	75.00	90.00
D 5736			
☐ Toby Philpots, large	1937-1969	125.00	150.00
D 5737			
☐ Toby Philpots, small	1937-1969	50.00	65.00
D 5753			
☐ Paddy, large	1937-1960	125.00	150.00
D 5756			
☐ Pickwick Papers Jug (Miscellaneous Dickens Jugs)	1937-1960	150.00	225.00
D 5757			
☐ Mephistopheles, large	1937-1948	2000.00	2500.00
D 5758			
☐ Mephistopheles, small	1937-1948	1000.00	1250.00
D 5768			
☐ Paddy, small	1937-1960	55.00	65.00
D 5788			
☐ Farmer John, large	1938-1960	140.00	175.00
D 5789			
☐ Farmer John, small	1938-1960	70.00	80.00
D 5823			
☐ Owd Mac, large	1938-1945	100.00	125.00
D 5823			
☐ Auld Mac, large	1938-	75.00	
D 5824			
☐ Auld Mac, small	1938-	39.95	

	Date	Price Range	
D 5838			
☐ Buz Fuz, intermediate size	1938-1948	140.00	165.00
D 5838			
☐ Buz Fuz, small size...............	1948-1960	100.00	115.00
D 5839			
☐ Mr. Pickwick, special size	1938-1948	140.00	165.00
D 5839			
☐ Mr. Pickwick, small	1948-1960	50.00	70.00
D 5840			
☐ Fat Boy, special size	1938-1948	150.00	175.00
D 5840			
☐ Fat Boy, small....................	1948-1960	90.00	100.00
D 5841			
☐ Sam Weller, special size	1938-1948	125.00	150.00
D 5841			
☐ Sam Weller, small	1948-1960	60.00	75.00
D 5842			
☐ Cap'n Cuttle, special size	1938-1949	140.00	165.00
D 5842			
☐ Cap'n Cuttle, small size...........	1948-1960	85.00	100.00
D 5843			
☐ Mr. Micawber, special size	1938-1948	110.00	160.00
D 5843			
☐ Mr. Micawber, small..............	1948-1960	75.00	100.00
D 5925			
☐ Old Charley (Ash Bowl)	1938-1960	100.00	125.00
D 5926			
☐ Paddy (Ash Bowl)	1938-1960	100.00	125.00
D 6006			
☐ Auld Mac (Ash Bowl)	1939-1960	100.00	125.00
D 6007			
☐ Farmer John (Ash Bowl)...........	1939-1960	100.00	125.00
D 6008			
☐ Parson Brown (Ash Bowl)	1939-1960	100.00	125.00
D 6009			
☐ Sairey Gamp (Ash Bowl)	1939-1960	100.00	125.00
D 6030			
☐ Old Charley (Toby Jug)............	1939-1960	160.00	225.00
D 6031			
☐ Happy John (Toby Jug)	1939-	95.00	
D 6033			
☐ Cardinal, small	1939-1960	65.00	80.00
D 6036			
☐ Old King Cole, large	1939-1960	225.00	275.00
D 6037			
☐ Old King Cole, small	1939-1960	80.00	125.00
D 6041			
☐ John Barleycorn, miniature........	1939-1960	65.00	75.00

	Date	Price Range	
D 6042			
☐ Paddy, miniature	1939-1960	50.00	65.00
D 6043			
☐ Toby Philpots, miniature	1939-1969	35.00	50.00
D 6044			
☐ Tony Weller, miniature.............	1939-1960	40.00	50.00
D 6045			
☐ Sairey Gamp, miniature............	1939-	29.95	
D 6046			
☐ Old Charley, miniature.............	1939-1983	29.95	
D 6047			
☐ Sairey Gamp (Bust)	1939-1960	65.00	85.00
D 6048			
☐ Buz Fuz (Bust)....................	1939-1960	75.00	100.00
D 6049			
☐ Mr. Pickwick (Bust)...............	1939-1960	75.00	100.00
D 6050			
☐ Mr. Micawber (Bust)	1939-1960	65.00	85.00
D 6051			
☐ Tony Weller (Bust)	1939-1960	65.00	85.00
D 6052			
☐ Sam Weller (Bust).................	1939-1960	65.00	85.00
D 6060			
☐ Mr. Pickwick, large	1940-1960	140.00	165.00
D 6062			
☐ Falstaff (Toby Jug)	1939-	95.00	
D 6063			
☐ Falstaff (Toby Jug)	1939-	50.00	
D 6064			
☐ Sam Weller, large	1940-1960	110.00	165.00
D 6069			
☐ Old Charley (Toby Jug)	1939-1960	150.00	200.00
D 6070			
☐ Happy John (Toby Jug)	1939-	45.00	
D 6088			
☐ Double XX or The Man on the Barrell (Toby Jug)	1939-1969	250.00	350.00
D 6107			
☐ The Best is Not Too Good (Toby Jug) .	1939-1960	225.00	275.00
D 6108			
☐ Honest Measure (Toby Jug).........	1939-	45.00	
D 6109			
☐ Jolly Toby (Toby Jug)	1939-	65.00	
D 6114			
☐ The Cavalier, large	1940-1960	125.00	150.00
D 6115			
☐ Drake (2nd version), large	1940-1960	150.00	175.00
D 6128			
☐ Dick Turpin (1st version), miniature ..	1940-1960	50.00	65.00

	Date	Price Range	
D 6129			
☐ Cardinal, miniature	1940-1960	50.00	65.00
D 6130			
☐ John Peel, miniature	1940-1960	45.00	55.00
D 6138			
☐ Mr. Micawber, miniature	1940-1960	45.00	55.00
D 6139			
☐ Fat Boy, miniature	1940-1960	60.00	70.00
D 6140			
☐ Sam Weller, miniature	1940-1960	50.00	60.00
D 6142			
☐ Fat Boy, tiny	1940-1960	110.00	135.00
D 6143			
☐ Mr. Micawber, tiny	—	110.00	135.00
D 6144			
☐ Old Charley, tiny.................	1940-1960	100.00	125.00
D 6145			
☐ Paddy, tiny	1940-1960	100.00	125.00
D 6146			
☐ Sairey Gamp, tiny................	1940-1960	45.00	60.00
D 6147			
☐ Sam Weller, tiny	1940-1960	100.00	125.00
D 6170			
☐ Churchill, large	1940-	9000.00	11000.00
D 6171			
☐ Sir Winston Churchill, large (Toby Jug)	1941-	95.00	
D 6172			
☐ Sir Winston Churchill, small (Toby Jug)	1941-	65.00	
D 6173			
☐ The Cavalier, small...............	1940-1960	75.00	85.00
D 6174			
☐ Drake (2nd version), small	1941-1960	90.00	110.00
D 6175			
☐ Sir Winston Churchill, miniature (Toby Jug)	1941-	45.00	
D 6198			
☐ Smuts, large	1946-1948	1750.00	2250.00
D 6202			
☐ Monty, large	1946-	75.00	
D 6205			
☐ Robin Hood (1st version), large	1947-1960	125.00	150.00
D 6206			
☐ Beefeater, large	1947-	75.00	
D 6207			
☐ 'Arry, large......................	1947-1960	175.00	200.00
D 6207			
☐ Pearly Boy, large	—	1200.00	1500.00
D 6208			
☐ 'Arriet, large	1947-1960	175.00	200.00

	Date	Price Range	
D 6208			
☐ Pearly Girl, large	—	1400.00	1750.00
D 6233			
☐ Beefeater, small	1947-	50.00	
D 6234			
☐ Robin Hood (1st version), small	1947-1960	70.00	90.00
D 6235			
☐ 'Arry, small . . . , ...	1947-1960	70.00	80.00
D 6235			
☐ Pearly Boy, small	—	700.00	800.00
D 6236			
☐ 'Arriet, small	1947-1960	70.00	80.00
D 6236			
☐ Pearly Girl, small	—	800.00	1000.00
D 6245			
☐ Mr. Pickwick, miniature	1947-1960	55.00	70.00
D 6249			
☐ 'Arry, miniature	1947-1960	70.00	80.00
D 6250			
☐ 'Arriet, miniature	1947-1960	65.00	75.00
D 6249			
☐ Pearly Boy, miniature	—	500.00	700.00
D 6250			
☐ Pearly Girl, miniature	—	600.00	800.00
D 6251			
☐ Beefeater, miniature	1947-	29.95	
D 6252			
☐ Robin Hood (1st version), miniature . .	1947-1960	50.00	60.00
D 6253			
☐ Auld Mac, miniature	1946-	29.95	
D 6255			
☐ 'Arry, tiny	1947-1960	200.00	225.00
D 6256			
☐ 'Arriet, tiny	1947-1960	175.00	225.00
D 6257			
☐ Auld Mac, tiny	1946-1960	185.00	225.00
D 6258			
☐ Cardinal, tiny	1947-1960	220.00	250.00
D 6259			
☐ John Peel, tiny	1947-1960	225.00	250.00
D 6260			
☐ Mr. Pickwick, tiny	1947-1960	175.00	250.00
D 6261			
☐ Mr. Pickwick (Toby Jug)	1948-1960	150.00	200.00
D 6262			
☐ Mr. Micawber (Toby Jug)	1948-1960	150.00	200.00
D 6263			
☐ Sairey Gamp (Toby Jug)	1948-1960	150.00	200.00

	Date	Price Range	
D 6264			
☐ The Fat Boy (Toby Jug)	1948-1960	200.00	225.00
D 6265			
☐ Sam Weller (Toby Jug)	1948-1960	200.00	225.00
D 6266			
☐ Cap'n Cuttle (Toby Jug)	1948-1960	150.00	200.00
D 6285			
☐ Oliver Twist Jug (Miscellaneous Dickens Jugs)	1936-1960	225.00	275.00
D 6286			
☐ Oliver Twist Tankard	1949-1960	200.00	250.00
D 6287			
☐ Falstaff, large	1950-	75.00	
D 6288			
☐ Jarge, large	1950-1960	275.00	300.00
D 6289			
☐ Samuel Johnson, large	1950-1960	225.00	250.00
D 6291			
☐ Old London Jug (Miscellaneous Dickens Jugs)	1949-1960	200.00	275.00
D 6292			
☐ Peggotty Jug (Miscellaneous Dickens Jugs)	1949-1960	275.00	350.00
D 6295			
☐ Jarge, large	1950-1960	150.00	185.00
D 6296			
☐ Samuel Johnson, small	1950-1960	150.00	175.00
D 6319			
☐ The Squire (Toby Jug)	1950-1969	250.00	300.00
D 6320			
☐ The Hunstman (Toby Jug)	1950-	95.00	
D 6321			
☐ Friar Tuck, large	1951-1960	400.00	450.00
D 6322			
☐ Clown, white hair, large	1951-1955	1100.00	1300.00
D 6335			
☐ Long John Silver, large	1952-	75.00	
D 6336			
☐ Lord Nelson, large	1952-1969	275.00	325.00
D 6337			
☐ Uncle Tom Cobbleigh, large	1952-1960	350.00	400.00
D 6372			
☐ Johnny Appleseed, large	1935-1969	235.00	260.00
D 6374			
☐ Simple Simon, large	1953-1960	525.00	575.00
D 6375			
☐ Dick Whittington, large	1953-1960	375.00	425.00
D 6384			
☐ Granny, small	1953-1983	40.00	50.00

	Date	Price Range	
D 6385			
☐ Falstaff, small	1950-	**39.95**	
D 6386			
☐ Long John Silver, small	1952-	**39.95**	
D 6403			
☐ The Pied Piper, large	1954-1980	**75.00**	
D 6404			
☐ Issac Walton, large	1953-	**75.00**	
D 6429			
☐ Poacher, large	1955-	**75.00**	
D 6438			
☐ Rip Van Winkle, large..............	1955-	**75.00**	
D 6439			
☐ Athos, large......................	1960-	**75.00**	
D 6440			
☐ Porthos, large	1956-	**75.00**	
D 6441			
☐ Aramis, large	1956-	**75.00**	
D 6452			
☐ Athos, small	1960-	**39.95**	
D 6453			
☐ Porthos, small	1956-	**39.95**	
D 6454			
☐ Aramis, small	1956-	**39.95**	
D 6455			
☐ Don Quixote, large	1957-	**75.00**	
D 6456			
☐ Sancho Panza, large	1960-1982	**65.00**	**85.00**
D 6460			
☐ Don Quixote, small................	1957-	**39.95**	
D 6461			
☐ Sancho Panza, small	1960-1982	**40.00**	**60.00**
D 6462			
☐ The Pied Piper, small	1957-1980	**39.95**	
D 6463			
☐ Rip Van Winkle, small	1957-	**39.95**	
D 6464			
☐ Poacher, small	1957-	**39.95**	
D 6467			
☐ Captain Henry Morgan, large	1958-1981	**65.00**	**95.00**
D 6469			
☐ Captain Henry Morgan, small	1958-1981	**40.00**	**60.00**
D 6470			
☐ Mine Host, small	1958-1981	**35.00**	**55.00**
D 6488			
☐ Mine Host, large..................	1958-1981	**60.00**	**80.00**
D 6496			
☐ Viking, large	1959-1975	**85.00**	**115.00**

	Date	Price Range	
D 6497			
☐ The Fortune Teller, large	1959-1967	**400.00**	**450.00**
D 6498			
☐ The Lawyer, large	1959-	**75.00**	
D 6499			
☐ Bacchus, large	1959-	**75.00**	
D 6500			
☐ Captain Ahab, large	1959-	**75.00**	
D 6501			
☐ The Mikado, large	1959-1969	**350.00**	**400.00**
D 6502			
☐ Viking, small	1959-1975	**55.00**	**70.00**
D 6503			
☐ The Fortune Teller, small	1959-1967	**350.00**	**400.00**
D 6504			
☐ The Lawyer, small	1959-	**39.95**	
D 6505			
☐ Bacchus, small	1959-	**39.95**	
D 6506			
☐ Captain Ahab, small	1959-	**39.95**	
D 6507			
☐ The Mikado, small	1959-1969	**300.00**	**350.00**
D 6508			
☐ Aramis, miniature	1960-	**29.95**	
D 6509			
☐ Athos, miniature	1960-	**75.00**	
D 6510			
☐ Captain Henry Morgan	1960-1981	**25.00**	**35.00**
D 6511			
☐ Don Quixote, miniature	1960-	**29.95**	
D 6512			
☐ Long John Silver	1960-	**29.95**	
D 6513			
☐ Mine Host, miniature	1960-1981	**20.00**	**30.00**
D 6514			
☐ The Pied Piper, miniature	1960-1980	**29.95**	
D 6515			
☐ Poacher, miniature	1960-	**29.95**	
D 6516			
☐ Porthos, miniature	1960-	**29.95**	
D 6517			
☐ Rip Van Winkle, miniature	1960-	**29.95**	
D 6518			
☐ Sancho Panza, miniature	1960-1982	**25.00**	**35.00**
D 6519			
☐ Falstaff, miniature	1960-	**29.95**	
D 6520			
☐ Granny, miniature	1960-1983	**25.00**	**35.00**

	Date	Price Range	
D 6521			
☐ Bacchus, miniature	1960-	29.95	
D 6522			
☐ Captain Ahab, miniature	1960-	29.95	
D 6523			
☐ The Fortune Teller, miniature	1960-1967	350.00	400.00
D 6524			
☐ The Lawyer, miniature	1960-	29.95	
D 6525			
☐ The Mikado, miniature	1960-1969	350.00	385.00
D 6526			
☐ Viking, miniature	1960-1975	95.00	125.00
D 6527			
☐ Robin Hood (2nd version), large	1960-	75.00	
D 6528			
☐ Dick Turpin (2nd version), large.	1960-1980	75.00	95.00
D 6529			
☐ Merlin, large	1960-	75.00	
D 6530			
☐ Town Crier, large	1960-1973	175.00	225.00
D 6531			
☐ Gone Away, large	1960-1981	65.00	95.00
D 6532			
☐ Robinson Crusoe, large	1960-1982	60.00	80.00
D 6533			
☐ Falconer, large	1960-	75.00	
D 6534			
☐ Robin Hood (2nd version), small	1960-	39.95	
D 6535			
☐ Dick Turpin (2nd version), small	1960-1980	40.00	50.00
D 6536			
☐ Merlin, small	1960-	39.95	
D 6537			
☐ Town Crier, small	1960-1973	100.00	125.00
D 6538			
☐ Gone Away, small.	1960-	40.00	60.00
D 6539			
☐ Robinson Crusoe, small	1960-1982	35.00	55.00
D 6540			
☐ Falconer, small.	1960-	39.95	
D 6541			
☐ Robin Hood (2nd version), miniature .	1960-	29.95	
D 6542			
☐ Dick Turpin (2nd version), miniature. .	1960-1980	30.00	40.00
D 6543			
☐ Merlin, miniature	1960-	29.95	
D 6544			
☐ Town Crier, miniature	1960-1973	125.00	150.00

	Date	Price Range	
D 6545			
☐ Gone Away, miniature	1960-	25.00	35.00
D 6546			
☐ Robinson Crusoe, miniature	1960-	25.00	35.00
D 6547			
☐ Falconer, miniature	1960-	29.95	
D 6548			
☐ Neptune, large	1961-	75.00	
D 6374			
☐ Simple Simon, large	1953-1960	525.00	575.00
D 6550			
☐ Gladiator, large.	1961-1967	550.00	600.00
D 6551			
☐ Old Salt, large	1961-	75.00	
D 6552			
☐ Neptune, small	1961-	39.95	
D 6553			
☐ Gladiator, small	1952-	375.00	425.00
D 6554			
☐ Old Salt, small	1961-	39.95	
D 6555			
☐ Neptune, miniature	1961-	29.95	
D 6556			
☐ Gladiator, miniature.	1961-1967	400.00	450.00
D 6557			
☐ Old Salt, miniature	1984	29.95	
D 6558			
☐ Scarmouche, large	1962-1967	425.00	475.00
D 6559			
☐ Regency Beau, large	1962-1967	550.00	625.00
D 6560			
☐ Gulliver, large	1962-1967	450.00	500.00
D 6561			
☐ Scarmouche, small	1962-1967	325.00	375.00
D 6562			
☐ Regency Beau, small	1962-1967	375.00	450.00
D 6563			
☐ Gulliver, small.	1962-1967	350.00	400.00
D 6564			
☐ Scarmouche, miniature	1962-1967	350.00	425.00
D 6565			
☐ Regency Beau, miniature	1962-1967	500.00	600.00
D 6566			
☐ Gulliver, miniature	1962-1967	350.00	400.00
D 6567			
☐ The Apothecary, large	1963-1983	75.00	
D 6568			
☐ Guardsman, large.	1963-1983	60.00	75.00

	Date	Price Range	
D 6569			
☐ Night Watchman, large	1963-1983	75.00	
D 6570			
☐ Goaler, large	1963-1983	75.00	
D 6571			
☐ Blacksmith, large	1963-1983	75.00	
D 6572			
☐ Bootmaker, large	1963-1983	70.00	75.00
D 6573			
☐ Gunsmith, large	1963-1983	60.00	75.00
D 6574			
☐ The Apothecary, small	1963-1983	39.95	
D 6575			
☐ Guardsman, small	1963-1983	40.00	50.00
D 6576			
☐ Night Watchman, small.............	1963-1983	39.95	
D 6577			
☐ Goaler, small	1963-1983	30.00	40.00
D 6578			
☐ Blacksmith, small	1963-1983	30.00	40.00
D 6579			
☐ Bootmaker, small	1963-1983	30.00	40.00
D 6580			
☐ Gunsmith, small	1963-1983	40.00	50.00
D 6581			
☐ The Apothecary, miniature	1963-1983	29.95	
D 6582			
☐ Guardsman, miniature.............	1963-1983	25.00	35.00
D 6583			
☐ Night Watchman, miniature	1963-1983	29.95	
D 6584			
☐ Goaler, miniature	1963-1983	29.95	
D 6585			
☐ Blacksmith, miniature	1963-1983	20.00	30.00
D 6586			
☐ Bootmaker, miniature	1963-1983	20.00	30.00
D 6587			
☐ Gunsmith, miniature	1963-1983	20.00	30.00
D 6588			
☐ 'Ard of 'Earing, large	1964-1967	900.00	1050.00
D 6589			
☐ Gondolier, large	1964-1969	500.00	550.00
D 6590			
☐ Punch and Judy Man, large	1964-1969	550.00	650.00
D 6591			
☐ 'Ard of 'Earing, small	1964-1967	700.00	800.00
D 6592			
☐ Gondolier, small..................	1964-1969	400.00	450.00

	Date	Price Range	
D 6593			
☐ Punch and Judy Man, small	1964-1969	350.00	400.00
D 6594			
☐ 'Ard of 'Earing, miniature...........	1964-1967	1500.00	1650.00
D 6595			
☐ Gondolier, miniature	1964-1969	425.00	475.00
D 6596			
☐ Punch and Judy Man, miniature	1964-1969	375.00	425.00
D 6597			
☐ Captain Hook, large	1965-1971	350.00	400.00
D 6598			
☐ Mad Hatter, large	1965-1983	50.00	75.00
D 6599			
☐ Ugly Duchess, large	1965-1973	230.00	260.00
D 6600			
☐ Walrus and Carpenter, large	1965-1979	75.00	100.00
D 6601			
☐ Captain Hook, small	1965-1971	300.00	350.00
D 6602			
☐ Mad Hatter, small.................	1965-1983	35.00	40.00
D 6603			
☐ Ugly Duchess, small	1965-1973	225.00	250.00
D 6604			
☐ Walrus and Carpenter, small	1965-1969	55.00	70.00
D 6605			
☐ Captain Hook, miniature	1965-1971	270.00	315.00
D 6606			
☐ Mad Hatter, miniature	1965-1983	20.00	30.00
D 6607			
☐ Ugly Duchess, miniature	1965-1973	225.00	275.00
D 6608			
☐ Walrus and Carpenter, miniature	1965-1979	35.00	50.00
D 6609			
☐ Trapper, large	1967-	75.00	
D 6610			
☐ Lumberjack, large	1967-1982	60.00	80.00
D 6611			
☐ North American Indian, large	1967-	75.00	
D 6612			
☐ Trapper, small....................	1967-	39.95	
D 6613			
☐ Lumberjack, small	1967-1982	35.00	55.00
D 6614			
☐ North American Indian, small	1967-	39.95	
D 6616			
☐ Smuggler, large	1968-1980	55.00	75.00
D 6617			
☐ Lobster Man, large	1968-	75.00	

	Date	Price Range	
D 6618			
☐ St. George, large	1968-1975	125.00	150.00
D 6619			
☐ Smuggler, small	1968-1980	35.00	55.00
D 6620			
☐ Lobster Man, small	1968-	39.95	
D 6621			
☐ St. George, small	1968-1975	65.00	90.00
D 6622			
☐ Yachtsman, large	1971-1979	75.00	100.00
D 6623			
☐ Golfer, large	1971-	75.00	
D 6625			
☐ Jockey, large.	1971-1975	175.00	200.00
D 6630			
☐ Gardener, large.	1973-1980	60.00	75.00
D 6631			
☐ Sleuth, large	1973-	75.00	
D 6632			
☐ Tam O'Shanter, large	1975-1979	75.00	100.00
D 6633			
☐ Veteran Motorist, large	1973-1983	55.00	75.00
D 6634			
☐ Gardener, small	1973-1980	40.00	50.00
D 6635			
☐ Sleuth, small.	1973-	39.95	
D 6636			
☐ Tam O'Shanter, small	1973-1979	60.00	75.00
D 6637			
☐ Veteran Motorist, small	1973-1983	35.00	50.00
D 6638			
☐ Gardener, miniature.	1973-1980	25.00	35.00
D 6639			
☐ Sleuth, miniature	1973-	29.95	
D 6640			
☐ Tam O'Shanter, miniature	1973-1979	30.00	45.00
D 6641			
☐ Veteran Motorist, miniature	1973-1983	20.00	30.00
D 6642			
☐ Henry VIII, large	1975-	75.00	
D 6643			
☐ Catherine of Aragon, large	1975-	75.00	
D 6644			
☐ Anne Boleyn, large	1975-	75.00	
D 6645			
☐ Catherine Howard, large	1978-	75.00	
D 6646			
☐ Jane Seymour, large	1979-	75.00	

	Date	Price Range	
D 6647			
☐ Henry VIII, small	1979-	50.00	
D 6648			
☐ Henry VIII, miniature	1979-	29.95	
D 6650			
☐ Anne Boleyn, small	1975-	39.95	
D 6651			
☐ Anne Boleyn, miniature	1981-	29.95	
D 6652			
☐ Lobster Man, miniature	1981-	29.95	
D 6653			
☐ Anne of Cleves, large	1980-	75.00	
D 6654			
☐ Mark Twain, large	1980-	75.00	
D 6657			
☐ Catherine of Aragon, small	1981-	39.95	
D 6658			
☐ Catherine of Aragon, miniature	1981-	29.95	
D 6659			
☐ The Cabinetmaker, large	1981-	60.00	75.00
D 6660			
☐ Sir Frances Drake (Toby Jug)	1981-	95.00	
D 6661			
☐ Sherlock Holmes (Toby Jug)	1981-	95.00	
D 6664			
☐ Catherine Parr, large	1981-	75.00	
D 6665			
☐ North American Indian, miniature . . .	1981-	29.95	
D 6667			
☐ Macbeth, large	1982-	75.00	
D 6668			
☐ Santa Claus, large	1981-only	75.00	
D 6669			
☐ George Washington, large	1982-	75.00	
D 6670			
☐ Romeo, large	1983-	75.00	
D 6671			
☐ Henry V, large	1982-	75.00	
D 6672			
☐ Hamlet, large	1982-	75.00	
D 6673			
☐ Othello, large	1982-	75.00	
D 6674			
☐ W. C. Fields, large	1983-	75.00	
D 6675			
☐ Santa Claus, large	1984-	75.00	
D 6688			
☐ Mae West, large	1983-	75.00	

	Date	Price Range
D 6689		
☐ Shakespeare, large	1983-	**75.00**
D 6690		
☐ Santa Claus, large	1983 only	**75.00**
D 6691		
☐ D'Artagnan, large	1983-	**75.00**
D 6692		
☐ Catherine Howard, small	1984-	**39.95**
D 6693		
☐ Catherine Howard, miniature	1984-	**29.95**
D 6694		
☐ Mark Twain, small	1983-	**39.95**
D 6695		
☐ Benjamin Franklin, small	1983-	**39.95**
D 6696		
☐ Loving Cup, Pottery of the Past	1984-	**75.00**
D 6697		
☐ Fireman, large	1983-	**75.00**
D 6698		
☐ U.S. Civil War/Grant and Lee, large (limited edition)	1983-	**95.00**
D 6699		
☐ Mr. Litigate, The Lawyer	1983-	**29.95**
D 6700		
☐ Miss Nostrum, The Nurse	1983-	**29.95**
D 6701		
☐ Mr. Furrow, The Farmer	1983-	**29.95**
D 6702		
☐ Rev. Cassock, The Clergyman	1983-	**29.95**
D 6704		
☐ Santa Claus, large	1984-	**75.00**
D 6705		
☐ Santa Claus, small	1984-	**39.95**
D 6706		
☐ Santa Claus, miniature	1984-	**29.95**
D 6712		
☐ General Custer and Sitting Bull (limited edition)...................	1984-	**95.00**
D 6713		
☐ Mr. Tonsil, The Town Crier..........	1984-	**29.95**
D 6714		
☐ Madame Crystal, The Clairvoyant ...	1984-	**29.95**
D 6715		
☐ Mrs. Loan, The Librarian	1984-	**29.95**
D 6716		
☐ Betty Bitters, The Barmaid	1984-	**29.95**

CHARACTER AND TOBY JUGS

It is thought by most persons who are collectors of "Toby Jugs" and "Character Jugs" that the idea of a pitcher or jug depicting either a full figure or head was first designed and made early in the eighteenth century by some potter believed to be a Staffordshire potter. These drinking vessels and flasks soon became very popular, spreading from England to all parts of the world. Although we know from museums around the world can be found various forms of pitchers, jugs, flasks and etc., although very crude in form, do resemble a living being. However, it was not until the eighteenth century that there began to appear a series of jugs in a more decorative and distinctive design pattern.

The Toby jug, which over the period of years, has become one of the more popular items for collectors usually depicts a seated character with a peculiar type hat with three points, one of which is used for the pouring spout. It is believed that this jug has carried down the name "Toby" from a song popular in the mid-eighteenth century in which there was a character called "Toby Fillpot."

It was not until the early 1930's that Charles J. Noke, then Art Director for the Royal Doulton Company, decided to model a design he had been working on for some time in the form of a pitcher with a face. This was titled "John Barleycorn" an imaginary being representing whiskey. Secondly, there was Old Charley, a night watchman . . . Saurey Gamp, a Dickens character . . . Dick Turpin, a notorious highwayman, and Parson Brown, all accepted with widespread popularity. Some of the other Doulton modellers for the character jugs were Leslie Harradine (who also modelled a number of figurines), Max Henk, Harry Fenton and David Brian Biggs.

From the artist mind comes the sketch, and from this sketch a master mold is made. The master mold is then taken and a "working" mold is made from it . . . from this working mold there might be as many as thirty molds made for pouring. These are plaster of paris and when the liquid is poured into them it is allowed to sit for a while as the plaster of paris will absorb the liquid and the mixture becomes a hardened clay molded figure. After the figure is removed from the mold it is cleaned up, any seams erased and the handle which is cast separately is then applied. The figure is then fired at a very high degree causing a great deal of shinkage. When removed and carefully inspected it is sent to the decorating studios where specially prepared paints are used in colors selected from the original design. It is then fired a second time for the hardening of the colors. The third firing is for the glossy finish which appears on most all of the figurines and mugs. There was a span of a few years in the late 1960's and 1970's when the character jugs were made of fine china instead of earthenware, and these figures have the translucent appearance of fine china.

Each character jug is titled and the name appears on the bottom along with the Royal Doulton trademark and a "D" number. The name also is embedded into the back of the jug. It is widely recognized among collectors that a jug bearing an "A" mark is of more value because of this mark which supposedly signified an earlier issue. However, it appears there is no basis to this as this mark was apparently used for factory identification purposes. Nevertheless the jugs bearing the "A" mark command a higher price.

As with the figurines a few prototype jugs were made but to the authors knowledge were never marketed. Sometimes prototypes are made as samples for the factory's use in determining if the subject is a saleable item or perhaps even to test market in areas throughout the world but quite often or probably most often these figures never are available to the public or to the collector, such as the character jugs titled Buffalo Bill, Maori and the Baseball Player. It has been reported that these jugs do exist in collections, although to my knowledge they were not marketed in any manner, perhaps a few escaped from the factory in an unexplained manner. Since it is not known how many truly exist one cannot put a dollar value on such a piece.

A few jugs have experienced some design changes over the years of production such as Auld Mac was "Owd Mac" during production years of 1938 through 1945; Beefeater appears with both "GR" and "ER" on the handles . . . from 1947 through 1953 the handle bears "GR" for George Rex and in 1953 the initials "ER" for Elizabeth Regina were used and is still in current production; Cavalier experienced a color change (though very slight) and a change in the collar in 1950; Dick Turpin in the earlier version has a mask on his hat but was changed in 1960 with a mask covering his eyes, a horse for a handle and a complete different color version . . . a total reconstruction of this figure; Drake, the very early version did not have a hat . . . this figure was test marketed but never put into general production . . . a few do exist in collections today and are known as the "Hatless Drake" . . . the second version redesigned with a hat and different coloring was introduced in 1940; John Barleycorn jugs in the early versions bear a different handle than the later pieces. Handle is molded down into the pitcher itself rather than leaving the appearance of an attached handle; earlier versions of Lumberjack, North American Indian and The Trapper bear the words "Canadian Centennial Series 1867-1967" and were produced for sale in Canada in 1967, however, in 1968 they were issued for sale world-wide without the backstamp; four Dickens characters were changed to a smaller size in 1949 with the style remaining the same . . . they were Buz Fuz, Cap'n Cuttle, Fat Boy, Mr. Micawber, Mr. Pickwick and Sam Weller; an earlier version of Old King Cole shows the character with a yellow crown.

On the bottom of the jug may appear a copyright date, register number and a Royal Doulton trademark . . . sometimes one, two or all three may be on the jug, however, the date that appears does not necessarily mean the date the jug was placed in production, it is merely the date of copyright for that particular piece. Normally release is sometime within a twelve month period of the copyright date.

CHARACTER JUGS

Character jugs were first introduced to the Royal Doulton line of products in 1933. They were made from their regular earthenware dinnerware body and fired in coal-burning bottle kilns which were in use at the time. The factory experienced some difficulty in the firing, and to cut down the loss, started to experiment with other earthenware bodies.

In 1939, a new earthenware body called Georgian was adopted for the making of character jugs and other earthenware dinnerware pieces. To identify those items made of the new Georgia earthenware bodies, the capital letter "A" was imprinted alongside the trademark.

In 1952, the factory installed electric tunnel kilns. After extensive tests, it was discovered that character jugs and other earthenware dinnerware pieces made of the Georgian body could be fired in the electric kilns using the regular earthenware dinnerware body.

Starting in 1955, the special earthenware body called Georgian was discontinued and the letter "A" next to the trademark eliminated. Therefore all character jugs that were produced prior to 1939 and after 1954 were made from the factory's regular earthenware dinnerware body which do not carry the "A" mark.

Prior to 1966, the United Kingdom did not have a copyright law, but did have a design registration act which in part corresponded to the copyright law in effect in the United States. To protect their new products from plagiarism, the Royal Doulton management in England registered all new products under England's design registration act. This registration also involved the countries of Australia, New Zealand, and South Africa.

Because the United States had a copyright law, the American company copyrighted new products in the United States. Since approximately 1950, all new products carry the copyright notice of the United States with the date and four registration numbers of the United Kingdom, Australia, New Zealand, and South Africa.

When the copyright act in the United Kingdom became law in 1966, it extended copyright protection to articles previously registered under the design registration act. As the periods of registration ran out, the relevant registration numbers disappeared from the respective article.

	Date	Price Range
ANNE BOLEYN		
Second wife of Henry VIII.		
☐ **D 6644,** large	1975-	75.00
☐ **D 6650,** small	1975-	39.95
☐ **D 6651,** miniature	1981-	29.95
ANNE OF CLEVES		
Fourth wife of Henry VIII.		
☐ **D 6653,** large	1980-	75.00
available in large size only		

APOTHECARY, The
A character from the Williamsburg series. Apothecary was the forerunner of what today is our drug store. The person who owned an Apothecary was allowed to dispense drugs for medicinal purposes, even going as far as treating a patient.

	Date	Price Range
☐ **D 6567,** large	1963-1983	75.00
☐ **D 6574,** small	1963-1983	39.95
☐ **D 6581,** miniature	1963-1983	29.95

Anne Boleyn, D6644, large, **75.00**

ARAMIS	Date	Price Range	
A character from the book "The Three Musketeers".			
☐ **D 6441,** large	1956-	75.00	
☐ **D 6454,** small	1956-	39.95	
☐ **D 6508,** miniature	1960-	29.95	
'ARD OF 'EARING			
A character with hand cupped to his ear indicating he is partially deaf.			
☐ **D 6588,** large	1964-1967	900.00	1050.00
☐ **D 6591,** small	1964-1967	700.00	800.00
☐ **D 6594,** miniature	1964-1967	1500.00	1650.00
'ARRIET			
Depicts a London Cockney street trader or costermonger as they are called in England.			
☐ **D 6208,** large	1947-1960	175.00	200.00
☐ **D 6236,** small	1947-1960	70.00	80.00
☐ same jug with an "A" mark		85.00	100.00

	Date	Price Range	
☐ **D 6250,** miniature	1947-1960	65.00	75.00
☐ same jug with an "A" mark		80.00	90.00
☐ **D 6256,** tiny	1947-1960	175.00	225.00

'ARRY

Companion to 'Arriet; also depicts a London Cockney street trader or costermonger.

☐ **D 6207,** large	1947-1960	175.00	200.00
☐ **D 6235,** small	1947-1960	70.00	80.00
☐ same jug with an "A" mark		85.00	100.00
☐ **D 6249,** miniature	1947-1960	70.00	80.00
☐ same jug with an "A" mark		80.00	90.00
☐ **D 6255,** tiny	1947-1960	200.00	225.00

ATHOS

A character from the book "The Three Musketeers".

☐ **D 6439,** large	1960-	75.00	
☐ **D 6452,** small	1960-	39.95	
☐ **D 6509,** miniature	1960-	29.95	

'Ard Of 'Earing, D6588, **850.00 – 900.00**

	Date	Price Range	
AULD MAC			

Depicts a thrift Scotsman. Also known as "Owd Mac", note listing under that title.

	Date	Price Range	
☐ **D 5823,** large	1938-	75.00	
☐ same jug with an "A" mark		85.00	95.00
☐ **D 5824,** small	1938-	39.95	
☐ same jug with an "A" mark		75.00	85.00
☐ **D 6253,** miniature	1946-	29.95	
☐ same jug with an "A" mark		45.00	60.00
☐ **D 6257,** tiny	1946-1960	185.00	225.00

BACCHUS

The Greek "god of wine", this character has a wreath of greenery and grapes representing the grape harvest.

	Date	Price Range	
☐ **D 6499,** large	1959-	75.00	
☐ **D 6505,** small	1959-	39.95	
☐ **D 6521,** miniature	1960-	29.95	

BEEFEATER

A popular name for a member of the Yeoman of the Guard, bodyguards for the Queen. Beefeater jugs with GR on the handle are more desirable for the collector as the initials were changed to ER in 1953. The value of the GR jug is determined to be approximately 50% higher than the jugs with ER embossed on the handle.

	Date	Price Range	
☐ **D 6206,** large	1947-	75.00	
☐ same jug with an "A" mark		85.00	115.00
☐ **D 6233,** small	1947-	39.95	
☐ same jug with an "A" mark		40.00	60.00
☐ **D 6251,** miniature	1947-	29.95	

BENJAMIN FRANKLIN

Depicting one of America's most famous statesmen in his famous experiment of flying a kite in a thunderstorm to demonstrate that lightning was a form of electricity. Handle is a kite in the clouds with a key at the base of the handle.

	Date	Price Range	
☐ **D 6695,** small.	1983-	39.95	

BLACKSMITH

A character from the Williamsburg series. Blacksmith was an eighteenth century ironworker. These characters have been recreated in the restoration of the town of Williamsburg, the original capital of Virginia.

	Date	Price Range	
☐ **D 6571**, large	1963-1983	**70.00**	**75.00**
☐ **D 6578**, small	1963-1983	**30.00**	**40.00**
☐ **D 6586**, miniature	1963-1983	**20.00**	**30.00**

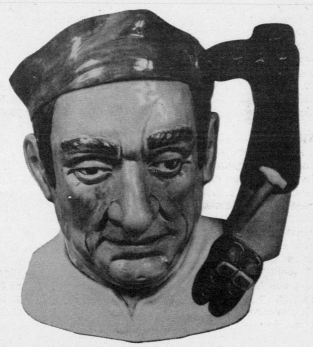

Bootmaker, D6572, large, **70.00 – 75.00**

BOOTMAKER

A character from the Williamsburg series. Bootmaker was the gentleman who made shoes and boots in the eighteenth century.

	Date	Price Range	
☐ **D 6572**, large	1963-1983	**70.00**	**75.00**
☐ **D 6579**, small	1963-1983	**30.00**	**40.00**
☐ **D 6586**, miniature	1963-1983	**20.00**	**30.00**

	Date	Price Range	

BUZ FUZ
A character from the book "Pickwick Papers" by Charles Dickens. Also note listing under Sergeant Buz Fuz.

	Date	Price	Range
☐ D 5838, intermediate size	1938-1948	140.00	165.00
☐ D 5838, small size.................	1948-1960	100.00	115.00
☐ Same jug with an "A" mark		125.00	150.00

CABINETMAKER, The
A character from the Williamburg series.

☐ D 6659, large	1981-1983	60.00	75.00

CAPTAIN AHAB
A character from the book "Moby Dick".

☐ D 6500, large	1959-	75.00	
☐ D 6506, small	1959-	39.95	
☐ D 6522, miniature	1960-	29.95	

CAP'N CUTTLE
A character from the novel by Charles Dickens titled "Dombey and Sons".

☐ D 5842, special size	1938-1948	140.00	165.00
☐ D 5842, small size................	1948-1960	85.00	100.00
☐ same jug with an "A" mark		100.00	125.00

CAPTAIN HENRY MORGAN
Probably the most famous British Buccaneer of his time. Born in 1635, died in 1688.

☐ D 6467, large	1958-1981	65.00	95.00
☐ D 6469, small	1958-1981	40.00	60.00
☐ D 6510, miniature	1960-1981	25.00	35.00

CAPTAIN HOOK
A villainous pirate in James M. Barrie's book titled "Peter Pan".

☐ D 6597, large	1965-1971	350.00	400.00
☐ D 6601, small	1965-1971	300.00	350.00
☐ D 6605, miniature	1965-1971	300.00	350.00

CARDINAL
A dignitary in the Catholic Church. This jug may represent a character from Shakespeare's Henry VIII known as Cardinal Woolsey.

☐ D 5614, large	1936-1960	110.00	135.00
☐ same jug with an "A" mark		120.00	145.00

	Date	Price Range	
☐ **D 6033,** small	1939-1960	65.00	80.00
☐ same jug with an "A" mark		75.00	90.00
☐ **D 6129,** miniature	1940-1960	50.00	65.00
☐ same jug with an "A" mark		60.00	75.00
☐ **D 6258,** tiny	1947-1960	220.00	250.00

CATHERINE HOWARD
Fifth wife of Henry VIII.

	Date	Price Range	
☐ **D 6645,** large	1978-	75.00	
☐ **D 6692,** small	1984-	39.95	
☐ **D 6693,** miniature	1984-	29.95	

CATHERINE OF ARAGON
First wife of Henry VIII.

	Date	Price Range	
☐ **D 6643,** large	1975-	75.00	
☐ **D 6657,** small	1981-	39.95	
☐ **D 6658,** miniature	1981-	29.95	

CATHERINE PARR
Sixth and final wife of Henry VIII.

	Date	Price Range	
☐ **D 6664,** large	1981-	75.00	

CAVALIER, The
During the reign of King Charles I his staunch supporters were given a title of honor and were known as "The Cavaliers".

	Date	Price Range	
☐ **D 6114,** large	1940-1960	125.00	150.00
☐ same jug with an "A" mark		160.00	175.00
☐ **D 6173,** small	1941-1960	75.00	85.00
☐ same jug with an "A" mark		75.00	90.00

CAVALIER WITH GOATEE
This character jug is different from the regular version. Although there are other distinctions the most noteable is a very prominent goatee. Considered rare.

	Date	Price Range	
☐ **D 6114,** large		5000.00	6000.00

CHURCHILL
Depicting the distinguished stateman Winston Churchill this jug is believed to have been in production for a short time only. It is not known the exact date it was withdrawn from the market. Considered extremely rare.

	Date	Price Range	
☐ **D 6170,** large	1940-	9000.00	11000.00

	Date	Price Range	

CLOWN, Red hair
Depicting a character from the circus.
Considered rare.

☐ D 5610, large	1937-1942	5500.00	6500.00

CLOWN, White hair.

☐ D 6322, large	1951-1955	1100.00	1300.00

D'Artagnan, D6691, large, **75.00**

D'ARTAGNAN
Depicting one of the colorful Dumas
characters. Attired in costume of the
period, plumed hat, lace trimmed
collar.

☐ D 6691, large	1983-	75.00	

DICK TURPIN
A notorious highwayman who was
eventually hanged. Released in two
versions.

First version - mask up on hat

☐ D 5495, large	1935-1960	125.00	150.00
☐ same jug with an "A" mark		140.00	180.00

	Date	Price Range	
☐ **D 5618,** small	1935-1960	60.00	80.00
☐ same jug with an "A" mark		70.00	90.00
☐ **D 6128,** miniature	1940-1960	55.00	70.00
☐ same jug with an "A" mark		70.00	85.00

Second version - Mask on face, horse handle.

	Date	Price Range	
☐ **D 6528,** large	1960-1980	75.00	95.00
☐ **D 6535,** small	1960-1980	40.00	55.00
☐ **D 6542,** miniature	1960-1980	30.00	40.00

DICK WHITTINGTON
Lord Mayor of London three times during the fifteenth century.

	Date	Price Range	
☐ **D 6375,** large	1953-1960	375.00	425.00

DON QUIXOTE
A character from the novel by Miguel de Cervantes' titled "Don Quixote".

	Date	Price Range	
☐ **D 6455,** large	1957-	75.00	
☐ **D 6460,** small	1957-	39.95	
☐ **D 6511,** miniature	1960-	29.95	

DRAKE
Depicting Sir Frances Drake, a distinguished figure in British sea power in the sixteenth century.

First version - Hatless Drake

	Date	Price Range	
☐		9000.00	11000.00

Second version - With hat and different collar.

	Date	Price Range	
☐ **D 6115,** large	1940-1960	150.00	175.00
☐ same jug with an "A" mark		165.00	190.00
☐ **D 6174,** small	1941-1960	90.00	110.00
☐ same jug with an "A" mark		100.00	125.00

FALCONER
Depicting a man who is trainer of birds. A falcon is the handle of this jug.

	Date	Price Range	
☐ **D 6533,** large	1960-	75.00	
☐ **D 6540,** small	1960-	39.95	
☐ **D 6547,** miniature	1960-	29.95	

	Date	Price Range	
FALSTAFF			

A character in the Shakespeare novel "Henry IV", Sir John Falstaff a fat and jolly character particularly liked for his wit and laughter.

	Date	Price Range	
☐ **D 6287,** large	1950-	75.00	
☐ **D 6385,** small	1950-	39.95	
☐ **D 6519,** miniature	1960-	29.95	

FARMER JOHN

Depicts the typical English farmer.

☐ **D 5788,** large	1938-1960	140.00	175.00
☐ same jug with an "A" mark		150.00	185.00
☐ **D 5789,** small	1938-1960	70.00	80.00
☐ same jug with an "A" mark		80.00	90.00

FAT BOY

Depicting a character from the Charles Dicken's novel "Pickwick Papers".

☐ **D 5840,** special size	1938-1948	150.00	175.00
☐ **D 5840,** small	1948-1960	90.00	100.00
☐ same jug with an "A" mark		100.00	110.00
☐ **D 6139,** miniature	1940-1960	60.00	70.00
☐ same jug with an "A" mark		65.00	75.00
☐ **D 6142,** tiny	1940-1960	110.00	135.00

FIREMAN, The

Created for the Griffith Pottery House, a company who sells gifts related to the fire fighting industry, this jug depicts a fireman in an authentic antique fireman outfit. Antique helmet with #1 appearing on the badge. Outfit has gold buckles and rivets. Fire hose is the handle.

☐ **D 6697,** large	1983-	75.00	

FORTUNE TELLER, The

Depicts a gypsy woman who roams the countryside who for a "piece of silver" will reveal the future for you.

☐ **D 6497,** large	1959-1967	400.00	450.00
☐ **D 6503,** small	1959-1967	350.00	400.00
☐ **D 6523,** miniature	1960-1967	350.00	400.00

	Date	Price Range	

FRIAR TUCK
A member of Robin Hood's band, he was the chaplain. Also a character in Sir Walter Scott's book titled "Ivanhoe".

	Date	Price Range	
☐ **D 6321**, large	1951-1960	400.00	450.00

GENERAL CUSTER AND SITTING BULL
The second in The Antagonists Series. Each double-faced jug in the series portrays two personalities involved in well-known conflicts. Chief Sitting Bull, Teton Dakota Indian Chief and General George Armstong Custer are depicted on this jug. Limited edition of 9,500.

	Date	Price Range	
☐ **D 6712**, large	1984-	95.00	

GEORGE WASHINGTON
Issued to commemorate the 250th anniversary of his birth. Designed by Stan Taylor this mug depicts the first President of the United States.

	Date	Price Range	
☐ **D 6669**, large size	1982-	75.00	

GARDENER
A character jug depicting the typical man who can be found working with the earth with the handle being a shovel and some vegetables.

	Date	Price Range	
☐ **D 6630**, large	1973-1980	60.00	75.00
☐ **D 6634**, small	1973-1980	40.00	50.00
☐ **D 6638**, miniature	1973-1980	25.00	35.00

GLADIATOR
Depicting a warrior of the Roman Empire.

	Date	Price Range	
☐ **D 6550**, large	1961-1967	550.00	600.00
☐ **D 6553**, small	1961-1967	375.00	425.00
☐ **D 6556**, miniature	1961-1967	400.00	450.00

GOALER
A character from the Williamsburg series.

	Date	Price Range	
☐ **D 6570**, large	1963-1983	75.00	
☐ **D 6577**, small	1963-1983	30.00	40.00
☐ **D 6584**, miniature	1963-1983	29.95	

George Washington, D6669, large, **75.00**

GOLFER	Date	Price Range	
Depicting an English gentleman out for a game of golf.			
☐ **D 6623,** large	1971-	75.00	
Small and miniature sizes were test marketed but not produced.			

GONDOLIER			
Depicts the romantic singing boat-man who guides his boat through the narrow canals of Venice singing his romantic songs.			
☐ **D 6589,** large	1964-1969	500.00	550.00
☐ **D 6592,** small	1964-1969	400.00	450.00
☐ **D 6595,** miniature	1964-1969	425.00	475.00

	Date	Price Range	

GONE AWAY
Depicts an English huntsman with his typical red coat and black silk hat. Handle is a fox.

	Date	Price Range	
☐ D 6531, large	1960-1981	65.00	95.00
☐ D 6538, small	1960-1981	40.00	60.00
☐ D 6545, miniature	1960-1981	25.00	35.00

GRANNY
Depicts an aged woman.

	Date		
☐ D 5521, large	1935-1983	60.00	75.00
☐ same jug with an "A" mark		90.00	100.00
☐ D 6384, small	1953-1983	40.00	50.00
☑ same jug with an "A" mark		110.00	125.00
☐ D 6520, miniature	1960-1983	25.00	35.00

An early version of Granny shows the characters face without the front tooth which appears on the currently produced jugs. Usually found on older "A" marked pieces.

☐ **Granny** jug without tooth		900.00	1000.00

GRANT AND LEE — THE CIVIL WAR
The first in a series titled "The Antagonists Collection" this mug represents the first double faced character jug since 1937. Both men wear the uniforms of their sides, navy blue for the Union and grey for the Confederacy. Their collars are embellished with bright golden stars of rank and the handle in their colourful flags. Limited edition of 9,500.

☐ D 6698, large	1983-	95.00	

GUARDSMAN
A character from the Williamsburg series.

☐ D 6568, large	1963-1983	60.00	75.00
☐ D 6575, small	1963-1983	40.00	50.00
☐ D 6582, miniature	1963-1983	25.00	35.00

GULLIVER
Depicting a character from the book "Gulliver's Travels", the handle is a castle with two Lilliputians on top.

☐ D 6560, large	1962-1967	450.00	500.00
☐ D 6563, small	1962-1967	350.00	400.00
☐ D 6566, miniature	1962-1967	350.00	400.00

Grant, D6698, **95.00**

	Date	Price Range	
GUNSMITH			
A character from the Williamburg series.			
☐ **D 6573,** large	1963-1983	60.00	75.00
☐ **D 6580,** small	1963-1983	40.00	50.00
☐ **D 6587,** miniature	1963-1983	20.00	30.00
HAMLET			
Depicting one of the characters from a Shakespearian play.			
☐ **D 6672,** large size	1982-	75.00	
HENRY V			
Depicting one of the famous kings of England.			
☐ **D 6671,** large size	1982-	75.00	
HENRY VIII			
Second son of Henry VII . . . he ruled England from 1509 to 1547.			
☐ **D 6642,** large	1975-	75.00	
☐ **D 6647,** small	1979-	50.00	
☐ **D 6648,** miniature	1979-	29.95	

Gulliver, D6560, large, **450.00 – 500.00**

	Date	Price Range	
IZAAC WALTON			
An author who has endeared himself to many . . . probably best known for his work titled "The Compleat Angler".			
☐ **D 6404,** large	1953-1982	60.00	85.00
JANE SEYMOUR			
Third wife of Henry VIII.			
☐ **D 6646,** large	1979-	75.00	
JARGE			
Depicts the original country boy, by no means handsome and often ridiculed.			
☐ **D 6288,** large	1950-1960	300.00	350.00
☐ **D 6295,** small	1950-1960	175.00	200.00

	Date	Price Range	

JESTER

A character known for his wit, he was often one who was instructed to use his wit to entertain nobility.

	Date	Price Range	
☐ D 5556, small	1936-	75.00	115.00
☐ same jug with an "A" mark		100.00	125.00

JOCKEY

Depicting a character who rides thoroughbred horses.

☐ D 6625, large	1971-1975	175.00	200.00

JOHN BARLEYCORN

Depicting a character in Old English ballads, familiar to many as the personification of whiskey or malt liquours. This jug was re-issued in 1978 as a limited edition of 7,500 for distribution in North America.

☐ D 5327, large	1934-1960	150.00	170.00
☐ same jug with an "A" mark		160.00	185.00
☐ D 5327, large signed by Doulton	1978-	110.00	140.00
☐ D 5735, small	1937-1960	75.00	90.00
☐ same jug with an "A" mark		85.00	100.00
☐ D 6041, miniature	1939-1960	65.00	75.00
☐ same jug with an "A" mark		70.00	80.00

JOHN PEEL

Immortalized in song by John Woodcock Graves in a song titled "D'ye ken John Peel" a man who had a passion for fox-hunting.

☐ D 5612, large	1936-1960	135.00	175.00
☐ same jug with an "A" mark		140.00	150.00
☐ D 5731, small	1937-1960	70.00	80.00
☐ same jug with an "A" mark		80.00	90.00
☐ D 6130, miniature	1940-1960	50.00	60.00
☐ same jug with an "A" mark		70.00	85.00
☐ D 6259, tiny	1947-1960	250.00	300.00

JOHNNY APPLESEED

Depicts the man John Chapman, whose nickname was "Johnny Appleseed", because he traveled on foot all across the Midwestern United States planting apple seeds near the cabins of early settlers.

☐ D 6372, large	1935-1969	250.00	300.00

	Date	Price Range
LAWYER, The Depicts an English lawyer with a quill for a handle.		
☐ **D 6498,** large	1959-	75.00
☐ **D 6504,** small	1959-	39.95
☐ **D 6524,** miniature	1960-	29.95
LOBSTER MAN Depicts a seaman, a jolly one, who sets out at night to set his pots for a lobster catch. Handle is a lobster.		
☐ **D 6617,** large	1968-	75.00
☐ **D 6620,** small	1968-	39.95
☐ **D 6652,** miniature	1981-	29.95
LONG JOHN SILVER Depicts one of the most famous fictional buccaneers. A character from the book "Treasure Island" by Robert Louis Stevenson. Handle is a parrot.		
☐ **D 6335,** large	1952-	75.00
☐ **D 6386,** small	1952-	39.95
☐ **D 6512,** miniature	1960-	29.95

Long John Silver, D6335, large, **75.00**

	Date	Price Range	

LORD NELSON
   Depicts Admiral Lord Nelson, one of
   England's great naval heroes.
☐ **D 6336**, large   1952-1969   275.00   325.00

Lord Nelson, D6336, large, **275.00 – 325.00**

LUMBERJACK
   Depicts the typical fellow who works
   in a lumber camp. His work was hard
   and often his only tool was an axe.
   Handle is a tree with an axe.
☐ **D 6610**, large   1967-1982   60.00   80.00
☐ **D 6613**, small   1967-1982   35.00   55.00

MACBETH
   Depicting one of the characters from
   a Shakespearian play.
☐ **D 6667**, large   1982-   75.00

Lumberjack, D6610, large, **60.00 – 80.00**

	Date	Price Range	
MAD HATTER			

MAD HATTER
Depicts a character from the book "Alice's Adventure in Wonderland" by Lewis Carroll. Handle is a mouse and a clock.

	Date	Price Range	
☐ **D 6598,** large	1965-1983	50.00	75.00
☐ **D 6602,** small	1965-1983	35.00	40.00
☐ **D 6606,** miniature	1965-1983	20.00	30.00

MARK TWAIN
Depicts the author of such well known classics as "The Adventures of Tom Sawyer" and "The Adventures of Huck Finn". His real name was Samuel Clemens, Mark Twain being a pen name.

	Date	Price Range
☐ **D 6654,** large	1980-	75.00
☐ **D 6694,** small	1983-	39.95

MEPHISTOPHELES

	Date	Price Range

A two faced jug showing a happy face and the sad face of the legendary figure most people associate with the devil to whom Faust sold his soul. It carries a verse on the bottom as shown in an illustration of this jug. Considered extremely rare.

	Date	Price Range	
☐ **D 5757**, large	1937-1948	2000.00	2500.00
☐ same jug with an "A" mark		2000.00	2500.00
☐ **D 5758**, small	1937-1948	1000.00	1250.00

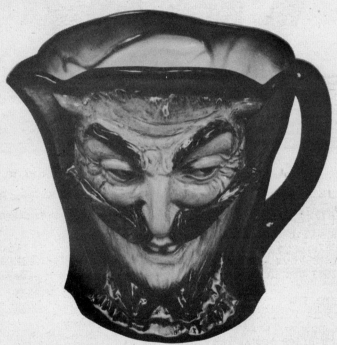

Mephistopheles, D5757, large, **2000.00 – 2500.00**

Mephistopheles, D5757, large, **2000.00 – 2500.00**

	Date	Price Range	
MERLIN			

Depicting the magician from the tales of King Arthur and The Knights of the Round Table. Has an owl for a handle.

	Date	Price Range	
☐ **D 6529,** large	1960-	75.00	
☐ **D 6536,** small	1960-	39.95	
☐ **D 6543,** miniature	1960-	29.95	

MIKADO, The

Depicts a Japanese Emperor. Probably most well remembered as a character in the opera "The Mikado" by Gilbert & Sullivan. Handle is a fan.

	Date	Price Range	
☐ **D 6501,** large	1959-1969	350.00	400.00
☐ **D 6507,** small	1959-1969	300.00	350.00
☐ **D 6525,** miniature	1960-1969	350.00	385.00

MINE HOST

Depicting a jovial and hospitable character from the nineteenth century.

	Date	Price Range	
☐ **D 6488,** large	1958-1981	60.00	80.00
☐ **D 6470,** small	1958-1981	35.00	55.00
☐ **D 6513,** miniature	1960-1981	20.00	30.00

The Mikado, D6501, large, **350.00 – 400.00**

	Date	Price Range	
MONTY			

Depicting the popular Field-Marshal Montgomery commander of the British forces who achieved great respect for his command of the 8th Army in North Africa and during the Allied invasion of Europe.

	Date	Price Range	
☐ D 6202, large	1946-	75.00	

MR. MICAWBER

Depicting a character from the Charles Dicken's classic tale "David Copperfield".

☐ **D 5843,** special size	1938-1948	110.00	160.00
☐ same jug with an "A" mark		135.00	160.00
☐ **D 5843,** small	1948-1960	75.00	100.00
☐ same jug with an "A" mark		85.00	110.00
☐ **D 6138,** miniature	1940-1960	45.00	55.00
☐ same jug with an "A" mark		55.00	65.00
☐ **D 6143,** tiny		110.00	135.00

	Date	Price Range	
MR. PICKWICK			

Depicting a character from another of Charles Dicken's classics "Pickwick Papers".

	Date	Price Range	
☐ **D 6060,** large	1940-1960	140.00	165.00
☐ same jug with an "A" mark		150.00	170.00
☐ **D 5839,** special size	1938-1948	140.00	165.00
☐ same jug with an "A" mark		150.00	170.00
☐ **D 5839,** small	1948-1960	50.00	70.00
☐ same jug with an "A" mark		55.00	75.00
☐ **D 6245,** miniature	1947-1960	55.00	70.00
☐ same jug with an "A" mark		65.00	85.00
☐ **D 6260,** tiny	1947-1960	175.00	250.00

NEPTUNE

Depicting the Roman God of the seas and rivers. Handle is a fish.

☐ **D 6548,** large	1961-	75.00	
☐ **D 6552,** small	1961-	39.95	
☐ **D 6555,** miniature	1961-	29.95	

NIGHT WATCHMAN

A character from the Williamburg series.

☐ **D 6569,** large	1963-1983	75.00	
☐ **D 6576,** small	1963-1983	39.95	
☐ **D 6583,** miniature	1963-1983	29.95	

NORTH AMERICAN INDIAN

Depicting the Chief of the Blackfoot tribe. Handle is a totem pole representing the thunderbird and bear mother.

☐ **D 6611,** large	1967-	75.00	
☐ **D 6614,** small	1967-	39.95	
☐ **D 6665,** miniature	1981-	29.95	

OLD CHARLEY

Depicting a night watchman of the eighteenth century.

☐ **D 5420,** large	1934-1983	75.00	
☐ same jug with an "A" mark		85.00	95.00
☐ **D 5527,** small	1935-1983	39.95	
☐ same jug with an "A" mark		75.00	85.00
☐ **D 6046,** miniature	1939-1983	29.95	
☐ same jug with an "A" mark		45.00	60.00
☐ **D 6144,** tiny	1940-1960	100.00	125.00

	Date	Price Range	

OLD KING COLE

Depicting the "merry old soul" from the familiar nursery rhyme Old King Cole. This jug is known to exist with a yellow crown instead of orange. It is also believed to have been made in both large and small size.

☐ D 6036, large	1939-1960	225.00	275.00
☐ yellow, large		1000.00	1500.00
☐ D 6037, small	1939-1960	80.00	125.00

OLD SALT

Depicting an old sailor whose face shows the many years he spent at sea, but smiling as he recalls the days he spend sailing. Handle is a mermaid.

☐ D 6551, large	1961-	75.00	
☐ D 6554, small	1961-	39.95	
☐ D 6557, miniature	1984-	29.95	

Old Salt, D6551, large, **75.00**

	Date	Price Range

OTHELLO

The Moor who murdered his beautiful wife Desdemona in a jealous rage having been convinced she was an adultress.

☐ **D 6673**, large   1982-   75.00

Othello, D6673, large, **75.00**

OWD MAC

The earlier version of Auld Mac. This jug depicts a thrifty Scotsman.

☐ **D 5823**, large   1938-1945   100.00   125.00

	Date	Price Range	

PADDY

Depicting a jolly Irish character. Paddy is the familiar nickname for Patrick. St. Patrick being the Patron Saint of Ireland.

	Date	Price Range	
☐ **D 5753**, large	1937-1960	125.00	150.00
☐ same jug with an "A" mark		135.00	165.00
☐ **D 5768**, small	1937-1960	55.00	65.00
☐ same jug with an "A" mark		65.00	75.00
☐ **D 6042**, miniature	1939-1960	50.00	65.00
☐ same jug with an "A" mark		60.00	75.00
☐ **D 6145**, tiny	1940-1960	100.00	125.00

PARSON BROWN

Depicting a typical Anglican parson of the eighteenth and nineteenth century.

	Date	Price Range	
☐ **D 5486**, large	1935-1960	95.00	115.00
☐ same jug with an "A" mark		110.00	135.00
☐ **D 5529**, small	1935-1960	60.00	70.00
☐ same jug with an "A" mark		65.00	75.00

PEARLY BOY

An early version of 'Arry except buttons are on the cap and around the collar. Known to be made in two colour variations. Blue variety considered rare.

	Date	Price Range	
☐ **D 6207**, large		1200.00	1500.00
☐ **D 6235**, small		700.00	800.00
☐ **D 6249**, miniature	1978-	500.00	700.00

PEARLY GIRL

An early version of 'Arriet except as in Pearly Boy buttons appear on the hat and the collar. Known to be made in two color variations. Blue variety is considered extremely rare.

	Date	Price Range	
☐ **D 6208**, large		1400.00	1750.00
☐ **D 6236**, small		600.00	800.00
☐ **D 6250**, miniature		600.00	700.00

PIED PIPER, The

Immortalized by Robert Browning, the Pied Piper of Hamelin was a figure of medieval legend.

	Date	Price Range	
☐ **D 6403**, large	1954-1980	75.00	
☐ **D 6462**, small	1957-1980	39.95	
☐ **D 6514**, miniature	1960-1980	29.95	

	Date	Price Range	

POACHER

Depicts a person who trespasses on other people's property illegally taking fish or game or personal property. Handle is a fish.

	Date	Price Range	
☐ **D 6429**, large	1955-	75.00	
☐ **D 6464**, small	1957-	39.95	
☐ **D 6515**, miniature	1960-	29.95	

PORTHOS

A character from "The Three Musketeers" by Alexandre Dumas.

☐ **D 6440**, large	1956-	75.00	
☐ **D 6453**, small	1956-	39.95	
☐ **D 6516**, miniature	1960-	29.95	

PUNCH AND JUDY MAN

Depicts the man who might resemble the original puppet showman. Handle is a puppet and the curtain.

☐ **D 6590**, large	1964-1969	550.00	650.00
☐ **D 6593**, small	1964-1969	400.00	450.00
☐ **D 6596**, miniature	1964-1969	375.00	425.00

REGENCY BEAU

Depicts a gentleman of the early nineteenth century who was instantly recognized for his fashionable clothes and elegant living.

☐ **D 6559**, large	1962-1967	550.00	625.00
☐ **D 6562**, small	1962-1967	375.00	450.00
☐ **D 6565**, miniature	1962-1967	500.00	600.00

RIP VAN WINKLE

Depicts a character from Washington Irving's "Sketch Book"

☐ **D 6438**, large	1955-	75.00	
☐ **D 6463**, small	1957-	39.95	
☐ **D 6517**, miniature	1960-	29.95	

ROBIN HOOD

Depicts the notorious outlaw who robbed the rich to feed the poor.

First Version

☐ **D 6205**, large	1947-1960	125.00	150.00
☐ **D 6234**, small	1947-1960	70.00	90.00
☐ same jug with an "A" mark		85.00	105.00
☐ **D 6252**, miniature	1947-1960	50.00	60.00
☐ same jug with an "A" mark		65.00	75.00

Punch and Judy Man, D6590, large, **575.00 - 650.00**

	Date	Price Range	
Second Version			
Different jug than the first version. Shows acorns and oak leaves on the hat and bow/arrow for the handle.			
☐ **D 6527,** large	1960-	75.00	
☐ **D 6534,** small	1960-	39.95	
☐ **D 6541,** miniature	1960-	29.95	
ROBINSON CRUSOE			
Depicts a character from the book "Robinson Crusoe" by Daniel Defoe.			
☐ **D 6532,** large	1960-1982	60.00	80.00
☐ **D 6539,** small	1960-1982	35.00	55.00
☐ **D 6546,** miniature	1960-1982	25.00	35.00

ROMEO

    Depicting the popular hero of centuries ago. Handle is the dagger which Juliet uses to stab herself on discovering her loved one's death.

	Date	Price Range
☐ **D 6670**, large	1983-	**75.00**

Romeo, D6670, large, **75.00**

ST. GEORGE

    Depicting the legendary character who saved the king's daughter by slaying the dragon. Handle is a dragon.

	Date	Price Range	
☐ **D 6618**, large	1968-1975	**125.00**	**150.00**
☐ **D 6621**, small	1968-1975	**65.00**	**90.00**

	Date	Price Range	
SAIREY GAMP			

Depicts the fat mid-wife from the Charles Dicken's book titled "The Life and Adventure of Martin Chuzzlewit".

	Date	Price Range	
☐ **D 5451,** large	1935-	75.00	
☐ same jug with an "A" mark		80.00	100.00
☐ **D 5528,** small	1935-	39.95	
☐ same jug with an "A" mark		60.00	75.00
☐ **D 6045,** miniature	1939-	29.95	
☐ same jug with an "A" mark		45.00	60.00
☐ **D 6146,** tiny	1940-1960	95.00	115.00

SAMUEL JOHNSON

Depicting the great English writer, most widely recognized for writing "Dictionary of the English Language".

	Date	Price Range	
☐ **D 6289,** large	1950-1960	250.00	275.00
☐ **D 6296,** small	1950-1960	175.00	200.00
☐ same jug with an "A" mark		210.00	240.00

SAM WELLER

Depicting a character from Charles Dicken's "Pickwick Papers".

	Date	Price Range	
☐ **D 6064,** large	1940-1960	110.00	165.00
☐ same jug with an "A" mark		125.00	150.00
☐ **D 5841,** special size	1938-1948	125.00	150.00
☐ **D 5841,** small	1948-1960	60.00	75.00
☐ same jug with an "A" mark		70.00	85.00
☐ **D 6140,** miniature	1940-1960	50.00	60.00
☐ same jug with an "A" mark		60.00	70.00
☐ **D 6147,** tiny	1940-1960	100.00	125.00

SANCHO PANZA

Depicting a character from Miguel de Cervantes book "Don Quixote".

	Date	Price Range	
☐ **D 6456,** large	1960-1982	65.00	85.00
☐ **D 6461,** small	1960-1982	40.00	60.00
☐ **D 6518,** miniature	1960-1982	25.00	35.00

SANTA CLAUS

Depicting the jovial character with his twinkling eyes and jolly expression. Handle is Rag doll.

	Date	Price Range	
☐ **D 6668,** large	1981 only	75.00	
☐ **D 6675,** large, handle is reindeer.	1982 only	75.00	
☐ **D 6690,** large, handle is Christmas stocking filled with toys.	1983 only	75.00	

	Date	Price Range	

SANTA CLAUS
A perfect interpretation of the character Santa Claus. He has a ruddy, wrinkled complexion, long white hair and full white beard. Scarlet red cap with matching red plain jug handle.

	Date	Price Range	
☐ **D 6704,** large	1984-	75.00	
☐ **D 6705,** small	1984-	39.95	
☐ **D 6706,** miniature	1984-	29.95	

SCARMOUCHE
Depicting a character probably from an Italian comedy, a buffoon.

☐ **D 6558,** large	1962-1967	500.00	600.00
☐ **D 6561,** small	1962-1967	375.00	425.00
☐ **D 6564,** miniature	1962-1967	350.00	425.00

SIMON THE CELLARER
Depicting the man who was in charge of the wine cellar. Shown in Elizabethan costume he was an expert on wines.

☐ **D 5504,** large	1935-1960	125.00	150.00
☐ same jug with an "A" mark		140.00	165.00
☐ **D 5616,** small	1936-1960	75.00	100.00
☐ same jug with an "A" mark		85.00	110.00

SIMPLE SIMON
Depicting the character in the well known nursery rhyme "Simple Simon".

☐ **D 6374,** large	1953-1960	525.00	575.00

SLEUTH
Depicting a character similar to the famous detective "Sherlock Holmes" from the books by Sir Arthur Conan Doyle. Handle is a pipe and magnifying glass.

☐ **D 6631,** large	1973-	75.00	
☐ **D 6635,** small	1973-	39.95	
☐ **D 6639,** miniature	1973-	29.95	

SMUGGLER
Depicting a member of a gang who smuggled goods into the country without paying duty, and whom dwellers along the coast feared.

☐ **D 6616,** large	1968-1980	55.00	75.00
☐ **D 6619,** small	1968-1980	35.00	55.00

	Date	Price Range	

SMUTS
Depicting Field Marshal Jan Christian Smuts.
☐ **D 6198,** large 1946-1948   1750.00 2250.00

TAM O'SHANTER
Depicting the character from the Robert Burns' poem "Tam O'Shanter". He was a farmer who barely escaped the witches.

	Date	Price Range	
☐ **D 6632,** large	1975-1979	75.00	100.00
☐ **D 6636,** small . . . . , ...	1973-1979	60.00	75.00
☐ **D 6640,** miniature	1973-1979	30.00	45.00

TOBY PHILPOTS
Depicting the familiar character from a mid-eighteenth century song. He has always been pictured as a seated male with a three cornered hat with the points being used as pouring spouts.

	Date	Price Range	
☐ **D 5736,** large	1937-1969	125.00	150.00
☐ same jug with an "A" mark		140.00	170.00
☐ **D 5737,** small	1937-1969	50.00	65.00
☐ same jug with an "A" mark		60.00	75.00
☐ **D 6043,** miniature	1939-1969	35.00	50.00
☐ same jug with an "A" mark		50.00	65.00

TONY WELLER
The father of Sam Weller, he was a coach driver.

	Date	Price Range	
☐ **D 5531,** large	1936-1960	125.00	150.00
☐ same jug with an "A" mark		125.00	150.00
☐ **D 5530,** small	1936-1960	50.00	60.00
☐ same jug with an "A" mark		60.00	75.00
☐ **D 6044,** miniature	1939-1960	40.00	50.00
☐ same jug with an "A" mark		50.00	60.00

TOUCHSTONE
Depicting the clown in Shakespeare's play "As You Like It".
☐ **D 5613,** large 1936-1960   225.00 300.00

	Date	Price Range	
TOWN CRIER			

TOWN CRIER
Depicts the eighteenth century man who called to the townspeople all the latest news, coming events, and meetings taking place plus many other important events before the event of newspapers.

	Date	Price Range	
☐ **D 6530**, large	1960-1973	175.00	225.00
☐ **D 6537**, small	1960-1973	100.00	125.00
☐ **D 6544**, miniature	1960-1973	125.00	150.00

TRAPPER
Depicting the northwoodsman of North America who trapped for fur bearing animals. Handle is a horn and snowshoes.

☐ **D 6609**, large	1967-	75.00	
☐ **D 6612**, small	1967-	39.95	

UGLY DUCHESS
A character from the Lewis Carroll book "Alice in Wonderland". Handle is a flamingo.

☐ **D 6599**, large	1965-1973	300.00	350.00
☐ **D 6603**, small	1965-1973	275.00	325.00
☐ **D 6607**, miniature	1965-1973	250.00	300.00

UNCLE TOM COBBLEIGH
Depicting a character from a nineteenth century song. Uncle Tom and others rode a horse to the Widdecombe Fair.

☐ **D 6337**, large	1952-1960	350.00	400.00

VETERAN MOTORIST
Depciting a driver in the Veteran Car Run held each year from London to Brighton.

☐ **D 6633**, large	1973-1983	55.00	75.00
☐ **D 6637**, small	1973-1983	35.00	50.00
☐ **D 6641**, miniature	1973-1983	20.00	30.00

VICAR OF BRAY, The
Depicting a country parson from an eighteenth century song.

☐ **D 5615**, large	1936-1960	175.00	200.00
☐ same jug with an "A" mark		180.00	225.00

VIKING

	Date	Price Range	
Depicting one of a band of Scandi-navian seafarers and explorers.
☐ D 6496, large	1959-1975	100.00	150.00
☐ D 6502, small	1959-1975	65.00	80.00
☐ D 6526, miniature	1960-1975	95.00	125.00

Viking, D6496, large, **100.00 – 150.00**

WALRUS AND CARPENTER

A character from the Lewis Carroll classic "Through The Looking Glass". Handle is a walrus.

☐ D 6600, large	1965-1979	75.00	100.00
☐ D 6604, small	1965-1979	55.00	70.00
☐ D 6608, miniature	1965-1979	35.00	50.00

WILLIAM SHAKESPEARE

Very recognizable with his Vandyke beard and bald head. Collar has the masks of comedy and tragedy. Handle is pen and quill.

☐ D 6689, large	1983-	75.00	

Walrus And Carpenter, D6600, large, **75.00 - 100.00**

YACHTSMAN	Date	Price Range	
Depicting a modern English sailing man. Handle is a sailboat.			
☐ **D 6622,** large	1971-1979	75.00	100.00

THE CELEBRITY COLLECTION

The Celebrity Collection introduced in the United States in 1983 will consist of well-known personalities from the entertainment field. Available in large size only.

W. C. FIELDS

	Date	Price Range

An excellent portrayal of the well-known personality. Black suit with pink carnation. Gray top hat, and the handle is the familiar black cane with silver top. Jug bears the inscription, "I was in love with a beautiful blonde once. She drove me to drink — it's the one thing I am indebted to her for." This was introduced as a Premier Edition for American Express which is stated on the base.

☐ **D 6674,** large 1983-   75.00

MAE WEST

Depicts the great platinum blonde with her liberal makeup and her silver fox wrap. This was introduced as a Premier Edition for American Express which is stated on the base.

☐ **D 6688,** large 1983-   75.00

LOUIS ARMSTRONG
☐ large............................. 1984-   75.00

GROUCHO MARX
☐ large............................. 1984-   75.00

CLARK GABLE
☐ large............................. 1984-   75.00

JIMMY DURANTE
☐ large............................. 1984-   75.00

Jimmy Durante, 75.00

TOBY JUGS

	Date	Price Range	
THE BEST IS NOT TOO GOOD Depicts a jovial character who loves his brew.			
☐ D 6107	1939-1960	225.00	275.00
CAP'N CUTTLE A character from the Charles Dicken's book "Dombey and Son".			
☐ D 6266	1948-1960	150.00	200.00
DOUBLE XX or THE MAN ON THE BARREL Depicts a person astride a barrel of brew yet still demanding another drink.			
☐ D 6088	1939-1969	250.00	350.00

The Best Is Not Too Good, D6107, **225.00 ~ 275.00**

FALSTAFF	Date	Price Range
Depicts a character in the Shakesperean plays "Henry VIII" and "The Merry Wives of Windsor".		
☐ D 6062	1939-	95.00
☐ D 6063	1939-	50.00

FAT BOY, The		
Depicts a character from Charles Dicken's "Pickwick Papers".		
☐ D 6264	1948-1960	200.00 225.00

HAPPY JOHN		
Depicts a seated character with a pitcher of ale in one hand and a glass full of ale in the other.		
☐ D 6031	1939-	95.00
☐ D 6070	1939-	45.00

Falstaff,
D6062,
95.00

	Date	Price Range
HONEST MEASURE Inscription reads "Honest Measure: Drink at Leisure". Sitting on the base and approximate 4½" tall this character is doing just that "taking it easy". ☐ **D 6108**	1939-	**45.00**
THE HUNTSMAN Depicts an English huntsman. ☐ **D 6320**	1950-	**95.00**
JOLLY TOBY Seated toby with a warm smile. ☐ **D 6109**	1939-	**65.00**
MISS NOSTRUM, THE NURSE Jolly lady with rosy cheeks. Wearing blue/black uniform with white apron. Hat same colour as uniform, grey hair. Fob watch on the bib of her apron. ☐ **D 6700**	1983-	**29.95**

Honest Measure,
D6108,
45.00

MR. FURROW, THE FARMER	Date	Price Range	
Depicting a man with weatherbeaten face indicating much time spent in the outdoors. Wears an old battered hat. He carries in one hand a riding crop and in the other corn. Coat is brown, his waistcoat yellow, green bow tie.			
☐ D 6701	1983-	29.95	
MR. LITIGATE, THE LAWYER			
Figure has long black coat, grey trousers, yellow vest. Gold watch chain. Traditional powdered wig.			
☐ D 6699	1983-	29.95	
MR. MICAWBER			
Depicts a character from Charles Dicken's book "David Copperfield".			
☐ D 6262	1948-1960	150.00	200.00

	Date	Price Range	

MR. PICKWICK
 A character from Charles Dicken's
 book "Pickwick Papers".
 ☐ **D 6261** 1948-1960   150.00   200.00

OLD CHARLEY
 Seated character depicting an early
 nineteenth century nightwatchman.
 ☐ **D 6030** 1939-1960   160.00   225.00
 ☐ **D 6069** 1939-1960   150.00   200.00

Old Charley,
D6030,
160.00 - 225.00

REV. CASSOCK, THE CLERGYMAN
 Dressed in a black jacket, wearing a
 clerical collar, grey uniform under
 jacket. Carrying an open bible.
 ☐ **D 6702** 1983-   29.95

SAIREY GAMP
 A character from Charles Dicken's
 book "Martin Chuzzlewit".
 ☐ **D 6263** 1948-1960   150.00   200.00

	Date	Price Range	

SAM WELLER
Depicts a character from Charles Dicken's "Pickwick Papers".

☐ D 6265 . . . . 1948-1960 200.00 225.00

SHERLOCK HOLMES
Depicting the famous sleuth from Sir Arthur Conan Doyle's many mystery books. Released to commemorate the fiftieth anniversary of the death of Sir Arthur.

☐ D 6661 . . . . 1981- 95.00

THE SQUIRE
Depicts a character known to exist in early medieval times He was all around assistant to a knight and often accompanied him into battle. In later years this title was given to young men of good family training who would later become knights themselves.

☐ D 6319 . . . . 1950-1969 250.00 300.00

SIR FRANCES DRAKE
Depicts this famous nobleman kneeling as if to bow before the queen. Released to commemorate the 400th anniversary of the arrival of Sir Frances Drake and his ship's landing at Plymouth.

☐ D 6660 . . . . 1981- 95.00

SIR WINSTON CHURCHILL
Depicting the statesman and Prime Minister of Great Britain. Earlier models bear the inscription "Winston Churchill Prime Minister of Great Britain 1940".

☐ D 6171, large 1941- 95.00
☐ D 6172, small 1941- 65.00
☐ D 6175, miniature 1941- 45.00

Sir Francis Drake,
D6660,
large, **95.00**

Winston Churchill,
D6171,
large, **95.00**

NEW DOULTONVILLE TOBY JUGS

	Date	Price Range
MR. TONSIL, THE TOWN CRIER Cries of "Hear Ye Hear Ye" can almost be heard as he rings his golden bell. Character is dressed in silver gray wig, plumed hat and purple coat.		
☐ D 6713	1984-	29.95
MADAME CRYSTAL, THE CLAIRVOYANT Character is wearing a purple skirt with pink shawl, green turban wrapped around her head.		
☐ D 6714	1984-	29.95
MRS. LOAN, THE LIBRARIAN Green skirt with light green blouse, brown hair. Character is sternly watching to keep the silence in the library.		
☐ D 6715	1984-	29.95
BETTY BITTERS, THE BARMAID Gaily dressed in purple skirt with green blouse. Accenting her blouse is a string of pearls.		
☐ D 6716	1984-	29.95

MISCELLANEOUS ITEMS

Royal Doulton has produced a number of miscellaneous items which do not fall into any of the major categories. These have mostly been in the class of novelties or novelty giftware, with adaptations of characters from its jugs. The Ash Trays and Ash Bowls (ash bowls are large receptacles for emptying pipe ashes) bear a variety of characters, following no special theme. All of the Busts feature Dickens characters, and these are supplemented by the Dickens Jugs and Tankards. The characters of Charles Dickens seem ideally suited to Doultonware; although fictional, they seem to typify traditional British "types" known all over the world. All the works listed in this section are out of production and have acquired solid collecto status.

ASH TRAYS

DICK TURPIN			
☐ D 5601	1936-1960	100.00	125.00

Left to Right: **John Barleycorn,** D5602, **85.00 – 125.00**
Dick Turpin, D5601, **100.00 – 125.00**

	Date	Price Range	
JOHN BARLEYCORN			
☐ D 5602	1936-1960	85.00	125.00
OLD CHARLEY			
☐ D 5599	1936-1960	100.00	125.00
PARSON BROWN			
☐ D 5600	1936-1960	85.00	125.00

ASH BOWLS

	Date	Price Range	
AULD MAC			
☐ D 6006	1939-1960	100.00	125.00

Left to Right: **Sairey Gamp,** D6009, **100.00 – 125.00**
Parson Brown, D6008, **100.00 – 125.00**

	Date	Price Range	
FARMER JOHN			
☐ D 6007	1939-1960	100.00	125.00
OLD CHARLEY			
☐ D 5925	1938-1960	100.00	125.00
PADDY			
☐ D 5926	1938-1960	100.00	125.00

PARSON BROWN	Date	Price Range	
☐ D 6008	1939-1960	100.00	125.00
SAIREY GAMP			
☐ D 6009	1939-1960	100.00	125.00

BUSTS

BUZ FUZ			
☐ D 6048	1939-1960	75.00	100.00
MR. MICAWBER			
☐ D 6050	1939-1960	65.00	85.00
MR. PICKWICK			
☐ D 6049	1939-1960	75.00	100.00
SAIREY GAMP			
☐ D 6047	1939-1960	65.00	85.00
SAM WELLER			
☐ D 6052	1939-1960	65.00	85.00
TONY WELLER			
☐ D 6051	1939-1960	65.00	85.00

DEWARS WHISKEY FLASKS

BEN JOHNSON			
☐ D		225.00	275.00
BONNIE PRINCE CHARLIE			
☐ D		200.00	250.00
FALSTAFF			
☐ D		200.00	255.00
GEORGE THE GUARD			
☐ D		200.00	250.00
JOVIAL MONK			
☐ D		250.00	300.00
MICAWBER			
☐ D		200.00	250.00
MR. MICAWBER			
☐ D	1983-	65.00	

	Date	Price Range	
MACNABB			
☐ D		250.00	275.00
JOHN DEWARS & SON			
☐ D Stoneware Egyptian design ..		175.00	225.00
OYEZ, OYEZ			
☐ D		275.00	325.00
PIED PIPER			
☐ D		200.00	250.00
SPORTING SQUIRE			
☐ D		225.00	250.00
WATCHMAN			
☐ D		225.00	275.00
TONY WELLER			
☐ D		200.00	250.00

DICKENS JUGS AND TANKARDS

	Date	Price Range	
OLD CURIOSITY SHOP JUG Figures in relief of Little Nell and her grandfather on one side, and the Marchioness on the other.			
☐ D 5584	1935-1960	125.00	175.00
OLD LONDON JUG Depicts London during the time of Charles Dickens with Old Charley on one side and Sairey Gamp on the other.			
☐ D 6291	1949-1960	200.00	275.00
OLIVER TWIST JUG.			
☐ D 5617	1937-1960	125.00	175.00
OLIVER TWIST JUG Oliver asking for more.			
☐ D 6285	1936-1960	225.00	275.00
OLIVER TWIST TANKARD Oliver watching the Artful Dodger picking a pocket.			
☐ D 6286	1949-1960	200.00	250.00

PEGGOTTY JUG	Date	Price Range	
Depicting a scene from David Copper-field.			
☐ D 6292	1949-1960	275.00	350.00

PICKWICK PAPERS JUGS			
Depicts the characters from Dickens book "The Pickwick Papers" outside the White Hart Inn.			
☐ D 5756	1937-1960	150.00	225.00

PLATES

This terminology is strictly British and is often misunderstood by Americans. A "head rack plate" is a plate designed to be displayed on a wall or in a cabinet ("rack"), rather than used as tableware. *Head* rack means that the plate carries a human likeness. Royal Doulton's Head Rack Plates have borne portraits of characters from the novels of Charles Dickens, as well as miscellaneous types both historical and fictional. In addition to Head Rack Plates, the factory has also made Scenic Rack Plates, which have landscape views, often including colorful wildlife.

Though we live in an age of plate collecting and might think decorative plates to be something new, the concept of Head Rack and Scenic Rack Plates dates back very far. Beautifully enameled majolica plates, with painted scenes, were made in Italy in the 15th century. English porcelain factories began putting them out in the 1700's, for use on elegant tables. But many were in fact purchased to use as wall decorations. In the early Victorian era (1840's) a vogue developed in England for encircling whole rooms with these plates, on upper walls near the ceiling. This gave further impetus to the manufacturers. Royal Doulton has been making decorative plates for many years. Interested collectors might want to seek out some of the early issues, in addition to the modern ones listed here.

These plates are issued without serial numbers.

Back in the early 1970's when the collector plate market was in somewhat of a turmoil, plaques with poor examples of what was supposed to be quality plates at high prices, and a seemingly get-rich quick attitude of many persons the Doulton Company conceived the idea of transferring quality works of art by good artists, some well-known, some not, on to plates of highest quality with great emphasis on the finished product being as near the artists original work as possible.

After considerable thought the Collectors International was established to issue products of Fine Art on Fine China. The first plate being introduced in 1973 with a series of Mothers Day plates by artist, Edna Hibel. Following is the entire series offered since 1973 bearing the secondary market prices as of the current date.

HEAD RACK PLATES
CHARLES DICKENS SERIES

	Size	Price	Range
☐ **Artful Dodger**	10¼ "	50.00	65.00
☐ **Barkis**	10¼ "	65.00	80.00
☐ **Cap'n Cuttle**	10¼ "	65.00	80.00
☐ **Fagin**	9½ "	45.00	55.00
☐ **Fat Boy**	10¼ "	50.00	65.00
☐ **Mr. Micawber**	10¼ "	50.00	65.00
☐ **Mr. Pickwick**	10¼ "	65.00	80.00
☐ **Old Peggoty**	10¼ "	65.00	80.00
☐ **Poor Jo**	10¼ "	50.00	65.00
☐ **Sairey Gamp**	10¼ "	65.00	80.00
☐ **Sam Weller**	10¼ "	50.00	65.00
☐ **Serjeant Buzfuz**	10¼ "	65.00	80.00
☐ **Tony Weller**	10¼ "	50.00	65.00

HISTORICAL BRITAIN SERIES

English Translucent China plates

	Size	Price	Range
☐ **Anne Hathaway's Cottage** Shottery Near Stratford-on-Avon	10½ "	40.00	50.00
☐ **Clovelly, North Devon**	10½ "	35.00	45.00
☐ **House of Parliament,** London	10½ "	35.00	45.00
☐ **Tower of London**	10½ "	45.00	55.00
☐ **Tudor Mansion**	10½ "	50.00	60.00

MISCELLANEOUS

	Size	Price	Range
☐ **The Admiral**	10¼ "	55.00	70.00
☐ **Arabian Knights**	10¼ "	70.00	85.00
☐ **Bradley Golfers** Pictures of men golfing with sayings printed around the plate very early 1900 era	10¼ "	150.00	200.00
☐ **Charles Dickens**	10¼ "	70.00	85.00
☐ **The Cobbler**	10¼ "	40.00	55.00
☐ **The Doctor**	10¼ "	40.00	55.00
☐ **Don Quixote**	10¼ "	50.00	65.00
☐ **The Falconer**	10¼ "	45.00	60.00
☐ **Falstaff**	10¼ "	50.00	65.00
☐ **Gaffers**	10¼ "	50.00	65.00
☐ **The Hunting Man**	10¼ "	70.00	85.00
☐ **Jackdaw of Reims**	10¼ "	50.00	65.00
☐ **The Jester**	10¼ "	60.00	75.00
☐ **The Mayor**	10¼ "	70.00	85.00
☐ **Omar Khayyam**	10¼ "	65.00	80.00
☐ **Ophelia,** Shakespeare	10¼ "	65.00	80.00
☐ **Othelo,** The Moor of Venice Act IV	10¼ "	70.00	85.00
☐ **The Parson**	10¼ "	40.00	55.00
☐ **Robert Burns**	10¼ "	40.00	55.00
☐ **Shakespeare**	10¼ "	40.00	50.00
☐ **The Squire**	10¼ "	40.00	55.00

SCENIC RACK PLATES

	Size	Price	Range
☐ **African Elephants**	10¼ "	25.00	35.00
☐ **Australian Aborigine**	10¼ "	20.00	25.00
☐ **Bow Valley**	10¼ "	30.00	40.00
☐ **Giraffes**	10¼ "	25.00	35.00
☐ **Koala Bears**	10¼ "	25.00	35.00
☐ **Lake Louise and Victoria Glacier**	10¼ "	22.50	35.00
☐ **Lioness**	10¼ "	35.00	45.00
☐ **Maritime Provinces**	10¼ "	25.00	35.00
☐ **Mother Kangaroo with Joey**	10¼ "	30.00	40.00
☐ **Mount Egmont**	10¼ "	20.00	30.00
☐ **Murray River Gums**	10¼ "	20.00	30.00
☐ **Niagara Falls**	10¼ "	25.00	35.00
☐ **Vermilion Lake and Mount Rundle**	10¼ "	20.00	30.00
☐ **Young Kookaburras**	10¼ "	35.00	45.00

ANIMAL PLATES

A dozen 10¼ " size plates bearing one or more full-body dogs were produced; also one signed Cecil Aldin. There was a series of 7½ " plates with head studies. Collectors have been able to find five breeds that are known, however, it has been suggested probably a dozen were made all prior to 1944.

☐ **Dogs,** signed Cecil Aldin	10¼ "	90.00	110.00
☐ **Dogs,** Cocker Spaniel	10¼ "	35.00	50.00
☐ **Dogs,** Cocker Spaniel Head Study	7½ "	50.00	75.00
☐ **Dogs,** English Setter	10½ "	40.00	60.00
☐ **Dogs,** Hounds	10¼ "	40.00	60.00
☐ **Dogs,** Irish Setter Head Study	7½ "	50.00	75.00
☐ **Dogs,** Labrador Retriever Head Study	7½ "	50.00	75.00
☐ **Dogs,** Pointer	10¼ "	40.00	60.00
☐ **Dogs,** Scottish Terrier	10¼ "	35.00	50.00
☐ **Dogs,** Sealyham Terrier Head Study	7½ "	50.00	75.00

SERIES PLATES

Title	Year	Edition Size	Issue Price
"BEHIND THE PAINTED MASQUE" by Ben Black			
☐ **Painted Feelings**	1982	10000	95.00
☐ **Make Me Laugh**	1983	10000	95.00
☐ **Minstrel Seranade**	1984	10000	95.00
"AMERICAN TAPESTRIES" by C. A. Brown			
☐ **Sleigh Bells**	1978	15000	70.00
☐ **Pumpkin Patch**	1979	15000	70.00
☐ **General Store**	1981	10000	95.00
☐ **Fourth of July**	1982	10000	95.00

"Painted Feelings"
Artist: Ben Black
95.00

"Sleigh Bells"
Artist: C.A. Brown
70.00

"Pumpkin Patch"
Artist: C.A. Brown
70.00

"General Store"
Artist: C.A. Brown
95.00

"4th Of July"
Artist: C.A. Brown
95.00

Title	Year	Edition Size	Issue Price
"FESTIVAL CHILDREN OF THE WORLD" by Brenda Burke			
☐ **Mariana** (Balanese)	1983	15000	65.00
☐ **Magdalena** (Mexico)	1984	15000	65.00
"REFLECTIONS OF CHINA" by Chen Chi			
☐ **Garden of Tranquility**	1976	15000	90.00
☐ **Imperial Palace**	1977	15000	80.00
☐ **Temple of Heaven**	1978	15000	75.00
☐ **Lake of Mists**	1980	15000	85.00
"ALL GOD'S CHILDREN" by Lisette DeWinne			
☐ **A Brighter Day**	1978	10000	75.00
☐ **Village Children**	1980	10000	85.00
☐ **Noble Heritage**	1981	10000	85.00
☐ **Buddies**	1982	10000	85.00
☐ **My Little Brother**	1983	10000	95.00

"Magdalena"
Artist: Brenda Burke
65.00

"Mariana"
Artist: Brenda Burke
65.00

"Garden Of Tranquility"
Artist: Chen Chi
90.00

"Imperial Palace"
Artist: Chen Chi
80.00

"Temple Of Heaven"
Artist: Chen Chi
75.00

"Lake Of Mists"
Chen Chi
85.00

"A Brighter Day"
Artist: Lisette DeWinne
75.00

"Village Children"
Artist: Lisette DeWinne
85.00

"Noble Heritage"
Artist: Lisette DeWinne
85.00

"Buddies"
Artist: Lisette DeWinne
85.00

"My Little Brother"
Artist: Lisette DeWinne
95.00

Title	Year	Edition Size	Issue Price
"MOTHER AND CHILD" by Edna Hibel			
☐ Colette and Child	1973	15000	500.00
☐ Sayuri and Child	1974	15000	175.00
☐ Kristina and Child	1975	15000	125.00
☐ Marilyn and Child	1976	15000	110.00
☐ Lucia and Child	1977	15000	90.00
☐ Kathleen and Child	1981	15000	85.00
"CHILDREN OF THE PUEBLO" by Mimi Jungbluth			
☐ Apple Flower	1983	15000	60.00
☐ Morning Star	1984	15000	60.00

"Colette And Child"
Artist: Edna Hibel
500.00

"Sayuri And Child"
Artist: Edna Hibel
175.00

"Kristina And Child"
Artist: Edna Hibel
125.00

"Marilyn And Child"
Artist: Edna Hibel
110.00

"Lucia And Child"
Artist: Edna Hibel
90.00

"Kathleen And Child"
Artist: Edna Hibel
85.00

"Apple Flower"
Artist: Mimi Jungbluth
60.00

"Morning Star"
Artist: Mimi Jungbluth
60.00

Title	Year	Edition Size	Issue Price
"PORTS OF CALL" by Doug Kingman			
☐ San Francisco, Fisherman's Wharf	1975	15000	**90.00**
☐ New Orleans, Royal Street	1976	15000	**80.00**
☐ Venice, Grand Canal	1977	15000	**65.00**
☐ Paris, Montmartre	1978	15000	**70.00**
"PORTRAITS OF INNOCENCE" by Francisco Masseria			
☐ Panchito	1980	15000	**300.00**
☐ Adrien	1981	15000	**85.00**
☐ Angelica	1982	15000	**95.00**
☐ Juliana	1983	15000	**95.00**
"GRANDPARENTS" by Mago			
☐ Grandfather and Children	1984	15000	**95.00**

"New Orleans"
Artist: Dong Kingman
90.00

"Venice"
Artist: Dong Kingman
65.00

"Panchito"
Artist: Francisco Masseria
300.00

"Adrien"
Artist: Francisco Masseria
85.00

"Angelica"
Artist: Francisco Masseria
95.00

"Juliana"
Artist: Francisco Masseria
95.00

Title	Year	Edition Size	Issue Price

"COMMEDIA DELL'ARTE" by LeRoy Neiman

☐ Harlequin	1974	15000	100.00
☐ Pierrot	1975	15000	90.00
☐ Columbine	1977	15000	80.00
☐ Punchinello	1978	15000	75.00
☐ Winning Colors. Although not part of the Commedia Dell'Arte Series, this plate was offered in recognition of the vast popularity of LeRoy Neiman's most notable subject matter	1980	10000	85.00

"JUNGLE FANTASY" by Gustavo Novoa

☐ The Ark	1979	10000	75.00
☐ Compassion	1981	10000	95.00
☐ Patience	1982	10000	95.00
☐ Refuge	1983	10000	95.00

"I REMEMBER AMERICA" by Eric Sloane

☐ Pennsylvania Pastorale	1977	15000	90.00
☐ Lovejoy Bridge	1978	15000	80.00
☐ Four Corners	1979	15000	75.00
☐ Marshlands	1981	15000	95.00

"LOG OF THE DASHING WAVE" by John Stobart

☐ Sailing with the Tide	1976	15000	115.00
☐ Running Free	1977	15000	110.00
☐ Rounding the Horn	1978	15000	85.00
☐ Hong Kong	1979	15000	75.00
☐ Bora Bora	1981	15000	95.00
☐ Journeys End	1982	15000	95.00

"FLOWER GARDEN" by Hahn Vidal

☐ Spring Harmony	1975	15000	80.00
☐ Dreaming Lotus	1976	15000	90.00
☐ From the Poet's Garden	1977	15000	75.00
☐ Country Bouquet	1978	15000	75.00
☐ From My Mother's Garden	1980	15000	85.00

"CELEBRATION OF FAITH" by James Woods

☐ Rosh Hoshanah	1982	7500	250.00
☐ Yom Kippur	1983	7500	250.00
☐ Passover	1984	7500	250.00

"CHARACTER" PLATES

Series limited to the period of issue each year. Entire series discontinued as of January 1, 1984.

☐ Old Balloon Seller	1979	year	85.00
☐ Balloon Man	1980	year	100.00
☐ Silk and Ribbons	1981	year	100.00
☐ Biddy Penny Farthing	1982	year	100.00

"Columbine"
Artist: LeRoy Neiman
80.00

"Punchinello"
Artist: LeRoy Neiman
75.00

The Ark
Artist: Gustavo Novoa
75.00

"Compassion"
Artist: Gustavo Novoa
95.00

"Patience"
Artist: Gustavo Novoa
95.00

"Pennsylvania"
Artist: Eric Sloane
90.00

"Lovejoy Bridge"
Artist: Eric Sloane
80.00

"Four Corners"
Artist: Eric Sloane
75.00

"Marshlands"
Artist: Eric Sloane
95.00

"Sailing With The Tide"
Artist: John Stobart
115.00

"Rounding The Horn"
Artist: John Stobart
85.00

"Hong Kong"
Artist: John Stobart
75.00

"Bora Bora"
Artist: John Stobart
95.00

"Journey's End"
Artist: John Stobart
95.00

"Spring Harmony"
Artist: Hahn Vidal
80.00

"Dreaming Lotus"
Artist: Hahn Vidal
90.00

"From The Poet's Garden"
Artist: Hahn Vidal
75.00

"Country bouquet"
Artist: Hahn Vidal
75.00

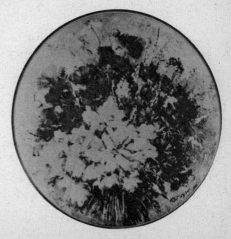

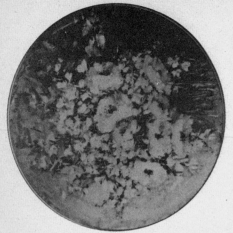

"From My Mother's Garden"
Artist: Hahn Vidal
85.00

"Rosh Hashanah"
Artist: James Woods
250.00

"Old Balloon Seller"
85.00

"Balloon Man"
100.00

"Silk And Ribbons"
100.00

"Biddy Penny Farthing"
100.00

Title	Year	Edition Size	Issue Price
"AROUND THE WORLD SERIES"			
Beswick Christmas Plates			
☐ Christmas in Old England.................	1972	15000	35.00
☐ Christmas in Mexico......................	1973	15000	37.50
☐ Christmas in Bulgaria....................	1974	15000	37.50
☐ Christmas in Norway.....................	1975	15000	45.00
☐ Christmas in Holland	1976	15000	50.00
☐ Christmas in Poland	1977	15000	50.00
☐ Christmas in America	1978	15000	55.00
"VICTORIAN ERA" CHRISTMAS PLATES			
Series limited to the period of issue each year.			
☐ Winter Fun	1977	year	55.00
☐ Christmas Day	1978	year	25.00
☐ Christmas................................	1979	year	30.00
☐ Santa's Visit............................	1980	year	33.00
☐ Christmas Carolers	1981	year	37.50
☐ Santa on Bicycle	1982	year	39.95
"VICTORIAN ERA" VALENTINE PLATES			
Series limited to the period of issue each year.			
☐ Victorian Boy and Girl	1976	year	65.00
☐ My Sweetest Friend	1977	year	40.00
☐ If I Loved You	1978	year	40.00
☐ My Valentine	1979	year	35.00
☐ Valentine	1980	year	33.00
☐ Valentine Boy and Girl...................	1981	year	35.00
☐ Angel with Mandolin	1982	year	39.95

"CHILDHOOD SERIES" CHRISTMAS PLATES
Series will consist of six plates each featuring a young child. Series limited to the period of issue each year.

☐ Silent Night	1983	year	

"Christmas In Old England"
35.00

"Christmas In Mexico"
37.00

"Christmas In Bulgaria"
37.50

"Christmas In Norway"
45.00

"Christmas In America"
55.00

"Winter Fun"
55.00

"Christmas Day"
25.00

"Christmas Sleigh Ride"
30.00

"Santa's Visit"
33.00

"Christmas Carolers"
37.50

"Santa On Bicycle"
39.95

"Christmas Carols"
39.95

"Victorian Boy And Girl"
65.00

"My Valentine"
35.00

"Valentine Boy And Girl"
35.00

"Valentine"
33.00

"Angel With Mandolin"
39.95

"To My Sweet Valentine"
39.95

FLAMBÉ

This article is excerpted from the Royal Doulton International Collectors Club Magazine with permission of Royal Doulton Tableware, Limited, Stoke-on-Trent, England.

Royal Doulton are justifiably proud of their famous flambé glazes. They were the first British firm to achieve consistent success with these exotic Oriental glaze effects and consequently to put them into commercial production. Experimentation began in the 1890's and since that date their discoveries have remained a closely guarded secret. According to C. J. Noke, the only outsider ever to have had the technique explained to him was King George V and he was certain it would be safe with him! Flambé artists have a gentlemen's agreement never to divulge details of the process and even today, visitors are never shown round the studio which specializes in this ware.

Why all this cloak and dagger intrigue? It dates back to the late nineteenth century when leading European ceramicists vied with each other to emulate the rich ruby glazes perfected by the Chinese. No recipes existed and each potter and chemist went through long periods of trial and error. At Doulton's the art director John Slater and the young Charles Noke had put their heads together and by 1900 had succeeded in producing the occasional good specimen. That year the manager's son Cuthbert Bailey joined the firm and he immediately became fascinated by the research. He set up a camp bed in his studio and stayed there day and night when a firing was going on. Essential ingredients of the flambé glaze, such as copper, had been established but the most important factor to gain control of was the kiln and how much and when to reduce the oxygen levels in order to make the copper turn red. Consistency in this field eluded them until they commissioned the help of Bernard Moore, a local consultant potter. He had already achieved some measure of success independently and so before long their combined expertise and resources came to fruition. Royal Doulton were able to launch their new flambé wares at the St. Louis Exhibition in 1904 and the reception was overwhelming. Even from the outset, they were considered to be collectors items, worthy of a place in the finest museums. Over the years, flambé glaze has been applied to hundreds of different Oriental style vases, bowls and plaques, as well as to a host of animal models. and occasional figures.

When Cuthbert Bailey, who had been the driving force in the rediscovery of flambé left Doulton in 1907, Charles Noke took on the responsibility for the further development of the transmutation glazes. During the first World War, when his modelling skills were less in demand, he evolved the *Sung* wares which are distinguished by more pronouced veinings in bright yellows, blues and greens. The scope of this new glaze, which was publicly launched in 1920, was vast. Artists such as Harry Nixon, Arthur Eaton and Fred Moore now had a wider color palette with which to create appropriate images of birds of paradise, fantastic dragons and tropical fish.

As well as the hand painted variety, there were many *Sung* wares which relied for their appeal on form and glaze alone. Texture also preoccupied Noke and by 1925 he had developed the most tactile of the transmutation glazes, the *Chang* Wares. The shapes were fashioned in a coarse refractory marl, often with the throwing rings left for effect. Over this trickled thick, viscous glazes in a myriad of colors. Collector interest in the distinctive *Chang* wares is enormous, so much so that unusual pieces have been selling at the rate of $200 per inch.

As well as the prestige wares such as *Sung* and *Chang* there were also less expensive flambé glazes. Mottled flambé, where the different metallic oxides were daubed on to create splashes of bright color when fired, were quicker and therefore less expensive to produce. Also very much in vogue since the thirties, has been landscape flambé in which pastoral scenes are part printed and part painted to form a silhouette under a deep red glaze. A more recent development of this style is the woodcut flambé which features the romantic landscapes of Thomas Beswick, the famous 18th century engraver. Woodcut flambé was introduced by art director Jo Ledger shortly after he joined Royal Doulton in 1955 and the flambé experimentation continues to flourish under his direction.

Alongside all the continuing research into the reduction fired flambé glazes, other experimental glaze effects were being developed. Lustre glazes also require a reducing atmosphere to create their metallic sheen from oxides of gold, silver, platinum and copper, so it is not surprising to find a wide range of effects dating from the same time as the flambé developments. Examples of 'peach blow', 'haricot', iridescent peacock hues, and silvery mother of pearl will all be included in the displays.

Royal Doulton's preoccupation with experimental glazes reflected the activities of many European and American potteries. All admired the crystalline glazes pioneered in Scandinavia which featured random groups of frost-like crystals. Bailey and Noke succeeded in controlling the cooling of a special glaze to create this effect in 1907. Most crystalline wares are in pastel shades but the technique was also occasionally used in conjunction with flambé and *Titanian* glazes.

The development of the latter in 1915 was yet another string to Mr. Noke's bow. Titanium was an essential component of the glaze, responsible for the ethereal blue coloring which formed an ideal background for evocative painting of birds, insects or fairy revels by artists such as Harry Nixon or Harry Tittensor. A much deeper ultramarine blue was also developed to simulate the semi-precious stone Lapis Lazuli, but very little of this turns up today, so production must have been limited. Equally hard to find is *Chinese Jade,* a white glazed ware with green veins imitating the translucent stone much venerated by the Chinese. Figure and animal models, as well vases and bowls based on chinese bronze prototypes, were decorated with Noke's new glaze which was introduced in 1920.

BOWL

	Price Range	
☐ Veined Sung, 8″ round	700.00	750.00

BUDDHA

☐ Veined Sung, 7″	1100.00	1200.00

CAT

☐ Rouge, No. 9, 4¾″	75.00	85.00
☐ Rouge, No. 2259, 12″	300.00	350.00

DRAGON

☐ Veined Sung, No. 2085, 8″	500.00	550.00

DRAKE

☐ Rouge, No. 137, 6″	85.00	95.00
☐ Rouge, No. 806, 6″	500.00	550.00

DUCK

☐ Rouge, No. 112, 1½″	55.00	60.00
☐ Rouge, No. 395, 2½″	55.00	60.00

$ 1. 40.

		Price Range	

ELEPHANT

☑ Rouge, 9″, tusks down	300.00	350.00
☐ Rouge, No. 489, white tusks, 7″	300.00	350.00
☐ Rouge, No. 489A, 5½″	115.00	150.00

FISH

☐ Veined Sung, 12″	1000.00	1100.00

FOX, LYING

☐ Rouge, No. 29, 12″	550.00	600.00
☐ Rouge 29B, 1″	60.00	75.00

FOX, SITTING

☐ Rouge, No. 12, (Head pointed down), 5″	75.00	95.00
☐ Rouge, No. 14, 4″	85.00	100.00

FROG

☐ 2″	135.00	175.00

HARE, LYING

☐ Rouge, No. 656A, 1¾″	60.00	75.00
☐ Rouge, No. 1157, 2¾″	85.00	100.00

LADY SEATED WITH FLOWING CLOAK

☐ Veined, rare, 5½″	1200.00	1300.00

LAUGHING CAVALIER SUNG PLATE

☐ 10″	150.00	200.00

LEAPING SALMON

☐ Rouge, No. 666, 12″	450.00	550.00

MONKEY

☐ Seated, arms folded, HN 118, 2¾″	200.00	250.00

MONKEYS

☐ Rouge, No. 486, two in embrace	250.00	300.00

MOUSE ON A CUBE

☐ Rouge, HN 255	250.00	300.00

NUDE ON A ROCK

☐ HN 604, 4½″ (considered rare)	700.00	800.00

OWL

Price Range

☐ Veined, No. 2249, 12″ 300.00   350.00

PENGUIN

☐ Rouge, No. 84, 6″ 95.00   115.00
☐ Rouge, No. 585, 9″ 700.00   800.00

PIPER MINSTREL

☐ 16″ 1350.00   1500.00

PUPPY SITTING

☐ Rouge, HN 128, 4″ 250.00   300.00

RABBIT, EAR UP

☐ Rouge, No. 113, 2½″ 85.00   100.00
☐ Memu Holder 175.00   225.00

RHINOCEROS

☐ Veined, No. 615, 12″ 800.00   850.00

SOW

☐ 2½″ x 5″ 300.00   350.00

TIGER

☐ Rouge, No. 809, 6″ 650.00   700.00

TRAY

☐ Veined, No. 1620, 4″ 45.00   55.00
☐ Veined, No. 1621, 6″ 75.00   85.00
☐ Woodcut, No. 1620, 4⅛″ 45.00   55.00
☐ Woodcut, No. 1621, 7½″ 100.00   125.00

VASE

☐ Landscape, 14″ high, 7″ round, old mark 750.00   900.00
☐ Landscape, No. 3879, 5¼″, signed O.C.K. 175.00   225.00
☐ No. 1622, large size 1100.00   1200.00
☐ No. 1623, large size 1100.00   1200.00
☐ No. 1624, large size 1100.00   1200.00
☐ Veined, No. 1605, 4¼″ 85.00   100.00
☐ Veined, No. 1612, 8″ 125.00   150.00
☐ Veined, No. 1614, 5¾″ 75.00   85.00
☐ Veined, No. 1616, 8¾″ 300.00   350.00
☐ Veined, No. 7798, artist signed, 11″ 550.00   600.00
☐ Veined Sung, fish design, artist signed, 8½″ 1000.00   1250.00
☐ Veined Sung, Pumpkin shape, 6″ 550.00   600.00

Left to Right: **"Veined Sung"** No.1618, No.1619 **300.00 – 350.00 each**

	Price Range	
☐ Veined Sung, No. 925, 7″	125.00	150.00
☐ Woodcut, Deer Scene, old mark, 11″................	600.00	700.00
☐ Woodcut, Desert Scene, 8½″	500.00	550.00
☐ Woodcut, No. 1603, 7¼″	75.00	85.00
☐ Woodcut, No. 1613, 6½″	85.00	100.00
☐ Woodcut, No. 1617, 13¼″	300.00	350.00
☐ Woodcut, No. 1619, 11″	300.00	350.00
☐ Woodcut, boat scene, No. 7203, 7½″	225.00	275.00
☐ Woodcut, landscape, No. 7754, 8″	275.00	325.00

Left to Right: **"Woodcut Flambeware"**
No.1618, No.1619 **300.00 – 350.00 each**

ABOUT THE AUTHOR

Mrs. Pollard has been a dealer in limited editions and collectibles for over twenty-five years. She was owner of Beru's, Inc., a store designed with the collector in mind for eleven years, and recently sold in order to devote more time to writing and traveling. She is the editor of the American Artist Print Price Trends for a national magazine.

She is a past charter member of the National Association of Limited Edition Dealers and the American Limited Audubon Society; President of the Irvington Businessmen's Association in Indianapolis for two terms.

She was awarded Dealer of the Year award by Frame House Gallery for outstanding sales and advertisement in 1973 and the President's Cup in 1977 for her continuing efforts in behalf of both dealer and collector in the limited edition print field.

Ruth M. Pollard

The author welcomes any comments, corrections or additions which will either be answered personally or used in any future updating of this price guide. Please write:
Ruth M. Pollard
P.O. Box 39038
Indianapolis, IN 46239

DESCRIPTION	DATE PURCHASED	COST	DATE SOLD	PRICE	CONDITION

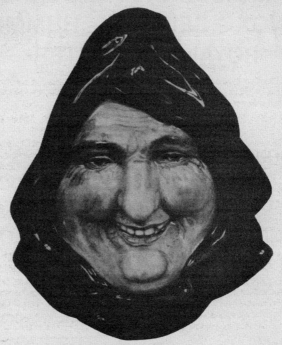

THE ROYAL DOULTON
INTERNATIONAL
COLLECTORS CLUB

U.S. Branch, Box 1815 Somerset, New Jersey 08873
Phone: 201-351-7880

☐ Please send me one John Doulton Character Jug, commemorating the founding of the Club, for $50. I understand that with my purchase I will automatically be enrolled for one year, at no extra charge, in the Royal Doulton International Collectors Club with full membership privileges. NJ residents add 5% sales tax.

☐ I wish to become a member of the Royal Doulton International Collectors Club, with all its privileges for one-year membership fee of $15.

Enclosed is my check ———— money order ———— for $ ————

SIGNATURE ————————————————————

Please Print
NAME ————————————————————

ADDRESS ————————————————————

CITY ————————————————————

STATE ———————— ZIP ————————
Please allow 4-6 weeks for delivery.

How did your plates do?

Reco's "Little Boy Blue" by John McClelland

UP 214% in 1 Year

Some limited edition plates gained more in the same year, some less, and some not at all...But *Plate Collector* readers were able to follow the price changes, step by step, in Plate Price Trends, a copyrighted feature appearing in each issue of the magazine.

Because *The Plate Collector* is your best source guide...has more on limited editions than all other publications combined...and gives you insight into every facet of your collecting...you too will rate it

Your No. 1 Investment In Limited Editions

Plate Collector, established in 1972, was the first publication to feature limited editions only. Since then it's expanded, adding figurines, bells and prints, earning such reader raves as "Objective and impartial," "...has great research," "...a major guide to the plates I buy," and "It is the best collector magazine on the market."

To bring you the latest, most valuable information every month, our editors travel the world. Sometimes stories lead them to the smaller Hawaiian islands, or to the porcelain manufactories of Europe.

Their personal contact with artisans, hobby leaders, collectors, artists and dealers lets you share an intimate view of limited editions.

Each fat, colorful, monthly issue brings you new insight, helps you enjoy collecting more.

You'll find *Plate Collector* a complete source guide. Consider new issue information and new issue announcements. Use the ratings of new releases and wide array of dealer ads to help you pick and choose the best.

Read regular columns and check current market values in Plate Price Trends to add to your storehouse of knowledge.

Learn about clubs (perhaps there's one meeting near you) and the growing number of collector conventions and shows. Profit from tips on insurance, decorating with limited editions, safeguarding your collectables...just a sample of recurring feature subjects.

Read *Plate Collector* magazine to become a true limited edition art insider. Order now. See new and old plates in sparkling color.

And now there's FIGURINE COLLECTOR...
Providing the same kind of objective reporting about the world of figurine collecting, this quarterly publication is the first in its field.

Figurine Collector lets you in on what's new in this rapidly growing area. A veritable

feast of information, it will instruct and entertain you with valuable information on a wide range of topics from how figurines are made to how they're doing on the secondary market.

To help you stay on top of what's happening in plate and figurine collecting, subscribe to both publications from Collector's Media, Inc., at the special combined rate.

16 issues (12 issues Plate Collector + 4 issues Figurine Collector) $30
Plate Collector only...12 issues (1 year) $24.95
Figurine Collector only...4 issues (1 year) $9.95

Collector's Media, Inc.
P.O. Box 1729-HS   San Marcos, TX 78667-1729

To use VISA and MasterCard, include all raised information on your card.

━━ TRADE PRICE GUIDE SERIES ━━

■ **Collectible Cameras** — Today **astonishing prices** are being paid for many **fine antique, classic,** and even **secondhand cameras.** • *More than 5,000 selling prices for all types of popular collector cameras.* • *Information on manufacturer, model name, model number, specifications, and date.* • *Advice on buying and building a collection.* • *A step-by-step guide through the hobby.* • *ILLUSTRATED.*
1st Edition, 320 pgs., 5⅜" x 8", Paperback, ISBN: 383-X, $9.95.

■ **Collectibles of the Third Reich** — **Phenomenal** is the only word to describe the **rising interest** in **Nazi militaria.** *Perhaps our desire never to forget the horror of Hitler is the root cause of this astonishing collectible field.* • *Included in this extensive guide are firearms, badges, insignia, flags, standards, banners, uniforms, bayonets, daggers, swords, and much more.* • *ILLUSTRATED.*
1st Edition, 320 pgs., 5⅜" x 8", Paperback, ISBN: 422-4, $9.95.

■ **Collectible Toys** — This is the **book** no toy collector can afford to be **without!** • *Over* **25,000 current values** *for trains, windups, autos, soldiers, boats, banks, guns, musical toys, Disneyana, comic characters, Star Trek, Star Wars, and more.* • *Major manufacturers from the Civil War to the present.* • *Valuable collecting tips.* • *Toy manufacturing in America.* • *The Evolution of toy collecting.* • *ILLUSTRATED.*
1st Edition, 576 pgs., 5⅜" x 8", Paperback, ISBN: 384-8, $9.95.

■ **Collector Cars** — The worldwide love affair with the automobile has **resulted in unprecedented profits.** • *Over* **37,000 actual current prices** *for 4,100 models of U.S. and Foreign antique and classic automobiles.* • *United States production figures — 1897 to date.* • *A list of reference publications, museums, and collector clubs.* • *Advice on how to buy and sell successfully at auctions, to dealers, and individuals.* • *ILLUSTRATED.*
5th Edition, 576 pgs., 5⅜" x 8", Paperback, ISBN: 408-9, $9.95.

■ **Collector Handguns** — No other book on the subject **comes close** to supplying the **concise** and **comprehensive information** found here. • *More than* **5,000 current retail prices** *for handguns of all styles and all calibers.* • *Every gun identified by manufacturer, model name, action, caliber, length, date, type of stock, weight, serial number, and markings.* • *Extensive ammo section.* • *Advice on buying and selling.* • *ILLUSTRATED.*
1st Edition, 544 pgs., 5⅜" x 8", Paperback, ISBN: 367-8, $9.95.

■ **Collector Knives** — **Endorsed by the American Blade Collectors.** • *Over* **14,000 current collector values.** • *1,250 worldwide knife manufacturers.* • *Special section for Case, Ka-Bar, and limited edition knives.* • *Valuable collector information.* • *Exclusive identification guide for pocket knife shields, knife nomenclature, and blade and knife patterns.* • *Up-to-date list of knife organizations and trade publications.* • *ILLUSTRATED.*
6th Edition, 736 pgs., 5⅜" x 8", Paperback, ISBN: 389-9, $9.95.

■ **Collector Plates** — The plate collector's bible! Contains the **most complete listing** of all U.S. and foreign plate manufacturers and distributors **in print!** • *Over* **18,000 current collectors values.** • *Includes thousands of collector plates from 1895 to date.* • *Tips on cleaning, shipping, storing, and displaying.* • *A glossary and complete list of plate publications and clubs.* • *How to buy and an investment review.* • *ILLUSTRATED.*
2nd Edition, 672 pgs., 5⅜" x 8", Paperback, ISBN: 393-7, $9.95.

■ **Collector Prints** — The **most accurate** and **authoritative work** on limited edition prints in publication today. • *Over* **14,750 listings of collector prints** *for more than* **400 of the world's leading artists.** • *A list of galleries, agents and publishers.* • *Information on buying, selling, storing, and caring for prints.* • *A glossary of printmaking and print collecting terminology.* • *Artists' biographies.* • *ILLUSTRATED.*
5th Edition, 576 pgs., 5⅜" x 8", Paperback, ISBN: 395-3, $9.95.

━━ *For your convenience use the handy order form.* ━━

TRADE PRICE GUIDE SERIES

MINI PRICE GUIDE SERIES

■ **Antiques & Flea Markets** — Do your antique browsing with the experts . . . take along this **super compact guide** to more than **15,000** old, rare, and unusual collectors' items! • Spot the bargains . . . **avoid the fakes** . . . make the best deals *when you buy or sell at antique shops, auctions, flea markets, and garage sales.* • Current market values *for thousands of collectors' items in all categories.* • Learn the professional approach to grading, storage, and restoration. • ILLUSTRATED.
2nd Edition, 320 pgs., 4" x 5½", Paperback, ISBN: 392-9, $3.95.

■ **Antique Jewelry** — The indispensable guide to **valuable, but affordable jewelry** — for collecting, wearing, and investing. • Over **2,500 current values** *for jewelry from 1750 to 1930.* • Complete descriptions *of styles, patterns, and identifying features.* • Date of manufacture. • Important collector's advice — *buying, selling, cleaning, storing, and displaying.* • **Grading information** *for diamonds, gold, and silver.* • Historical background *of jewelry.* • ILLUSTRATED.
2nd Edition, 288 pgs., 4" x 5½", Paperback, ISBN: 442-9, $3.95.

■ **Baseball Cards** — For thousands of fans, young and old, baseball card collecting is **a year round hobby.** This newly revised edition is the collector's standard reference. • *Over* **100,000 current market values.** • **Valuable collecting information** — *The history of card manufacturing in the U.S., tips on buying and selling, and how to grade condition to determine the value of your collection.* • A special price column indicates which items have increased in value. • **Exclusive checklist "grading" system.** • ILLUSTRATED.
4th Edition, 352 pgs., 4" x 5½", Paperback, ISBN: 438-0, $3.95.

■ **Beer Cans** — Collectors agree this handy carry along guide contains everything you will ever need to know about one of America's fastest growing hobbies! • Over **6,000 actual selling prices** *for old, modern, rare, and common beer cans.* • **All brands** *and all types of cans. Includes all label design variations, with information for identifying every variation.* • **History of brewing** *through 6,000 years!* • Tips on how to find valuable cans and how to buy, sell, and trade • ILLUSTRATED.
2nd Edition, 288 pgs., 4" x 5½", Paperback, ISBN: 440-2, $3.95.

■ **Bottles** — Never before in pocket-size! Here is the **most convenient** guide to collectible **bottles** in print! *Thousands of values given for all types of old and new bottles.* • *Includes ale & gin, beer, bitters, cure, flasks, fruit jars, Hutchinson, ink, medicine, mineral, poison, Pontil, soda, spirits, Avon, Jim Beam, Brooks, Old Fitzgerald, and many more.* • *Also valuable collecting tips on buying and selling, grading condition, conducting a dig, background histories, bottle clubs, basic bottle shapes, trademarks, and investment advice.* • ILLUSTRATED.
1st Edition, 288 pgs., 4" x 5½", Paperback, ISBN: 431-3, $3.95.

■ **Cars and Trucks** — You could have a fortune parked in your own garage! *Over* 10,000 current auction and dealer prices *for all popular U.S. and foreign made antique, classic, and collector cars.* • **Each detailed listing includes:** *the model name and year of production, engine specifications, body style, and a price range value from fair to excellent condition.* • Learn how to evaluate *the condition of a collector car the way the professionals do!* • ILLUSTRATED.
1st Edition, 240 pgs., 4" x 5½", Paperback, ISBN: 391-0, $2.95.

For your convenience use the handy order form.

MINI PRICE GUIDE SERIES

■ **Collectible Records** — One of the **most enjoyable and profitable hobbies** today. • *Over 11,000 current market prices* for *Rock and Country recordings. A chronological listing of discs from 1953 to date.* • *Listed by their original label and issue number.* • **Collecting tips** — *How to begin a collection, buying, selling, and grading the condition of records and jackets.* • *A handy guide to "Golden Oldie" shops, conventions, flea markets, and garage sales.* • *ILLUSTRATED.*
1st Edition, 240 pgs., 4" x 5½", Paperback, ISBN: 400-3, $2.95.

■ **Collector Guns** — This **handy pocket guide** contains *over* **9,000 dealer prices** compiled from nationwide sales records for handguns, rifles, and shotguns. *Covers American and foreign manufacturers.* • **Complete data** *on model names, barrel lengths, calibers, and sight types.* • *Information on the history of firearms, biographies of famous gunmakers, and collecting techniques!* • *ILLUSTRATED.*
1st Edition, 240 pgs., 4" x 5½", Paperback, ISBN: 396-1, $2.95.

■ **Comic Books** — Join the **thousands** who have discovered the fascinating world of comic collecting, one of the nation's fastest-growing hobbies. • **Current market values for over 5,000 old and new comics.** • **Learn how** *to start a comic collection and watch it grow into a* **profitable investment.** • **Tips on buying, selling, and swapping your comics.** *Start a comic collection with purchases from the newsstand.* • *ILLUSTRATED.*
2nd Edition, 288 pgs., 4" x 5½", Paperback, ISBN: 382-1, $3.95.

■ **Dolls** — Reap pleasure and profit! • **Over 3,000 current market prices** *for dolls of all types and all manufacturers.* • **Positive identification** *by maker, name of doll, markings, hair color, eye color, type of eye, date of manufacture, and size.* • **Valuable collector information** *on buying and selling, fakes, repairs, and how to care for your dolls.* • **Extensive glossary** *of doll making and collecting terms.* • *ILLUSTRATED.*
2nd Edition, 288 pgs., 4" x 5½", Paperback, ISBN: 434-8, $3.95.

■ **Football Cards** — Call the right signals every time with the most **authoritative** guide to football cards **in print today! This revised edition features all the latest cards and price changes.** • *Over 50,000 current market values for collectible football cards.* • **Valuable collector information** — *tips on trading, buying and selling, and how to grade condition to determine the value of your collection.* • **Exclusive checklist system.** • *ILLUSTRATED.*
3rd Edition, 288 pgs., 4" x 5½", Paperback, ISBN: 388-0, $2.95.

■ **Glassware** — The handiest guide to collectible glassware on the market today! *Contains thousands of values for the five major types of collectible glass — art, carnival, cut, depression, and pattern.* • *Includes history of each period, manufacturer's marks, pattern and motif identification guide, extensive glossary, and much more.* • *Plus valuable collector advice on buying, selling, care, display, collector publications, clubs, organizations, and museums.* • *ILLUSTRATED.*
1st Edition, 288 pgs., 4" x 5½", Paperback, ISBN: 432-1, $3.95.

■ **Hummels** — Handy pocket guide with *over* **2,000 current collector prices** *for the most common and most popular Hummels. All the latest releases are included.* • **A Hummel encyclopedia** — *from Berta Hummel's beginnings to the growth of the Goebel firm, plus a collector's glossary.* • **Valuable collector information** *on buying, selling, storage, and display.* • *Pictures for each listing from 1923 to date.* • *ILLUSTRATED.*
2nd Edition, 256 pgs., 4" x 5½", Paperback, ISBN: 435-6, $3.95.

For your convenience use the handy order form.

OFFICIAL PRICE GUIDE SERIES

■ **Collector's Journal** — *This is the most* **valuable** *book any collector could own! Use it to record dealers, collectors, clubs, museums, and reference materials.* • *Special inventory forms allow the recording of individual collectibles in minute detail.* • *Value development chart provides space for keeping track of investment value.* • *Vital information is provided on appraisal, insurance, taxes, and buying and selling.*
1st Edition, 256 pgs., 5¼" x 7⅞", Paperback, ISBN: 445-3, $4.95.

■ **The Official Encyclopedia of Antiques and Collectibles** — More than 10,000 **definitions.** • **Plus** — *U.S. automobile production figures.* • *bottle trademarks.* • *clock chronology.* •*collector plate backstamps.* • *pottery and porcelain marks.* • *U.S./ firearm trademarks.* • *precious metal purity and weight conversion tables.* • *silversmith's marks.*
1st Edition, 704 pgs., 5⅜" x 8" Paperback, ISBN: 365-1, $9.95

■ **The Official Guide to Buying and Selling Antiques and Collectibles** — *covers every phase of collecting from beginning a collection to its ultimate sale* • *Examines IN DETAIL the collecting potential of approximately* **200 different categories IN ALL PRICE RANGES.** • *Learn how the collectible market operates and what makes an item valuable. Every possible source of collector's items is explored IN-DEPTH.*
1st Edition, 608 pgs., 5⅜" x 8", Paperback, ISBN: 369-4, $9.95

IDENTIFICATION GUIDE SERIES

■ **Identification Guide to Early American Furniture** — A comprehensive guide **to identifying antique American furniture** *dating from 1603 to the 1840's.* • *Provides instant access to hundreds of pieces with superb line drawings.* • *Includes Jacobean, Pilgrim, William and Mary, Queen Anne, Chippendale, and Neo-Classical Revival.* • *Features the famous cabinetmakers Adam, Hepplewhite, Sheraton, and others.* • *ILLUSTRATED.*
1st Edition, 320 pgs., 4" x 8", Paperback, ISBN: 414-3, $9.95.

■ **Identification Guide to Glassware** — *Over* **100 types** *of glass are completely described.* • *Hundreds of illustrated marks and line drawings.* • *Includes Agata, Amberina, Blown, Burmese, Cameo, Carnival, Cranberry, Crown Milano, Custard, Cut, Depression, Durand, Fry, Galle, Kew Blas, Lalique, Loetz, Mercury, Milk, Napoli, Nash, Paperweights, Peach Blow, Pressed, Ruby, Silveria, and dozens more.* • *ILLUSTRATED.*
1st Edition, 320 pgs., 4" x 8", Paperback, ISBN: 413-5, $9.95.

■ **Identification Guide to Gunmarks** — An important "companion" identification guide to both **The Antique and Modern Firearms** and the **Collector Handguns Price Guides.** • *Over 1,500 of the most commonly encountered trademarks on modern and antique guns.* • *Learn which marks are valuable and how to spot fakes and forgeries.* • *An alphabetical listing of trade names and codes for firearms without trademarks.*
1st Edition, 256 pgs., 5⅜" x 8", Paperback, ISBN: 346-5, $6.95.

■ **Identification Guide to Pottery and Porcelain** — Absolutely the most **comprehensive guide to identifying pottery and porcelain in print today!** • *Includes manufacturers in the United States, Austria, Belgium, Denmark, Holland, England, France, Germany, Ireland, Italy, Prussia, Russia, Scotland, Spain, Sweden, and Switzerland.* • *Complete descriptions of characteristics and all known marks are given for each of the hundreds of individual types listed.*
1st Edition, 320 pgs., 4" x 8", Paperback, ISBN: 412-7, $9.95.

■ **Identification Guide to Victorian Furniture** — There is a **tremendous surge of interest** in the ornate furniture of the **Victorian Period.** • *Complete descriptions of every piece and hundreds of line drawings make identification quick and easy.* • *Also contains manufacturers' histories and an extensive furniture glossary.* • *Includes Victorian, Renaissance Revival, Rococo Revival (Belter), Spool-turned, Cottage, Louis XVI Revival, Arts and Crafts, Wicker, Cast Iron, and Indian Teak.*
1st Edition, 320 pgs., 4" x 8", Paperback, ISBN: 415-1, $9.95.

For your convenience use the handy order form.

NUMISMATIC SERIES

■ **1984 Blackbook Price Guide of United States Coins** — A coin collector's guide to current market values for all U.S. coins from 1616 to date — over *16,500 prices.* **THE OFFICIAL BLACKBOOK OF COINS** has gained the reputation as the most reliable, up-to-date guide to U.S. Coin values. This new edition features, an exclusive gold and silver identification guide. Learn how to test, weigh and calculate the value of any item made of gold or silver. Proven professional techniques revealed for the first time. Detecting altered coins section. Take advantage of the current "BUYERS' MARKET" in gold and silver. *ILLUSTRATED.*
$2.95-22nd Edition, 288 pgs., 4" x 5½", Paperback, Order #: 385-6

■ **1984 Blackbook Price Guide of United States Paper Money** — Over *9,000 buying and selling prices* covering U.S. currency from 1861 to date. Every note issued by the U.S. government is listed and priced including many Confederate States notes. Error Notes are described and priced, and there are detailed articles on many phases of the hobby for beginner and advanced collector alike. Comprehensive grading section. *ILLUSTRATED.*
$2.95-16th Edition, 240 pgs., 4" x 5½", Paperback, Order #: 387-2

■ **1984 Blackbook Price Guide of United States Postage Stamps** — *Featuring all U.S. stamps from 1847 to date pictured in full color.* Over *19,000 current selling prices.* General issues, airmails and special delivery. United Nations, first day covers, and more. New listings for the most current commemorative and regular issue stamps, a feature not offered in any other price guide, at any price! Numerous developments in the fast moving stamp market during the past year are included in this *NEW REVISED EDITION. ILLUSTRATED.*
$2.95-6th Edition, 240 pgs., 4" x 5½", Paperback, Order #: 386-4

INVESTORS SERIES

■ **Investors Guide to Gold, Silver, Diamonds** — *All you need to know* about making money trading in the precious metals and diamonds markets. This practical, easy-to-read investment guide is for everyone in all income brackets. How to determine authenticity and values. *ILLUSTRATED.*
$6.95-1st Edition, 208 pgs., 5⅜" x 8½", Paperback, Order #: 171-3

■ **Investors Guide to Gold Coins** — *The first complete book* on investing in gold coins. Exclusive price performance charts trace all U.S. gold coins values from *1955 to date.* Forecast price trends and best bets. *ILLUSTRATED.*
$6.95-1st Edition, 288 pgs., 5⅜" x 8½", Paperback, Order #: 300-7

■ **Investors Guide to Silver Coins** — *The most extensive listing* of all U.S. Silver coins. Detailed price performance charts trace actual sales figures from *1955 to date.* Learn how to figure investment profit. *ILLUSTRATED.*
$6.95-1st Edition, 288 pgs., 5⅜" x 8½", Paperback, Order #: 301-5

■ **Investors Guide to Silver Dollars** — Regardless of your income, you can *become a successful silver dollar investor.* Actual sales figures for every U.S. silver dollar *1955 to date.* Comprehensive grading section. *ILLUSTRATED.*
$6.95-1st Edition, 192 pgs., 5⅜" x 8½", Paperback, Order #: 302-3

For your convenience use the handy order form.